ALVAR AALTO

AND THE INTERNATIONAL STYLE

ALVAR AALTO
AND THE INTERNATIONAL STYLE

BY PAUL DAVID PEARSON

WHITNEY LIBRARY OF DESIGN,
an imprint of Watson-Guptill Publications/New York

To my parents, Fritz and Annie Bell Pearson

Note: In the captions the architect, unless otherwise cited,
is Alvar Aalto.

Copyright © 1978 by Paul David Pearson

First published 1978 in New York by Whitney Library of Design,
an imprint of Watson-Guptill Publications,
a division of Billboard Publications, Inc.,
1515 Broadway, New York, N.Y. 10036

Library of Congress Cataloging in Publication Data
Pearson, Paul David, 1936-
   Alvar Aalto and the international style.
   Bibliography: p.
   Includes index.
   1. Aalto, Alvar, 1898-1976.   2. International style
(Architecture) I. Title.
NA1455.F53A255   720'.94'4 [B]   77-20029
ISBN 0-8230-7023-9

Manufactured in U.S.A.

First Printing, 1978
Second Printing, 1980

Edited by Sarah Bodine and Susan Davis
Designed by James Craig
Set in 10 point Helvetica

Contents

Acknowledgments

It is the nature of any work based upon scholarship that authors, if they are to handle the material smoothly, must receive counsel and aid from their friends and colleagues. In my own case this aspect is not only true, but it is a pleasure to have such people encouraging me at every step. This citation, though humble and factual, is from the heart, and I thank the following for their timely support:

The late Raija Liisa Heinonen, who was for many scholars of Finnish architecture and art a window through which her country's culture could be clearly observed and adequately evaluated. Her unselfish aid to me in this project was the key to an understanding of the material that enabled me to bring the work to fruition. I know she did as much for others and all of us will miss her.

Johanna Hecht, who revealed to me the nature a manuscript must take and whose counsel convinced me that the subject was correct for me. Susanne Churchill, who unselfishly gave of her time in the technical preparation of the manuscript and photographs. Eugene Santomasso, who made vital criticisms and suggestions regarding the foundation of the text.

Vitto Acquafredda and Thomas Bittner, two of my former students, who in their devotion and diligent assistance on translations and photoprinting, respectively, gave more than could be expected. Marja Roth, who along with her husband David cleverly translated many of the quotes into a clear, sound, architectural-style English.

Dean Bernard P. Spring and the Administration of City College of New York for granting me a leave to commence the study. Professor Newton-Watson of the University College London for seeing me through the study. Margot Wittkower and her late husband Rudolf who supported my idea of a study even before it took form.

Marian Page whose sensitive approach to editing makes me think she must be the best in this world. Samuel H. Kress Foundation, particularly Mary Davis, who supported my travels to gather information. Tatu Tuohikorpi and the Finnish Consulate of New York, who assisted me in true supportive form in the final moments of preparation.

My colleagues at the City College School of Architecture for enduring me over the years of preparation.

My publishers and editors, especially Susan Davis and Sarah Bodine for their tireless effort and counsel which enabled me to realize the project as a finished work.

Anne and Peter Ceresole of London in whose house this work was largely written. My two sons David Brian and Paul Christopher who aided me in the thankless task of processing photographic prints for the original manuscript.

Finally and perhaps most importantly, to Reyner Banham, my mentor, who characteristically first saw that the time had come for the subject matter and its study.

Chronology, 1894–1949

Second date where used denotes completion date of previous project or competition entry.

1894	Born Aino Marsio, January 12.
1898	Born Hugo Alvar Henrik Aalto, February 3.
1916	Graduation, Jyväskylä Normal School.
1918	Alajärvi. Renovation of parents' house.
1918	Kauhajärvi. Remodeling of church and bell tower addition.
1919	Naantali. Student project; preparation of church survey drawings.
1919	Alajärvi. Youth Society Building.
1920	Helsinki. Tivoli Area Finnish National Fair assisted by Carolus Lindberg.
1921	Helsinki. Diploma project: Finnish National Fair Hall. Diploma, Helsinki Technical University.
1921	Traveled to Stockholm and Gothenburg seeking employment.
1921	Gothenburg. Assisted Arvid Bjerke: prepared design for main assembly or congress hall at Gothenburg Fair site.
1922	Tampere. Industrial Exposition: exhibition pavilions, craft sheds, choral and band shell, and snack bar.
1922	Traveled to Tallinn, Estonia, for *Arkkitehti* magazine.
1923	**Accepted for membership in SAFA as qualified architect.**
1923	Jyväskylä. Multifamily house with shop in Taulumäki area.
1923	Helsinki. Entry, Houses of Parliment Site Plan competition.
1923	Jyväskylä. Railway employees Garden apartment block.
1924	Äänekoska. Church restoration.
1924	Anttola. Church renovation.
1924	Jyväskylä. Workers Club.
1924	Marriage to Aino Marsio.
1924	Honeymoon to Italy, Greece, and Vienna.
1924	Helsinki. Entry, National Parliament House Competition.
1925	Seinäjoki. Civil Guard s House complex.
1925	Vitasaari. Church restoration.
1925	Jyväskylä. Casa Lauren, design project for a two-family house.
1925	Jämsä. Entry, church competition. Entry, Furniture Design Competition for *Aitta*.

1925	Alajärvi. Villa Flora by Aino Aalto.
1926	Alajärvi. Villa Väinölä.
1926	Geneva. Entry, competition for League of Nations Headquarters.
1926	Helsinki. Entry, Union Bank Headquarters and Office Building Competition.
1926	Jyväskylä. Monumental Plaza layout for City Plan.
1927	Alajärvi. Municipal Hospital.
1927	Jyväskylä. Entry, Civil Guard House Complex Competition; 2nd Prize.
1927	Helsinki. Entry, church competition for Töölö area.
1927	Tampere. Entry, church competition for Viinika area; 2nd prize.
1927	Jyväskylä. Entry, church competition for Taulumäki area.
1927	Pylkönmäki. Church restoration and remodeling.
1927/9	Muurame. Parish church.
1927/9	Wooden stacking chair.
1927/9	Turku. Entry, Southwestern Agricultural Co-operative Multi-use Building Competition; 1st prize.
1927	Viipuri. Entry, Municipal Library Competition; 1st prize.

1927 Relocated office in Turku during summer months.

1927	Two entries, small summer house competition for *Aitta;* 1st prize
1927	Entry, larger summer house competition for *Aitta.*
1927	Vaasa. Entry, Office Block Competition, with E. Bryggman.
1928/9	Turku. Standard apartment block for J. Tapani.
1928	Korpilahti. Church restoration. Traveled to Holland and Paris.
1928/30	Turku. Itämeri Restaurant, interior in Agricultural Co-op Building.
1928/30	Turku. Newspaper plant and offices for *Turun Sanomat.*
1928	Helsinki. Entry, Independence Monument Competition (stadium).
1929	Kemijärvi. Church restoration.
1929	Paimio. Entry, Tuberculosis Sanatorium Competition; 1st prize.
1929	Turku. 700th Anniversary Exposition with E. Bryggman. Plywood chairs with laminated wood legs or pipe legs; five drawer unit with recessed handles for Korhonen; traveled to Frankfurt to attend CIAM Conference.
1929	Santo Domingo. Entry, Monumental Light House Competition.
1929	Helsinki. Entry, church competition for Vallila area.
1930	Turku. Entry, municipal water tower competition.
1930	Vierumäki. Entry, Physical Education Institute Competition; 3rd prize.
1930	Helsinki. Entry, church competition for Tehtaanpuisto area.
1930	Traveled to Brussels for CIAM Conference and presentation of examples of modern design from Finland. Traveled to Stockholm for opening of Functionalist Exhibition and later to Trohdheim, Norway, with Swedish architects for Nordic Building Conference.
1930	Entry, furniture competition for Vienna organization.
1930/3	"Paimio" chair made of birch veneers.

1930	Helsinki. Minimum apartment Exhibition held jointly with Pauli and Marta Blomstedt, Erik Bryggman, and Werner West.
1930	Zagreb. Entry, University Hospital Complex Competition.
1930	Oulu. Exterior Design, Pulp mill for Toppila.
1930	Viipuri. Second version, Municipal Library.
1931	Helsinki. Entry, University Expansion Site Plan Competition.
1931	Helsinki. Entry, Lallukka Area Artists Housing Competition.
1932	Helsinki. Entry, National Stadium Competition, part I; entry, weekend house competition for Insulite Co.; entry, weekend house competition for Enso-Gutzeit.

1933 Relocated office in Helsinki.

1933/5	Patent development for bent wood leg used in stools.
1933/5	Viipuri. Final version, Municipal Library.
1933	Paimio. Physicians' and staff members' residential blocks.
1933	Stockholm. Entry, Urban Design Competition for Norrmalm area.
1933	Helsinki. Entry, National Stadium Competition, part II for Olympics.
1934	Tampere. Entry, Railway Station Facade Competition.
1934	Helsinki. Housing proposal in Munkkiniemi for Stennius Co.
1934	Helsinki. Entry, National Exhibition Hall Competition, 3rd prize.
1934	Helsinki. Entry, National Postal Telegraph Headquarters Competition.
1935/6	Karhula. Pulp mill for Sunila combine.
1935/6	Karhula. Village layout and first stage apartment development for Sunila pulp mill.
1935	Patent development of Spring leaf supported chair of molded plywood.
1935	Moscow. Entry, Finnish Embassy Competition.
1936	Helsinki. Entry, Plant and Office Complex Competition for ALKO.
1936	Helsinki. Aalto's personal residence and studio in Munkkiniemi.
1936	Paris. Two entries Finnish Pavilion Competition for 1937 World's Fair; 1st and 2nd prizes later shared with A. Ervi and V. Rewell.
1937	Tallinn. Entry, National Museum of Art Competition.
1937	Helsinki. Two entries, university library competition, Swedish glassware competition.
1937	Turku. Savoy Restaurant interior.
1937/9	Noormarkku. Villa Mairea.
1937	Karhula. Nordic United Bank.
1938	Kauttua. Residential area plan and stepped housing block for Ahlström plant.
1938/9	Karhula. Stepped apartment block for Sunila pulp mill.
1938	Laupa. Forestry Pavilion, Agricultural Fair.
1938	Helsinki. Film Studio project for Bloomberg in Westend area.
1938	Inkeroinen. Papermill for Anjala.
1938/9	Inkeroinen. Employees' village and housing units for Anjala paper mill.
1938/9	New York. Three entries, Finnish

	Pavilion Competition for 1939–1940 World's Fair, 1st, 2nd, and 3rd prizes.
1938	New York. Exhibition, Museum of Modern Art. Traveled to New York on Fair business in autumn.
1939	Karhula. Apartment projects for Ahlström. Traveled to New York for opening of World's Fair and toured U.S.A., including Golden Gate Exposition display of Aalto furniture.
1940	Helsinki. Entry, housing development competition for HAKA.
1940	Helsinki. Entry, entrance pavilion and tram plaza competition for Errotaja arga, 1st prize.
1940	Traveled to U.S.A. for second opening of World's Fair and secured visiting research professorship at Massachusetts Institute of Technology. Formed "For Finland," foundation dedicated to post-war rebuilding in Finland. Report published.
1940	Model town for Finland executed with MIT students.
1941	Kokemäki. Master plan development for Kokemäki River valley for Harry Gullichsen.
1942	Säynätsalo. Town center project for Enso-Gutzeit.
1942/3	Kauttua. Dormitory for Ahlström plant.
1943	Oulu. Entry, town center and rapid area competition; 1st prize.
1943	Oulu. Entry, Merikoski Power Plant Facade Competition.
1944	Avesta. Entry, town center competition with Albin Stark.
1944/7	Vaasa. Meter factory for Stromberg.
1944/7	Housing units for Stromberg.
1944/5	Rovaniemi. Comprehensive city plan for urban redevelopment.
1944	Kauttua. Addition to Ahlström plant.
1944/5	Karhula. Mechanical workshops for Ahlström.
1945	Kauttua. Additional housing and sauna for Ahlström plant.
1945/6	Varkaus. Sawmill extension for Ahlström.
1945/6	Varkaus. Single family house neighborhood for Ahlström.
1946	Nynäshamn. Entries, master plan and housing development competitions.
1946	Pihlava. Single family house.
1946	Noormarkku. Sauna for Villa Mairea.
1947	Vaasa. Sauna and laundry for Stromberg employees' village.
1946/9	Cambridge. Seniors' Dormitory (Baker House) for MIT.
1947/53	Imatra. Regional development plan for Enso-Gutzeit.
1948	Helsinki. Two entries, National Pension Bank Headquarters Competition; 1st prize.
1949	Death of Aino Aalto.
1949	Helsinki. Entry, Technical University at Otaniemi master plan and main classroom competition, 1st prize.
1949	Karhula. Glass products warehouse for Ahlström.
1949	Helsinki. Entry, Sea Harbor Passenger Terminal and Facilities Competition.
1949	Säynätsalo. Entry, town center competition for Enso-Gutzeit.

Introduction

When Alvar Aalto died in May of 1976, the followers of the International Modern Movement in architecture were for the first time since the twenties without a leader or design philosopher. In the decade containing both Le Corbusier's and Mies van der Rohe's deaths, Aalto had become known as the most unique of the "second generation" of modern architects as well as the last surviving member of that group.[1]

This study, meant to cover the first half of his long creative life, is hopefully only the first of many such evaluative works by a wide range of scholars who will address themselves to the study of various aspects of Aalto's works.[2] Too frequently during his life the appreciation of his work had to be based on observations and suppositions made by enthusiastic but superficial analysis.[3] It was we architects who after all idolized and placed him in the high position of a tacit guru. Although Aalto perhaps humorously did little to dispel this adulation and its incumbent myths, he was, all things aside, an enigma in his own right. This work is an attempt to sort out the first word and not the last about his most formative and creative period. Too long and too thinly has the information regarding Aalto's sources been spread over periodicals and catalogs, and to this date not one work of critical analysis has appeared in the breadth of Aaltoiana.

There will be some who find this study an irreverent one, but nothing could be further from the truth, for my own work unabashedly bears traces of inspiration from the Finnish maestro.[4] Aalto has been for a significant number of architects and enthusiasts not only the last modern designer who was capable of producing a heroic level of architecture, but a unique contributor of romantic modes that challenged the latter day International Style of our post-war era.

I have examined Aalto's formation as a young man and traced his entrance into a mastery of the International Style, even to the heroic levels of that mode. Furthermore I have identified and codified Aalto's disenchantment with that philosophy and catalogued his emergence from it into the personal and unique design style for which he has become identified and been so highly praised.

There are two categories of material on which this study is based: the identification of new and key works in the evolution of Aalto's practice and the critical evaluation of those previously published designs and buildings long associated with his name. It is intended that the scholarly study of these two categories of material together will give a new overall understanding to a subject too long neglected.

In any analytical survey it is necessary to cover the methodology of research and recording in an orderly fashion, and since some eccentricities still exist in the field of architectural history and criticism, it is necessary to characterize those with respect to their use and appearance herein.

In establishing a date for Aalto's projects and buildings I have used the following as a guide: for competition projects in all cases I used the date of submission as the date of the completed design; for drawings and proposals of commissioned works I have used the date as signed by Aalto on the drawings; and for buildings I have unless otherwise stated used the completion date since Aalto's working method permitted changes until construction was realized.

With respect to terminology, several stylistic labels have been employed in a slightly modified manner. "National Romanticism," a term that may be applied to many countries in the same or related period, here applies to Finland unless stated otherwise. "Expressionism," pertaining to the German architecture of the period following the turn of the century, has been used in the wider sense as employed by Dennis Sharp and Wolfgang Pehnt to include the work of some modernists in the twenties such as Hugo Haring and Hans Schroun.[5] "International Style" not only refers to the term as defined by Hitchcock and Johnson, but is expanded to encompass Scandinavian and Russian design activity of that period as well. "Functionalism," a term of longstanding confusion, is used to refer to the Scandinavian version of the International Style that first had its introduction at the Stockholm Exhibition in 1930 and was later adopted by architects in that region as a term to define the first wave of antitraditional modernism. "Constructivism" refers strictly to that style as practiced by the Russians during the late teens and twenties.[6] "Classical Style" or "classicism" refers to the broad range of precedents in the tradition of European architecture growing from and added to the ancient Greek and Roman architecture. "Neoclassical" not only relates to the style of early 19th-century Europe but to its revival around the early 20th-century, particularly as practiced by Germans such as Peter Behrens between 1910 and 1917.[7]

Finally, it must be noted what for most of us is a new supporting cast of characters, in modern architecture, those predecessors and contemporaries of Aalto, architects who played a role in his and Finland's new architectural styles. Many, introduced here for the first time, will receive a larger and more individual treatment in coming studies by others.[8]

AALTO AND
FINLAND
COME OF
AGE

1
Aalto's Early Years

Alvar Aalto once half-jokingly said of his early years that even before he left Jyväskylä it was told in Helsinki that a young genius would come from the north to the Polytechnic Institute there to train for a career in architecture.[1] At the time of Aalto's arrival in Helsinki, however, this genius had not manifested itself. At the Jyväskylä Normal School he had been the student of Toivo Salervo, an architect whose chief claim to fame was in the widespread use of a pedagogical script alphabet he designed for the state school system. Such recognition that Aalto got there was evidently based on his possession of outstanding verbal gifts, rather than his talents in the area of design. He was reminded many years later (at a banquet speech by architect Väinö Tuukkanen) that upon graduation Salervo had advised him to pursue a career as a journalist and not to waste his time trying to become an architect.[2]

Aalto's Background

Aalto was born on February 3, 1898, in Kuortane, a small village in Ostro-Bothnia, but the family soon moved to Alajärvi where the young Aalto's mother, Selly Mathilda (born Hackstedt), died in 1903. His father, Juho Heikki, shortly thereafter married Selly's sister to provide a suitable home for his family. Some time before 1907 they moved to Jyväskylä,[3] where the elder Aalto, a surveyor, had taken a post with the county

government. Jyväskylä was the unofficial capital in the densely forested lake district in the central area of the country that is to this day identified by Helsinkians as being most wholly and typically "Finnish." Aalto himself must surely have felt this area, the "heart of Finland," to be the authentic Finnish habitat. He maintained his ties with it until his death, building many projects there, including his own summer retreat.

Jyväskylä provided Aalto with his first close association with town life. There he beheld a range of buildings that, while anything but modern, were nevertheless larger, more complex, and more recently built than any to be found in the traditional hamlets around Alajärvi. Splendid examples of Jugend and National Romantic styles were much in evidence in Tampere, which, however, was 80 miles (120 km) away (1).

Aalto placed his earliest recollected responses to architecture in this period, recalling his discovery, at the age of nine, of some works of Eliel Saarinen illustrated in color in the magazine *Nuori Suomi*.[4] This influence, by his own testimony appears short-lived, however, for while acknowledging Saarinen's pavilion (2) for the 1900 Paris World's Fair as an important building for Finland, Aalto failed to execute even a single building in that romantic style.[5] The importance seems to have been the mere existence of that building as a declaration that Finland could pro-

duce a distinctive national style at an international level. In later years Aalto steadfastly disclaimed any personal interest in what he called the "Saarinen clique."[6]

After graduation from secondary school in 1916, he went to work for his teacher Salervo during the summer and autumn of that year. From that time dates his first recorded venture into the realm of architecture—the addition of a wooden portico to his parent's summer house in Alajärvi (3), an indigenous wooden house clad in board and batten. Certainly his father's profession was to provide Alvar with an elementary exposure to native construction materials and techniques (especially in wood) as well as a nominal acquaintance with drawing and technical factors related to land surveying. The small entry portico is a temple-form pediment fused in an abrupt manner to the upper part of the house, seemingly without formal regard to the fenestration or moldings. It is supported on two square bracketed posts offset from the corner of the pediment, creating a somewhat unclassical cantilevered effect.

This was a time of intense political and social upheaval in the Baltic, precipitated by the pressures of the First World War and the Russian Revolution. The period of Aalto's childhood and adolescence had been a time of rising concern with Finland's national identity. The basic struggle throughout the nine-

1. Top: Tampere Cathedral, Tampere, 1904. Architect: Lars Sonck.

2. Above: Finnish Pavilion, World's Fair, Paris, 1900. Architect: Eliel Saarinen.

3. Left: Aalto's parents' home, Alajärvi, 1918.

teenth century was a cultural one, directed against the Swedish language and the domination of the nation by the Finno-Swedish segment of the population. This group had traditionally exerted influence far out of proportion to its numerical representation, even after the political hegemony of Finland had shifted from Sweden to Russia at the beginning of the century. The Russian Empire, into which Finland was incorporated as a Grand Duchy, had for the most part allowed the Finns a very considerable amount of political and cultural autonomy, and it was in this context that the struggle against the age-old Swedish influence was waged.[7]

However, with the opening of the twentieth century, Russian nationalists suddenly mounted an offensive against the quasi-independent status the Finns had enjoyed, and the country was subjected to increasingly serious inroads on its cultural and political autonomy. The upheaval of the war and the revolution provided Finland with the opportunity to break this oppressive domination decisively. In the wake of the overthrow of the Czarist regime on December 6, 1917, Finland declared its independence and the Bolshevik government was quick to grant the new nation recognition. At that point, however, a civil war was precipitated over the form and direction to be taken by the new Finnish government.[8]

Aalto interrupted his apprenticeship to join this struggle which divided Finland. It might appear to some observers that this moment of rising socialism in the world was a time for him to be swept into that cause. The fact is that Aalto fought on the ultimately victorious side of the "Whites," or nonsocialists,[9] perhaps because the support of the "Red," or extreme left forces, by 40,000 Bolshevik Russian troops aroused fears of renewed domination by the mammoth eastern neighbor.[10] Stationed in Jyväskylä, Aalto saw little military action, for the key battle in that part of the country was centered around Tampere. During the conflict, however, he was thrown into the company of Swedish volunteers who came to assist in the fight against a Communist takeover. Among these he met Sten Pranzell, an architect from Stockholm, and when the peace was declared in May, they traveled together to the Swedish-speaking town of Vaasa on the west coast of Finland. There Pranzell introduced him to Matti Björklund (later called Visanti), a designer-builder for whom Aalto worked during the remainder of the summer.[11] When he traveled by train to Helsinki in the autumn to begin his professional studies, he arrived at Saarinen's newly completed railroad station.

Student Days in Helsinki

In Helsinki Aalto proceeded to immerse himself in the cultural life of the capital. He made many friends in theatrical circles and even designed the sets for a dramatic production.[12] At the Polytechnic Institute he was taken personally by Armas Lindgren to his studio. The latter saw promise in Aalto's work but felt that his training had not been adequate and that he should receive special attention in the preparation of architectural drawings.[13]

Lindgren, who had left the partnership of Saarinen and Gesellius in 1905, was a recognized force in the Helsinki scene and one of the chief proponents of National Romanticism, a style related in some respects to the international Art Nouveau and English Arts and Crafts movements but generated in Finland as a direct function of the struggle for national identity. The principal architects furthering the National Romantic style were Eliel Saarinen and Lars Sonck. The movement drew most of its design inspiration from two basic sources: the Karelian log house and indigenous medieval architecture, namely churches and fortresses.[14] This style reached is pinnacle in the first decade of the twentieth century with Saarinen's National Museum in Helsinki and Sonck's Tampere Cathedral.[15] Both of these buildings combine rough-hewn stonework with sharply pointed towers, balanced with picturesque asymmetry over horizontal wings embellished with medieval Finnish motifs. The development of this style was significantly altered by a number of external and internal pressures which can be most clearly observed in the heated controversy that surrounded the competition for the Helsinki Railway Station in 1904.

Architectural Background

The railway station contest, according to Marika Hausen, attracted the attention of virtually every prominent architect in Finland including the team of Gesellius, Lindgren, and Saarinen. When, however, the jury announced its selection, it was a project submitted by Saarinen alone (4) with a graphic motto of a winged wheel that took first prize.[16] The project and the entire style was vehemently denounced by Sigurd Frosterus and Gustaf Strengell in lengthy press installments. Frosterus was an architect who had worked abroad for Henri van de Velde.[17] His belief that the new building should reflect rational thinking related to the nature of a railway station and should be less romantic and emotionally nationalistic in tone was expressed by his own project for the railway station, which was rejected by the jury as "an importation, foreign, and not very attractive" (5).

Strengell, a prominent journalist and critic as well as an architect who would continue to battle for the rationalization and simplification of Finnish architecture throughout his career, condemned Saarinen's project in similar terms. When Saarinen submitted his final design late in 1904 (6), the sweeping changes, clearly made in response to the criticisms of Frosterus and Strengell, indicated that National Romanticism as it had been developed to that point was dying.

4. Top: Railway station competition entry project, first prize, Helsinki, 1904. Architect: Eliel Saarinen.

5. Middle: Railway station competition entry project, Helsinki, 1904. Architect: Sigurd Frosterus.

6. Bottom: Railway station, final design, Helsinki, 1906. Architect: Eliel Saarinen.

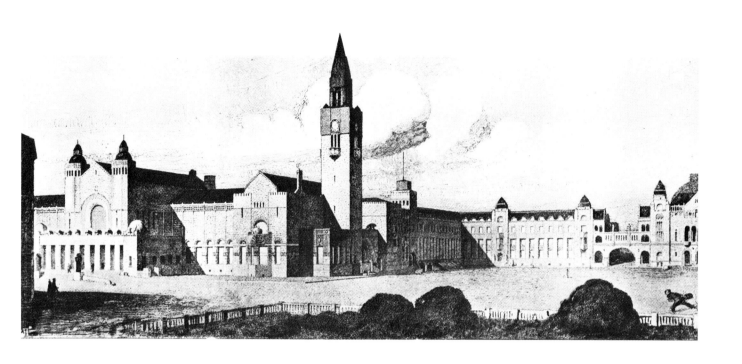

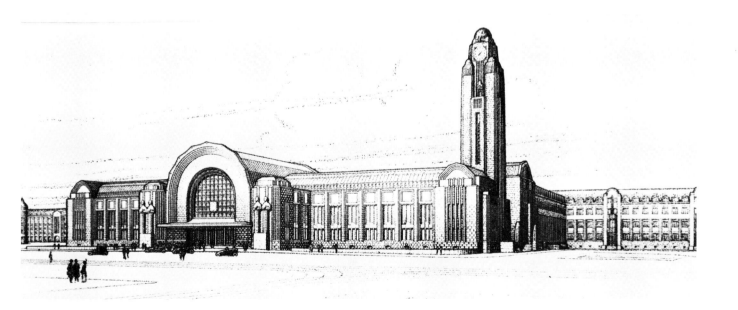

7. Top: Hypoteksbanken, Helsinki, 1908. Architect: Lars Sonck.

8. Above: Villa Väinölä, Alajärvi, 1925.

9. Opposite page above: Naantali Church, survey drawing of the facade, Naantali, 1919. Architectural students: Aalto, Holmberg, and Laine.

10. Opposite page below: Tivoli area National Fair, Helsinki, 1920. Architect: Carolus Lindberg.

The original prize-winning solution by Saarinen was an amalgam of National Romantic mannerisms with a castellated profile pierced by Romanesque arches and even topped with a spired tower nearly identical to the one used on the Finnish National Museum by Saarinen and his partners just around the corner on Mannerheimintie. The final design as built more closely reflected the thinking shown in Frosterus's own entry. The qualities of National Romanticism expressed in this building represent the movement's more international phase in which it was stripped of much of its eccentric, whimsical embellishments and folkish qualities, while retaining some freedom in planning and the massing of volumes.

National Romanticism was a style that had few constraints and was in general manageable only in the hands of the most imaginative and competent designers. Its sometimes fancifully employed open-planning techniques were ill-suited to the design of apartment blocks which constituted a major portion of the growing country's new construction requirements. The final version of the National Romantic style (described by some as the style of "big business"),[18] as practiced by Lindgren (7) and Sonck, expressed a far more restrained and conservative mood, even to the point of employing faintly classical elements. At this time in Finland, as in much of Northern Europe, commercial architecture had come under the strong influence of the Chicago School.[19]

Lindgren's influence on Aalto, it would appear, was to lead him away from the emotional roots of Finnish design in a simple and more classical direction. On the basis of his later works it might be inferred that Aalto derived from Lindgren some of his enormous facility in creative open planning as well.[20]

In the area of theory it seems likely that Aalto fell under the intellectual influence of two men who were never actually his teachers. They were Gustaf Nyström, an architectural historian and design critic at the Polytechnic, and Yrjö Hirn, an aesthetician at Helsinki University.

Nyström, who was an avid enthusiast of Greek architecture and culture, died shortly after Aalto began his training, but he did learn Nyström's approach to classical detailing.[21] Hirn, basically a theorist, seems from his published writings to have espoused a thoroughly anthropological approach to the history of art and design as well as religion. His major books, *The Origins of Art* (1900) and *The Sacred Shrine* (1909), were both published in English and became standard reading at many art schools in the early part of the century.[22] Hirn's major concern was "to determine the part which the *production* and *enjoyment* of works of art play," in aesthetic standards. His main thesis was expressed in *The Origins of Art* as follows:

Art can no longer be deduced from general, philosophical and metaphysical principles; it must be studied . . . as a human activity. Beauty cannot be considered as a semi transcendental reality; it must be interpreted as an object of human longing and a source of human enjoyment.[23]

This rejection by Hirn of "objective" aesthetics and his concern with the nature of the psychological interaction among art, its creator, and its audience prefigure in many ways the attitudes expressed by Aalto in his own mature writings and designs. But for the moment at least some of the academic instruction that Aalto was receiving is more likely to have been influenced by Nyström's classical and archeological leanings as well as by the classicizing direction of contemporary architecture in Central Europe. It is therefore not suprising that the addition to the Alajärvi house bears this out if only in a folk manner. The house he built there later for his brother Väinö contains a fairly correct Doric order executed in wood (8).

At the same time, however, certain buildings in the indigenous vernacular style (not always distinguishable from the medieval-styled buildings designed by the National Romantic revivalists) would appear to have held some attraction for the young architect. This is witnessed by the wooden bell tower Aalto designed in 1921 and constructed in 1923 as an addition to the Kauhajärvi Church. He had previously been exposed to this folk tradition in a structured academic context. We know of at least one student exercise in 1919 in which Aalto was teamed with Herbert Holmberg and Yrjö Laine to produce a set of measured drawings of the fifteenth-century Naantali Church (9), located in a small town north of Turku.[24] The drawings are by Laine, but the title block identifies Aalto as a member of the team, and it is certain that he made on-site measurements for at least parts of the building.[25]

First Professional Projects

Among the most interesting and probably least known projects and buildings from his student days are several designs for the Finnish National Fair held in Helsinki during 1920 and 1921. Aalto is credited with "helping" Carolus Lindberg,[26] another of his teachers at the Polytechnic Institute, in the planning of the "Tivoli" (amusement) area (10) of the fair in 1920. A previously unpublished set of Lindberg's drawings for this Tivoli area shows a most unusual and romantic character in the rendering of a vernacular-styled series of board and batten booths and pavilions. Also detectable is a distinct Baltic Baroque flavor in the profile of the main gateway, which bears a striking resemblance to a building of Aalto's from the following year, the bell tower for the church in Kauhajärvi. The tower is a fusion of differentially sloped roofs and straight and curved walls, yielding a unique shape not unlike some Ostro-Bothnian bell towers in overall shape, but more playful and less orthodox in form than anything found in conventional Baroque architecture of Northern Europe.

Young Aalto's participation in the design of these buildings must have given him an unusually open idea of how the vocabulary of architectural history could be used to produce amusing and interesting forms and

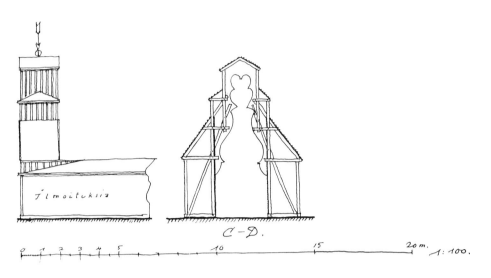

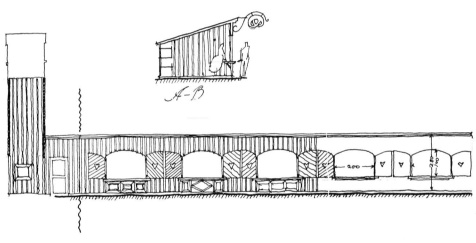

effects. The playful curvilinear entrance portal and the edge of the bandstand structure are composed of a series of linked Baroque shapes. The board and batten texture is painted a contrasting bright color scheme to complete the gaiety of the free-style complex (11). Just as interesting as the profile and curves of the entrance gate is the framing method used to support it. The informal truss configuration is a precursor of many later efforts on Aalto's part to solve structural problems with wooden truss and interlocking braced frames. In fact a similar technique in much more sophisticated terms was employed on the giant pylons of the Gothenburg Fair, in the design of which he was to participate in 1921.

The largest of the early fair designs is his diploma project at the Poly shown in a drawing dated 1921 (12) and signed "Alvar." It is a perspective rendering of a large fair hall, probably the earliest known example of his personal style of draftsmanship. The design for the building, which was to cost 54 million Finn Marks,[27] called for a large quadrangle open to the sky, surrounded by a high, vertically articulated facade, vaguely reminiscent of a classical peristyle temple ruin. In one corner of the building rises a high massive tower topped by a disproportionately small, thin spire. This entire complex, intended as exhibition space, was bordered on one side by a vast railroad right of way in the central area of Helsinki and on each of the other sides by a network of proposed green allées with trees.

The quality of the drawing is like that of a cartoon found in newspapers of the time. Aalto utilized a curvilinear scheme of entourage, not unlike that employed on Saarinen's winning entry in the Helsinki station competition, to set off the rectangular massings of the buildings by employing circles to suggest the sweeping clouds and ovoids to characterize the trees adorning the walks and streets. The tower ornament and profile that characterize this design also seem to prefigure a project on which Aalto would work that coming summer, the fair in Gothenburg (13).

After his graduation in 1921 from the Polytechnic Institute, qualifying him to practice architecture in his native land, Aalto set off for the west with Stockholm as his major goal. In that city he tried to secure work in the office of a young Swedish architect then coming to prominence, Gunnar Asplund, but not finding any opening there, he pushed on to Gothenburg where the buildings of the fair's Tivoli area were under commission to Arvid Bjerke and R. O. Svenson. He found work in Bjerke's office.[28]

In speaking of his experience in Bjerke's office, Aalto said that he made many sketches and drawings for buildings at the fair. He characterized his employer as "primarily an administrator," who had spent most the six weeks of Aalto's employment in Paris.[29] In that period, he claims, he executed the design for the large Congress Hall[30] (14), later used as an acknowledged source for the Royal Horticulture Hall in London (15). The Congress Hall was a giant clear-span auditorium structure supported on wooden composite trussed parabolic arches. The span was 30 m while the maximum clear height was just over 17 m. From each panel point a strut was extended radically outward to form support and bracing for the stepped roof and clerestory glazed window system. This stepped profile was incorporated into the main facade of the building, and in that respect it is truly a function of the mathematical nature of the parabola and the proportions of the straight line segments tangentially projected from the arch (16).

Aalto's acquaintance with this type of wooden construction had begun with the Helsinki Fair projects of the two previous years, but it is rather likely that his interest in such techniques was related to the temporary, rustic structures and equipment required in the backwoods land surveying in which his father had been engaged in Jyväskylä.[31] He also designed a summer theater that was never realized.[32] In a comparison of the drawing of the towers in the Gothenburg and Helsinki Fair projects, it is not difficult to believe that they might both have been the work of the same designer (12).[33] Both these fair towers, in fact, seem to reflect a new trend for the twenties, and while they might be loosely characterized as "classical" with respect to their simplicity and angularity, they are certainly not Greek in flavor.[34]

11. Opposite page above: Tivoli area National Fair, details, Helsinki, 1920. Architect: Carolus Lindberg.

12. Opposite page below left: Pavilion, National Fair, Aalto's diploma project, Helsinki, 1921.

13. Opposite page below right: Entrance pylons, World's Fair, Gothenburg, 1923. Architect: Arvid Bjerke.

14. Below: Congress Hall in the Tivoli area, main entrance, Gothenburg, 1923. Architect: Arvid Bjerke.

15. Bottom: Royal Horticultural Hall, interior, London, 1925. Architects: Easton and Robertson.

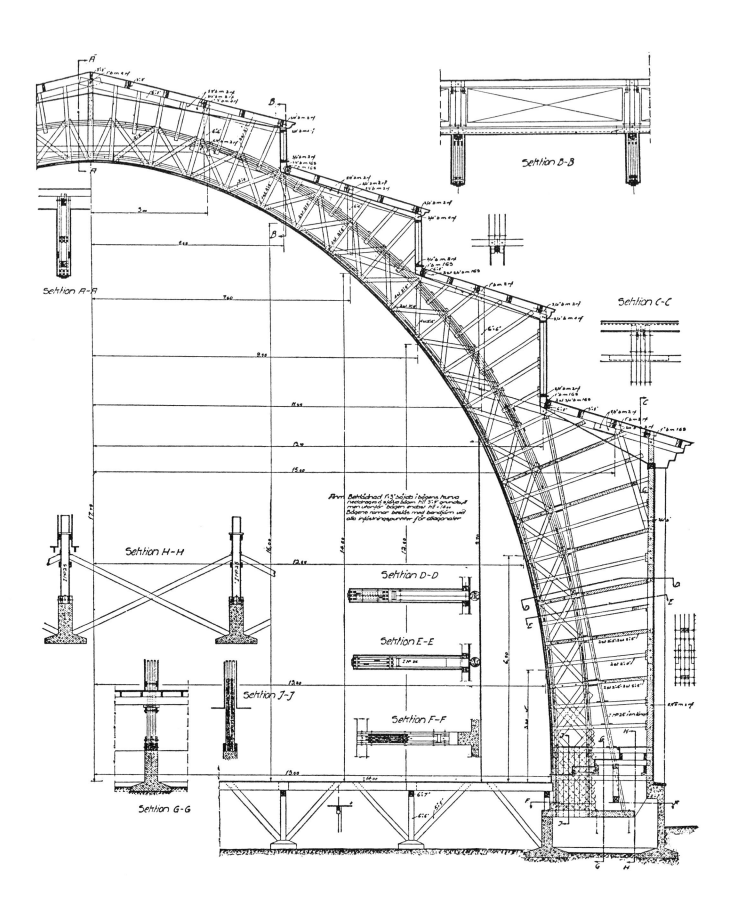

Sektion B-B

Sektion A-A

Sektion C-C

Sektion H-H

Sektion D-D

Sektion E-E

Sektion J-J

Sektion F-F

Sektion G-G

Anm Beklädnad f:3° böjda i bågens kurva
nedragas å sjelva bågen till 3:9 grundsyll
men utanför bågen endast till 1:400
Bågens ramar brették med bandjärn vid
alla infästningspunkter för diagonaler

Classical Spirit for a New Nation

During the first two formative decades of Aalto's career, his growth and development can be observed in his designs for fair facilities. It might be thought rash, in a scholarly sense, to refer to this classicizing as Italianate on the basis of a couple of towers, but one need not look further than the popular architectural journal *Arkkitehti* to find other indications of contemporary interest in that direction. In the February 1923 issue of *Arkkitehti,* there appeared an article entitled "Italia la Bella" by Hilding Ekelund. In it Ekelund described the fresh, simple virtures of the provincial Renaissance style architecture as well as of a few carefully selected simple antique and Early Christian buildings of minor merit that could be seen in the towns and countryside of North and Central Italy. This survey, illustrated with travel sketches by Erik Bryggman and Ekelund, clearly points out the relevance of this architecture for a country just beginning to search for a replacement for the National Romantic style. This rustic version of classicism was popular with architects such as Heinrich Tessenow during the early twenties.[35] The expression of classical motifs as folk art, growing out of the English Arts and Crafts movement, probably symbolized in Germany as it did in Finland, the rising importance of the middle class in the cultural life and democratic movements of European societies.[36] The motifs featured in these drawings are echoed in contemporary architectural projects. Ekelund's drawing of the interior of San Giovanni in Lucca (17) and the profile of Perugia with San Domenico in the background (18) could be cited as adequate sources for Aalto's competition project for the Toolo Church in Helsinki of 1926 (19) were it not that Aalto himself traveled to Italy in 1924.[37]

Aalto returned from Sweden to supervise the construction of his design for the industrial exhibition in Tampere (20). This fair, housed in simple frame buildings, appears to have impressed those who saw it as

16. Opposite page: Congress Hall, structural detail, Gothenburg, 1923. Architect: Arvid Bjerke.

17. Left: Travel sketch of San Giovanni in Lucca, Italy, 1922. Drawing: Hilding Ekelund.

18. Below: Travel sketch of San Domenico in Perugia, Italy, 1922. Drawing: Hilding Ekelund.

19. Bottom: Töölö church competition entry, perspective, Helsinki, 1925.

something unique for Finland. Ekelund remembers it as seeming classical (it employed an arch over the entry) and at the same time new and different. The quality of this design—being on the brink of something new, while possessing a traditional quality—is attributed by Ekelund to Tessenow.[38] The new and different idea of the construction rests in the simple use of slender vertical poles joined by tall sheets of plywood, probably of the same standard size, which act as both the exterior wall and the gusset. This would make it an early example of modular design and construction. The wall was topped by a high glass strip window running around the entire perimeter of the pavilion to admit light to the interior. This building, Spartan and void of any ornament, could be regarded as a display for the plywood industry in Finland. This unusual employment of a bare industrial product as a design element does seem to support Ekelund's point. The overall system also resembles that of some of the Vienna Ringbahn stations.[39]

It may be, though, that for source and inspiration for this building Aalto had to look no farther than Sweden and the work of Asplund, Markelius, and Bergsten, all of whom became fighters for Functionalism and later authors of the Functionalist Manifesto in 1930.[40] His friendship with these figures was to intensify over the years, at least until he himself became a well-known figure outside Scandinavia. In contrast to this use of industrially inspired design elements, the crafts pavilion—a small, open stand covered with a steeply pitched thatched roof with primitive spiral forms adorning the end gables (21) —clearly points to Aalto's preoccupation with simultaneously expressing both machine and "natural" traditions in his designs at this time.[41] In later years he was to successfully employ both modes on many of his buildings in a style that became uniquely his own.

Another unpublished pavilion at the Tampere industrial exposition was the large thatched roof exhibition hall (22), which utilized the same modular wall construction as the main pavilions discussed above. The unique aspect of this pavilion was the system of diagonal bracing it incorporated to give the extra strength to the exterior columns needed to support the heavy thatch that Aalto employed.[42] In this building he combined the two modes of the other fair pavilions: a bucolic and romantic roof as on the craft pavilion and snack bar and an expressed structural esthetic as used on the main pavilions. This pavilion, smaller and lower in height than the main pavilions, sat on a pedestal constructed of timber framing. The bracing members, painted a contrasting color to both the dark columnar members and the lighter plywood infill, give the building a decidedly modern and even structurally expressive appearance.

The other (and heretofore unpublished) architectural element for which he was responsible was a small acoustical "shell" (23) for the performance of musical ensembles, demonstrations, and shows. The structure, made entirely of wood, is an approximation of a giant seashell turned on its hinged edge to focus sound, from the stage in front of it, evenly and directly toward the audience beyond. This shows that at an early period of the twentieth century, as well as an early age for him, Aalto was both concerned with and knowledgeable about acoustics and the problems of sound projection out-of-doors. The construction of this form, while not following the more scientific curves known to architects later in this decade, is a fair version of what is needed to adequately perform the main required function of even sound dispersal from a single point.[43] The inner surface is planked between the slender struts that give the shell rigidity, but the backing material is certainly plywood. While this structure was meant to stand for a matter of days or weeks at most, it is a sophisticated and, for its scale, even daring experiment in the technology of faceted wood shell structures. It presented problems that were not easily solved, for the base form of the shell had to be shored up by a strut at the outer edge of the base on either side to provide extra stability.

The Tampere Fair buildings, prefigure, probably more clearly than any other building or project in Aalto's early career, the varied and complex nature of his mature work. They demonstrate his concern with the small and intimate aspects of designed environments, while revealing his parallel concerns with technical problems of construction and design as well as the emotional and rational expression of the designs themselves. Though increasingly under the influence of first classical and then rational sources, he did not cast away this unique combination of design attitudes.

20. Opposite page top: Main pavilion of Industrial Exposition, Tampere, 1922.

21. Opposite page middle: Snack bar pavilion, Industrial Exposition, Tampere, 1922.

22. Opposite page bottom: Exhibition hall, Industrial Exposition, Tampere, 1922.

23. Below: Bandstand and choral shell, Industrial Exposition, Tampere, 1922.

2
Professional Practice

Jyväskylä

In the early part of 1923 Aalto established an office in his hometown of Jyväskylä. In May, the competition for the Houses of Parliament site selection and preliminary design was announced. Once again Aalto joined the ranks of aspirants who in the next few years sought to establish and maintain their practices based on opportunities arising from the needs of the newly independent state and its policy of open contests.[1] In June, when the competition results had been announced, he did not win a prize, but his proposal did receive a mention (it actually was "bought"). It was the only entry outside the first three prizes to be so honored. The design (24), a project unassociated with Aalto until now, was submitted under the title "Piazza del Popolo." If built it would have occupied the same harbor marketplace site on which his Enso-Gutzeit headquarters (25) was ultimately built in the late fifties and early sixties.[2]

The project was probably so named because of the nature of the site. As a main entrance way into the city it was similar to that of the Piazza del Popolo in Rome. Directly on the main harbor and adjoining the marketplace around which the other main civic buildings of Helsinki are centered, the site was clearly a prime location for such an important building. In later years Ekelund recalled that Aalto had "a very beautiful project." The proposal (26) called for the site on the eastern extremity of the open marketplace to be developed as a single horizontal mass with a giant order stretching up, through what is probably three stories, to match the height of the existing classical buildings on the harbor front, the most revered of which is the city hall by Carl Ludwig Engel. Aalto's building would have completed this existing space in a classical "Baltic" or, more precisely, Petersburgian manner. The drawings, it should be noted here, are titled with the same Roman style lettering he used for many years set into a shell-like title block form that was also used on the site plan drawings for the Gothenburg Fair.[3]

Aalto had a certain degree of national pride in and reverence for projects such as this, and in an article written two years earlier, he cited a fellow artist's emotional outcry as the basis for the furtherance of art in Finnish society:

I recently heard from one of our best known artists, "Finnish art cannot develop properly until we have a large national building project to do." Helsinki needs a city hall, but Finnish cultural life needs above all "a city hall as a building project."[4]

Though he designed many civic centers for communities in Finland, he was not given a chance to design with this emotional dedication until he secured the commission for the Finlandia Concert Hall, completed only in the last phase of his career.

Aside from this early competition, Aalto's development as a designer can only be seen in the progression from one executed building to another. The interpretation of a young architect's practice must necessarily be made on the basis of a very few works. This is even more true with respect to Aalto's practice, for the retarded or only slowly accelerating economy of the new nation, clamoring for attention in the aftermath of the European wars and revolutions, yielded fewer opportunities than might have been expected. Aalto survived, but it wasn't until his move to Turku that he found any degree of financial success as an architect.

At the end of 1923 and the beginning of 1924 Aalto participated in the building competition for the Finnish Houses of Parliament. This contest, following the site plan competition, placed the young Aalto early in his career in the most important and densest level of national competition. The site, where the winning solution by J. S. Siren was built, is on Mannerheimintie near the center of Helsinki.[5] Aalto's entry, called "Flagello," is a grouping of buildings asymmetrically arranged on the site around the square form of the main auditorium or parliament assembly hall.[6] Aalto obviously didn't win, but it was surely unusual to have such a young competitor vying with the older architectural establishment of Helsinki.

In his first year in Jyväskylä, he

24. Above: Houses of Parliament competition entry, perspective, Helsinki, 1923.

25. Left: Houses of Parliament competition entry, site plan, Helsinki, 1923.

26. Below: Houses of Parliament competition entry, elevation, Helsinki, 1923.

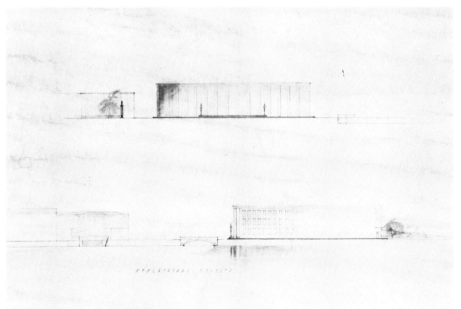

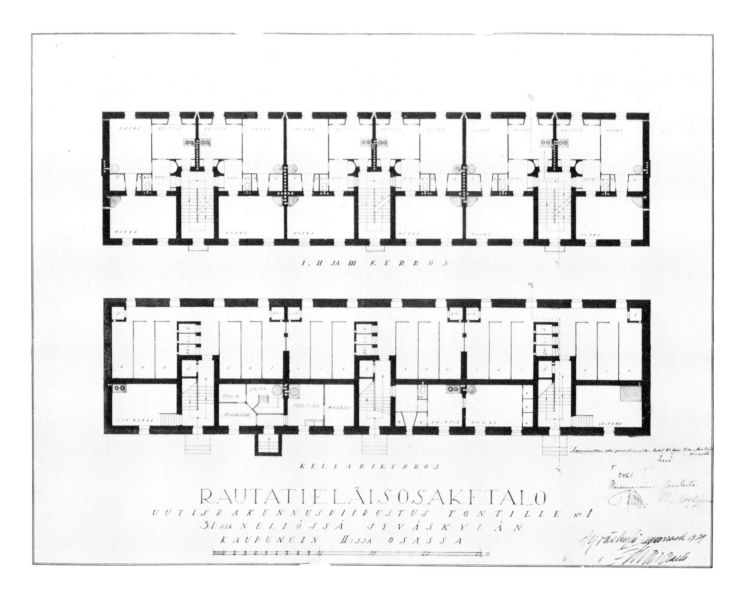

RAUTATIELÄISOSAKETALO

UUTISRAKENNUSPIIRUSTUS TONTILLE № 1

31:ssa NELIÖSSÄ JYVÄSKYLÄN

KAUPUNGIN II:ssa OSASSA

27. Top: Railway employees housing plan, Jyväskylä, 1924.

28. Above: Railway employees' housing, garden facade, Jyväskylä, 1924.

secured two important commissions —an apartment house and a workers' club. These represented the first buildings of any size or architectural complexity that he was to tackle on his own. The apartment block (27, 28) is a row type of building with three doorways providing access to six flats, each pair stacked one on the other. The block, with its entrance garden located on the opposite side of the building from the street or main approach, is an English-type garden apartment introduced in Germany by Hermann Muthesius.[7] By 1922 the Muthesius garden apartment had certainly appeared in the design magazines, and Aalto would have been able to see these publications in the library of the Technical High School in Helsinki.[8] Even though one might think Finland's long, severe winters might make the garden apartment less plausible than in England or Central Europe, this form is the most popular type of multiple dwelling found in Finland today.

The unique aspects of Aalto's building, however, are to be found in its architectural detailing. The trim around the doorways is still painted in the original subdued basic color scheme of red and green with accents of blue. The downspouts (29) of the roof drainage system are wrapped through their entire length with a spiraling steel band whose bright red color contrasts sharply with the light green of the pipes. The downspout's shoes are shaped like classical pedestals completing the evocation of an attenuated polychromatic order. These polychromatic touches, found in much Jugend architecture in Finland, seem in this case more suggestive of a familiarity with the application of decorative colors in the buildings of ancient Greece.

Aalto's use of color here is similarly intended to accent specific details and call attention to their uniqueness in the total scheme of plain painted brick walls and trimless window openings, rather than to integrate them within an overall decorative scheme. The end chimneys (30), projecting slightly from the end walls, are expressed to a

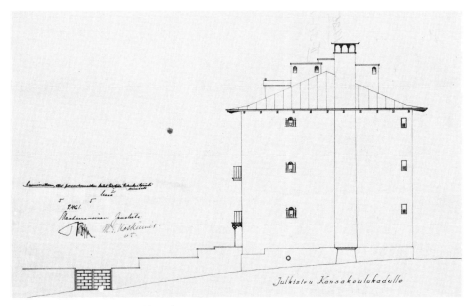

29. Top: Railway employees' housing, general view, Jyväskylä, 1923.

30. Above: Railway employees' housing, end elevation, Jyväskylä, 1923.

31. Top: Railway employees' housing, end wall detail, Jyväskylä, 1923.

32. Right: Railway employees' housing, detail, Jyväskylä, 1923.

33. Above: Railway employees' housing, detail, Jyväskylä, 1923.

34. Opposite page: Workers Club, main facade, Jyväskylä, 1924.

greater depth of reveal in the textured concrete basement story (31). This idea is again repeated at the junction of the roof, which produces the total effect of a corbeled masonry stack. The low metal roof is essentially a flat line broken by three intermediate chimneys that appear to be taller than would be required even in such a deep-snow climate as Finland's. This may possibly be understood as the architect's method of expressing the party wall to retain a more individual identity for each stack of flats, but it is a traditional device often found on buildings in parts of Scandinavia. This shows that Aalto's interest in vernacular motifs was active even during the design process of his classical works.

On the garden facade (32), the vertically ordered entry doorway and steps are capped by the alignment of a small dormer window on the roof. Though built to an obviously austere budget, the ornamentation has been composed in such a way as to capitalize on the Spartan nature of the whole and, by such simple means as color and inexpensive metal work, to produce an effect of quality (33). The folkish nature of the actual motifs would tend to render them palatable to a general public which would not necessarily appreciate the elements of classical style in the architect's conception. This building bears a marked similarity to two contemporary buildings in Helsinki: Martti Välikangas' Käpylä "garden city" suburb, a group of brightly painted board and batten houses and apartments; and the apartment group built by the Helsinki municipal architect's office (Gunnar Taucher, Designer). Both of these examples are distinguished from Aalto's by their more consistent application of classical styling, albeit in a somewhat vernacular manner in Välikangas' case. The maverick quality of the Jyväskylä building is an early indication of Aalto's resistance to the straitjacket of established vocabulary, whether classical or National Romantic.

Marriage and Partnership

In the late months of 1923, Aino Marsio, a woman four years Aalto's senior and trained as an architect at the Polytechnic at Helsinki, started to work in his office. In the spring of the following year the two were married.

Before the marriage, Aalto took a trip to Italy and Austria. In a speech delivered to the Association of Austrian Architects in Vienna in 1965, he noted that this city was one of the first places he had visited as a "student." This must have been the period to which he was referring, for before this date he did not have the money to travel so extensively. According to Teuvo Takala, draftsman and modelmaker in Aalto's office, he and Aino did travel to the Mediterranean on their honeymoon in 1924.[9] The travel sketches he made on this trip show, if nothing else, his observance of and respect for the stones and physical beauty of the southern European environment.[10]

After their marriage, Aalto listed Aino as his partner, but it is a matter of question whether she played a major role in the design of many of his projects. Except for certain ones, some of which carry only her name, the credit given in periodicals and even in competition reviews was to Aalto alone. It seems likely, however, that Aino assisted him on the Railway Workers Housing and even more probable that she played a role in the design and development of the Workers Club building in Jyväskylä.

The Workers Club (34), on the main commercial street of the city and only a short distance from Aalto's apartment block, was built to a significantly larger budget than the earlier building and is evidence of a classical consciousness equal to that of any architect practicing in such a vein in Finland at that moment. In fact it is at this point in Aalto's career that we can see, in the purest version to be found in his

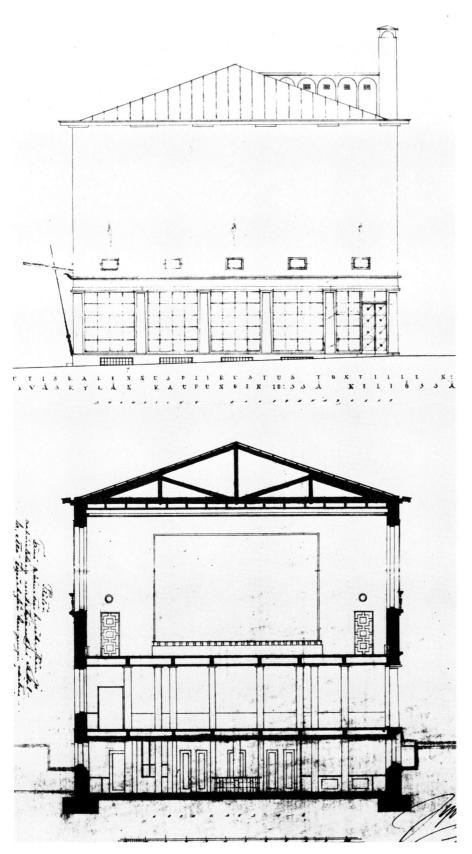

35. Above: Workers Club, section and elevation, Jyväskylä, 1924.

36. Opposite page top: Workers Club, plans of main and basement floors, Jyväskylä, 1924.

37. Opposite page bottom: Workers Club, auditorium plans, Jyväskylä, 1924.

work, the reaction to the sentimentality of National Romanticism which the neoclassical revival constituted.

The progression between the Railway Workers Housing and the Workers Club is one of transition from a stripped-down classicizing shell to a more elaborate Germanic version of Greek detailing. The latter building, which has been discussed as one of the key works of Aalto's early career, has generally been known only on the basis of the esthetic qualities of its exterior, and then mainly through the medium of a few overall photographic views. A set of drawings, only recently found at the Jyväskylä City Archive, now makes it possible to analyze the exact character and specifically unique aspects of the building's interior organization in a way that has not been done so far. An examination of these drawings will allow us to correct some standard misconceptions of just how the building was organized—misconceptions resulting partially from the fact that the ground floor has been remodeled.

The building is essentially a double-storied assembly hall located on top of a glazed, open, columned ground-floor level housing a restaurant and coffee bar. The drawings (35), dated July 1924, show how Aalto was able to come to grips with the problem of placing the heavy weight of the theater, with its seating for 300 people, on top of this open restaurant level. The fairly short spans (36), needed on the ground floor to support the theater floor's weight, were disguised by shaping the interior space of the coffee bar as a round room with a column at the center. This avoids the feeling of a maze of columns that a rectangularly organized room would have given to the ground floor. The relatively light load of the stage is supported on somewhat longer spans in the main restaurant area toward the front of the building. A row of floor-to-ceiling glazing between the columns allows the light from the north and west to penetrate to the inside and gives the effect of a completely open room. The building, originally designed to act as a freestanding

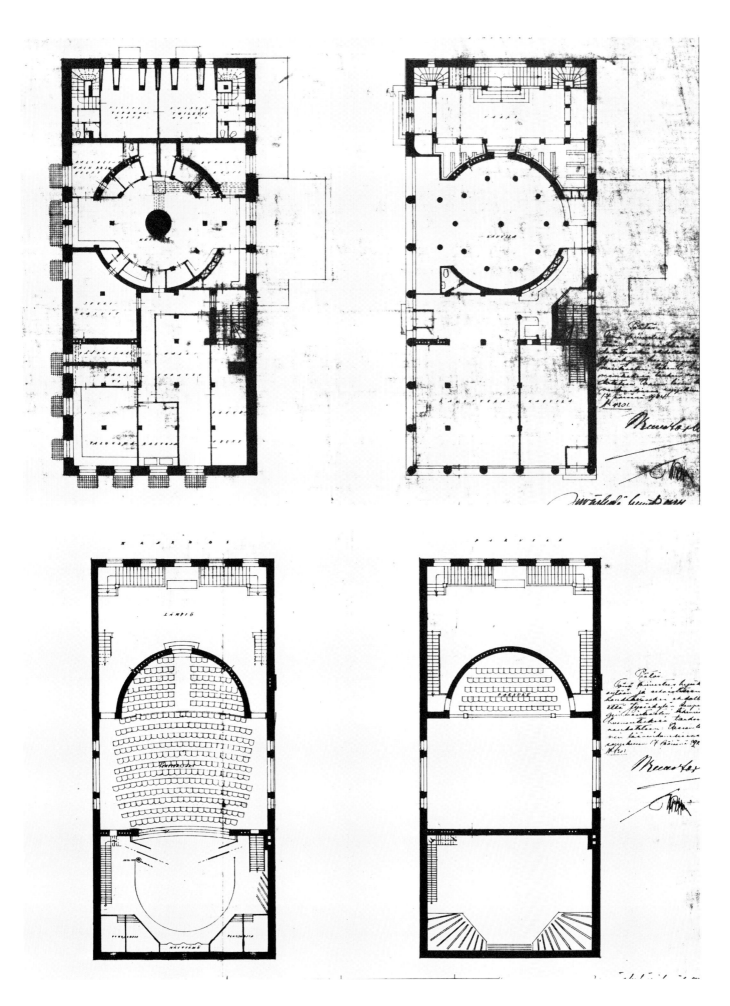

38. Top: Workers Club, auditorium interior toward stage, Jyväskylä, 1924.

39. Above: Workers Club, auditorium interior toward rear wall, Jyväskylä, 1924.

40. Opposite page: Workers Club, theater entrance facade, Jyväskylä, 1924.

structure with windows on all four sides, has since been abutted by new construction to the south, thus cutting off the light through the windows located on that exposure.

The second level (37) of the theater auditorium is reached by an entrance facing the secondary street at the northeast corner of the building. The doorway leads to a lobby where the divided stairway along the east wall, opposite the coatrooms and the entrance to the coffee shop, leads up to the foyer of the theater. The main impact of this space is made by the juxtaposition of the cylindrical rear wall of the auditorium within the rectangular volume. This curved wall, of course, corresponds to and is supported by the east half of the curved wall in the coffee shop below. The main portion of the auditorium is a rectangular volume lighted on either side by a curious version of a Palladian window.[11] The proscenium stage (38), shown on the drawings, was set up with a semicircular cyclorama to symmetrically complement the rear wall of the auditorium (39). The dressing rooms were located to the rear of the stage along the front wall facing the main street, each with a small glazed opening near the floor level.

The external stylistic organization of the building in terms of its decoration and details is just as unique as its internal spatial arrangement. The low, flat roof of the club building is concealed behind a knife-blade cornice which projects over the sidewalk. Below that is a starkly plain white stucco wall punctured by tiny square portholes, each set in a molded surround and arranged in vertical pairs directly above one of the squat rectangular vent windows at the second floor line. This upper portion, a two-story mass, is supported weakly, in a visual sense, by an external row of Doric columns which are faithfully reproduced, though proportionally stunted, giving the building a dwarfed sense of scale overall. On the main elevation (34) all the elements and the related distances between them are either squares or multiples of a square. This method of proportioning, it has

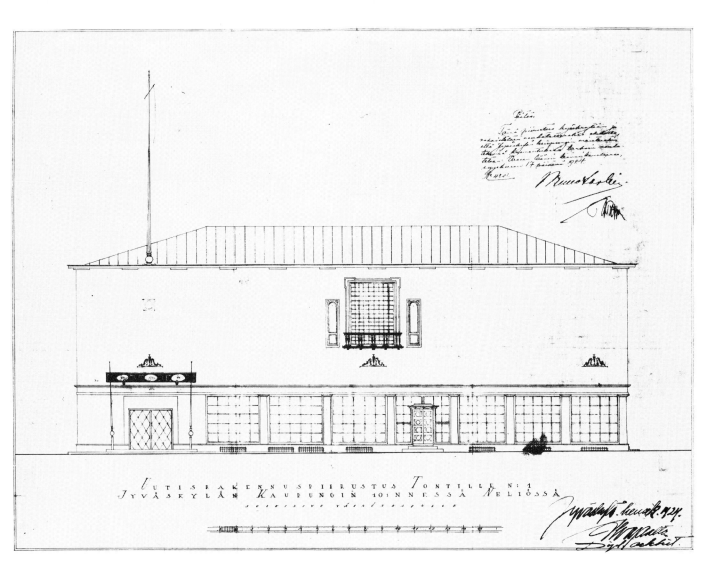

been suggested, was the standard *Hochschule* practice in use in Germany throughout most of the nineteenth century and persisting in some places into the 1920s.[12]

The unfluted Doric order is more an abstraction of a classical element, and the small shallow entablature seems barely adequate to support itself, being no deeper than the width of the columns. The small rectangular windows located just above the midspan of each bay are the strangely low dressing room windows referred to above. Two rows of small round portholes in square molded surrounds are aligned with these windows; the lower row is at approximately eye level of the dressing rooms, and the top row permits the entrance of light into the scenery storage rooms above. These small openings are not shown on the original design and were apparently substituted for

the ornamentation that appears in the early drawings in each of the end bays and over the center. The side elevation shows one of them sketched in its final location.

Here, as in the apartment building, Aalto was concerned about the ventilation in view of the fixed glazing and closed nature of the spaces below. The stale air exhaust system can be readily detected from the plan where the vents are expressed as tiny holes in the interior walls.[13] Through these holes used air was directed into vents that took it up and out of the roof of a wing wall connected to the single chimney through which it exited.

The side elevation (40) presents us with a most curious collection of neoclassical revival elements, and as in the case of the apartment it must be kept in mind that this was the climactic moment of that movement as witnessed by the decora-

tions on Ragnar Östberg's Stockholm Town Hall. For the three urn-and-garland forms on the smooth upper stage, Aalto finally substituted roundels. The giant modified Palladian window, however, remains as the principal element in the upper stage. Here Aalto curiously abandoned the usual idea of agreement between the two divisions of the facade, and some of his devotees have privately speculated that he set the axis of the window off that of the colonnade below to achieve some purposely unorthodox visual quality. The drawings, however, suggest that he set the window exactly in the center of the main auditorium space to maintain the strict symmetrical balance of the classical interior. Obviously it presented problems that were insoluble, and at this point he relinquished the effort to resolve all considerations and conflicts simul-

41. Top: Workers Club, theater entrance portal, Jyväskylä, 1924.

42. Above: Workers Club, auditorium doorways, Jyväskylä, 1924.

taneously. The theater entryway (41), however, offers the observer a chance to witness just how deep Aalto's concern for correctness of technique and matching of lines went. The doors to this entryway, each one exactly half a square, are clad with hammered bronze plates, echoing a long-established Scandinavian tradition.[14] The pattern of low relief diagonal beads, forming a regularized diamond system, is broken only by a pair of unusual hooded door pulls apparently designed to prevent the accumulation of ice, but looking more like medieval weapons than pieces of architectural hardware. The doorway is a simple, trimless opening in the stucco wall, but the joints of the stonework sill and their alignment with the door jambs and edges indicate a marked familiarity with the classical architect's desire to achieve geometric integration of each element to the total design.

The interior details reveal the same careful attention to classical taste. The curved rear wall of the second-floor foyer with its square panel grid executed in plaster recalls both revetmented facades and marble-clad walls of Romanesque and ancient Roman buildings. The open-railed stairs to the balcony have black cove strips running continuously along each tread and up the risers. This detail of coving each tread individually in parallel rather than following the sloped line of the stringer was a basic technique of decoration and detailing in wooden vernacular houses in the Baltic and was to be conserved by Aalto and used as a signature motif from the Turun Sanomat on.

The arched auditorium entrance (42) has doors paneled to match the adjoining wall. The interior of the auditorium, though straightforward and even plain, carries through the classical idea by the employment of standard lighting fixtures that complement the paneled doors and swags of fabric trim under the lower edge of the balcony.

It is surprising at this time to find such an increasingly classicizing trend as is exhibited by these two buildings in a town like Jyväskylä.[15]

Aalto had brought the most recent international architectural developments to Central Finland, and it was not entirely predictable that he should have been able to express and continue to perfect this classical vein at a pace in keeping with and even ahead of his Helsinki contemporaries.

This building makes it clear that National Romanticism had died and that emotion, at least in the work of young Aalto, was suppressed at this time. The state of Finland was now 5 years old, and the need for romantic avenues of expression, once independence had been achieved, was greatly reduced. But there was no immediate or rational direction clearly related to the new status of the land; rather we find a generalized national desire to appear more professional and less provincial. The new freedom from prescribed or accepted nationalistic dogma and the increased ease of travel gave designers and architects the chance to import theories and styles previously inaccessible or deemed unacceptable. The establishment of a new style for the independent state and the leadership of its theory were up for grabs.

Ekelund's article of 1923 was quite surely a product of this search for a new and appropriate design philosophy. It is interesting, therefore, to find Aalto delving in a different direction—into the realm of classical theory and relating the democratic nature of Greece to his newly liberated homeland and its government. He was not the first architect to find a satisfying correlation between the architecture of ancient Greece and a newly formed nation's desire for an expression of democracy in its buildings. Classicism, moreover, was no stranger to Finland. Carl Ludwig Engel, Finland's greatest architect before Aalto, had spent most of his life producing neoclassical buildings that were to be valued highly by each succeeding generation of local architects and were a vivid reminder of a period when Finnish architecture was developing well within the broad mainstream of Europe.[16] Now classicism was once again a sort of

"international style," and as such it was sure to appeal to Finnish progressives as well as establishment types who were eager to embrace a style that would give their nation a more professional and less provincial appearance.

The first project, publicly credited to both Alvar and Aino, was a 1925 entry in a furniture design competition for the arts and crafts journal, *Käsiteollisuus.*[17] Their entry (43) mottoed "Trianon Americaine," provided the design for a basic group of simple household furnishings which were more than nominally of classical lines. Most of these designs were revivals in spirit of seventeenth-century English and Northern European styles which had been preserved to some extent in vernacular furniture forms. This in itself might not seem surprising, but contrary to the retarded design trends one might expect in Scandinavia given its position outside the mainstream, the designs of the other competitors reflect an agreement with the revived Biedermeier style then popular on the Continent. Careful study reveals that Aino's and Alvar's furniture designs represent a significant departure and according to one critic, "were quite adventurous in taste for 1925."[18]

The competition, which was entitled "Furniture for Common Homes," was originally intended to provide furniture designs for a one-room worker's house, but the organizers felt that it would be too condescending to indicate this explicitly in the title. The Aaltos appear to have been the only entrants to have actually arrived at a version of simple furniture in their adaptations of traditional cottage-style pieces. The other published entries were essentially toned-down versions of the currently fashionable mode. Except for the Grecian-style divan the other pieces in the Aalto group reflect the style of objects in the catalog of the William Morris Company during the same period.[19] The hoop-back Windsor chair, though upholstered, along with the gate-legged table and glass-front cupboard are almost faithful copies of Morris Company designs. The major deviation

seems to be in the details. The drawer fronts on the chest, for example, appear to be a loose interpretation of a rusticated stone wall from the architectural vocabulary of the Italian Renaissance. The Windsor chair, while typical, employs parts of bent wood, a feature that Aalto was to incorporate into chairs he would design much later. This follows, more or less, designs of Thonet which he may have seen in Vienna the previous year.[20] The development of this range of furniture designs indicates a rough agreement with the architecture of Aalto at the same time. The same blend of stylistic metaphors such as Italian Renaissance and English Arts and Crafts in a single collection indicates a lack of clear direction or unified design values. But this soon changed, and for a while the Arts and Crafts tradition disappeared from the Aaltos' work altogether.

Aalto's next building, one long associated with his early career, is the House of the Civil Guard, a private paramilitary club, built in Seinäjoki in his home district of Ostro-Bothnia. The work has previously been known to the world on the basis of one view of a single structure, which is only one of three located around a courtyard on a well-landscaped site. The heretofore published building is, in fact, the barracks located at the rear of the site and the last of the three to be constructed.[21] The main building (44), which houses the administrative offices and ceremonial spaces, stands on the street side of the site, and a stable and garage complex (45) is located on the eastern end of the parade field/courtyard (46) which has a semicircular form at its western end.

The main building (47), designed in 1925 and finished the following year, still bears evidence of an extraordinarily refined spirit of classicism in both its organization and its details. Comparing the drawing of the main elevation with the building, one can see that here Aalto was able to realize almost all the design as recorded. The attenuated pediment with its prominent acroterion atop the roof line is missing from the actual building as are the corner pi-

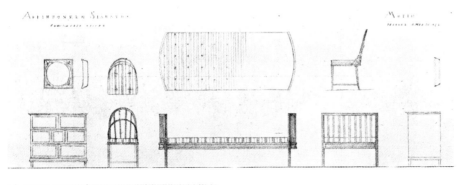

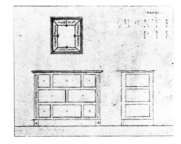

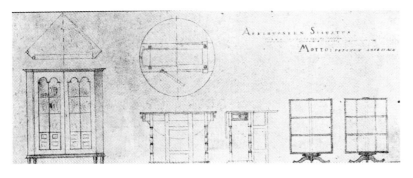

43. Furniture competition entry design for *Kasiteollisuus* by Aino and Alvar Aalto, 1925.

lasters, but the board and batten fabric of the wall is the same. Six giant order Corinthian pilasters stretch the height of the main facade from the top of the paneled battered concrete base that continues around the entire building. The paneled doors and transom of the main entrance are still visible in contemporary photographs of the complex (although the door paneling is now expressed as a lozenge or diamond pattern rather than the squares of the original drawing). It is, however, from the drawings of the original design, published here for the first time, that the fine-grained nature of these exterior details can best be judged.[22]

The drawings also permit one to see, from the plan and interior details, that the building represents the most splendid example of neoclassical revival detailing Aalto ever produced (48). The giant circular assembly room located in the rear, half of whose mass projects out into the parade ground (49), is the dominant space both spatially and stylistically. Its round shape was employed more for its ceremonial qualities than anything else, but its presence here and in the coffee shop and auditorium of the Workers Club represents Aalto's growing interest in the accent and dynamic qualities of curved forms. In the center of the room two massive inverse-sloped, Minoan-styled piers (50) are placed to support the load of the rear wall above.[23] The stairhall, leading from the main entrance to the assembly room as well as the office complex on the upper floors, is a pastiche of eccentrically classical elements. The wall surface of the entire room is decorated with a system of horizontal lines that correspond in dimension to the riser height of the stairs, while the ceiling above is coffered.

The stair balusters (51) are paneled with a shape that approximately reproduces the outline of the building in plan, while the newels are decorated with standard classicizing motifs. The focus of attention, because of their size and position, is a pair of metal light standards possessing an extraordinary serpentine base and mounted at the top by a splayed cluster of five lamps. They are mounted on the entrance landing newels but extend to the head line of the doors on the floor above. The overlushness seems almost Victorian in flavor and strangely out of place in the rustic hinterlands of Northern Finland.[24] The semisubterranean assembly room was covered with a sod covering, perhaps to give it a truly underground feeling from a psychological point of view. The stable in the rear is less exciting architecturally but displays a definite classical feeling in its use of small segmentally arched ventilation openings and in the crowning pediment of the central portion, which is recessed and supported on two wooden columns to give the effect of a portico.

By comparison these design elements make the barracks building, constructed some time later in a smooth white stucco and employing only a minimum of classicizing motifs, seem to be a building of a different style and even perhaps for a different site. The original design for this building, erroneously dated 1928 by some sources, does show some of the same classicizing elements—the base, the spring points of the entrance arch, and the guard house. The high style classical details were perhaps eliminated for a more utilitarian tone when it was designed and constructed in 1925. It is probable that when these buildings were brought to light years later Aalto chose not to have the more classically refined buildings published since they clearly show that at this point in his career he was as far away from his future destiny as a modern master as one could imagine. However, it would take him less than four years to make the breakthrough complete.

The ability of Alvar Aalto to turn out such refined contemporary versions of classical, or more properly neoclassical revival, buildings is difficult to rationalize since the one teacher who might have imparted this training, Gustaf Nyström, died too early to be influential in his de-

44. Top: Civil Guards House, main building, Seinäjoki, 1925.

45. Above: Civil Guards House, stable and garage, Seinäjoki, 1925.

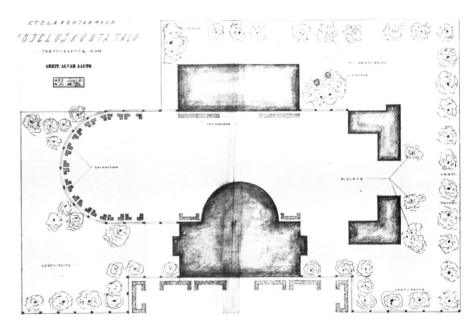

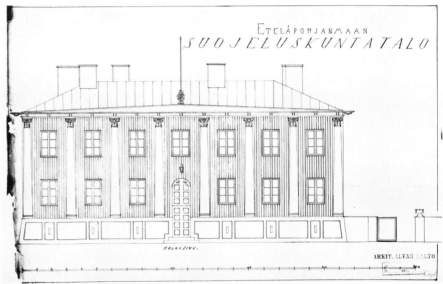

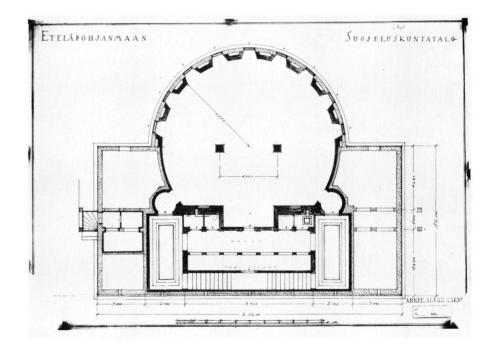

46. Top: Civil Guards House, overall plan, Seinäjoki, 1925.

47. Middle: Civil Guards House, main building facade, Seinäjoki, 1925.

48. Bottom: Civil Guards House, main building basement plan, Seinäjoki, 1925.

49. Opposite page top: Civil Guards House, main building rear view, Seinäjoki, 1925.

50. Opposite page middle: Civil Guards House, main building section, Seinäjoki, 1925.

51. Opposite page bottom: Civil Guards House, main building stairway detail, Seinäjoki, 1925.

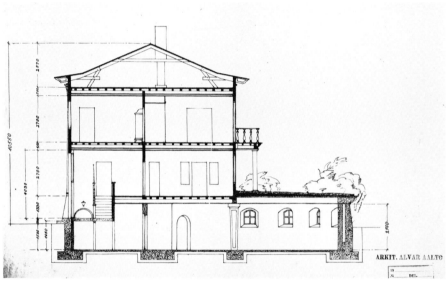

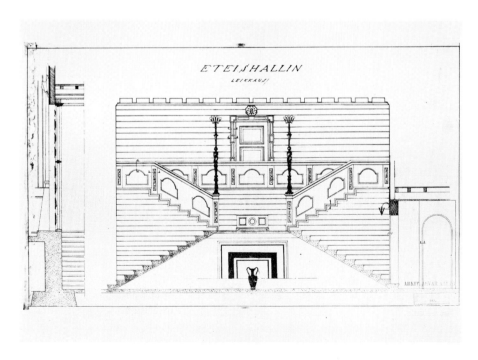

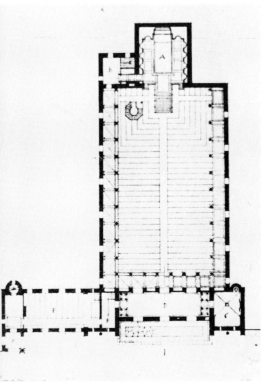

52. Top: Church competition entry, interior perspective, Jämsä, 1925.

53. Above: Church competition entry, plan of sanctuary, Jämsä, 1925.

velopment. Even taking into account the fact that Aalto was well acquainted with Asplund's popularization of classicizing forms and details in Sweden and that he himself had followed, if only briefly, in Asplund's footsteps, the facility he showed in inventing and creating new classical forms was unusual. It is more probable that Aino, also a graduate of the Poly, was a student of Nyström's for a number of years, and since she was older than Alvar, she would have been able to fully experience his unique and inventive approach to the classical design vocabulary. This can be readily observed in many of her designs and drawings recently discovered in the Aalto Atelier. Her ability as a draftsperson and classical detailer during this period seems to have exceeded that of Aalto himself. Her collaboration with her husband is certainly a possible explanation for the facility in handling the classical vocabulary which is exhibited in so many of Aalto's works of this period.[25]

At the end of 1925 Aalto was invited to participate in the limited competition for a church in Jämsä, one of Jyväskylä's neighboring towns. The interesting aspect of this contest, with respect to the development of a national style, is the extent to which all three of the published designs display Italian influence.[26] The winner of the commission, K. S. Kallio, produced a Palladian or, more precisely, a "Burlingtonian" centrally planned rotunda design. Armas Lindgren's entry called for a low cruciform church with plain stucco walls and a dome on a square crossing, the entire mass punctured only by simple rectangular windows topped with glazed roundels. Aalto's design (52), by far the most Italianate, was the only proposal that called for a basilica plan. The scheme (53) projected a baptistry located just off the narthex and a high central-aisled nave flanked by lower arcaded side aisles. Most church plans in Finland had previously been designed in either centrally planned or Greek-cross forms. This building with its basilican plan, while designed for a Lutheran congregation, would have

pleased the most conservative Roman Catholic clergy in its liturgical correctness. The building was to be sited adjacent to a piazza located, Assisi style, on a hilltop (54) and reached by a long monumental staircase on the opposite side of the open space. The facade (55) rendering recalls the revetments found on Romanesque churches, such as San Miniato in Florence.[27]

Aalto's church design, like the others, has an expressed Italianate spirit, but his is taken more or less directly from the primary sources rather than from any reinterpreted international style of traditional Renaissance forms. As has already been noted, it is probably fair to say that Ekelund, as evidenced by his article "Italia la Bella," had been searching for a fresh architectural style for Finland within this Italian mode. It would seem from the competition drawings that Aalto, among others, was prepared to carry Ekelund's suggestions into actuality. Aalto's project (56) was clearly admired by the editorial staff of the *Arkkitehti* for they placed one of his interior sketches on the lead page of the article reporting the competition results. It is likely that this gesture of recognition from his peers in Helsinki gave Aalto a certain amount of satisfaction. The interior space, as he delineated it on the section and perspectives, would have been a large, light volume with plain walls emphasizing the high arched choir which is raised and set off by a prayer rail (57), very much in the style of that element in San Clemente in Rome. Aalto must have been thinking about this kind of space when in the same year he wrote:

The church does not need art, the church does not need decoration. . . . It needs something else and needs it badly. It needs pure and earnest form, no matter what the forms are. . . . It is more beautiful to see a humble modest room, where a small detail, a crucifix on the grey limestone wall represents religious devotion.[28]

At this stage Aalto must have fancied himself a theorist on the nature of religious architecture. Within the next year and a half he entered com-

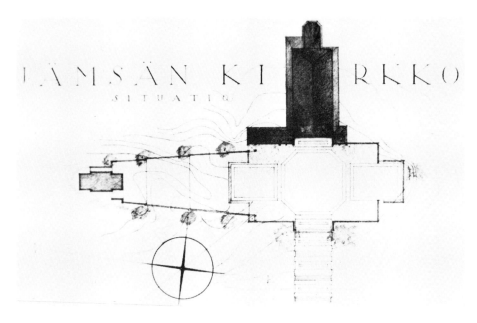

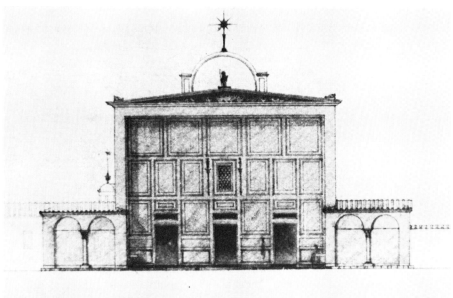

54. Top: Church competition entry, site plan, Jämsä, 1925.

55. Middle: Church competition entry, elevation, Jämsä, 1925.

56. Above: Church competition entry, perspective of entry plaza, Jämsä, 1925.

57. Left: Church competition entry, section looking to altar, Jämsä, 1925.

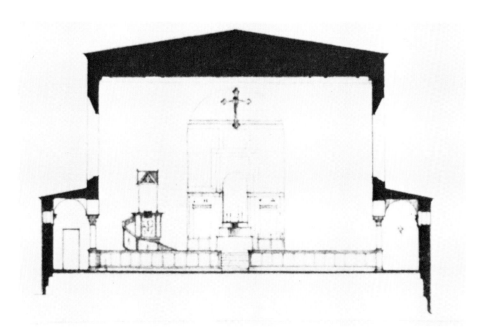

58. Finnish Industrial Exposition, Helsinki, 1876.

petitions for churches in Helsinki, Tampere, and Jyväskylä, while renovating one at Viitasaari and beginning the construction of his first complete church building at Muurame.

Wooden Houses

Paralleling the mainstream of Aalto's development—what might be termed his "trained tradition" as manifested primarily in his stucco and masonry buildings—is the almost separate manner revealed in his early wooden buildings. These must be handled apart from the major buildings of Aalto's neoclassical period and such examples as the Seinäjoki Civil Guard building, for their sources are different. As opposed to the generally established and official mainstream classicism that derives from Engel, and the later Wagnerschule, these wooden buildings are a part of the vernacular Baltic wooden house tradition with its own classical derivatives.[29]

Wood had always occupied a prime position in Finland as the most available and utilitarian building material. It was the country's chief structural material even in the age of the Industrial Revolution's greatest impact on architecture, the mid-to-late nineteenth century. At the National Industrial Exhibition held in Helsinki in 1876, the major spanning material of the main pavilion (58) was wood.[30] The trussed dome utilized ferrous metal as only part of the lower chord in a steel tie rod. This is characteristic of Finland for even today wood and related products remain the country's chief industrialized export. This adherence to tradition becomes especially noteworthy at a moment in history when the fairs held at Philadelphia and Paris were making a major impact on visitors by demonstrating the use of ferrous metal as a means to longer and lighter spans for exhibition purposes.

The Baltic tradition with respect to wooden domestic, and even civic, architecture is long and rich in Finland, and many examples still remain. The tradition is a classical one that basically imitated the finely proportioned stucco buildings of the early to midnineteenth century. In some cases classical detail and proportion were converted directly and fairly accurately into wood, but for the most part a naive interpretation of the style persisted. But while the vernacular style of these wooden buildings depended on the classical tradition, the style was often welded to nonclassical and more strictly utilitarian modes such as board and batten sidings. Parts of towns and villages such as Porvoo still exist that are built primarily of wood and often possess a fine classical tradition and a rugged folk mode side by side and sometimes even in the same building. Aalto would have been thoroughly exposed to this tradition even if he had not trained to be an architect.[31]

The number and size of buildings he constructed during the twenties in this general vernacular vein demonstrates a developed facility with and even affection for the mode. In March 1919, following the renovation of his parents' house and the addition of the bell tower to the Kauhajärvi Church, he executed a design for a Youth Society Building in his home village of Alajärvi (59). This building is clad in a fine board and batten and has a fairly high metal hip roof adorned with a small cupola at the ridge line. The main entrance is through a recessed colonnaded porch which, however, seems to have been added later. The outside of the structure offers little of interest but is firmly in the combined style mentioned before. The building's interior, however, shows slightly more in the way of detail. In the sections drawn by Aalto (60) both large and small assembly rooms are indicated. The upper section is drawn through the main salon and shows that the main wing is spanned by a scissors truss concealed behind a ceiling, partially contoured to take advantage of the increased height possibilities afforded by the trusses. Above the shaped ceiling Aalto indicates insulation material. The structural system, while formal and defined, utilizes the type of lumber trusses that

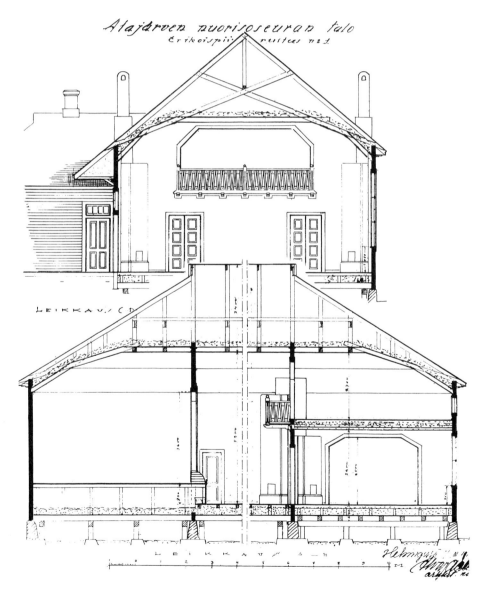

59. Top: Youth Society Building, remodeled main entrance facade, Alajärvi, 1919.

60. Above: Youth Society Building, sections, Alajärvi, 1919.

2.

61. Above: Multifamily house with shop, side view, Jyväskylä, 1923.

62. Opposite page top: Casa Lauren, two-family house, elevation, Jyväskylä, 1925.

63. Opposite page bottom: Casa Lauren, two-family house, end elevation, Jyväskylä, 1925.

Aalto and his classmates would have been exposed to during the survey drawings for the Naantali Church.[32] The resulting two-story space is linked on the lower level to the rest of the building by paneled double doors and on the upper level, at least visually, by a balconied opening. At the opposite end is a large, raised stage with a proscenium opening visible in the lower section drawing. The beveling off of the large openings, which echoes the shape of the trussed ceiling, contributes to the building's rustic feeling. The balcony and railing detail, although made of wood, seems to be a stylized rendering of a rope and pulley and is nonclassical in every sense of the word. In general the interior, with its giant corner fireplaces, resembles an Alpine chalet more than anything in the native Baltic domestic tradition.

In 1923 Aalto executed a simple two-story multifamily house at Jyväskylä. This building originally had a small shop on the ground floor and four modes apartments located on two levels. This house (61), published before as a two-family house, is again a blend of vaguely classical traditions with the return on the end gables making a refer-

ence to a classical Renaissance pediment and straightforward domestic techniques. On the main facade facing the street, Aalto executed an open base broken pediment supported on stylized corner boards, giving a refined character to the simple wooden structure. Aside from the end elevation, the most interesting aspect of the design is the cantilevered balcony (now much altered) attached to the second floor level along the southern side. While it is clad in the same sheathing as the main body of the house, the under structure has been expressed in a vaulted-style profile, reminiscent of Alpine balconies in Central Europe. This inclusion of a folk motif on an otherwise classical exterior is in the mainstream of his architectural development during this period.[33]

On November 17, 1925, Aalto produced a set of drawings for a two-story block of flats in Jyväskylä known as the "Casa Lauren" (62). As might be expected the style of the building was not far removed from the generic style of its Baltic counterparts, but a few details are worth mentioning. The swagged garlands, presumably made of wood, divide the primary facade into six bays each containing stacked windows. The end elevation (63) shows an arrangement of exterior stairs giving access to the upper apartments. The stairway has a colonnaded shed covering over the landing and stair treads which give it the look of a mountain dwelling, again similar to those found in the Alps. Examining the plans one can see that there were to be only two apartments in the building, each having a service entrance on the facade away from the street. An interesting feature is the corner entrance hall which, in each apartment, stretches through the two main stories linking the living-dining level with the sleeping level. The basement plan indicates the typical Baltic stone foundation for exterior walls. What is surprising is that there is no visible through-wall ventilation such as he had planned for the Railway Workers Housing constructed just prior to this.[34]

The following year Aalto published an article in *Aitta* magazine on the nature of housing design in Finland and the state of the art in general. The house that he used as an example of good and responsive design was a projected design for his brother Väinö's house mentioned previously. The interesting aspect of the house was the combination, in a single building, of various classical details which are truly Mediterranean, but adapted for North Central Finland. The plan (64) proposed for the Villa Väinölä, as it was referred to, has a simple, covered courtyard open to the second story. Around this double-height volume two levels of dwelling spaces are arranged in a somewhat pinwheel fashion. Along one side Aalto located a large portico that had wooden columns arranged in pairs and groups of three. They were originally painted pink and the ceiling above was a dark blue.[35] The configuration of the courtyard volume and its interior (65) is quite Roman in feeling and detail, but the outside of the house is a modest low-key, closely spaced batten arrangement with bright contrasting trim. The actual house as built (66) has been altered a great deal but the original details that remain confirm the plan as drawn.

Perhaps the largest building Aalto executed during this period was the hospital at Alajärvi (67). Its complexity of program and architectural massing distinguish it slightly from the typical wooden buildings discussed above, but the amalgamation of the two major traditions which Aalto was to carry in varying degrees throughout his design career are splendidly present in this civic building. The design drawings, which reveal the general organization of the building (68), were signed on the last day of September 1927 and presumably construction started immediately thereafter. The drawings reveal that the building is organized in two parts along an L-shaped layout. The administration, kitchen, and service function, as well as the operating theater, were located along the entrance side while the patients'

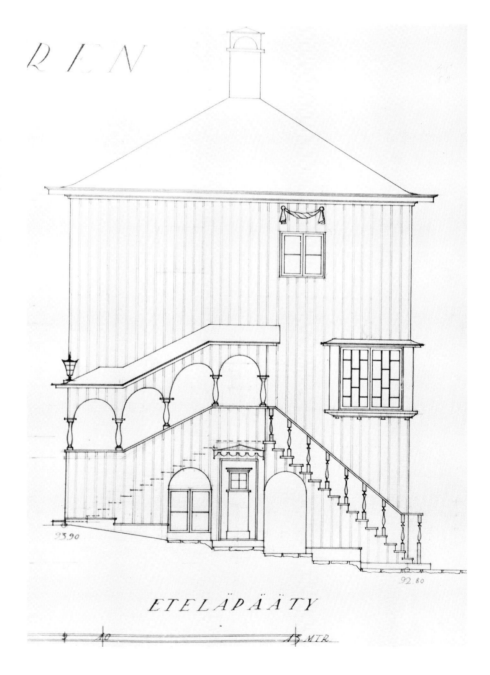

ETELÄPÄÄTY

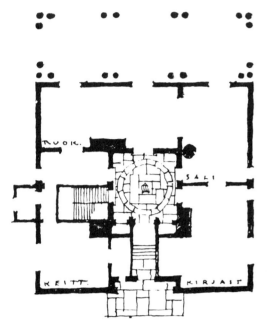

64. Above: Villa Väinölä, proposed plan, Alajärvi, 1926.

65. Above right: Villa Väinölä, interior perspective, Alajärvi, 1926.

66. Right: Villa Väinölä, main portal, Alajärvi, 1926.

rooms, wards, and toilets were located around a wide central hall in the larger wing. In the courtyard formed by the two wings of the L, Aalto placed the entrance loggia. This colonnaded porch (69) contains four Tuscan Doric columns which are the richest part of the ornament of the hospital building. Their classical nature contrasts gently with the finely battened surface walls, which were accented by dark window surrounds and panels at the corner of the building's wings. The courtyard has a central round point of hedges opposite the middle bay of the loggia, well concealed in a square-shaped hedge which is exactly aligned with the projecting kitchen wing. The sections (70) reveal that the central hall is lighted by a large quadruple-sashed window located in a segmentally headed surround, giving it an almost Palladian feeling and certainly one of openness and light. Although the hospital has been altered slightly, the overall detailing, such as the tiny port window on the rear facade (also found in the Villa Väinölä), and the unsymmetrical fenestration, indicate that Aalto was not bound exclusively by Baltic or any other tradition in that sense. The timber rafter scheme is again a rather lightweight and, for a heavy snow climate, rather brave treatment to gain the maximum use of the attic volume. The building, though constructed late in his early phase, demonstrates a mastery of the time-honored building traditions of the Baltic's wooden architecture.

The two major traditions present in Aalto's wooden structures were to play a decided role in his later years, but there would be a lapse of nearly a decade before he would reap the rich harvest of these vernacular and naive classical motifs and again take them into the mainstream of his conscious design style.[36]

Classical Projects

In the latter part of 1926, Aalto was still immersed in traditional architectural thought to such a degree that even an isolated examination of

67. Left: Municipal hospital, rear view, Alajärvi, 1927.

68. Below: Municipal hospital, plan, Alajärvi, 1927.

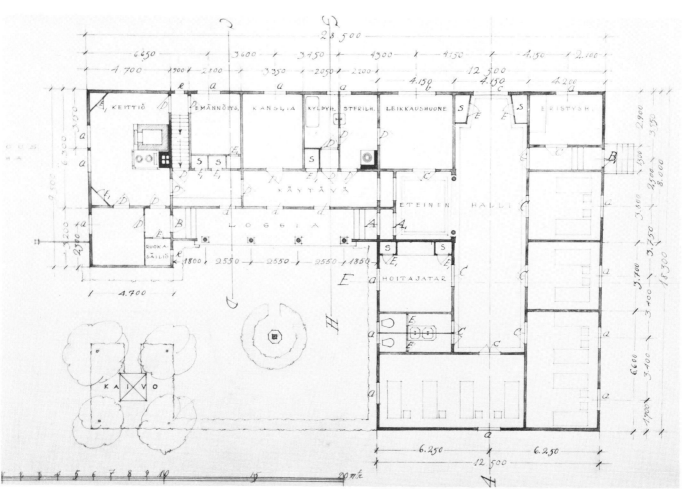

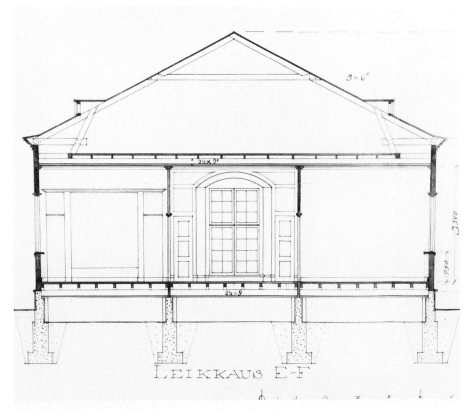

69. Top: Municipal hospital, entrance portico, Alajärvi, 1927.

70. Above: Municipal hospital, section, Alajärvi, 1927.

71. Opposite page top: Monumental plaza layout for urban development, Jyväskylä, 1926.

72. Opposite page middle and bottom: World Headquarters Competition entry for League of Nations, preliminary sketches, Geneva, 1926.

any single project by a trained eye would not be able to discern in his planning designs that he was on the verge of a breakthrough to a more progressive style. This can be seen in two projects designed at that time: the street development plan for the center of Jyväskylä and the competition proposal for the League of Nations.

The study executed for the city of Jyväskylä was a proposal for a system of planting and urban development for the expanding town toward the Taulumäki region to the north. Aalto's plan (71), based on the existing street pattern of the town, called for the establishment of a monumental plaza focused on a projected pair of large buildings of identical mass and presumably civic importance, reminiscent of the twin churches that are the focal points of certain great Italian squares.[37] The plaza was meant to provide an appropriate transition from the old regularized grid of the town to an established angular artery to the north. The tree-lined boulevard did not actually terminate at the plaza drawn by Aalto but rather ended timidly at another, smaller plaza at the juncture with Kauppakatu, the main commercial street of the town.[38] Near this confluence stood Aalto's newly completed Workers Club just off axis with the diagonal boulevard. He made no attempt to bring his building into the interplay with the diagonal Puistokatu.

Around the existing market square in the top center of the plan, he designed an extensive series of formal gardens reminiscent of European palace gardens.[39] This would form a link between the marketplace complex and the larger green space of the hillside park to the west.

To the southwest, around the main square of the town, he designed a scheme to enhance the city's civic center. Along one edge of the church square he indicated a long narrow porticoed building to stand on the opposite side of Vapaudenkatu from the existing nineteenth-century city hall, which he apparently planned to replace. To the rear of this building, facing the 1880 church of L. I. Lindqvist,[40] he located a group of planting bays in the shape of meanders. Axially facing his proposed new city hall, along a reclaimed edge of the main square, he indicated a large paved plaza to tie the two civic buildings to the city church which stands directly in the center of the existing open square.[41] Strangely, he seemed to ignore his recent design for the Civil Guard House which was to be more or less on axis with the church mass, although he did make an indentation in the curb line to indicate some special consideration for that site.[42] It does not, however, correspond to his solution as finally built. To the east of this he indicated a lakefront plaza as a point of primary access, since water transportation in the summer months is a reality.

The overall extent of Aalto's contribution might be misinterpreted if it is not kept in mind that the existing street pattern was entirely retained and that Aalto only proposed a device for blending the two systems at the north, as well as some modifications around existing squares. His proposal, while simple in its Baroque definition of plaza and street alignment, is awkward and unstudied in its relation to the street patterns he had observed on his travels in southern Europe. That the plan is incompletely studied is understandable for a preliminary sketch, but still it offers only a meager, standard Baroque treatment for the design of urban spaces.

The second project of that year, the League of Nations competition entry was actually due for submission on January 25, 1927.[43] The competition, however, had been announced by September in the *Arkkitehti,* along with the publication of the program, and Aalto had actually begun work on July 25. The flavor of his entry is in keeping with the Mediterranean nature of the town plan and the Civil Guard House, but in this case the headquarters of the world body is shown in a decidedly Grecian style.[44] The headquarters was to sit high on an acropolis outside Geneva (72), and it would be approached by way of a series of

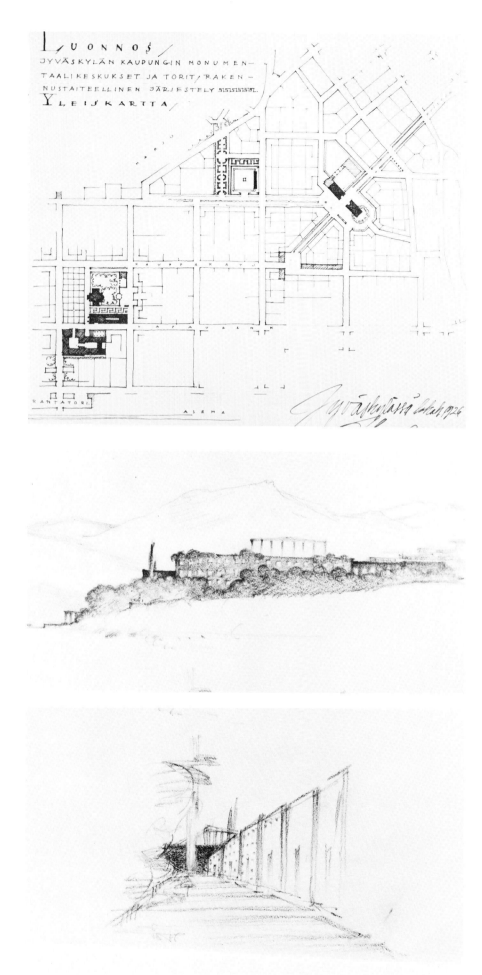

73. World Headquarters Competition entry for League of Nations, preliminary sketches, thumbnail perspective, Geneva, 1926.

First Competition Success

Aalto's last two buildings to be firmly in the classical-Italian period were the competition project and building for the Club House of the Civil Guard in Jyväskylä, built 1927–1929, and the Muurame Church, located some 15 miles (24 km) to the south. Both buildings, or rather the original designs for them, had been conceived at about the same time, during the first half of 1926. The entries for the Civil Guard House were due on May 15 of that year. Aalto's entry (74) was his first successful one in an open competition. He received second prize, 10,000 Finn Marks (old Finn Marks), and eventually the commission.

Since the building was later to be extensively remodeled upon its conversion into a post office, the only critical judgment that can be undertaken must be based on the evidence of the competition drawings. The scheme (75) for the Guard House is essentially a variation on a Florentine palazzo, with a three-part facade that fronts on the central square of the town. The ground floor at the sidewalk level is given over to a row of glass-fronted shops with a tall, slot-like formal entry located in the center. This entrance leads up a long, straight-run stair to the first floor where the main functions of the club would take place.

All but one of the published entries allowed for a later expansion that would double the area of the first stage of the building and yield an enclosed courtyard located away from the street. The courtyard was reached only by a narrow drive through the facade of the building.[46] Aalto's design (76) provided for this option and was shown complete with landscaping and four Lombardy poplars (77). Also contributing to the bucolic effect were two rusticated cylindrical towers, one of which was built and still stands (78). The building was intended to be a military compound of some degree of security. At the end, Aalto placed a dining terrace with an elegant straight-run stair with a low baluster open to the garden.[47] The facade is symmetrically balanced around the

stepped ramps more like those of Assisi than the Athens Acropolis. Nevertheless, the style of the building as shown in a recently discovered series of sketches has a pronounced Greek form (73), complete with a colonnade along one side and a giant high portal flanked by columns at the main entrance. The design, however, is not truly Greek and can best be described as neoclassical in its restrained and stilted detailing. Also among the discovered sketches are indications that Aalto toyed with other neoclassical ideas and a literal adaptation of Asplund's Stockholm Municipal Library complete with a giant flat-topped rotunda.[45] The rotunda appears again in what seems to be a mannered version of the Pantheon in Rome.

The decided classical spirit of these two projects shows how far Aalto was in 1926 from the transition which would take place so soon afterward.

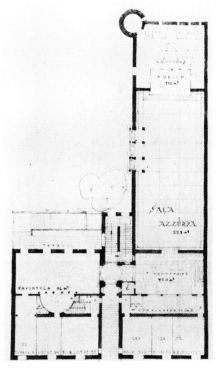

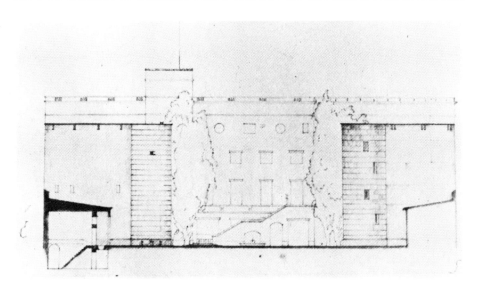

74. Top: Civil Guards House, view from square, Jyväskylä, 1927–1929.

75. Middle: Civil Guards House, competition entry, facade, Jyväskylä, 1926.

76. Above: Civil Guards House, competition entry, plan of ground floor, Jyväskylä, 1926.

77. Left: Civil Guards House, competition entry, section of court, Jyväskylä, 1926.

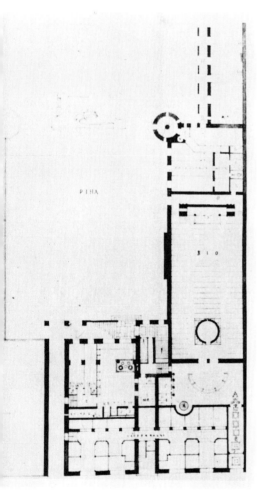

78. Top: Civil Guards House, detailed view of stairtower, Jyväskylä, 1927–1929.

79. Above: Civil Guards House, competition entry, plan of main floor, Jyväskylä, 1926.

grand entry on the left by the courtyard portal and on the right by the entrance to a cinema located on the ground floor. Above this base stage the middle portion is treated simply with a flat wall and square window openings. The lintel above each window projects slightly to define the void. The entire facade is capped by a frieze.

The cinema complex is located directly under the clear span of the large hall on the main floor (79). Just as the courtyard towers were given a round form for mood, the cinema employs round projection and ticket booths and a semiround lobby furniture ensemble to achieve contrast of form for visual amusement and relief to the more rigid rectangularity of the overall design. The main floor is given entirely over to the major rooms of the Guard's organization. From the cylindrical vestibule on the main floor, access is provided on the left to the restaurant and on the right to the main meeting room or lounge. Straight ahead to the rear a stair tower leads to the remaining smaller rooms on the upper floors. The restaurant and dining terrace are dramatically separated by a row of four high doors, which constitute one wall of the courtyard beyond. A large, semicircular niche recessed into the exact center of the interior wall appears to have been an attempt to transform the restaurant into something more than just a rectangular room. This overall form, as well as the row of posts across the open end, should probably be read as a preoccupation with a version of Italianate elegance rather than any expression of modern curvilinear design. The large meeting room of the Guard, poetically labeled "Sala Azzurra," is splendidly lighted by a giant Palladian window facing out to the courtyard and contains a "podium" at the far end. In the drawings Aalto has sketched on this element a design for some theatrical sets or backdrops that are possibly inspired by Palladio's Teatro Olimpico in Vicenza.

Viewing the rear elevation from the aspect of the courtyard it is possible to see that the entire composition pivots asymmetrically around the rectangular stair tower rising above the roof, giving a friendly and romantically Mediterranean feeling to the courtyard, at least on the drawings. This direct contrast with the cold, formal, and even military facade is in keeping with the spirit of the palazzo prototype. The capping frieze on the facade with its marching, sitting, and bending figures, was never built, but was pared down to a simple band of vertical flutes stretching across the entire width (80, 81). The other piece of ornament on the facade is a pair of bronze doors leading to the cinema complex (82). These cladded doors show a personally stylized tree, composed of a traditional spiral motif, common since ancient times in Scandinavia and throughout Europe.[48] This building gave Aalto an opportunity to experiment with relationships necessary to solve a multifunction architectural program on a larger scale than the Workers Club had provided. The Civil Guard House project, moreover, was a good primer for the even larger multipurpose scheme for the Southwestern Agricultural Coop building competition in which he won first prize in 1927.

The other building of this period, the Muurame Church (83), though far simpler and much more modest in budget, nevertheless allowed Aalto to express his newly found enthusiasm for Italian design in the realm of church architecture; this was his first commission to design a complete ecclesiastical building. If this church did not possess a certain Finnishness, it might be mistaken for a church on a similar lonely hilltop site in or near almost any small town in North-central Italy. The general massing of the composition is a three-part assembly of long hall, balanced on one side by a high, square-plan campanile and a low arcaded administrative wing on the other. The campanile is topped by a molded entablature, on top of which a slightly narrower extension rises with slotted bell openings in each of the four faces and above that a low-pitched roof. The entire exterior surface is finished in a fine, light-colored stucco. The main fa-

80. Top: Civil Guards House, detailed view of main facade, Jyväskylä, 1927–1929.

81. Middle: Civil Guards House, frieze detail on main facade, Jyväskylä, 1927–1929.

82. Bottom: Civil Guards House, main facade cinema entrance, Jyväskylä, 1927–1929.

83. Above: Muurame Parish Church, main facade, Muurame, 1927–1929.

84. Opposite page top: Muurame Parish Church, interior view to choir loft, Muurame, 1927–1929.

85. Opposite page bottom: Muurame Parish Church, interior view to altar, Muurame, 1927–1929.

cade owes a simple debt to Alberti's San Andrea in Mantua, with its understated white pediment broken by the superimposed boxy white niche.[49] Aalto's version seems almost an abstraction of the original. At the rear there is only the simple projection of an unadorned apse.

The interior could have been inspired by the medieval churches spread throughout Southern Finland; the single space, accented by the use of simple wooden furniture, and the exposed wooden rafters which frame the view into the vault above all help to create a primitive, rural Gothic feeling. It may be that local architectural traditions were beginning to encroach on his classical inclinations. On this point it must be kept in mind that, while this church was designed in 1926, it was not finished until 1929,[50] and since the interior was among the final stages of construction, it probably owes little if anything to this early, classical phase of his career.[51]

The choir loft (84) stands on posts which rise from the floor and does not touch the side walls. It is located just over the main entrance, producing the effect of a narthex but also giving a dramatic feeling to the interior volume. This drama was heightened by the use of an open row of candles on both sides of the narrow center aisle leading right up to the altar (85). Natural lighting for the altar comes from the full-height side window facing east. The nave is artificially lit by ten Poul Henningsen fixtures, pendant-mounted from the soffits along the side walls.[52] This type of direct-indirect fixture, made in Denmark, was similar to those that Aalto was to produce and utilize in most of his later buildings.

By the time this building was completed he had turned out the prize-winning design for the Paimio Sanatorium, which, along with the Turun Sanomat building, launched him as a major modern architect.

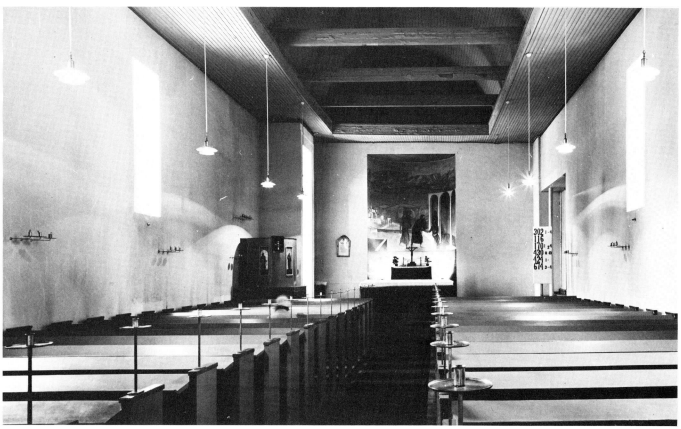

Classical Maturity

In the summer of 1927, Aalto moved his office to Turku, a major port city in the densely populated and rapidly expanding commercial area of Southern Finland, to prepare for the construction of the largest building in his early career, the Southwestern Agricultural Co-operative. The move occurred in the same year as the tenth anniversary of Finnish independence, and the future must have looked very bright. Finland's old desire for recognition as a member of the world community now took on new meaning.

Aalto had come of age during a period of architectural uncertainty. As a student and young practitioner he had worked in a number of styles and had taken part in the general development from the highly embellished National Romanticism to an increasingly stripped-down classicism which, however, had not been resolved into an appropriate national style. It could be said that taste was evolving toward the simple clarity of the International Style, but in any case the interim simplicity of the classicism of the twenties undoubtedly prepared people for the next rationalizing phase.

In moving to Turku, Aalto had taken more than a nominal step toward the outside world; not only would he have more access to the new modern architecture of Europe, but he had relocated in a predominantly Swedish-speaking part of Finland. This base, nearer to Sweden culturally and geographically, enabled him to travel more readily and inexpensively and to witness the Functionalist developments taking place only a few hours away in Stockholm.

The method of awarding commissions during the Russian domination, which favored architects sympathetic towards the Imperial government, was altered by the new Finnish state to a democratic system of open competitions that determined how commissions for the new state's buildings were to be distributed. This procedure seems to have been arranged voluntarily by the Society of Finnish Architects (SAFA),

and no legislation to sanction or enforce it was required. Many architectural commissions continued to be awarded privately and by means of limited or closed competitions, but architects for the key buildings, especially those of a civic nature, were most often selected after the due process of a published, public contest. As the sanctioning body, SAFA insured that universal rules of fair play and reasonable notice would provide any qualified architect in Finland with a chance to compete.[53] Jury members were drawn from a wide range of interested parties, including the project client, SAFA representatives, and the first-prize winners of previous competitions. Many countries during the period utilized this traditional method for selecting architects for various projects of national importance, but in this respect Finland led all others by far.

Very few of the contests in Finland were open to architects of other countries. The architects for every type of building, from vacation houses to churches, hospitals, sports facilities, transportation facilities, and government buildings on both national and municipal levels, were determined by this procedure. The competition for these commissions became a way of life for Finnish architects, and a pattern was developed that has lasted to this day. The idea that a young designer with only a minimum amount of experience might, after qualifying, not only be able to compete with established professionals for these commissions but have an equal chance at winning them, is one that has fascinated architectural students and graduates since the training of architects in a formal sense began. In this respect Finland is truly unique in the realm of architectural practice.

Alvar Aalto was certainly one of those students who was inclined to see himself in a position of equality with the established professionals, if not superior to them. He probably didn't feel so confident when he took part in the 1923 competition for the site plan for the Houses of Parliament. In 1925, however, he took

part in the limited competition for the Jämsä Church mentioned earlier. In fact Eliel Saarinen was to have taken part, but as a consequence of his relative success in the Chicago Tribune Tower competition and the American opportunities that appeared in its wake, as well as a general disenchantment with National Romanticism in Finland, he immigrated in 1923 to the U.S.A.[54] Impressed with the young Aalto's abilities, Saarinen recommended him to take his place in the invitational Jämsä competition.

This invitation, despite the failure of his entry, must certainly have bolstered Aalto's self-esteem and probably made the winning of the open Co-op and Viipuri Library competitions seem like a natural development in the career of a "young genius," which to some extent it was. His success spurred him on to enter even more competitions and later in his life he blandly observed:

During those years I entered many competitions and won many prizes, mostly first prize but usually something. . . .[55]

Indeed he did win prizes, and while not always first, the ones in which he did led to major and crucial commissions in his career.

Church Competition Projects

In the first part of 1927, the year of his move to Turku, Aalto entered no less than three competitions for the design of parish churches, the Töölö Church in Helsinki, the Viinikka Church in Tampere, and the County Congregation's Church on the edge of Jyväskylä.[56] The first design was executed in March, the second in April, and the third in June—just before he moved to Turku. During this period he was involved in the renovation of several churches in Central Finland as well as the commission for the Muurame Church. The three projects, as might be expected, have many aspects of design in common. All are of the basilican type with free-standing bell towers; all are situated on a hill or other high place in the land; all have elements composed in an informal, asymmetrical layout on the site; and all exhibit the same low-key classical treatment found in his other works of that year. Perhaps because of their similar siting requirements, the Töölö Church and the Jyväskylä Church are closer in feeling to each other than to the Viinikka Church. The Töölö project was labeled "Job" (19). The Jyväskylä project was called "Taulumäki" (after the place in which it was to be located). Both projects were sited near a road system with the basilica mass projecting well into the site and the ground level falling away from the grouping to give the effect of a rural Italian hilltown church.[57] The Töölö project, if built to Aalto's plans, would have been a four-part complex located around a piazza and set on a terraced hillside garden. The contours of the hill would be delineated with interlocking diagonal and orthogonal walkways (86) leading up to the church from the street below. The Taulumäki project (87) shows a more elemental church with its flanking campanile standing beside an orchard on a rural hilltop amidst a group of dwellings.

Despite the difference in scope of the programs, the architecture of these two church designs is the same with respect to style and proportion. Aalto, in selecting an appropriate style for each of these buildings, seems to have tried to give one an urban and the other a rustic feeling, but the basic Italianate source of both is too strong to allow for a significantly different interpretation. The Töölö Church design, unified by the use of simple rectangular solids with stuccoed surfaces, is arranged in a well-balanced composition of three distinctly different volumes (88) grouped around a courtyard with a slender campanile located at the visual fulcrum. Both campaniles were designed to rise to a height equal to seven times the width of their square bases, and each had the same slot-type opening found on the Muurame Church. The Taulumäki tower (89) was to be a smooth white shaft resting on a cubical base trimmed with rustications and a cornice, while the tower of the

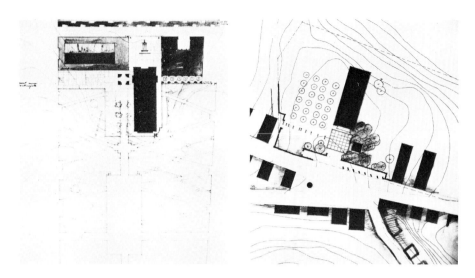

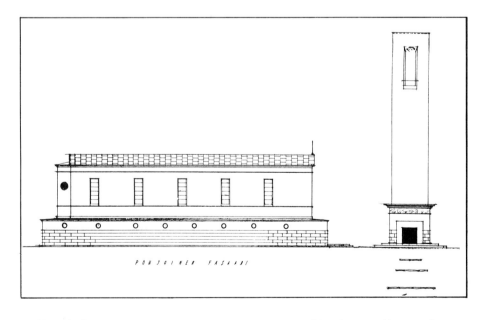

86. Top left: Church competition entry for Töölö area, site plan, Helsinki, 1927.

87. Top right: Church competition entry for Taulumäki, site plan, Jyväskylä, 1927.

88. Middle: Church competition entry for Töölö area, elevation, Helsinki, 1927.

89. Above: Church competition entry for Taulumäki area, elevation, Jyväskylä, 1927.

VIINIKAN
KIRKKO

THE CHURCH
OF MANCHESTER

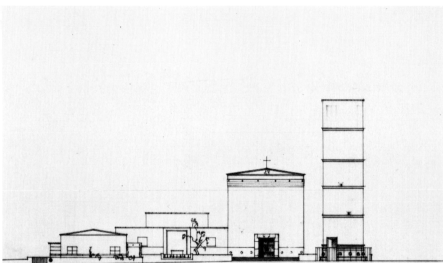

Töölö Church was designed to stand on four corner piers, with the shaft above marked by a molding at each floor line and a shallow capping cornice. Metaphysically, both are akin to the Muurame Church discussed earlier, and the interior of the Taulumäki sanctuary is essentially the same as that proposed for the Jämsä Church two years earlier.[58]

The project for the Viinikka Church, labeled "The Church of Manchester"[59] (Tampere, an industrial city in Finland, is often called "Manchester" after the English industrial city), exhibited a more restrained sense of neoclassical detailing than either of the other two designs from that year. The site (90), a triangular plot located in the central area of Tampere, is bordered on all sides by streets. To a lesser degree than in the other two churches, the ground slopes away from the rear of the complex, terracing down to a street bordering on a sports park. The site plan shows that the rectangular courtyard arrangement —comprised of the church, its attached parish house, and the parsonage—is counterbalanced by a free-standing cylindrical campanile at the corner of the site, which is actually out in the street itself like some early Christian or medieval relic left in its original position and

90. Top: Church competition entry for Viinikka area, site plan, Tampere, 1927.

91. Middle: Church competition entry for Viinikka area, elevation, Tampere, 1927.

92. Above: Church competition entry for Viinikka area, perspective, Tampere, 1927.

protected by a fence.

The composition (91) does not demonstrate the same classical equilibrium that the Töölö Church design does, although the distribution of elements was also asymmetrical. The overall composition displays a slightly nervous tone which is reinforced by the strange quality of the neoclassical details found on the otherwise simple planar faces of the buildings. These details, concentrated for the most part at the ground level, are in low relief and exhibit a curiously original idea of ornament which utilizes classical motifs in a mannered style. The base of the church and campanile are banded and carry a row of circular bosses, creating the effect of a riveted layer of material. The capping pediments on the sanctuary and the parsonage are so shallow in height as to deny the special nature of that shape. The perspective from the playground below shows an attempt to create the same informality and dramatic effect by placing the complex on the highest ground, which couldn't have been more than a few meters above the street level, and by taking advantage of the foreshortening effect gained by so doing (92). In overall terms the Viinikka Church design resembles the Taulumäki proposal, but the windows and doorways are in all cases square, which, in the context of the design, adds to the uneasy sense of proportion and geometry already described (93).

The one element that is truly unusual is the bell tower; proportionally more squat than that of either of the other churches, it is not unlike the stair tower on the Civil Guard House being constructed at that time in Jyväskylä This form, although found in the Romanesque towers of Pisa and Worms, was seldom used by classical-minded designers of any age except for the purpose of housing attached stair towers. The moldings, which divide the stack horizontally and break up its height, are closer together in the midsection, making that stage shorter than those above and below it. Although this is not solely a medi-

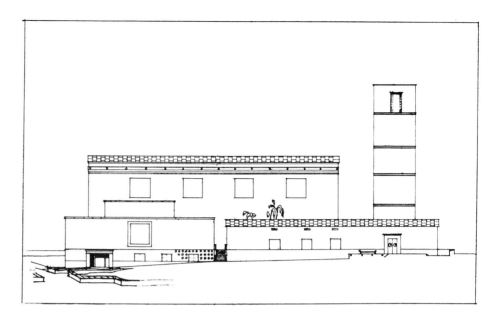

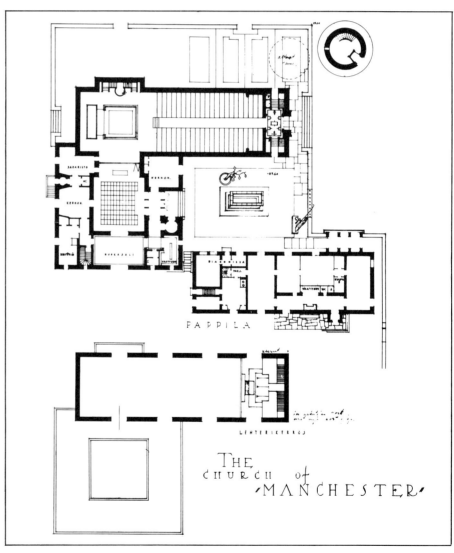

93. Top: Church competition entry for Viinikka area, side elevation, Tampere, 1927.

94. Above: Church competition entry for Viinikka area, plan showing parish house, Tampere, 1927.

95. Top: Church competition entry for Taulu-maki area, interior showing organ loft, Jyväs-kylä, 1927.
96. Above: Church competition entry for Töölö area, interior showing altar and organ screen, Helsinki, 1927.

eval pattern, it is definitely an un-classical one.[60] The progression of stages ends abruptly in a slotted top with only the thinnest of moldings and a flat top. On the site plan draw-ings, as if anticipating a lack of sympathy from the client for the ec-centric location of the belfry, Aalto placed a note explaining that a rec-tangular one might be used if de-sired and in that event it would not be necessary to locate it in the cor-ner of the street intersection. It could be placed instead back against the corner of the church building proper. If the jury didn't understand his reasoning they would have available an understandable alter-native.

The details of the Viinikka Church project present a picture of Aalto's evolving design taste at that mo-ment. The basement of the parish house was to be rusticated with a grid of miniature roundels echoing the bossed friezes on the cathedral and tower. These forms later appear in the doors of the Co-op as glazed perforations and steadily thereafter in many buildings as a paneled screen or divider; they can even be compared with the ceiling of the Vi-ipuri Library. The doorway from this basement level is trimmed with a pi-laster and lintel arrangement that re-sembles the neoclassical door sur-round that Aalto placed on the Korpilahti Church when he reno-vated it in 1928.[61] The details from that as well as from the Viitasaari Church reconstruction of 1925 and the Pylkönmäki Church restoration of 1927 reveal exactly the same level of neoclassical detailing as do these drawings.

Another classical element in the Viinikka Church proposal can be observed in its plan (94), which shows Aalto joining the structures of church, parish house, and parson-age, rather than keeping them sepa-rate as he did in the Töölö project. Instead of grouping them around a piazza in the Italian style, here Aalto chose to link the three by a format recalling the plan of the Roman atrium house. The main buildings enclose a courtyard whose focus is a rectangular cistern; its axis runs

parallel to the nave of the church on its right and back to the entrance of the atrium-centered parish house. This building's square central hall, with its ceiling rising above those of the surrounding rooms, opens di-rectly into the choir area of the church through a large square por-tal in the party wall. Opposite is the pulpit niche in the south wall. The niche formed by this portal (to be screened off by a movable partition during services), together with the south niche, creates the effect of a shallow transept.

Enclosing the courtyard on the north is the parsonage, structurally separated from the parish house by a flight of stairs running down to the terraced hillside at the back. The greater forward projection of the parsonage, with its entry portico jut-ting south toward the campanile di-rectly opposite, gives the parish house courtyard a feeling of enclo-sure which is complemented by the siting of the free-standing tower. But despite the classical elements, the asymmetrical lapping and massing of the disparate volumes is highly anticlassical, looking back to the freedom of the National Romantic style and forward to Aalto's later works.

Within two years he would fully shed the tightly ornamented style in favor of the Functionalist philoso-phy, but even after the switch in thinking had commenced and was beginning to show up in the design and execution of his secular works, he apparently continued to find the classical mode appropriate as far as church design was concerned. The transition between classical de-sign and the beginnings of modern-ism, analyzed and documented by scholars specializing in this peri-od,[62] is clearly exemplified in Aal-to's practice at this moment. An ex-amination of his work at this stage reveals a gradual thinning of the veil of classical detail as the modernist strain takes over.

The interior designs of Aalto's churches exhibit the same creative approach to refined neoclassical details as do those of the exteriors. The sketch for the altar piece of the

Taulumäki Church project (95), like that of the Jämsä Church (96), shows a series of banded organ pipes decorating the wall. Perspectives of both reveal Aalto's concern for the total visual effect of the end wall of the sanctuary. Both drawings indicate a raised altar platform and walls recessed in a deep square apse. The Taulumäki design, with the pure semicylindrical reeded form of pulpit cantilevered from the blank wall of the apse with the form of the Angel Gabriel framed by bands of flat classical decoration, shows a more keenly developed sense of neoclassical forms as they were used outside Finland. The proposed Viinikka altarpiece appears to be a mural decoration comprised of figures from the Parthenon frieze arranged in a pyramidal composition crowned by the figure of a flying angel (97).

Aalto's style of drawing at this stage of his career is clearly adequate to impart the spirit of the intended design to any observer. His reliance on established techniques can be seen in the planar definition given to the praying group surrounding the communion table in the Jämsä sketch which is treated, with its interlocking circular forms, in the same manner found in the cloud formation of the Helsinki Fair sketch of 1921 (12).[63]

After moving to Turku, Aalto regularly submitted entries in the continuous string of competitions open to Finnish architects and later in 1927 entered and won the competition for the Viipuri Library. In the Turku years alone, he entered eleven competitions, and while he only managed to win a few (aside from the sanatorium and library that were to give him an international reputation), the competition process served to develop the ideas and theories with which he was experimenting.

97. Church competition entry for Viinikka area, interior showing altar decoration, Tampere, 1927.

AALTO
DISCOVERS
A NEW
WORLD

3
Turku: Classical Foundation

To understand Aalto's impact as a force in modern architecture, it is necessary to appreciate in a detailed sense the five major commissions he secured and built during his practice at Turku, the old capital city located on Finland's southwestern coast. It was in this city that he transformed himself from an architect of local fashion to a member of the Modern Movement who would never be satisfied with any design that merely reflected current popular trends. The ostensible motive behind the move to Turku was the Agricultural Co-op building, which also provided the financial basis to support the move. However here, and in two later instances as well, Aalto was to take advantage of the opportunities presented by such occasions. He utilized the relocation to evolve his practice on a higher plane than it had previously been.[1]

Upon arriving in Turku, which was still the commercial center of Finland and its major port, Aalto immediately experienced a sense of the city's accelerated building activity. In the 6 years of his residence there, architectural development in Finland underwent a transformation with relation to style and rational execution of building plans, which can be characterized simply as the introduction of the International Style into Finland's mainstream. At the same time that a general modernizing tendency was alive in the land, Finnish architects were beginning

to shed their new-nation status and search for a more mature attitude in relation to the outside world. That general development can be measured in Aalto's career on two primary levels: first, in the fairly continuous progression beginning with the somewhat classical Co-op, through the Standard Apartment block, the Turun Sanomat plant and offices, the 700th Anniversary Fair, and culminating with the Paimio Sanatorium; and second, in the series of steps spanning the same years from 1927 to 1934 that comprised the total development of the design of the Viipuri Library. The end result of each of these lines of progression was the realization of a "heroic" example of modern architecture.[2]

Erik Bryggman and the Turku Scene

Turku had been destroyed by fire in the first quarter of the nineteenth century. At the time of Aalto's arrival in 1927, its architecture was characterized by wide, straight streets lined with low classical buildings and interspersed with a system of green fire lanes. Though the capital had been moved by the Russians to Helsinki, Turku remained Finland's principal cultural and commercial center until the turn of the century. With the main center of intellectual action moved or in the process of moving to Helsinki (it takes only a century or so to complete this transition), the architects of Turku must

have felt somewhat abandoned, especially since the national publication, the *Arkkitehti*, was published in Helsinki and the only school training architects was the Polytechnic Institute of Helsinki.[3]

In April 1928, a special issue of the *Arkkitehti* was devoted to buildings and projects of contemporary date in the Turku area. One can imagine that this special issue, entitled "Turku numero 1,"[4] was conceived as a sort of gesture of comradeship to show the Turku architects that their associates in the capital city hadn't entirely forgotten them. The issue shows several completed designs for apartment buildings or blocks of flats, most of which are about five stories high. All of them exhibit the typical Northern European profile with a high ground floor embellished with classical columns or pilasters and squarish rectangular windows stacked and spaced in a repetitive grid pattern that gives the buildings a highly regularized appearance. The work shown is metaphysically akin to the clean, crisp neoclassical building style of Carlo Bassi (also called Charles), the Turin-born architect trained at the Royal Academy in Stockholm whose Empire creations give Turku architecture its dominant tone.[5]

The buildings erected in Turku in the twenties and thirties apparently had to live up to the refined classical quality of Bassi's style. This, of course, was accented by the fact

98. Atrium apartment block, Turku, 1925. Architect: Erik Bryggman.

that the classical spirit discussed earlier was widespread in Finland by the late twenties, chiefly because the one seat of architectural training was, by virtue of its small size and its location, a controlled source of design inspiration.

Over half of the buildings and projects shown in the special issue were the work of a Turku native, Erik Bryggman. A graduate of the Polytechnic in Helsinki and a proven architect with a number of prize-winning designs to his credit, Bryggman had returned to Turku in 1923 after working for Frosterus, Lindgren, and Walter Jung in Helsinki to become the principal architect of residence there. Two of his most noted buildings, the Atrium cooperative apartment and the almost completed Hotel Hospits Betel (101), were linked by a system of parallel stairs on adjacent sites in the center of the town.

The facades of both buildings exhibit the same two-part design scheme described above as typical for the town; in each of them, the two stages are separated by a plain, smooth, banded entablature. The Atrium is a large apartment complex with an interior courtyard and flats facing inward and outward over the streets. The facade, a smooth stuccoed surface, is organized with shops and entry on the ground floor; the main section incorporating the windows of two flats is capped with a restrained cornice (98). The hotel, constructed some 2 years after the

98. Atrium apartment block, Turku, 1925. Architect: Erik Bryggman.

99. Top: Caricature of Erik Bryggman, Turku, 1929. Drawing: Elsi Borg.

100. Middle: Hotel Seurahuone, dining room and dance floor, Turku, 1927. Architect: Erik Bryggman.

101. Above: Hospits Betel with walking street common to Atrium apartment block, church bell tower in background, Turku, 1927. Architect of entire complex: Erik Bryggman.

apartment block, shows a cleaner facade, with cubical projecting balconies that give it an almost International Style look. The entire composition is balanced formally by a bell-and-clock tower, also designed by Bryggman.

By no means a provincial architect who moved back to the oblivion of his home district and was forgotten, Bryggman earned the respect of his contemporaries and critics for the "calm flow" of his creativity.[6] "Brygge," as he was known to his friends, was a quiet, Bohemian, self-reliant person who based his work and life on simplicity and exuded a "refined aristocratic character" (99).[7] While the works he created lay in the mainstream of architectural taste, they possessed an ageless beauty that could be comprehended by layperson and professional alike. Turku already had a significant place in the classical tradition, but Bryggman gave it new stature within the development of the modern style. He was acknowledged in later years as a man who both led and resisted that development, recognizing its good and evil qualities, and as one whose nearly perfect control of new and traditional elements gave a timeless quality to his works (100, 101).

But Turku's architecture was not the only beneficiary of Bryggman's activity there; it was especially fortunate for the newly arrived Aalto that Finland's second city was the home of such a well-developed, flexible architectural mind. He was to find in Bryggman a colleague of unusual value whom he could consult and observe to great advantage in the course of their separate and joint practice.

Agricultural Co-operative of Southwestern Finland

In the special number of the *Arkkitehti* dealing with Turku architecture the results of the competition for the Co-op building were listed and the three prize-winning designs were published. Aalto took first prize with his entry entitled "Acer" (102), Hilding Ekelund took second, and Erik Bryggman third. This was Aalto's

first top prize in a major open competition, and it must have sweetened the effect to have accomplished it in the company of two more mature and proven figures of the big city scene. Each of the entries shown in the magazine provided for a large office block five stories high with an interior courtyard and a full dramatic theater along the interior corner of the plan. Except for the circular plan of the theater in Erik Bryggman's proposal, the top three solutions exhibited a surprising amount of agreement with respect to the modular nature of the planning and the overtly classical qualities of the major spaces and the exterior articulation. Aalto's design (103) is definitely the simplest of the three, incorporating the fewest identifiable classical embellishments. Both Bryggman and Ekelund employed curves and ovals to accent the formal quality of stairs and circulation spaces, but in Aalto's scheme (104) only the circular utility stairs indicate any preoccupation with design forms other than the rectangle. The elevation in particular seems to adhere quite rigidly to some accepted dictum of the 90° angle.

This rectangularity would not seem especially worthy of remark except for the fact that Aalto, after having secured the commission, implemented the final design with circular and semicircular shapes to denote many key points of organization and circulation. Instead of holding to his original simple plan, he augmented it with the sort of traditional forms found in the other two prize winners' solutions. In fact, his final plan (105) included more of these elements than Ekelund's and Bryggman's combined.

Aalto's personal responsibility for the design presented in the competition, however, is unquestionable. While he would have been familiar with the style of the Turku architectural environment, and probably with some of Bryggman's works as well, it is unlikely that he had a chance to visit the proposed site before the projects were due. Hence he adjusted his normal inclination to follow the course of his develop-

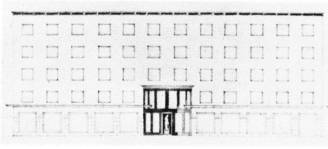

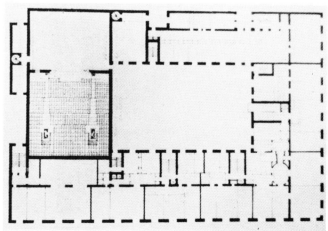

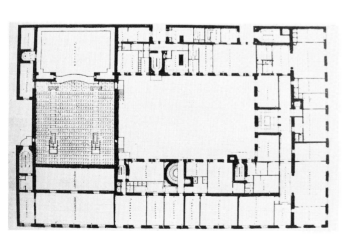

102. Top: Southwestern Agricultural Co-operative Building, Turku, 1928.

103. Middle: Southwestern Agricultural Co-operative Building, competition entry, facade, Turku, 1927.

104. Above: Southwestern Agricultural Co-operative Building, competition entry, plan of theater level, Turku, 1927.

105. Left: Southwestern Agricultural Co-operative Building, final plan, Turku, 1928.

ment as a neoclassical designer to the local style.

A comparison of his final plan with his competition entry reveals that little in the way of spatial arrangement is different. The stairways of the final version are located in the same positions, the theater arrangement is virtually the same, the interior court is the exact size and proportion as in the earlier drawings. One noticeable change is the addition of small ventilation risers in the fabric of the exterior walls facing the streets and those in the courtyard. These exhaust ducts, like those of the Jyväskylä housing for railroad employees, were located at the juncture of the outside wall and the adjacent interior partition line. Each vent is a duct through the exterior wall and is expressed on the face of the building as a small grilled opening located halfway between each window along the line of the lintels. This seems to have been a standard approach to apartment ventilation at the time, for the same scheme appears on the facade of Bryggman's Atrium mentioned above (98).[8] The interior supporting walls of the load-bearing masonry are more pronounced on the final version, being roughly the equivalent of the outside wall in thickness. The thickness of the structural wall of the theater is increased considerably to carry the clear-span roof, but since at least one back wall, a nonstructural wall, is also drawn larger, it may be presumed that this was done more for sound isolation than a need for stronger supports. The ceiling of the theater is suspended from a parabolic arch made of wood, a type of support found in bridges of a simple, rustic nature but also found in highway and rail bridges since the turn of the century.

Examining the facade drawing of the competition entry (103), one can observe that the constructed building is essentially that of the original design. The square windows on the upper stage are in keeping with the local classicism and are balanced by an axially aligned row of square display windows in the ground floor, exactly 1½ times as great in dimension. Each window on the facade is separated from the rest by a distance equal to the size of the smaller windows. The original design shows a partially rusticated lower stage, but this was eventually expressed by a triple stripe of dark paint, located at about door height, stretching between the molded frames of the display windows and around the entire outside. This polychromatic touch seems to be similar to some examples of the Viennese school.[9] There were to be two thin projections from the otherwise planar facade, one just at the ceiling line of the ground floor stage and the other at the top of the entire facade. In the final design of the building (102), the lower cornice was considerably increased in prominence by deepening the edge thickness of the projecting canopy that cast a deep shadow and gave a powerful base effect for the rest of the building. The top cornice is very much as Aalto planned it originally but lacks the breaks that punctuate it on the project drawing.

The most significant change on the facade is the revision of the main entrance portal. The original was planned to be a double-story, semicircular, flat-topped niche with a square profile facing the street. The fenestration pattern in the upper level of the entrance was divided in six equal radial parts while the supporting entry level below was to be divided into five, creating a rhythmical tension at the facade's bold center of interest. The entire white plaster facade composition rests on a contrasting gray stone base-course that acts simultaneously as a buffer to the sidewalk and a sort of concealing cove.

For the portal niche Aalto substituted a volumetric void of a half cube, symmetrically arranged with a single door in the exact center of the lower level of the square grand entrance. The overall conception of the ground floor with its lower projecting cornice extending into and interrupted by the grand entry is a gesture reminiscent of Alberti and one used later by Erich Mendelsohn.[10]

The decoration on the main facade's top extremity (102), which flanks the name of the organization for which it was built, is another of those forms derived from the primitive spirals of prehistoric and medieval European art. The motif on the facade may, however, be derived only indirectly from ancient forms, for it closely resembles the design found on the balcony face of Gunnar Asplund's Skandia Cinema of 1923 in Stockholm (106), a place that Aalto had visited with Asplund.

The overall building is a simple mass with an understated facade that denies the existence of its multifunctioned internal nature. It may be viewed as the ultimate classicizing step at a time when Aalto and others practicing in Finland were about to take the step into Functionalism. It is a refined example of stripped-down classical modes, with the molded windows that were quite pronounced in the original design now clean and surroundless. The disappearance of those elements can be clearly read as a beginning of a transition in his thinking. If the facade facing the street shows this progression to a limited degree, the final design for the interior courtyard goes further and signals the transition into a more complete Functionalist mode. The early plan would seem to show nothing that reveals any elements other than the traditional profile of the rest of the outside walls. But, when this plan is compared with the final scheme, it becomes clear that in the course of its design, Aalto felt impelled to "rationalize" the handling of the out-of-the-way courtyard, adopting a manner in line with Bryggman's Hotel Hospits Betel facade, complete with projecting balconies and cubic balusters (101). It is evident that here, away from the street, he had ventured forth for the first time as a practicing architect into the world of modern design. The courtyard style is utilitarian in a way that would certainly have been normal for 1929, but the configuration of the four horizontal balconies in the southwest corner, carefully fitted against the square vertical boiler stack with its full length set of service ladders, is an abstract composition in the vein of the Interna-

106. Skandia Cinema, balcony rail decorations, Stockholm, 1923. Architect: Gunnar Asplund.

tional Style[11] as it was then being taken up by progressive architects in Central Europe. Pipe railings on the other balconies (107) lend a feeling of modernity to the courtyard that the facade fails to reach.

With respect to the interior of the building, both the theater and the restaurant are of special interest. In its early design, the theater was to include a surprising number of traditional motifs. The basic scheme, though spatially the same as it was subsequently built, originally comprised no more than a sequence of "decorated" rooms. The entrance stair, which switches the circulation back toward the entrance as it conveys its users to a mezzanine-level cross aisle before thrusting them upward into the auditorium proper, was to be articulated with four pairs of decorated panels and capped by a coffered vault (108). The access from the cross aisle up to the main space was via a pair of vomitoria, decorated with a row of urns along each side and topped by an entablature with a row of dentils. The entire room was to be capped by a painted frieze with near life-size figures, reminiscent of the similar element proposed to top the facade of the Civil Guard House in Jyväskylä. There was also to be a row of spherical glass lighting fixtures along the side walls and a large recessed circular cove in the ceiling to complete the restrained Wagnerschule elegance.

The final design as built demonstrates that in the two years between winning the competition and the final construction, Aalto underwent a change of design spirit that would make it impossible for him to return to traditional classicizing modes. The long stairway leading to the mezzanine (109) was converted to a simple straight-run, 28-riser flight without any midpoint landing, and except for a mannered version of a Greek key over the stairway, the only ornamentation was two round openings starkly set into the wall to allow a view back to the front lobby. Inside the auditorium (110) the changes were more dramatic with the vomitoria becoming simple volumetric solids set boldly and clearly into the room more as sculptural shapes than anything else. The walls of the vomitoria were covered with gray- and rose-colored plush, and the interior of the auditorium was painted a deep blue without any ornamentation whatsoever.[12] The lighting in this building, completed in June 1929, was provided as in the Muurame Church, by the Poul Henningsen direct-indirect fixture that was gaining popularity with modern architects throughout Europe and Scandinavia.[13] The overall shape of the seating arrangement for 500 persons is the same in each case. The double-aisle, stepped seating is very much like that used for the auditorium in Hälsingborg, Sweden, by Aalto's friend Sven Markelius. Aalto may not actually have seen the auditorium (which was designed in 1926 and finished in 1932) when he traveled through Sweden in 1928, but he would surely have been shown drawings of it on his trips to Stockholm, where he often visited both Markelius's and Asplund's offices.[14]

The Itameri Restaurant (111), located in the main part of the building, was designed to utilize the Henningsen lamps and tubular metal furniture. It had an open baluster (112) to the main lobby that demonstrated Aalto's sympathy with the crisp, simple white forms of the French Purists.

In completing the multifunction building for the Agricultural Co-operative of Southwestern Finland—by any standards a major building in a major population center—Aalto placed himself at 31 in the ranks of the most respected and seasoned designers of his homeland. He had completed a large commission won in open competition with the best and most progressive thinkers of the time. Influenced to an extent by Erik Bryggman he had obviously readjusted his designs to fall in line with the Turku style of simplified classicism. Within the years of the Co-op's construction he had matured as an independent thinker and designer to a point where he was setting out to augment his knowledge through outside travel and contacts with others who were taking or had taken a similar course as the one on which he was about to embark. If his first venture into the modern world, the interior courtyard of the Co-op, had to be undertaken in some degree of seclusion from public and architectural scrutiny, his success in this building meant that he would never again have to conceal his love of the modern International Style. It not only raised his status, it certainly raised his hopes.

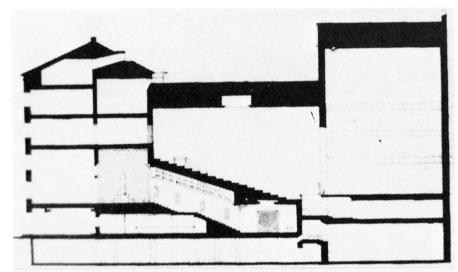

107. Top: Southwestern Agricultural Co-operative Building, detail, Turku, 1928.

108. Middle: Southwestern Agricultural Co-operative Building, competition entry, section through theater, Turku, 1927.

109. Bottom: Southwestern Agricultural Co-operative Building, entrance stair leading from lobby to seating, Turku. 1928.

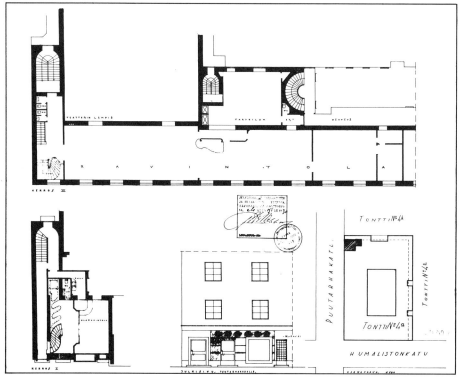

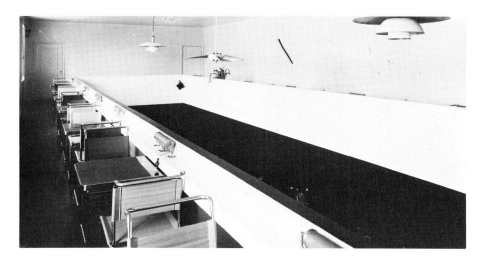

110. Top: Southwestern Agricultural Co-operative Building, interior of theater, Turku, 1928.

111. Middle: Southwestern Agricultural Co-operative Building, Itameri Restaurant, Turku, 1930.

112. Bottom: Southwestern Agricultural Co-operative Building, Itameri Restaurant, interior from balcony, Turku, 1930.

4
Housing Designs

Standard Apartment

In 1927, while the Agricultural Co-op was under construction, Aalto was asked by a local entrepreneur, Juho Tapani, to undertake the design of a row of flats (113) utilizing a system of precast concrete units for the primary structure. The Tapani system, first used in 1913, must have excited Aalto as it was this type of standardized unit that occupied the thoughts of many theorists during the late twenties and thirties.[1] Like the railway employees housing in Jyväskylä, the so-called Standard Apartments were divided into six stacks of living units organized around three stairhalls. There are one- and two-bedroom apartments that stretch the entire depth of the building, the larger apartment size being predominant. The layout of the apartments (114) shows evidence of the free-plan design already in use in Central Europe.[2] The plan (115) of a typical apartment centers around a multipurpose room that can be closed off to function as a separate spare room or opened up to more than double the size of the living room which faces the street. It was this spatial arrangement for which Aino designed the basic furniture layout that was published in the September 1929 *Arkkitehti* and may have created some uneasiness for the then-conservative architectural reader. This structure has indeed been declared the first Functionalist building in Finland.

The rest of the apartment layouts, while not revolutionary, do appear to be competent and clean examples of modern, compartmentalized efficiency. It seems that virtually all the plumbing for the large apartments lies along one wall that is common with the neighboring living unit. Though the main entrance to the stairhalls is from the street, the stairs themselves are located along the rear of the building, giving the flats maximum exposure toward the street (in this case the southwest). On the ground floor, flanking each stairhall entrance, Aalto provided basic rental space for commercial establishments. On the intermediate landings of each stair were attached cantilevered concrete balconies (a traditional element in Finland) surrounded with ship-type pipe railings. To properly understand this, one must think of the siting of the block of flats in its original context with its straight uncluttered view back to an open park less than 30 m away.[3]

The facade of the building is the main reason it was declared a pioneering effort in the development of Functionalism. The broad steel window sashes, mostly divided into three parts with at least one operational panel, create such a strong feeling of horizontality that it seems only a small step is needed to link up the windows edge to edge and create a complete glass band from one end to the other. The continuous window band is of course one of the five points proposed by Le Corbusier as necessary for rational building.[4] It would be misleading, however, to attribute any direct relationship between this building and those theoretical requirements. Essentially the facade expresses a different visual spirit since it is quite definitely broken into three more or less equal parts along the main structural bearing points by a system of downspouts leading from a large, recessed gutter in the roof intended to prevent water from marring the planar stucco facade.

The modular units used to build the walls and floors are based on a standard width of $\frac{1}{2}$ m. The wall units—roughly $\frac{1}{3}$ m or about 15″ in thickness—are made of high-strength concrete. Each one is double celled to permit ease of erection and ductless installation of conduits and pipes during construction. This is significant because one of the obvious selling points of any such system would certainly be ease and speed of construction. The floor slab units (116), again $\frac{1}{2}$ m wide, are based on a channel slab system with a leg turned down along each lengthwise edge. It is a system that appeared in buildings of an industrial nature in many parts of Europe once concrete had appeared as a suitable material.[5] The spans for the floor loads average about 5 m, and in the case of the center spans are about 7 m, clearly not adventurous in a structural sense, but for Turku, it represented an experimental act for domestic use. As in the Co-op

113. Standard apartment block for Tapani,
exterior view, Turku, 1929.

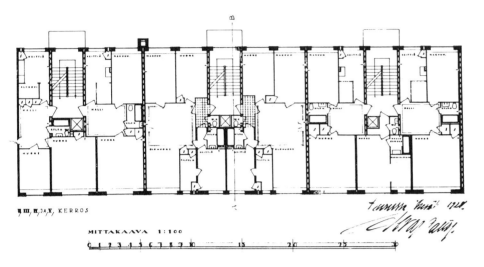

MITTAKAAVA 1:100

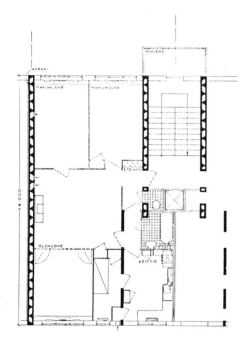

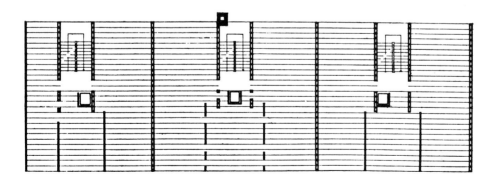

114. Top: Standard apartment block for Tapani, plans, Turku, 1929.

115. Middle: Standard apartment block for Tapani, apartment plan, Turku, 1929.

116. Above: Standard apartment block for Tapani, framing plan, Turku, 1929.

building, the facade away from the street is more utilitarian, and the evidence of the cantilevered balconies and ground stairs (117) gives it an appearance as daring as any structural slab of its vintage.[6] The interiors designed by Aalto are simple trimless spaces; the windows have a slender profile and a simple shelf that would act as an interior sill.

This unit was interpreted by the Aaltos to be the basis of a standard apartment for a Finnish society. The Standard Apartment building may have been in Aalto's mind when he said,

I once stated that the best standardization committee in the world was nature herself; but in nature standardization appears, above all and almost exclusively in small units, the cells. This results in millions of elastic combinations in which there is no trace of formalism. . . .[7]

However, for all its standardization, an examination of the building's facade reveals that the structural bays are different, and the window pattern from one section to the other is different. When this is correlated to the plan, it is clear that there are five different sizes of apartments on each floor out of a total of six. Aalto has achieved flexibility with a standard cellular structure.

This construction left Aalto squarely on the threshold of undertaking an entire career as a modern architect in his own homeland, and surely that thought could not have occurred to him even two years earlier.

Aitta Weekend House

In the spring of 1928 *Aitta* magazine, a popular journal (published by the large Finnish publisher Otava) that dealt with aspects of design related to modern life, sponsored a two-part competition for the design of houses. Part A dealt with vacation cottages and Part B with a full three-bedroom villa.[8] The jury, Martti Välikangas and Oiva Kallio, two of Helsinki's most progressive designers, awarded Aalto's designs the top prize in both categories.

Part A of the contest, for a weekend or summer house, called for basic accommodations for a small family over the temporary periods of residence. The program requirements were a central space where the main living activities of the family would take place, a kitchen, and two distinct sleeping areas. Aalto entered two different schemes for Part A, or rather one scheme with two philosophically different interpretations. Of the eighty-two entries submitted, both of Aalto's entries placed in the published results; his label "Konsoli" (118) won first prize and "Kumeli" (119) was bought. Antero Pernaja took second prize, Hilding Ekelund took third, and a project he submitted with Erik Bryggman was bought. The cottage had a budget of 30,000 marks, about 150 pounds or $750 in 1928.[9]

The scheme common to both of Aalto's entries was essentially a double-square rectangular plan with a large fireplace at the midpoint of the span at one end of the main living space. One of the sleeping areas was behind the masonry stack while the kitchen and other sleeping area occupied the opposite end of the cottage. This scheme was taken from a design for a summer house by Aino Aalto, the Villa Flora (120), built in Alajärvi in 1926. A comparison of Aino's house and Kumeli shows the design of their plans and many aspects of their elevations to be the same. The difference is that the later design has been divested of the earlier expressive, romantic, arched overhanging roof and veranda running the length of the front facade in favor of a more sedate and stripped-down look. The asymmetrical entry, the two chimney locations, the stucco walls, fenestration, and double-pitch sod roof are identical.[10] The design in both instances, however, does express a romantic notion of a humble summer dwelling, and the sod roof strikes an emotional note in keeping with the strongest traditional images of bucolically isolated Finnish summers. This basic idea must have appealed to Kallio who, though a progressive, was at the same time one of the leading romantic designers of the period.

In light of the differences between

117. Standard apartment block for Tapani, rear view, Turku, 1929.

the Villa Flora and Kumeli, Aalto's winning design Konsoli is especially interesting, for while it retains the overhanging roof and portico of Aino's earlier construction, the style of the building is completely changed. Though the layout is essentially the same—with the two chimneys, etc.—Konsoli has a completely flat profile concealing a slightly sloped sod roof. The front wall is recessed from the roof line to create a covered porch under the long horizontal leg of an inverted L-shaped facade. This stark geometric definition, produced in the spring of 1928 simultaneously with the first stages of the Turun Sanomat design drawings, pinpoints this period as the earliest stage of development in Aalto's evolution in which

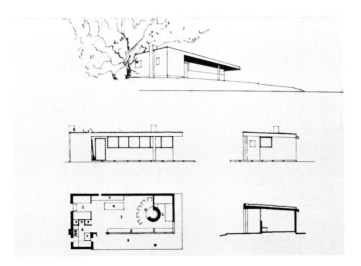

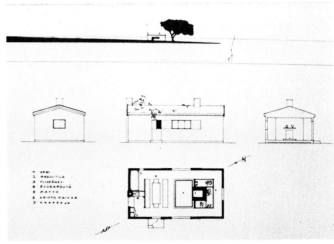

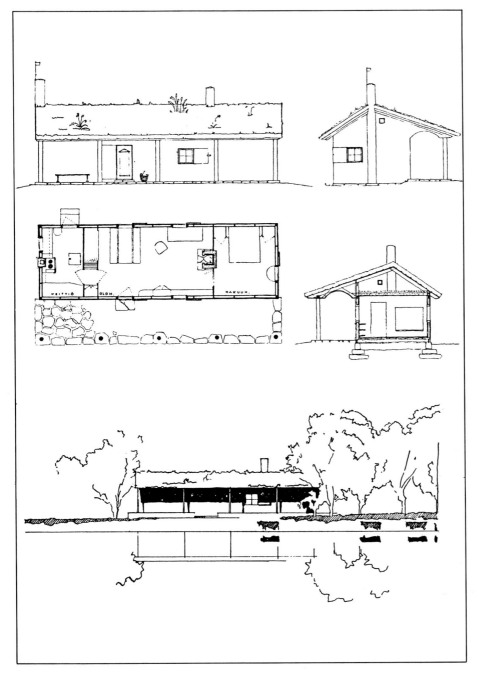

118. Top left: Summer house competition entry for *Aitta,* first prize winner entitled Konsoli, 1927.

119. Top right: Summer house competition entry for *Aitta,* entitled Kumeli, 1927.

120. Left: Villa Flora, Alajärvi, 1925. Architect: Aino Aalto.

121. Above: Summer house competition entry for *Aitta,* rendering of Konsoli, 1927.

he can properly be described as a modern architect. The deep shadow of the porch reduces the entire cottage to an abstract composition and even the small chimney at the end has been pulled out to define its shape as a solid element on that face. The strip fenestration ending in a corner window reinforces the overhang while the location of the single column in line with the main chimney seems to have been determined more by its function as a relieving vertical element in the composition than as a required structural support.

The only major change on the interior is the replacement of the square masonry fireplace with one that is rounded in form, giving an unusual and therefore more modern look to the scheme. This deliberate insertion of a rounded mass into the rectilinear volume of the room echoes the use of the curving column elements that are the leitmotifs of the Turun Sanomat building, contemporary with this design. The editors of *Aitta* were so pleased with Konsoli that they ordered a special watercolor made of it for the cover of the book they issued on the results of the design competition (121). The watercolor seems to sum up in a visual manner the state of design in Finland at that time, and particularly in Aalto's work. It shows a traditional summer scene with happy children playing in the sunlight by the sea with the flag of Finland flying proudly and independently over the home ground (flags have always been popular in Scandinavia), while the small, unpretentious house with its neat, simple, almost minimal character sits nearby on a low granite bluff under a large tree facing the water.

Part B of the competition, the design of a villa for a family, was won by Aalto, with Erik Bryggman winning second prize, and Veikko Leisten third. This contest was to provide a dwelling located on open land consisting of a large living room, a kitchen, three bedrooms, and a bath that would cost no more than 80,000 marks, 420 pounds, or just over $2,000 to build. Aalto's

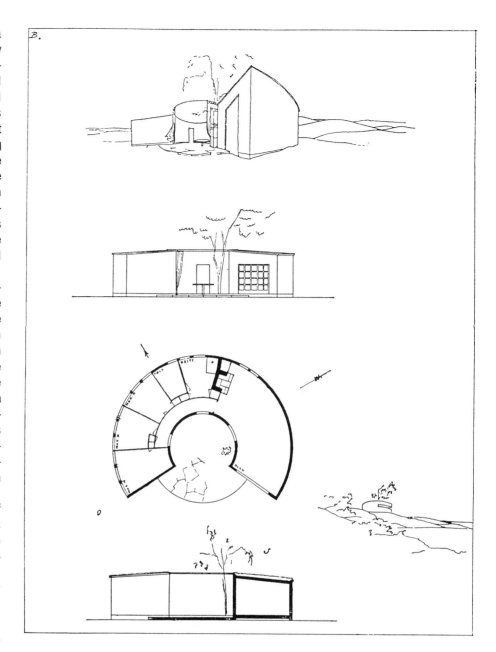

project, dubbed "Merry-Go-Round" (122) because of its circular shape, was in many ways no more than the conventional design for a single family dwelling found in the architectural publications of the late twenties. However, its shape renders it a novel treatment of the atrium house—a recurring form in the history of Western housing. Both features, the atrium and the circular shape, anticipate what were to become major themes in Aalto's mature architectural work. In one way or another, they reveal a preoccupation with nature and the outdoors—natural materials and forms that are found in nature—themes that were to dominate Finnish architecture in

122. Larger house competition entry for *Aitta*, entitled Merry-Go-Round, 1927.

the later part of the century. In an earlier article for *Aitta*, Aalto had written:

Northern climate that requires clear separation between the warmer inside spaces and outside has become a stumbling block to the architect. . . . The garden (courtyard) belongs to the home just the same way as any of the rooms. Let the step from the herb garden be a much smaller contrast than from the street or road to the garden. . . . A Finnish home should have two faces.[11]

Aalto had used an interior courtyard or atrium scheme in a design for a villa built for his brother Väinö in Alajärvi in 1926,[12] and he would later repeat the form in his own sum-mer house built in the fifties at Muuratsalo in Central Finland. How-ever, in the *Aitta* design, the atrium space is not completely enclosed, but is formed by bending a long rec-tangular house around three sides of a circular courtyard. This court-yard, open on one-third of its cir-cumference, would be oriented to the southeast. Because the living room bends around a full quarter of the circle (the end wall faces south and the wall adjacent to it bends around to face north), the room has the advantage of receiving light from both directions without admit-ting a direct view through the length of the room. In opening three differ-ent parts of the house to the court-yard Aalto creates a visual interplay between the interior of the house and its immediate natural environ-ment as he had previously advo-cated. The house plan is essentially a single-loaded corridor with the liv-ing room located at one end and the master bedroom at the other. The corridor itself leads along the edge of the atrium court, with all rooms relating directly to it.

I would like to mention the long de-spised corridor design form. As an entrance to a house it offers invalu-able possibilities for beauty, it is a natural centralizer for the inner rooms and it allows even in a small building a location for bold monu-mental linear measure.[13]

However, the adaptation of the corri-dor plan to this rounded, fan-like ar-rangement brings an extraordinary new element into the scheme and may show some measure of the ar-chitect's uneasiness with the strictly rectangular module.

The atrium house, primitive though it was in some respects, would apply directly to his pub-lished theories on the subject, and it is clear that he was beginning to put aside the superfluous aspects of his training as well as the styles of the time. It is also clear that he was be-ginning to put together the basics from his background with the range of modern design theory available to him and evolve designs that did not depend on established styles or dogmas.

5

International Modernism

Turun Sanomat

On the basis of Aalto's new-found prominence as architect of both the Co-op and the apartment block, and probably a considerable amount of self-promotion as well, he was commissioned to design the new offices and plant for the Turun Sanomat newspaper in January of 1928.[1] The development of this project took place during the key growth period by which architectural historians have judged Aalto's early career. In the process there has been a tendency to continually reevaluate the building as more significant and earlier in date than it might otherwise be considered. The program for the Turun Sanomat building is one of dual purpose. In fact, as Aalto conceived it, it embodied commercial shops on the ground floor as well as the journal's editorial, advertising, and printing functions. Whatever implications may be derived from the working schedule, there is no evidence on file that would place any phase of this project as early as 1927. Construction had definitely begun in August 1928 and continued for over two years. This long construction period allowed for some interesting developments in both the design of the building itself and in Aalto's career. Within the preceding twelve months the Aaltos had won over 60,000 marks, and this, combined with payments from three commissions in Turku and two in the Jyväskylä area, placed them for the first time in a comfortable financial position.

The year was a very busy one for Aalto. He had two buildings under construction—the Agricultural Co-op and the Standard Apartment building—had secured two new commissions—the Turun Sanomat and the Viipuri Library—had placed at the top of one more competition, and had been nominated for the jury of another. Immediately ahead were the competitions for the National Independence Monument and the Paimio Sanatorium. These interruptions would lead one to expect the development of the design of the Turun Sanomat newspaper building to have been an unusually fragmented one, which is exactly the case.

To qualify the building in terms of modern architecture one must say that it is the earliest building in Finland that meets the five points set forth by Le Corbusier and, what is more, accomplishes this in a remote corner of the Western world only a short time after Le Corbusier first published them. The key accomplishment for Finland, in a theoretical sense, is probably the construction of a concrete building that actually had a concrete column skeleton. In the minds of most observers, however, it is not the skeleton that stands out; rather it is the smooth concrete facade with its asymmetrically balanced fenestration which employs continuous horizontal strip windows framed in metal used for the first time in Finland. But interestingly, this facade, which has intrigued so many and made Aalto's name a spoken word among architects and art historians, has in fact a precedent in Finland itself.

In a competition for an office block in the town of Vaasa, an entry submitted late in 1927 by Bryggman, assisted by Aalto, broke the barrier of traditionalism and launched the modern style in the commercial architecture of Finland. His project, "Waasas" (123), was published in a small sketch in a review of the competition results in January 1928. It didn't win a prize because it was considered to be against the program and was disqualified by the jury. Martti Välikangas, the new editor of *Arkkitehti* and the progressive designer of the Käpylä garden suburb, noted Bryggman's design as a significant departure from the more traditional and conservative prize winners that were selected by the jury, headed by J. S. Siren, the conservative classicizing architect of the Houses of Parliament.

In speaking about Bryggman's drawing years later, Asko Salokorpi, a Helsinki critic, wrote:

In the window strip of the perspective plan, in the lines of the cars speeding by, the image of a new era is evident for the first time; it is modern in the same way as a continental railway station with its trains and sensibly dressed, hurrying people, had been modern to Frosterus and Strengell at the turn of the Century.[3]

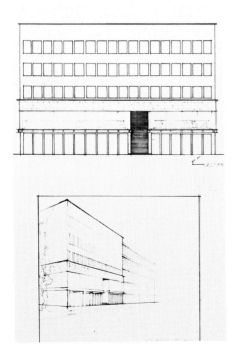

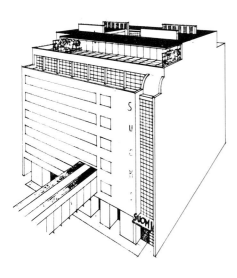

123. Top: Office block competition entry, Vaasa, 1926. Architect: Erik Bryggman.

124. Above: Suomi insurance headquarters extension competition entry, Helsinki, 1927. Architect: Erik Bryggman.

If Aalto had not been associated with Bryggman on this project, he still would have known of its development, for among the small architectural fraternity of Turku, it can be surmised that there was more than mere social contact. The drawings of the Waasas elevation and perspective (123) reveal a striking similarity in an overall compositional sense to the later fenestration of the Turun Sanomat facade. The organization of this facade is, though unmistakably modern, essentially the same as that of the Atrium apartment building—a row of shop windows along the ground level capped by a smooth section without any fenestration and, finally, cellular windows aligned above that. However, if one imagines the large square window of the Turun Sanomat inserted in the lower right corner of the Bryggman facade, the main portal of the latter shifted to the opposite end, and the remaining blank portion above the ground floor filled in with a band of windows at the mezzanine level, the entire drawing appears to be a mirror image of the Turun Sanomat facade.

During the course of design and construction of the Turun Sanomat building, however, Aalto certainly encountered yet another Bryggman project that bears a striking similarity to the newspaper plant. In July 1928 the competition for the Suomi Insurance Company headquarters annex was announced, and Aalto was listed as one of the jury members. This was customary, for the practice of selection entailed the inclusion of at least one member from the winners of recent competitions. Thus for the first time in his career, Aalto was put in the position of judging his peers. Among the other jurors were Uno Ullberg, a well-known designer, and Aalto's former teacher, Armas Lindgren. When the time came for Aalto to view the entries for the Suomi Insurance Company addition, he would have been presented with one design which, if he hadn't seen it before in Bryggman's office, would certainly have been the subject of discussion between the two men in relation to the problems posed by

the Turun Sanomat commission.

Except for a row on the jury, however, we might never have known what Aalto felt about this similar version of the newspaper plant (124). Aalto quarreled with the rest of the jurors, all of whom felt Bryggman's scheme to be unfit, stating that he wanted to be on record as voting that it should be the winner.[4] This published jury proceeding was somewhat rare in its candor, but for Aalto to take advantage of the privilege of sitting on a panel of a major open competition to speak so forcefully against his ideological opposition, in this case Ullberg and Lindgren, was characteristic of his behavior from that point on. The result was that there was no first prize and Bryggman, while not receiving the commission, tied for second place. However, the editors of the *Arkkitehti* did use Bryggman's project as their lead illustration in reviewing the competition, implying at least sympathy and possibly signaling a general erosion of confidence in the conservative nature of recent juries.

Aalto must have found it somewhat sobering to finally come face to face with the backroom politics of competitions and the overall conservative nature of their juries. But he did not shy away from the conflict, and when later that year he traveled to Helsinki, he took advantage of the occasion while attending a meeting of SAFA to show the photographs of modern architecture he had made in Holland and France.[5] This was just before the due date for the Paimio Sanatorium competition, and it is not hard to construe this action as part of a campaign to embarass the jury publicly and deter them from choosing a traditional scheme which would place Finland even further behind in the sequence of development of modern architecture.

In any case, a comparison of the Suomi Insurance Company building project facade with Aalto's own design (125) shows a direct relationship between the two. The alternately indented floor-to-ceiling vitrines on the ground floor are the same free-standing elements punc-

tuated by recessed passages; the difference is mainly in the functional use to which each front was to be put. In Bryggman's design, they served mainly as a light lens to a lower floor, and in the Turun Sanomat they actually were built as display cases for the row of shops behind, which, however, were remodeled at the owner's request shortly after the building was finished. Over and above the similarity of composition in the facades of these two designs, the front half of the ground floor plan of Aalto's building is laid out like the ground plan of the Bryggman proposal.[6]

Looking at the overall composition of the Sanomat facade, one sees that the strips of windows are broken periodically by ventilator

125. Above: Turun Sanomat newspaper plant and offices, Turku, 1928.
126. Left: Turun Sanomat newspaper plant and offices, Turku, 1929.

sash made of glass louvers (126). Aalto's characteristic concern for the ventilation of rooms would certainly have been thwarted by a complete row of fixed glass, but the louvers were required by local building regulations. From early sketches it appears that he wanted the width of this louver unit to be the same modular width as that of all the fixed glass panels on the facade, but it is probable that the only type of sash available in Turku at the time was that being used on the Standard Apartment block, then under construction across town. In addition to the louvered panels, the sash does have operable sections; of the total of five units in any one length, two open. Amazingly, there seems to have been no double glazing, a standard technique to combat infiltration of cold air in Finland for many years. The placement of the louver vent sash was originally on axis with the ground floor display cases and therefore on the column lines of this part of the building, but when the shop-front section was altered, this rhythmical unity was lost.

The main division between the fenestration occurs above and in line with the edges of the giant window on the left, a rationally based detail corresponding to the division of structural bays in the building's front portion. The column-free space behind the giant window was meant to be an open office space for the newspaper's advertising department. It is doubtful that any attempt was ever made to construct the display screen that was to be mounted in front. The space behind the giant window, in fact, was protected from the cold by a vestibule of exact size. The screen (127), as published in many catalogs and books, was to have a copy of the daily front page of the newspaper projected on it, thus serving at once as advertisement and billboard for the newspaper and an assertion of the building's identity since no other graphics were planned. This concept was of course exactly what the Vesnin brothers had planned for the Pravda building in Leningrad (128) in 1924, a project never built.[7]

Outside this window there was to

127. Above: Turun Sanomat newspaper plant and offices, large display window, Turku, 1929.
128. Right: Pravda newspaper building, design project, Leningrad, 1924. Architects: Vesnin brothers.

be a one-riser-high platform step to stand on while reading the projected page. The platform extended across the window to the main doorway that led to the upper stories where the editorial departments were to be housed. This single doorway is located within a tall, vertical opening glazed with giant louvers on which Aalto placed the signs and names of firms occupying space in the building. At the very top of the front face is a ship-type railing. It is located at the edge of a terrace fronting the glazed wall of the executive offices and is recessed from the face much as in Bryggman's proposal for the Suomi Insurance Company. Also like the insurance company project, there is a vehicular portal at the right edge of the facade that leads slightly up a ramp to a service yard along one side of the building. In the original design this yard was to be located at the first floor level and it was to be paved with ferro-cement skylight panels in order to illuminate that part of the ground floor below it, but it was not realized that way.

The service courtyard for the most part is constructed with the same wall section and fenestration scheme that Aalto used on the Standard Apartment but with a few notable exceptions. The front wings (129), forming one of the three faces of the courtyard, has an engaged cylindrical tower next to the portal leading from the street. This tower, reminiscent of a similar element in the courtyard of the Civil Guard House at Jyväskylä, stands against the facade in a different relationship at virtually each floor level. The facade on the upper levels is indented in places and a pipe railing creates a shallow balcony across the wing. In spite of the somewhat traditional employment of canted slot windows on the tower, the total effect of the volumetric composition is relatively more advanced in terms of modern architecture than the facade of the building. The wing which houses the loading dock and forms the rear wall of the courtyard is much less adventuresome in its surface treatment. It is quite flat and, in its elements, could be mistaken

for a standard industrial building. However, the most curious aspect occurs in connection with the rear stair. The switchback staircase, located at the junction to the main portion of the building, is lighted by a four-story-high window and capped above the roof line by a partially cylindrical penthouse bearing little or no geometric relation to the stair beneath. The inexplicable manner in which Aalto composed these hidden elements leads the trained observer to wonder about their genealogy and to question their role in his stylistic repertoire some thirty or forty years later when he contrived such designs consciously and with premeditation.

The ventilation is apparently via the small grills used on his previous buildings, and the rainwater is brought to the ground by a system of gutters and downspouts. This was the last time in his career that Aalto was to employ these devices.[8]

Beyond the organization of its facade and the structure of the front portion, the Turun Sanomat is nevertheless different from any other building in Finnish architectural history in its total expression of modernity. Though some of the details might betray traditional techniques, a look of simplicity and newness

129. Above left: Turun Sanomat newspaper plant and offices, service court view, Turku, 1928.

130. Above: Turun Sanomat newspaper plant and offices, main entrance stair, Turku, 1928.

131. Above: Turun Sanomat newspaper plant and offices, press room interior, Turku, 1928.

132. Opposite page: Turun Sanomat newspaper plant and offices, final plan of press room level, Turku, 1928.

prevailed in 1928, or rather 1930 when it was actually finished. The long, straight-run stairway (130) leading up to the first floor introduces this straightforward tone. Those who use it are deposited at the information desk for immediate rerouting should they require it. Halfway up the stairs is the porter's desk, where one may deposit a message or package and quickly return to the sidewalk without inconveniencing staff or visitors.

In designing the interior of this building Aalto gave consideration to each object, fixture, and surface. This concern for final details was to become in itself a kind of trademark of his architecture. From time to time, other architects in the Modern Movement tried to achieve the same ideal, but with Aalto it became the standard. Here he designed the doorpulls using graphics with simple letters constructed of band iron. Working for the first time with a client who allowed him a free hand and without any apparent economic restraint, the building became a proving ground on which he could employ all his knowledge as well as experiment with the techniques he had observed on his travels to Holland and France.[9] The design of the handrail, with offset supports of chrome-plated steel fitted to a low baluster, created a sanitary and light feeling. Aalto emphasized the shape of these elements by painting the rail and top of the baluster in

colors that contrast with the light-toned walls. This reinforcement of geometry was continued in the cove base and on the treads and risers where it took on a more traditional feeling but, again, formed a precedent for the design of such details in all his subsequent buildings.

In his scheme for lighting the building he employed some fixtures then available, but for the first time he also ventured into the realm of lighting design. In the design of a simple shade and ceiling mount he provided a section drawing indicating the exact nature the light should take as it radiated from the bulb. Perhaps the most striking aspect of Aalto's lighting design was his placement of the electrical conduit in plain view, either in a groove or bead embedded in the ceiling. This harmony between the fixture and its service line might seem obvious in the context of an industrial application, but Aalto has carefully adjusted the esthetics of placement and size to agree with the clarity of the design of the building.

Perhaps the most singular aspect of this building is the design of the shaped column supports in the clear-span structure of the press room (131). Such a large span, 7½ m, supporting eccentric column loads from above, was necessitated by the need to plan for the future installation of increasingly larger presses. In fact this trend has continued. In order to support the latest press installation, the machinery had to be connected directly to the columns, and on all but one column the profile was squared off and covered with ceramic tile. The inverse canting of the columns corresponds to the properties of shear in concrete design theory; where the greatest shear occurs, the section of the column must be larger and so forth. Aalto probably observed this in use for the first time in the design for the Hälsingborg Auditorium by Markelius. The structure of the Turun Sanomat press room is different in that the structure resting on the columns is a flat slab design requiring a smooth undersurface. With contemporary reinforced concrete technology it was possible to support heavy loads with such a system by using a drop panel and bell capital, usually round or square, over a correspondingly shaped column.

This is exactly what Aalto selected for the paper storage vaults located to one side of this structure on the next floor below. But here on the main floor, in plain view through the observation window, he shaped the bell capital to blend beautifully with the shape of the canted columns.[10] He gave the bell a longer gusset where the span was greater and a shorter one in the lateral direction, and cleverly stiffened the unbraced length of the columns by installing a paper-roll rack at midheight just beneath a series of skylights to the west of the press bay. The large rolls of paper were brought up from below via a ramp at the rear of the building. The unique aspect of this columnar system lies in the degree to which the modeling of the columns is expressed. They are rounder and more fluid in their expression of internal stress than Markelius's.[11] They even seem dramatic because at least on one side they are almost free-standing. This design evidently gave Aalto a lot of trouble for there are many different versions of the press room structure in the files at the Atelier Aalto in Helsinki which were made as the design development drawings were being prepared. The final scheme was not resolved until the last day of 1928 (132),[12] almost a year after the commission had been awarded. Surely Aalto's visits that summer to Holland where he saw the works of Duiker, particularly the Zonnestraal Sanatorium, must have brought him back to Turku with renewed enthusiasm for the possibilities that were now open to him.

With the construction of the Turun Sanomat building Aalto became the first Finnish architect to break the bonds with traditionalism to any degree. It not only gave him a weapon with which to press on towards his ambitions at home, but it was sufficiently modern to earn him respect and gain him admission to the circle of organizers of thought and criticism of modern European architecture.[13]

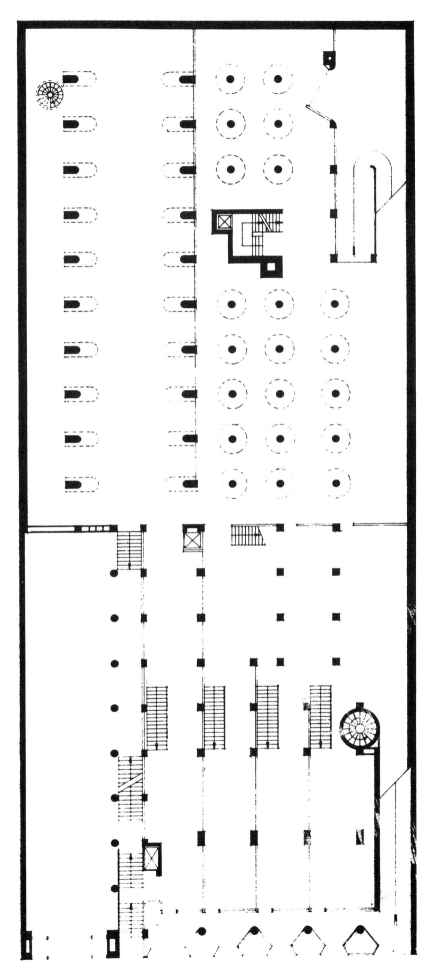

6

Heroic Age: Mastery of the Style

Paimio Sanatorium

Between the judging and the final design for the Turun Sanomat plant and offices, Aalto entered the competition for the design of the tuberculosis sanatorium at Paimio, 30 km east of Turku. The program announcement was published in the November issue of *Arkkitehti,* and he probably began work later that month. The final design, in any case, was finished quickly for it was due in January 1929, barely two months later. Aalto won the first prize of 20,000 marks with his project called "Piirretty ikkuna"—graphically mottoed by an L-shaped window unit (133,134). K. Brog, O. Flodin, and Paavo Hansten won second place while Ragnar Ypyä and Antero Pernaja took third. Erik Bryggman's project was bought and published along with the prize winners in March of that year.

Securing this commission, the most important he had ever aimed for, was of crucial importance to Aalto at this stage, and the temptation to disguise his adherence to the new architecture and to submit a noncontroversial design may have been great indeed. He avoided this temptation, however, and his victory over the established leaders was on his own terms and placed him in a lone status in Finland. This caused hard feelings that only vanished slowly.[1]

The resulting building has been described by every critic who has recorded his thoughts about it as a true example of the heroic period of modern architecture, or some equivalent accolade. In general terms, the project represents the building pretty much as it was finished in 1933, but closer examination of two stages of design drawings, reveals a spiritual difference of some magnitude in the final form (135, 136).

The basic organization of the hospital complex remained unchanged throughout the design development. The scheme is a variant of Duiker's Zonnestraal Tuberculosis Sanatorium (137) which Aalto had seen at Hilversum in Holland earlier in 1928.[2] The plan of Duiker's complex was based on a three-part nursing wing unit (138), consisting of a nursing service core with one block of patient's rooms arranged at right angles to it and the other block of rooms at a 45° angle to the first two elements. This design was faithfully adopted by Aalto, even down to the pinwheel arrangement of the stairs at the corner of the angled wing, although at Paimio the stairs were located on the corner of the service unit. Comparing the two arrangements functionally makes it apparent that Aalto used the geometric solution of Zonnestraal to fit his needs in a slightly different organization. The central administrative unit at Zonnestraal is in a separate building that was designed as the nucleus of a projected swarm of these tripartite units, situated along an axial courtyard of a "campus type" siting arrangement. In Paimio,

however, the administrative wing is joined to the patients' wing by a connecting link containing the main entrance hall and vertical circulation.

Essentially what Aalto did was to combine the two lengths of Duiker's patients' wings into a single slab, the total number of rooms being the same. Duiker provided nursing access at the end of the wing; in Aalto's it turned out to be the middle. Aalto increased the height by doubling the number of stories to four, thus centralizing his hospital to a greater extent. In the case of Paimio, Aalto eliminated any idea of a separate administrative element by using a series of angled units attached to the connecting circulation element, the closest to the patients' wing being the dining/consultation, the second the laundry and service facilities, and eventually a third element not in the original plan and not really connected by route of access, the heating plant. Aalto had undoubtedly observed Zonnestraal, just finished in 1928, in full operation, for his own conceptual drawings of the kitchen with its large steam-heated cooking caldrons show an operational knowledge of those spaces.

In medical terms both Paimio and Zonnestraal were founded on the theory of tuberculosis treatment popular in the late twenties—isolating the patient from the urban environment of smoke and pollution and effecting a cure by allowing him to sit in the sun absorbing solar rays and breathing in fresh air.[3] This system reached its pinnacle in the creation of facilities such as those at Davos, Switzerland, with giant terraced residence hospitals which, until the development of drug therapy, were filled to capacity the year round. Duiker's rather horizontal scheme, located in a forest of low-growth trees, utilized a balcony for sunning at the window of each patient's room, while Aalto, needing to get above the taller forest of Finland, concentrated this activity in high-rise suntraps located at the end of each corridor floor. In spite of this difference, aerial views reveal that both building complexes were sited on the same principles.

As much as Paimio is a takeoff of Zonnestraal in terms of planning, the similarity is even closer with respect to detail. The main use of concrete in both cases is in the construction of the structural skeletons. As it happens, there is not all that much wall surface in Duiker's building that isn't glazed, while the more severe climate of southwestern Finland required considerable covering of the frame by stuccoed brick walls, which were less expensive to build than concrete. The clarity and exposed nature of the concrete construction at Zonnestraal (139, 140) enabled Aalto to observe at first hand a formed and monolithically poured product as complex as any in Europe at that moment. The walls of glass framed by shaped cantilev-

133. Below: Tuberculosis sanatorium competition entry, site plan, Paimio, 1929.

134. Middle and bottom: Tuberculosis sanatorium competition entry, elevations, Paimio, 1929.

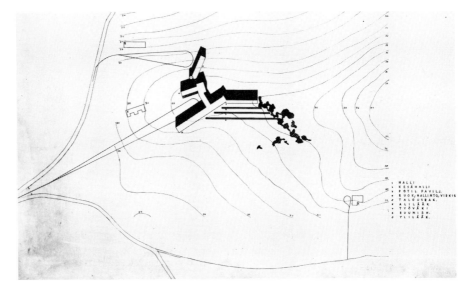

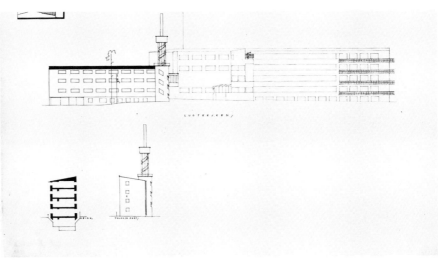

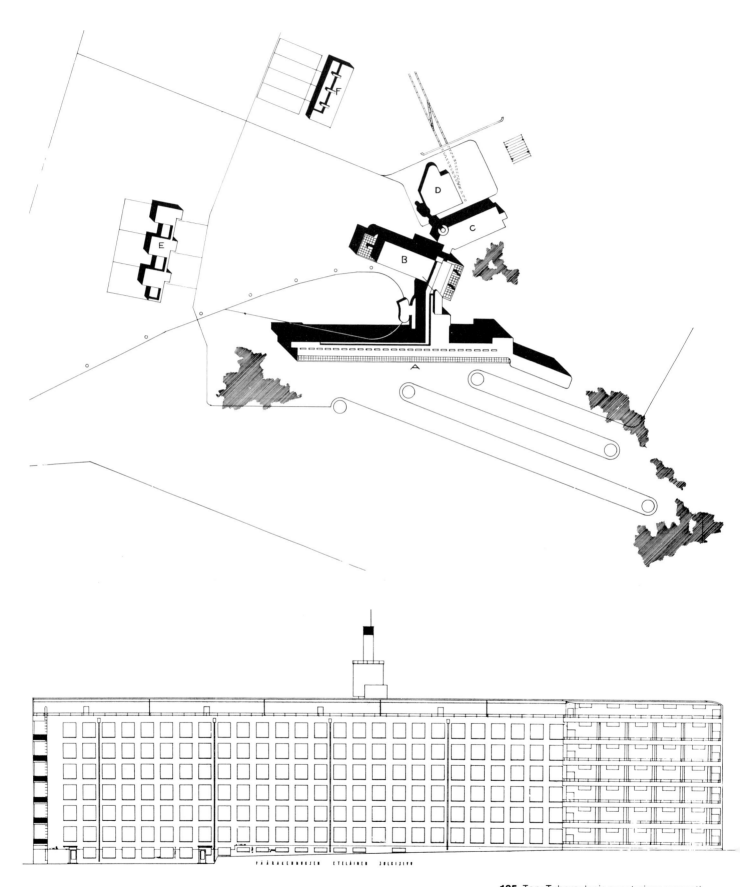

135. Top: Tuberculosis sanatorium competition, final design, site plan, Paimio, 1930.

136. Above: Tuberculosis sanatorium competition, final design, elevation, Paimio, 1930.

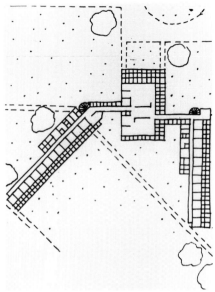

ered beams providing maximum exposure to the healing out-of-doors and the special effects of helical spiral staircases capped with an omnidirectional, flat concrete umbrella roof, seem striking enough achievements 50 years later, and Aalto could not have helped being impressed by them in 1928.

Aalto's borrowing of elements found in Duiker's work was not limited to the design of Paimio,[4] and his sources were not limited to Zonnestraal. The corner window in the courtyard of the Turun Sanomat (129) has in fact many precedents, but it could easily have come from Duiker's residence for A. Suermondt in Aalsmeer designed and built in 1924 (141). Though it could be established that other modern architects had utilized two-height, L-shaped window openings, the simple treatment of those in Duiker's work was certainly the type of stark multiplex opening Aalto had in mind when he spiritually dubbed his hospital a "drawn window." This would, in the mind of a designer, call special attention to an element he considered essential in the appreciation of such a proposal. On the competition drawings, each one of the patients' rooms was to be lighted and ventilated by such an opening in the south facade (134). This form, most assuredly linked to the ventilation of the patients' rooms, had been in use in southern Europe for centuries;[5] but in its pur-

137. Above left: Zonnestraal Tuberculosis Sanatorium, aerial view, Hilversum, 1926–1928. Architect: Jan Duiker.

138. Above: Zonnestraal Tuberculosis Sanatorium, nursing unit plan, Hilversum, 1926–1928. Architect: Jan Duiker.

139. Left: Zonnestraal Tuberculosis Sanatorium, concrete details, Hilversum, 1926–1928. Architect: Jan Duiker.

140. Below: Zonnestraal Tuberculosis Sanatorium, concrete details, Hilversum, 1926–1928. Architect: Jan Duiker.

141. House for A. Suermondt, side view, Aalsmeer, 1924. Architect: Jan Duiker.

142. Above: Zonnestraal Tuberculosis Sanatorium, water tank detail, Hilversum, 1926–1928. Architect: Jan Duiker.

143. Below: Tuberculosis sanatorium, interim drawings with water tank smoke stack detail, Paimio, 1930.

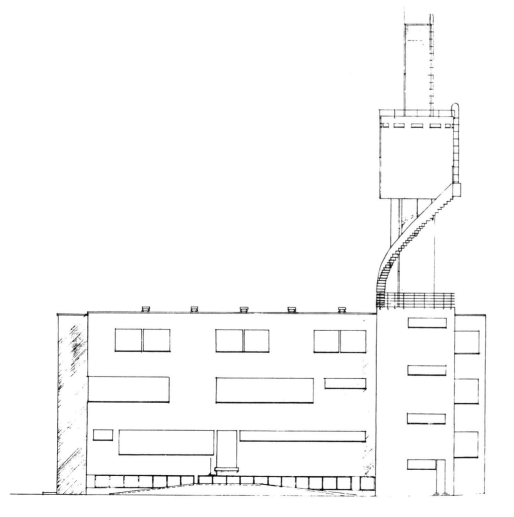

poseful modernity, it was something new at that time, at least for Aalto, and of course it became a signature motif for him in later years.

Because critics have called Paimio a true example of his genius, the most interesting aspect of his borrowing probably centers around the design of the service stair, smoke stack, and hot-water tower (134). The form of the base, as in the case of the Turun Sanomat service stair, had been used earlier by Aalto as a rusticated element in Jyväskylä.[6] The way it is executed at Paimio, as a closed, stuccoed cylinder on the corner as at Zonnestraal, and surmounted by an exposed, glass-enclosed continuation of the spiral case inside, precisely like those of Duiker, prevents it from any other credit. The lower two elements in this assembly of Zonnestraal motifs are fittingly capped by an exact copy of the hot-water tower tank (142) from the roof of the central service building at the same location. It is a clever reworking of another designer's vocabulary (143). In the final built version of the tower, at the corner base of the service wing (144), Aalto altered the cylinder, removing the spiral fenestration and assuming the circular ramped form of the top of the stair tower on the house at Aalsmeer (141). The stacking of this base, beneath the water tower of Zonnestraal is the profile that Aalto constructed.[7]

When the final design was produced the L-shaped window, so much a key to Aalto's image of the project, was eliminated in favor of a large square opening that was divided into three equal casement units (136). Another change that altered the spirit was a 40 percent increase in the number of patient rooms, requiring a six-story wing instead of four. This made it possible to push the wing further toward the southwest in relation to the circulation link, resulting in a more informal feeling. The suntraps, as originally planned, ended at the first floor in a series of terraced gardens oriented to the south and stepped down in four half levels to the lawn below. Sadly, this plan was discarded for a

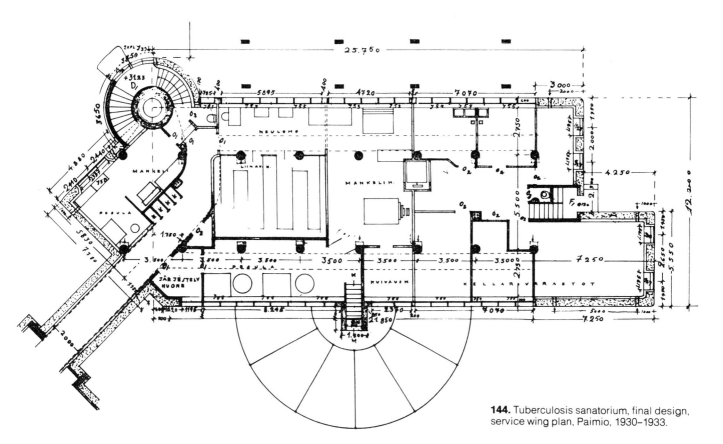

144. Tuberculosis sanatorium, final design, service wing plan, Paimio, 1930–1933.

much less workable and less maintainable flat walkway zigzagging formally toward the forest and arbitrarily circling around a series of small round pools (135). The suntrap was built to a height of seven stories, and the top level of the deck continued across the entire length of the patients' wing. This top level possessed a Davos-type proportion, and it was used as the standard in the design of similar spaces elsewhere in Finland and Scandinavia (145).

The design of the suntrap at Paimio is of particular interest for it was undoubtedly the largest monolithic concrete undertaking in a public building of its day in Finland.[8] The entire building, as it stands, looks like a masterful job of reinforced concrete technology, but, in fact—except for the skeleton, floor slabs, and the sun-deck structure—the exterior walls are insulated brick, cavity wall construction.[9] The suntrap is supported by six massive reinforced concrete piers tapering upward out of the earth and held down by a giant, continuous, pyramidal footing less than one-half story deep beneath the surface of the

ground (146). Though he was undoubtedly assisted by a structural engineer, it is to Aalto's credit to have executed this construction in the early thirties. The placement of the reinforcing is up to the standard of any subsequent theory. Despite the fact that mass is reduced at higher levels by reduction of the column section, and the fact that it was backed with a solid wall, its sheer weight seems to provide its only resistance to being overturned by the wind. The design of the platform was pitched forward and crowned to shed rain and melting snows by means of a terminal downspout at each end of the structure. Along the top-level suntrap above the patients' wing, the drainage was carried off by a downspout system buried in the walls of the corridors. This caused a great deal of difficulty when the downspouts froze and broke the walls open during the first winter of occupation.

The refinements developed between the competition project and the constructed design are too numerous to cover in anything but a monograph on this building alone, but some of the additions are the es-

sence of what must be recognized as unique about the building in terms of modern architecture. The three major changes that occurred are the detailing of the famous west gable of the patients' wing, the development of the entrance lobby and canopy, and the character of the east facade on the dining/consultation wing. Approaching the hospital, one is presented with its classic view, the entrance in the center, the dining hall on the left, and the stark end elevation in nearly pure orthographic projection on the right. In the original drawings this low four-story wing was designed to end with a blank wall with floor-length windows at the ends of the corridors, a long terrace cantilevered northward over the entrance courtyard, and the fire stair set in from the end in the third structural bay.

When the design reached its final form, the stair had been moved to the end of the wing, and at the end of each corridor was added a nurses' living quarters (now abandoned) with an adjacent balcony forming the third element on the end face. The remaining elements were

145. Below: Tuberculosis sanatorium, interim drawings of suntrap perspectives, Paimio, 1930.

146. Right: Tuberculosis sanatorium, interim drawings of suntrap structural section, Paimio, 1930.

147. Bottom: Tuberculosis sanatorium, final design, patients' wing end gable stairway and elevator shaft, Paimio, 1933.

148. Opposite page: Tuberculosis sanatorium competition entry, ground level plan, Paimio, 1929.

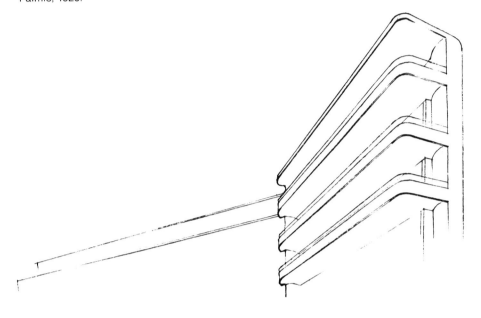

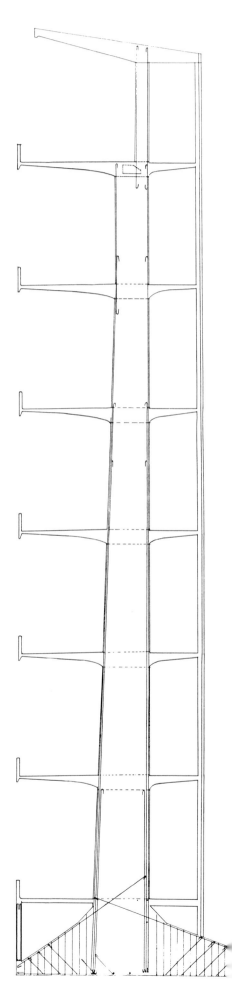

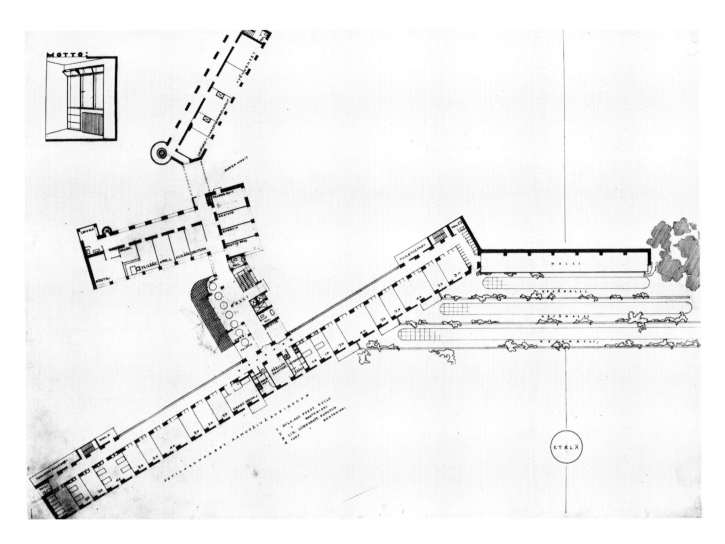

framed in concrete structural members giving the illusion, at least, that the entire building had been sliced to reveal the guts of a total concrete system.

The double cantilevering (147), so spectacular in its profile, does, however, obscure the truly dramatic element of this gable—the glazed elevator cage located at the outside end of the stairwell and in full view of all who see the building for the first time. This use of an element of machinery in such an exposed and visible sense places the Paimio sanatorium firmly in the first machine age.[10] It is a loose interpretation of the elevator that the Vesnin brothers had planned for the full-height glass lobby of the Pravda building project in Leningrad (128) in 1924.[11] Aalto's elevator, like many of the elevators built in United States hotels in the sixties and seventies, celebrates the motion relative to the ground outside while being protected inside by the build-

ing. It is a trick that was built into much exhibition architecture from the Eiffel Tower onward, but it was seldom expressed in a building as a straightforward reading of its utilitarian function. The panels that form the railings and baffles for the nurses' balconies are flat and seem to be placed there solely to give visual bulk to the composition of columns and slabs that makes up the gable end.

The next element that catches the eye of an approaching visitor is the entrance canopy (135). This element is totally lacking in the original scheme as presented in the competition. The entrance hall or the connecting link to which it is attached was described on the drawings as a small, simple, rectangular link where the entrance drive turned back toward the road. This "grand piano" shape as some have called it, or something similar to it, is found as an accent element in other early examples of modern architecture.

During this period, the free-form shape against the straight-line design was taken into Aalto's repertoire of signature form, but this was not the first time he executed such a composition.[12] In the design development stage (148) Aalto apparently searched for a fitting solution for this connecting link that had to welcome people at the ground floor level. At one point he projected an entrance terrace with a rounded end that corresponded to the final shape of the waiting lobby. It is likely that the canopy, which complements the curve of the lobby in an exact opposite manner, was one of the last elements to be derived. By 1933 when the building was completed, this type of element was in popular use by architects and painters of the Modern Movement. Another free-form element, the dual fireplaces in the main salon across the corridor from the dining room, did not in fact appear on the plan diagrams in the visitors' booklet,[13] indicating perhaps that they were among the last elements to be incorporated into the design. Inside the lobby Aalto provided an arrangement of cubicles for the storage of hiking shoes—one H-shaped, the other semicircular, and each centered under one of the round skylights above.[14] This layout was reinforced by a graphic system of wide gray stripes inlaid in the bright yellow linoleum of the floor-covering to direct traffic. This early use of what has come to be called "super graphics" was also found on the adjacent main stairway walls, painted in the same warm gray color at the corners and behind the outer stair railings where people would most often mar the wall with hand-prints. The evolution of this entry scheme from a small, straightforward lobby to an organized, maintainable, and at the same time light and cheery area, enabled him to impress upon the visitor and arriving patients that the rest of the hospital complex had been designed along the same lines.

The changes on the east face of the pavilion that contains the patients' lounge are the last to be discussed here. Comparing the original site/roof plan (133) with the final version (135), one notes the additional presence of a roof terrace enclosed within the framework of exposed concrete columns and beams extending from the skeleton frame of the exterior wall and roof structure. The volumetric nature of the design is in some ways the most interesting. This is because it may be the most original derivation of designed segments in the entire project; at any rate it demonstrates the greatest degree of variety within a single face. Structurally the pavilion (149) is supported on three main column lines set in from the side edges of the cantilevered floor slabs by something like half of a bay. This enabled the corners to be completely opened up where the need was justified. On the first floor this meant that the lounge could have a nearly unobstructed view of the forest as well as a maximum amount of radiation from the sun in the mornings. The two large

"picture" windows (150) in the center of the lounge were flanked by a diagonal pane that formed a sort of triangular double-glazed plant case with corner windows. On the upper levels of the pavilion the facade is opened up with either a balcony or a terrace stretching across the entire width. Standard flat casement sash defines the basic geometry of the block within which Aalto was to sculpt this unusually informal and varied, almost De Stijl-type, design. Many precedents could be cited for this type of abstract approach to architecture. In Duiker's work, the Cineac cinema project would seem to be close enough for comparison, and the cranes on one of his apartments could have suggested the outstanding beams at the top of the Paimio pavilion. But it is probably the emergence of Aalto's own design talents that accounts for the free nature of expression in this facade.

The patients' rooms located behind the facade of triple-mullioned windows were the subject of much discussion by the designer. Rarely in the history of Finland has any building occasioned such rationalization in hindsight. Aalto composed and edited a complete fifty-page booklet on the sanatorium which included articles by the hospital's director, Severi Savonen, who had been a member of the awarding jury, and the architect himself. In a series of diagrams and pictures the design theory of nearly every aspect of the building is covered. The need for this was probably created during the construction period when a row arose among the SAFA stalwarts in Helsinki, many of whom took advantage of the fact that Paimio was a commission for the state to take their turn at Aalto. In his defense came a voice that had battled the same forces once before, Sigurd Frosterus. Frosterus, amid a climate of heated emotions, cooled tempers until he could visit the construction site and make a full and soothing report back in Helsinki, and eventually all those who were interested followed Frosterus's example by visiting the sanatorium.[15] However,

tradition and resentment of the outspoken Aalto dissipated slowly in Helsinki. In fact it is conceivable that had he chosen the capital as his place of operation after Jyväskylä, Finland's conversion to the modern style might have been somewhat different. In the creation of Paimio Aalto left few items to chance, and though it is certainly a building firmly in the International Style, its considerations are so extensive in scope as to place it with the most complete *Gesamtkunstwerk* created during the Art Nouveau or any other comparable period. He explained this partly in the following passage:

When I received the assignment for this sanatorium I was ill myself and therefore able to make a few experiments and find out what it is really like to be ill.[16]

This is obviously a piece of designer's poetry, but Aalto steadfastly held throughout his life to the notion that people were the most important recipients of the designer's art. He continues:

I did not include, for example, artificial ventilation which causes a disturbing draught around the head, but designed a system whereby slightly warmed air entered from between the panes of the windows.[17]

In the space between the double glazing of the three-part window he placed a heating element that tempers the air as it passes from the outside through an open casement along the center cavity and enters the patient's room via the opposite side of the inner casement. This might be only a small improvement for one who had probably lived his entire life in houses and buildings fitted with double-glazed casements, but he was certainly bringing into play in Paimio all the tricks and refinements that he had ever learned, whether from his teachers, from architects around the world, or from his life in a country where people, healthy as well as sick, spent a large portion of their lives indoors. Paimio incorporated many new ideas in hospital design and epidemiology when it was constructed, but for us today, as its designer claimed, it is the consideration of the patient's needs and the process of health administration that made it unique. In this respect, whether driven by ambition to make a name in the world of architecture, or simply to fulfill his promise to his client, Aalto created a building of greater than heroic proportions. By his own documentation, few buildings in modern architectural history equal the timeless quality of its totality.

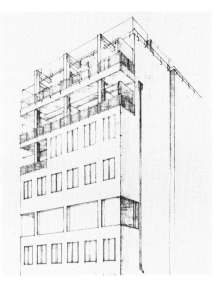

149. Left: Tuberculosis sanatorium, final design, eastern face of doctors' wing and lounge, Paimio, 1930–1933.

150. Below: Tuberculosis sanatorium, final design, eastern face of doctors' wing and lounge, Paimio, 1930–1933.

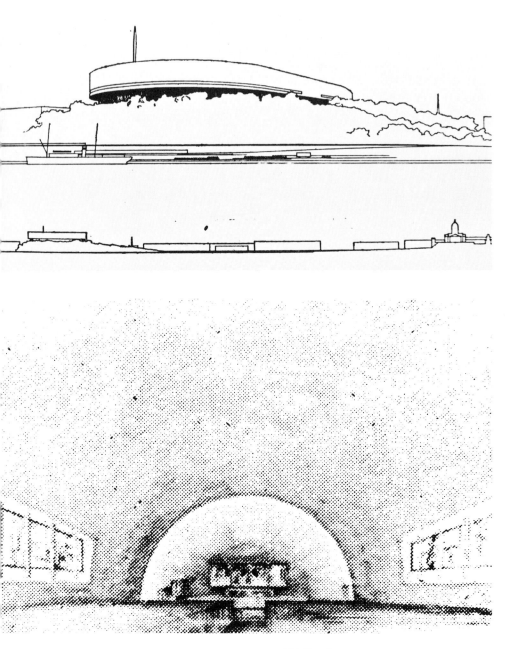

151. Top: Independence Monument competition entry, perspective, Helsinki, 1928.
152. Above: Church competition entry for Vallila area, perspective, Helsinki, 1929.

Independence Monument Competition

The Independence Monument competition, which had been announced in the spring of 1928, was divided into categories or types of monuments that would be appropriate to celebrate the second decade of the Finnish nation. Category A1 was for monuments in the nature of belvederes or ones located on high ground; A2 was for those of a freer interpretation to be located anywhere; and B was for designs of a traditional monumental nature. In all there were thirty-two entries, but only third prizes were awarded in B and in A1. Among the ideas presented were traditional towers, ornamented towers, and carillon towers, in all a disappointing response to such an emotional theme. Adding to the lack of clear resolution was the makeup of the jury which consisted of ten members, among them Armas Lindgren, J. S. Siren, and Gunnar Taucher, who were strong personalities developing in different directions from each other.

Although it didn't win a prize, Aalto's entry—from the point of view of the editors of *Arkkitehti* who reviewed the results of the judging—appears to have been the one project worthy of consideration.[18] His submission, calling for the building of a sports stadium as the National Monument, was certainly prescient in light of the later stadium projects that were to preoccupy the Finnish architectural scene over the course of the next decade and finally culminate in the building of the Olympic Stadium.

Aalto's project, falling under category A1, was labeled "Helsingin horisontti" (151), a reference to the quality of the Helsinki skyline as well as to the long, low fascia of the stadium floating above the trees of the purposed hilltop site known as Observatory Hill adjacent to the main harbor in Helsinki. While the siting on Observatory Hill, the highest spot in that part of the capital, would render the structure clearly visible from any point around the harbor, the entire conception reveals Aalto's sensitivity to the special qualities of the Helsinki littoral with its constantly shifting interplay of inlet, peninsula, and bay along the line of the horizon. Highly visible, yet at one with the environment, the smooth, simple line of the fascia of Aalto's design must have seemed strangely out of step with the times in the context of the other entries, which displayed traditional monument profiles with crowning statues and other classical motifs. However, the other entries were soon to be seen as outmoded, and Aalto's stadium was among the first buildings proposed for Helsinki in the International Style and thus in the mainstream of contemporary architectural development.

Vallila Church Competition

The competition for the Vallila Church—with Armas Lindgren, Gunnar Taucher, Bertel Jung, and Erik Bryggman among the jury members—certainly presented a chance for a significant change in spirit in its awards. While over fifty-one entries were submitted, it is likely that at least some of Finland's more enterprising architects were occupied with the larger, and for some, more interesting Paimio Sanatorium competition being conducted simultaneously and consequently did not enter the Vallila contest. Even if the two were not in conflict with respect to their preparation, the timetable for presentation required that they be handed in within two weeks of each other which would have made it difficult for one architect or firm to make a respectable showing in both. This was certainly the case with Aalto, for while running away with the first prize for Paimio, he didn't even receive an honorable mention in the awards list for the church competition. In fact, there was no first prize, and Bertel Liljeqvist who took second eventually obtained the commission. The jury, however, did cite Aalto's entry, dubbed "Gloria" (152), as an interesting project.[19] This entry was unsigned (as are most competition projects) and has never been published under Aalto's name. Only recently has it been identified as his work. The Vallila design, in keeping with the newly emerging modern style, was quite simple and provided a minimum of elements to conflict with the worship service. The striking feature of the project lies in Aalto's basing his design, as he had in the *Aitta* project "Merry-Go-Round" and in the Independence Monument, on circular or curved volumes. The high ceiling was curved down to form a vault that opened up from the pulpit toward the seating like a megaphone. The windows, placed above the congregation's eye level at the transition from wall to ceiling, are long horizontal strips that lead the worshiper's eye back to the semicircular end wall behind the simple altar. The idea is undeveloped, and it is clear that Aalto neglected this entry in favor of the sanatorium, but it is an early example of his interest in acoustical architectural devices. The jury noted that

> *The entry is based on the acoustical experiments that were used for the construction of Salle Pleyel. The entry is designed logically according to these experiments, but since this kind of acoustics provides that the sound is directed from the pulpit and altar towards the congregation, the acoustics from the organ loft on the opposite end are not considered.*[20]

This type of criticism may well be what inspired Aalto to introduce a two-directional acoustical ceiling a few years later when he designed the Tehtaanpuisto Church and Viipuri Library lecture hall.

During 1929 Aalto was busy preparing for the opening of the 700 Year Fair, beginning the Paimio design development drawings, and squabbling over the design and siting of the Viipuri Library project. He found time to travel to Germany and Greece, however, as competitions were scarce. In 1930 he entered four.[21]

7
International Style Becomes Functionalism

Turku's 700 Year Fair

In the summer of 1929 the city of Turku celebrated its 700th year as a population center, and Erik Bryggman and Alvar Aalto jointly received the commission to design and supervise the construction of an entire campus of buildings for a trade fair to commemorate the event. This was the only project or building on which Aalto ever collaborated with Bryggman. In fact, except for his partner and wife Aino, he was to do so with only one other person in his fifty-five year career.[1] This fair was characterized by a series of rather inexpensive pavilions, mainly lightweight wood frame buildings covered with fabric and plywood, an abundant material in Finland.[2] Perhaps the most interesting building in the scheme was the main restaurant (153). Designed by Bryggman, its round shape was a spiritual embodiment of the restaurant projected for the Stockholm exhibition the following summer. The fact that Bryggman reserved this special pavilion for his own attention indicates that he was in the senior position in the collaboration. However, based on similarities and duplications in his later works, it is clear that Aalto had a major role in many design decisions in the project.

The main complex was located on a hill in a park. Access to it was provided by two gates, each flanked by an exhibition of display stalls filled with Finnish products. Ascending stairs or ramps, the visitor was led up to the highest level of the park where the main exhibitions and activities were housed. At each corner of the main pedestrian crossings were small buildings topped with tall, slender pylons. These pylons, along with a forest of others, were in essence the design theme of the fair, and they served a useful purpose because they could be seen from any major vantage point in downtown Turku. Pylons, especially of this squarish cross section, had been used earlier by Aalto in the Tivolis of the Helsinki and the Gothenburg Fairs.[3] They were decorated with large lettering and graphics to announce the names of individual exhibitors as well as the fair in general. The site plan (154) shows a subtle misalignment of a row of what one might have expected to be parallel buildings. If these gently splaying lines are seen as radians, they would have to be located thousands of meters from their single center. The effect is of an organized group while the faintly perceptible lack of parallelism prevents it from being overtly so.

The ends of these buildings served as one edge of a large court formed by the major pavilions. The idea of using pylons must have been a fresh idea for Finland at that time and corresponds favorably with the more avant-garde techniques being used abroad and by the Russian Constructivists in the Soviet Union.[4] The low one-story pavilions (155) with their sharp corners and edges were opposed by long boxlike shaped pylons guyed by cables. On the surfaces of these lofty signs the two architects composed a series of horizontal and vertical letters and motifs in a manner that could be linked to any of several different groups working during the previous decade. Both the Dadaists and members of De Stijl, though to a limited extent, applied graphics directly to architecture, and Le Corbusier's demountable pavilion for Nestle, probably the best-known example of this use of graphics in Western Europe at the time, was erected in Paris in 1928.[5] Though it is quite possible that Aalto had seen this building on his trip to Paris that year, the towers at Turku must be seen as essentially Constructivist in nature. The overall divisions of colored tones on which the lettering was placed is very close in spirit to many of the projects for propaganda towers, popular subjects for architects and students alike in Russia's early revolutionary period. Lettering was an important and integral consideration in permanent buildings such as the Pravda building project (128) as well as in exhibition design. An early example of this was the group of pavilions at the 1923 Agriculture Fair held in Moscow (156).

A design that exhibits the effect of the towers proportionally is Leonidov's Isvestia Tower project of 1926 (157). The main difference between the Turku pylons (158) and their

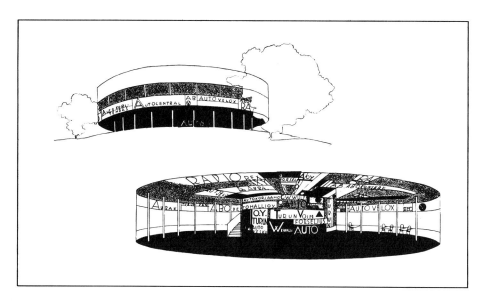

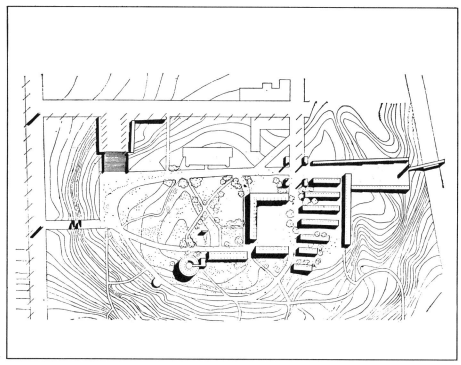

153. Above: Turku's 700 year fair and exposition, restaurant design drawings, Turku, 1929. Architect: Erik Bryggman.

154. Left: Turku's 700 year fair and exposition, site plan, Helsinki, 1929. Architect: Erik Bryggman.

155. Below: Turku's 700 year fair and exposition, pavilion design, Turku, 1929. Architect: Erik Bryggman.

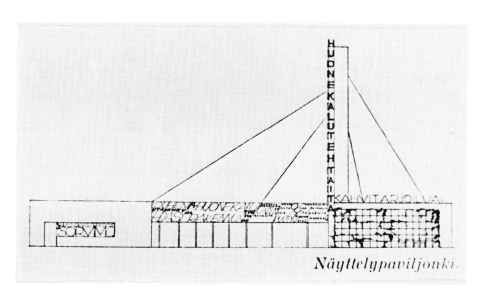

156. Above: Restaurant at Agricultural Fair, general view, Moscow, 1923. Architect: V. Suko.

157. Right: Tower project for Isvestia Newspaper, perspective, Moscow, 1926. Architect: Ivan Leonidov.

158. Far right: Turku's 700 year fair and exposition, pylons, Turku, 1929. Architects: Alvar Aalto and Erik Bryggman.

159. Below: Turku's 700 year fair and exposition, choral shell, Turku, 1929.

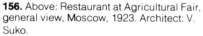

Russian predecessors was that the towers of Aalto and Bryggman failed to define in any external way the lightweight structure to which the surface material was attached. The Constructivist designs, however, forcefully declared their internal structures, identifying rigid members and cables as well with a dark linear system that outlined each member. The unavoidable use of cables in the Turku Fair thus contributes to its Constructivist quality.

The only main elements that stood apart from the main quadrangle were Bryggman's restaurant-in-the-round and Aalto's choir concert podium (159). The latter building was perhaps the structure that in one sense stood out the most; it contained no graphics or lettering and was constructed entirely of wood. The podium was a low wedge-shaped platform on which the performing singers stood. At the rear, just behind the stepped risers, was an acoustical reflecting wall, shaped at the top in a series of small, concave, flat bands that projected the voice waves out toward the audience. Aalto would have known about developments in acoustical design theory as expressed by the shell in Sven Markelius's auditorium in Halsingborg, but the outdoor concert shell was well known in the Baltic where the tradition of choir concerts and song festivals is perhaps the oldest form of public entertainment still in wide use today.

The wooden aspect of this structure is its striking feature for, in spite of the painted surfaces, the nature of the material and Aalto's use of it is expressed in a straightforward manner. On the side panels he created a series of vertical battens, closely spaced to give depth and interest to the flat sheets of plywood. The floor of the platform curves gently down toward the audience to provide for better voice propagation.

If Aalto didn't feel the equal of Erik Bryggman during his first two years in Turku, by the time the fair rolled around he quite likely felt that he knew more of, or understood more about, the world of modern architecture outside Finland than any other Finn. He was a dashing, active young man (160), outspoken and freewheeling. Having achieved a number of designs, impressive in quantity and quality, within his first two years in the big time, he was about to make a clean jump to the pinnacle of Finnish architecture.

Turku Water Tower Competition

In the middle of January 1930[8] it was announced that Turku would build a new water treatment plant and storage tower to provide better service for the recently expanded metropolitan area. It was, naturally, to be located on a plot of high ground on the northeastern edge of the city. The competition called only for the designs of facades for the structures, and although it was a local and somewhat modest project as buildings go, more than forty architects from all over Finland entered the contest. The character of the entries shows a widespread difference in architectural design theory. Almost one of each style that had ever been popular in Finland was represented. However, among the published entries there appears for the first time what seems to be a nucleus of designs that exhibit only the minimum of traditional modes and that are fairly clearly based on rational or Functional principles. Erik Bryggman of course was among the entrants and his project was bought. Pauli Blomstedt won

160. Caricature of Alvar Aalto at age 31, 1929. Drawing: Elsi Borg.

third prize, but Aalto did not place, though his project was published in the *Arkkitehti*'s review.[9] The design he entered was humorously titled "Wolstead Act" (161), after the notorious prohibition law that banned the sale of alcoholic beverages in the United States. A similar law also existed in Finland until 1932.[10]

Once again, in this small-scale project, we find Aalto shying away from the simple rectangular form and embracing a gently curved wall. The trapezoidal-shaped volume of his project is by no means hydrostatically rational.[11] If it is related to anything at all, it may refer to the flow properties of fluids. The form sits in a monumental fashion on a low base directly on top of the hill. The flat vertical walls, linked by gently curving corners, seem to become an extension of the softly rolling hill on which it rests. This soft-edged design is contemporary with the free-form shapes discussed in the context of Paimio and is one of the earliest manifestations of his interest in such forms in architecture. Whereas previously he had relied on circular, cylindrical, and other geometrically curved shapes as alternatives to the rectangle, the Water Tower project seems to express a more organically inspired, intuitive conception.

The design, freely shaped without evident regard for construction methods or programmatic input—perhaps because it was only intended as a screen wall around the

tank structure—draws its inspiration directly from a design by Sven Markelius for an open-air funeral chapel designed in 1923 for Simrishamn, Sweden (162). Though a more regularized oval form in plan,[12] the constantly changing radius of the walls gives an impression of free form. This wall is interrupted at the flattest point in the curve by a high V-shaped opening. The opening corresponds to the rolled tuck in Aalto's water tower. The massing of the water tank is, in bulk and proportion, the same as Markelius's chapel, and it is similarly raised on a base, as mentioned above. Though the water tank base is different in form from that of the chapel, the way it creates a platform on which the curvilinear walls rest at the top of the rising slope is the same as in the cemetery chapel. In both cases, the effect from a distance is the same— a gently curving form with a monumentally static quality dominating all surrounding forms but relieved by a break in the smooth, imposing, monolithic shell which creates a point of interest for the observer.

Vierumäki Sports Institute

At the end of March, judging for another major competition took place —a sports park with training facilities for a year-round physical education college. Erik Bryggman won first prize, Antero Pernaja and Ragnar Ypyä, second, and Alvar Aalto took third prize (carrying an award

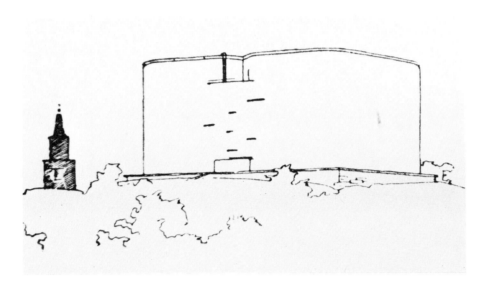

161. Top: Water tower competition entry, perspective, Turku, 1930.

162. Above: Crematorium proposal, perspective, Simrishamn, 1926. Architect: Sven Markelius.

of 8,000 marks) with his project titled "Mens"; Hilding Ekelund's project was bought. Aalto's old teacher from Jyväskylä, Toivo Salervo, now a practicing architect in Helsinki, was among the jury members. The program called for a large sports park incorporating five fields for organized events and practice, with one of them having a concrete stadium. The main building complex required housing for a large gymnasium, training rooms, classrooms, dining and sleeping facilities, and administration. A further consideration was to provide for the location of a series of student dormitories on the site.

Aalto's proposal (163) showed the fields in a staggered line parallel to the main building. The chief consideration of the competition was the building itself, with special emphasis on its main space, the gymnasium. Aalto cleverly fused the stadium and main building into one unit (164), organized in a modified asymmetrical pinwheel arrangement like many of his other designs from this period. The entrance courtyard, rather than leading into the building, surprisingly leads through it to the sports fields located at the rear, for they were the primary area open to the public. The building itself, except for some viewing galleries of the gym, was meant to be used mainly by the athletes who trained there.

The perspective—rendered in the style popular in Finland at that time among progressive architects—was executed in dark fine lines and solid black shadow to reveal the volumetric nature of the design.[13] From the vantage point of the perspective (165), the building appears to be two rectangular solids arranged in echelon, in plan as well as profile, but the juncture is ambiguous because the lower, longer element of the support facilities wing is composed of three distinct and directionally different parts fused at the corners. This pinwheel arrangement and lapping of volumes in some respects appears to anticipate the final design of the Viipuri Library and even appears to utilize the device of the circular staircase as the center of the radiating wings. The sports park project antedates the final Viipuri design, and it may well be that the new ideas which appear in that version were actually developed here.

The chief element of concern in the building is the gymnasium itself. The long, high volume (165) is spanned by a row of parabolic arches, each with a pair of sun reflectors joined back to back at the midspan, forming a continuous ceiling that curves up and out to the edge of the roof. At that point on each long side, a row of tall windows forms a clerestory effect with the curving support walls. The combination of vertical fin walls and the concave ceiling provides for the admission of natural light into the room without any direct transmission of the sun's rays to any part of the floor or any area where an athlete might practice (166). This structure, to be executed in reinforced concrete, was similar to the wooden structure of the large Congress Hall he designed in Gothenburg, Sweden, but considerably more refined in terms of the lighting.[14] He had seen a similar idea executed in timber trusses and plywood baffles in the open woodworking shop at Duiker's Zonnestraal Sanatorium (167). This arrangement was utilized by Aalto in the natural lighting of many subsequent projects such as the libraries at Wolfsburg and Rovaniemi and the lecture hall of the Technical University at Otaniemi.

The outside expression of this unique interior arrangement makes this building as fully developed an example of expressionist architecture as any of the contemporary works of Hans Scharoun or Hugo Häring. The building, finally built in 1936 after the design by Bryggman, is a fine example of Functionalism, but the bold and straightforward manner in which the technical aspects are expressed would have placed Aalto's design in a completely respectable position in the development of architectural theory if it had been 5 or perhaps 10 years later.[15]

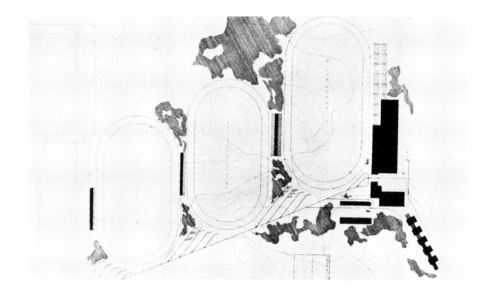

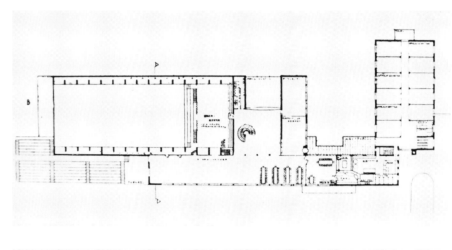

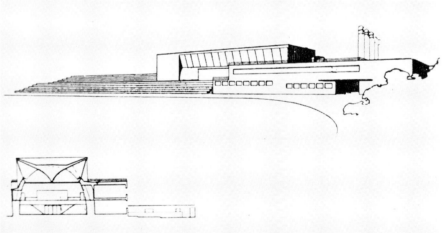

163. Top: Sports Institute competition entry, site plan, Vierumäki, 1930.

164. Middle: Sports Institute competition entry, floor plan, Vierumäki, 1930.

165. Above: Sports Institute competition entry, perspective and section, Vierumäki, 1930.

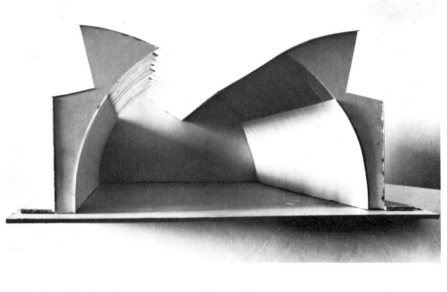

Ideal Stadium and Sports Park Site Plan

Running virtually simultaneously with the Vierumäki Institute competition was the competition for the Ideal Stadium and Sports Park-Site Plan in Helsinki. In this site planning competition, he entered two projects, "Parking Park" and "Petäjä kruunu." The former was bought and published, while the latter listed by Aalto as an alternative received no mention and has unfortunately been lost.

The stadium competition probably grew out of the seed which Aalto ironically had planted himself with his unsuccessful entry in the Independence Monument competition. His suggestion, a novel one for a monument, had, as previously noted, impressed the journalists covering the competition, and the stadium enterprise was one that would continue to preoccupy the Finnish architectural world throughout the next decade. The site designated for development was north of Töölö Bay in central Helsinki where the present Olympic Stadium was finally built. The site, as defined in the competition, was hilly and had very little street frontage, making the building design and access a problem.[16]

In their comments published in the *Arkkitehti,* the jury, of no particular note in its makeup, praised Aalto's "Parking Park" (168) as the only entry to address itself to the problem of vehicular access and parking. These considerations were apparently not of great importance to many architects in 1930, for no other entry paid any attention to them.[17] Aalto's plan provided auto drives from the two major streets just as in the present stadium and allowed for the direct access of vehicles by means of a grand porte-cochere separated from the parking bay by a long island which stretched in front of both the large stadium and the football stadium. The parking lot, somewhat resembling the Circus Maximus in plan, is a long, flat plaza along which the major fields and stadia are located; it would be cut into the earth at the northern end

166. Top: Sports Institute competition entry, study model, Vierumäki, 1930.

167. Above: Zonnestraal Tuberculosis Sanatorium, woodshop, Hilversum, 1926–1928. Architect: Jan Duiker.

and project out on a filled berm at the southern end. In the case of the various subsidiary stadia, Aalto tried to incorporate the natural contours of the rolling site into his designs which called for the minimum of cut and fill elsewhere. The remainder of the facilities were to be scattered around the site wherever contour and orientation would permit and without direct adjacent relationship to the vehicular access.

The design he shows for his main stadium is basically the one he used for the Independence Monument competition—a long oval dished up to allow the pedestrian flow to lead into the lowest level of the seating via a series of vomitoria. Perhaps the stark simplicity of Aalto's design caught some of the jury members off guard; in spite of the fact that it was lauded for its considerations of vehicular access and traffic design, they placed it in the lowest category of awards. Among the other participants listed in the awards was Aalto's old teacher and employer, Carolus Lindberg, whose project, executed with Lauri Pihkala, was bought. Another architect whose entry was bought was Martti Välikangas who, as a progressive designer, had replaced the conservative-minded Lindberg as editor of the *Arkkitehti* when the latter was eased out of that position in 1927.[18] Second prize went to a newcomer on the competition scene in Finland, Erkki Huttunen, one of the architects who in the thirties, along with Aalto, Bryggman, Ekelund, and a few others, followed the lead of the Swedish Functionalists and through his buildings introduced rationalism into the fabric of Finnish architectural thought. When the competition for the design of the stadium was held 3 years later, most of these same architects and some of the jury members participated.

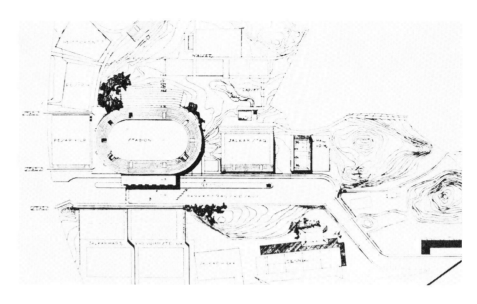

168. Stadium and sports park site competition entry, plan, Helsinki, 1930.

8
International Friendships and Travels

At this point in his life Aalto was beginning to be caught up in what must have been a period of increasing professional frustration within Finland, which led him to seek alliances and supportive connections outside the country. The first step in this quest was marked by the development of his relationship with the Swedish Functionalists. Possibly because of the lack of sympathy he must have felt from his fellow Finns, Aalto spent a good deal of time in Stockholm during these years.[1]

One of the advantages of Turku was that it was only a few hours by boat from Stockholm, giving Aalto the opportunity to witness at first hand the genesis of the key strain in modern architectural thought developing there.

At Aalto's invitation, Sven Markelius and Gunnar Asplund came to the opening of the Turku Fair in the summer of 1929,[2] and in the summer of 1930, Aalto attended the opening of the Stockholm Exhibition as the invited guest of Markelius. After the opening festivities, accompanied by Asplund and his guest Ekelund, he went to a conference on architecture in Trondheim, Norway.[3] When Aalto returned to Finland, he wrote a review of the exhibition and comments on the "Functionalist Manifesto" for the *Arkkitehti*. His friendship with the Swedish Functionalists lasted for many years and led him further into international professional conference circles.

CIAM

It was certainly through Markelius that Aalto learned of the existence of CIAM (Congrès Internationaux d'Architecture Moderne) and with him attended the second meeting of that body held in Frankfurt in 1929. At the time he was undoubtedly unknown to Le Corbusier, Siegfried Giedion, or any of the other Central European architects who actually operated the conferences. The main statement of the CIAM document—its renunciation of willingness to, "follow principles of shaping, dating from former epochs and past structures of society"[4]—fell closely in line with the attitudes Aalto had exhibited at home during the previous year. To register his credentials as a modern architect, he brought photographs to the CIAM meeting of the not yet completed Turun Sanomat.[5] He evidently fitted in well there and was accepted by the group, despite the fact that he was not officially representing any Finnish group.

In the summer of 1930 he also attended the CIAM conference in Brussels[6] and presented several items for exhibit and publication relative to the conference theme—the design and planning of housing for lower income groups. Representing Turku (or Åbo as it was given in Swedish by Aalto), he showed four examples of his recent designs. On the surface, the largest example would appear to be purely imagi-

nary in conception; in fact it is an amalgamation of three distinctly separate sources. The super block site, where the housing of three and two stories was presumably located, is in actuality the site on the edge of Vartiovuori (Watch Hill) Park where the handicrafts museum is now located. Aalto showed the observatory relocated at the park's edge to fit within his apartment neighborhood; otherwise the streets and pathways remain as they existed. On the dead-end border street he placed an entrance courtyard breaking a long line of apartment blocks that follows precisely the configuration of Bryggman's stairway and courtyard between his hotel and Atrium apartment block (169, 101).

Finally, the overall layout shows two long, only slightly broken, rows of two-story garden apartments without any direct street access, recalling his own Jyväskylä railroad employees' housing. This type of English garden apartment planning was safe enough to present to an international body. He also gave a small section presumably showing that the rows of dwellings were located at distances, in line with the best Gropius theories already known in CIAM circles.[7]

Another of Aalto's contributions was an apartment floor plan taken from the Standard Apartment block with references to construction methods deleted, perhaps to make it appear as if it were constructed of monolithic concrete (170). He also presented a type of project not commonly found in his or any other Finnish architect's work: a group of attached row houses separated from their private gardens (171) by the main access path, which is located, as in the railroad employees' flats, away from the street. The path thus bars any direct passage from the individual row house dwelling units to their respective gardens. Aalto may have had some idea of giving each dwelling unit the option of having a garden or not, but in the flurry of CIAM activity the scheme would probably not have been subjected to such detailed examination. The fourth example was the layout for a worker's flat designed for Paimio.

Application for Professorship

In the winter of 1930–1931 Aalto applied for the Chair of Architecture in Helsinki.[8] The only other applicant for the post was J. S. Siren, the architect whose heavily neoclassical design for the Houses of Parliament, then still under construction, had placed him in a sentimentally advantageous position in Finland. Though Aalto had by this time certainly revealed himself to aware observers as an emerging force in the world of architecture, the committee passed over him in favor of his older colleague.[9] While this decision could be easily rationalized on the

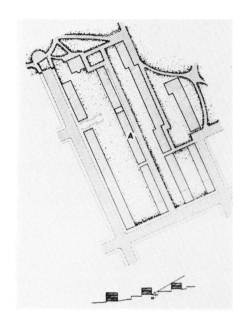

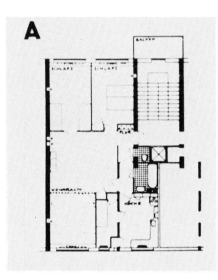

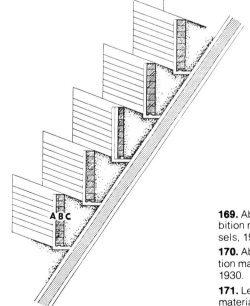

169. Above left: Apartment and housing exhibition material for CIAM conference, Brussels, 1930.

170. Above: Apartment and housing exhibition material for CIAM conference, Brussels, 1930.

171. Left: Apartment and housing exhibition material for CIAM conference, Brussels, 1930.

172. Photograph of Alvar Aalto and Laslo Moholy-Nagy on return voyage of *Petros II*, 1933. Photographer: Erno Goldfinger.

grounds that Aalto, at 32, was too young and as yet unproven and generally unknown, the selection of Siren was a politically and theoretically conservative choice on the committee's part.

The following summer, in 1931, Aalto traveled with Hilding Ekelund to the Deutsche Bausstellung in Berlin where Finland's Architectural Society had placed an exhibit. While there he made the customary call on Gropius and was introduced to other members of Berlin's architectural community.[10] As time went on, however, Aalto seems to have found himself increasingly out of tune with the CIAM line. He is remembered in CIAM circles as being a cheery, boisterous, and lively figure,[11] but one who did not always appear serious at conferences. While drawn to the cosmopolitan milieu and desiring moral support from his involvement with the international architectural avant garde, Aalto appears to have grown progressively detached from CIAM's more substantive activities as he began to develop his own style. His pattern was to appear at the conferences, to socialize and take part in the festivities, but to spend little time with any of the official proceedings. In Athens in 1933 he arrived late with an elaborate excuse and without any of the pledged exhibition materials,[12] and he missed the historic voyage of the Patros II from Marseilles to Athens. He did, how-

ever, make the return trip with the group after the conference was over (172).

Tehtaanpuisto Church

At the end of 1930 a competition was held for the design of a church in the Tehtaanpuisto section of Helsinki. Although it is by no means surprising to find that the design of churches is a favorite task for Finnish architects, it is amazing to find that this contest attracted twice the number of entries as the Stadium Site Plan.

The Michael Agricola church, as it was called, was not constructed to the design of the first prize winners, T. H. Strömberg and Gunnar H. Wahlroos, but to a design by Lars Sonck which came out of the second competition for the church in 1932. In the first competition Erik Bryggman placed second, Ilmari Ahonen and E. I. Sutinen third, and Martti Välikangas's design was among those that were bought.

Aalto's competition record was becoming progressively worse, and in this contest he did not even receive a mention, although his entry was placed in the higher class. His design (173) is based upon a long, high, open hall, which is rectilinear in cross section and plan, but combines his inclination to ameliorate the rigidity of the rectangle with a significant amount of consideration for the acoustical qualities of church interiors. The jury, in their review, commented on this pronounced design quality which is revealed most explicitly in the longitudinal section. The apse is basically an acoustical shell with a parabolic shape projecting sound from the altar toward the congregation as the Vallila Church design had attempted to do.[13] The ceiling as drawn, would be a row of segmental vaults stretching across the span of the nave. These vaults were not inherently structural but rather decorative and recall the technique of ceiling construction in fireproof loft buildings from the early part of the twentieth century where the spanning structural depth of a T beam was concealed by a series of curves.

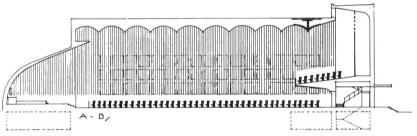

A - B/

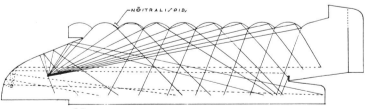

NÕITRALISOID/

AKUST. KONSTR, ÄÄNIAALLOT KUORISTA/
SOUNDWAVES FROM THE CHOIR

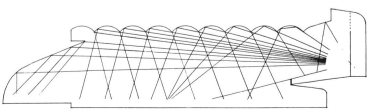

AKUST KONSTR ÄÄNIAALLOT URUISTA/
SOUNDWAVES FROM THE ORGAN

173. Church competition entry for Tehtaan-puisto area (later called Michael Agricola Church), interior perspective and section, Helsinki, 1930.

Acoustically Aalto's design would have created a concentration of sound at certain points and almost none at others (i.e., dead spots) resulting from the reflection of the cusps where the vaults adjoin.[14] This, however, is just one step in resolution from the final profile used in the ceiling of the lecture room in the Viipuri Library, which evolved in the next two years. If for no other reason these competitions were invaluable to his career because they allowed him to test his theories before designing the projects in which they were finally, successfully used.

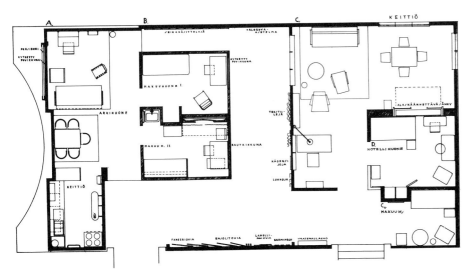

174. Above: Minimum standard apartment exhibition, plan, Helsinki, 1930. Architects: Alvar and Aino Aalto, Pauli and Märta Blomsted, Erik Bryggman, Werner West.

175. Opposite page top and middle: Minimum standard apartment exhibition, model kitchen layout, Helsinki, 1930.

176. Opposite page bottom: Aalto family apartment in Co-op Building, children's room, Helsinki, 1928.

Minimum Apartment Exhibition

In the autumn of 1930 at the annual exhibition of the Finnish Arts and Crafts Society in Helsinki, a special exhibit of the so-called minimum apartment was included. This exhibit was designed and installed by Aino and Alvar Aalto, Pauli and Märta Blomstedt, Erik Bryggman, and Werner West.[15] The Aaltos handled the coordination of the exhibit as well as the largest number of display rooms in it.[16] They were responsible for a unit comprised of a kitchen and living room with a small dining area between and a small bedroom. Bryggman designed a larger combined living and dining room. The Blomstedts' layout was for a hotel room, and they also designed a small bedroom, as did West. The exhibit was made up of a series of sample rooms or booths installed with furniture, carpets, utensils, lamps, artwork, and appliances in a set of simulated apartment arrangements (174). A serious attempt was made to use only furnishing items of the most modern design; many of them were designed by the exhibit designers themselves and were available on the market in Helsinki. The exhibition represented a significant break with the esthetic qualities of the traditional modes of homelife. It was patterned on similar exhibits held in other European capitals and specifically owed a direct debt to the Frankfurt CIAM conference held the previous year.[17]

The Aaltos reserved the kitchen for themselves, undoubtedly seeing it as the room that presented the greatest opportunity to demonstrate the change that would soon take place in domestic design. Their design showed a galley-type kitchen with two sinks, a counter for food preparation, and storage cabinets above and recessed below the counter. The adjacent wall had a range in the corner away from the sink, and a rotating ironing board was mounted along the wall opposite. This arrangement, with its wall-hung cabinets and racks, was seen to be a significant step forward. The sketches illustrate the use of the kitchen by a woman who could sit down to perform many household tasks (175). The figure shown is that of Aino Aalto herself, complete with her closely cropped hairdo fashionable at that time. This level of minimum design—i.e., the minimum number of elements necessary to sustain a full and satisfying style of life—was maintained by the Aaltos in the apartment they occupied in the Co-op building in Turku (176). The furnishings they lived with were the products of good industrial design, and many of the items were of their own creation. They actually lived the lifestyle of the exhibit theme.[18]

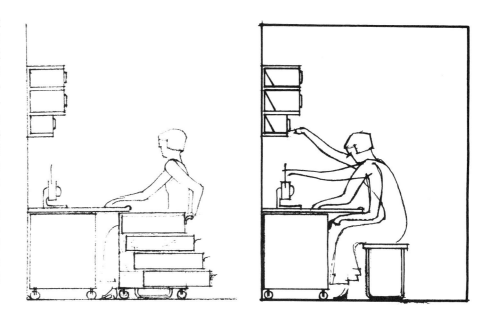

Prototype House Competitions

In the spring of 1932 the Nordic Building Conference, a pan-Scandinavian event that dealt with all aspects of building and architecture in that part of the world, was held in the city of Helsinki, and many special events and exhibitions were organized to coordinate with it. In the preceding winter two local companies announced competitions for house designs that would employ their products as the main feature of the building. The prototype designs were obviously to be used in their respective advertising campaigns after the conference. The first competition, that of the Insulite Company of Finland, called for the design of a house, of 75 to 90 sq m, that utilized prefabricated, insulated wood wall panels. Aalto didn't win, but his entry "Bio" was published in the Insulite brochure and in the special conference catalog, along with many other entries.[19]

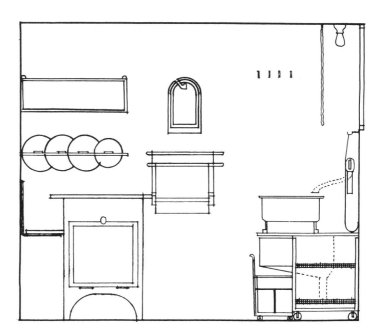

Aalto's design was based on the idea of the separation of functions in two parts of the house. Unlike Marcel Breuer's later "Bi-nuclear" house, which separated the sleeping from the other functions, Aalto separated the served and serving spaces.[20] This by no means twentieth-century notion is the basic division of much traditional domestic architecture for the upper classes of the world, but it was indeed a novel idea to apply to housing for the average citizen. The division in this

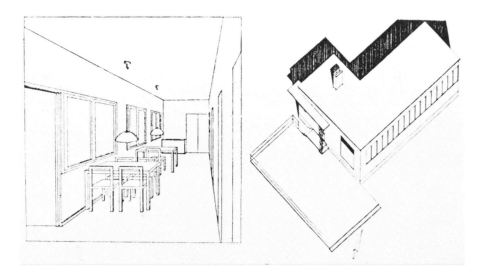

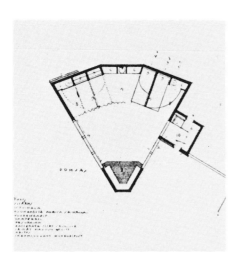

177. Top: Prototype house competition entry for Insulite Co., perspective, 1932.

178. Middle: Weekend house competition entry for Enso Gutzeit Co., perspective, 1932.

179. Above: Weekend house competition entry for Enso Gutzeit Co., plan, 1932.

design occurs between the kitchen and maid's room, which are separated from the rest of the house by the main entrance hall. The main block is dominated by a large sitting room that opens into a broad, windowed, single-loaded corridor (177) that is large enough to house dining functions as well as ancillary activities of family life such as sewing and studying. All the bedrooms are aligned along this corridor and, at the end, next to the master bedroom, is the bathroom. The corridor could if desired be divided into sections by curtains.

The second prototype house competition was sponsored by the Enso-Gutzeit Company, Finland's largest manufacturer of plywood, and involved the design of weekend cottages.[21] It was a two-part competition for a small weekend house of about 20 to 35 sq m and another of 50 to 60 sq m, both, of course, requiring the use of plywood as the primary wall material. There is no evidence that Aalto entered the contest for the larger house, but his project in the smaller category was bought.

Aalto's design, which he entitled "Tuli" (178), meaning fire, is actually a single, large, fan-shaped room with a massive open hearth fireplace located at the acute corner. The fireplace is left unobstructed so that heat can radiate through the entire room without interference. The fan shape (179), which was to become his most fre-

quently employed and widely varied signature motif in later years, is used here for the first time to capitalize on the nature of its geometric form. In order to prevent heat loss, the open hearth fireplace is placed at the apex of the fan. Where a wide expanse for sleeping is needed the splay of the shape is used. Throughout his life, Aalto was able to take this simple form and adapt it functionally to apply to virtually any architectural program that might arise. He could turn it to use in a concert hall, a cemetery, or a library, but always something of the pure nature of the fan shape remained.

The sleeping arrangement in Tuli is designed to permit flexibility in size and number of private areas needed on any given occasion, with a maximum of two singles and a double, formed by hinged panels that fold back against the wall and conceal three separate lavatories when they are not in use. Flexibility was one of the themes on which Aalto harped throughout his career, usually citing standardization as its natural enemy. But here he justifies it by creating an arrangement flexible enough to be used in many ways and by many different personalities literally within the framework of a standardized, mass-produced prototype.

At this point in Finland's development, architectural design began to exhibit evidence of change on a broad level. This meant that for a period Aalto and the other progressives would take their place among the community of modern architects who rose around them, thus softening the effect of their former uniqueness. The period during which Aalto entered all these competitions witnessed a change in his concern for the theoretical basis of architecture. This ended on one level with the construction of Paimio but was not brought to resolution until the final drawings for the Viipuri Library were finished.

BEYOND
FUNCTIONALISM

9
Viipuri Library

Competition Project

Perhaps any one of the buildings from the Turku period discussed above would serve as a subject for detailed examination of Aalto's development into a master of the modern style, but the building of this period that presents the greatest opportunity for such analysis is the Municipal Library at Viipuri, the largest city in Eastern Finland and the capital of southern Karelia (now in the USSR and called Vyborg). The design and building of this project stretched over a period of 9 years, from 1927 to the latter part of 1935, during which time Aalto's perception of the nature and mode of architectural design underwent a radical transformation. The change evinced in the progression from the Agricultural Co-op to the Paimio Sanatorium is paralleled in the development of the designs for the Viipuri Library, from project to final building.

Sometime before he moved his office to Turku, Aalto would have heard about the forthcoming competition for the library; however, after the original announcement in October 1926, some difficulty was encountered in arriving at a suitable program. Finally on June 27, 1927, the program was ready for distribution. The deadline for submission of entries was the first day of October, and Aalto would therefore have produced the greater part of the design after he moved to Turku that summer. The competition project was

drawn during the same period in which the first drawings for the construction of the Agricultural Co-op were produced. The library drawings were labeled "W W W" (180). The letter "W" stood for the archaic spelling of the city's name—Wiipuri.

It is doubtful that Aalto really expected to gain a prize, for although he had just won the Co-op, he was still trying hard to establish himself as an integral part of the Turku scene. In winning the first prize of 15,000 marks for the library,[1] he was again able to gauge his worth against the best Helsinki had to offer. Hilding Ekelund won second prize with his project "Codex."

The site for the library was on Aleksanterinkatu, one of Viipuri's main thoroughfares (181), just where it bisects the long green space of Torkkelinpuisto which stretches back for several blocks from either side of the street through much of the city's center just north of the existing civic and government area.[2] The site for the proposed House of Culture was across the way, situated, like the library site, within the park. As there had been no definite decision on just how this building was to be built, the program for the library required that its site plan encompass the proposed House of Culture; and each competitor was expected to provide a ground plan shape for this building as well. Both Aalto and Ekelund decided to give the House of Culture an L-shaped mass that would in-

scribe a plaza facing the main street and thus their libraries as well. Aalto's project shows a large statue in the center of his plaza. The site dictated by the program called for both buildings to be located near one of the main tramline intersections of Viipuri. Aalto's site plan (182) in fact suggested that the streetcar loop around to the rear of the House of Culture, thus providing a stop away from other vehicular traffic.

His library building was to be a simple rectangular solid in mass, with a long narrow entrance wing leading from the street. The scheme he presented (180) included several features arranged in a fashion previously unknown in Finland. Principally, these consisted of the stairway and entrance spaces, the main interior volume with its stairways and control system, and the west or main elevation which faced the House of Culture. Each of these components is related to the same design source, Asplund's Municipal Library in Stockholm, first designed in 1921 and under construction until 1928.[3] In the preliminary and final versions of his design, Asplund had employed a grand, straight-run entry stair which was expressed on the interior as an open stairwell, which led up into a large rotunda brilliantly lit by high windows above. Aalto's scheme made use of a similar concept but employed a turn of axis to orient arriving readers to the stairway leading to the main control desk located at the end of the large-

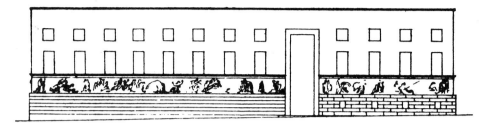

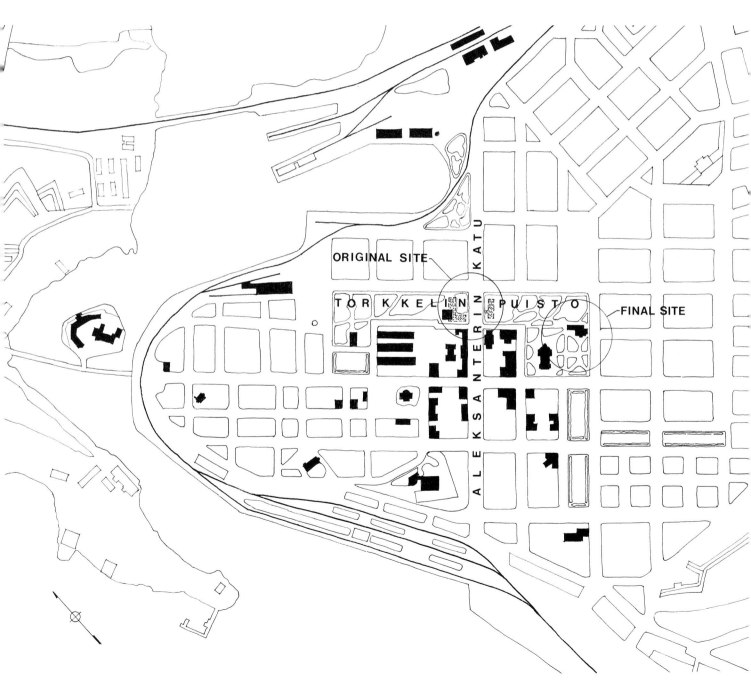

180. Left: Municipal library competition entry, elevation, Viipuri, 1927.

181. Below: Map of Viipuri, circa 1935. Drawing: Paul David Pearson.

ORIGINAL SITE

T O R K K E L I N   P U I S T O

A L E K S A N T E R I N   K A T U

FINAL SITE

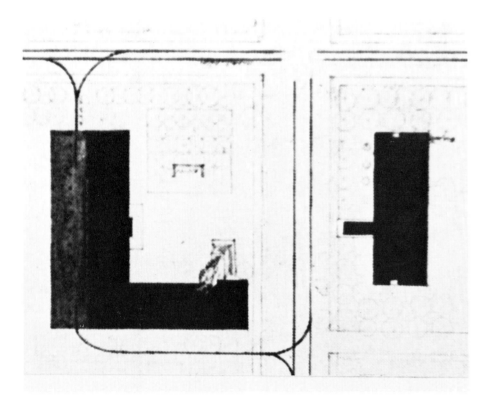

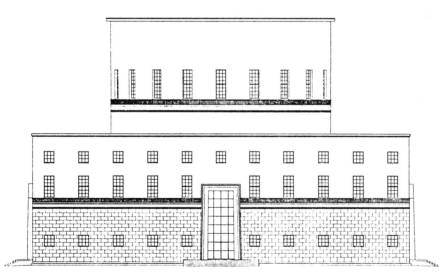

182. Top: Municipal library competition entry, site plan, Viipuri, 1927.

183. Above: Municipal library project, elevation, Stockholm, 1923. Architect: Gunnar Asplund.

volume, skylit room (although not a rotunda). This motif of a sunken space within a larger space open to the sky, a variant of Asplund's rotunda with sunken stairway, was used in some form in every library that Aalto executed.[4]

He might just as well have borrowed this form from the atrium of a Roman house with its depressed cistern or from any of a number of Renaissance palace designs with two-level interior courtyards open to the sky,[5] or even from precedents in his own early career.[6] But a comparative analysis of the Viipuri facade with that of Asplund's in Stockholm (183) demonstrates that the plan similarities are more than just coincidental. While the design for Viipuri is asymmetrical and the Stockholm building contains a giant, axially planned rotunda on top, the remaining elements are so similar they might have been produced by the same hand.

The primary horizontal division of each facade occurs just below the midline course, and the area below that is articulated in ashlar stone coursing, while that above is a smooth stuccoed band. The fenestration of the upper part is handled by stacking a square window in the top story over a double-height window of the same width on the main level. The sills of these large windows are located just at the string course. Although Aalto's project contained on the first floor level the same type of frieze of marching figures proposed in his competition drawing for the Jyväskylä Civil Guard House the previous year, and Asplund's building contained only a series of basement windows, the general agreement of proportions of the lower parts, including the main entrances, indicates that the facades are essentially the same. The portal of Asplund's building, inspired by the Erechtheum, is a trimmed vertical opening proportionally about one unit wide and over two-and-a-half units high. In Aalto's building the portal is transformed into an untrimmed volumetric form, having the same external proportions as Asplund's, but projecting far out from the facade of the main structure. The Viipuri portal was to be fitted with a straight-run stair inside the projecting entry, the walls and ceiling of which were to be decorated with a frieze of the same posed figures as the facade.[7] These figures may be a loose reference to the Parthenon or some other Greek frieze, although they are shown in so mannered a style as to bear little direct relationship to classical vocabulary.

The influences on the original version of the Viipuri Library are certainly from Asplund, but Hakon Ahlberg, another Swedish architect whom Aalto met when he worked on Bjerke's fair buildings at Gothenburg, must also have had considerable impact on his thinking about the building. One building, or rather group of buildings in particular, can be seen as a precedent for the Viipuri Library design—Ahlberg's Arts and Crafts building at the Gothenburg exhibition. Ahlberg, something of a historian and critic himself,[8] executed a fascinatingly eclectic building that had a high, wide facade with square stucco panels and a giant, narrow doorway in the center, not unlike the Erechtheum profile used by Asplund and later Aalto. More importantly, the interior of Ahlberg's pavilion had a number of rooms executed in a wide variety of decorative geometric patterns of a basically restrained neoclassical spirit. The room that is of interest with respect to the Viipuri Library is the giant colonnaded atrium centered around a cistern and open to the sky. This, the central space, must have been observed by Aalto when the building was under construction in 1921–1922. The cistern area, with its stepping sides, undoubtedly struck a responsive note and provided Aalto with one of the basic inspirations for the motif of the depressed space within a skylit room which became so persistent in his work from Viipuri on.

Directly on axis with this space, but higher up the hill and set alone, was another space of interest in light of Aalto's later work. Over a round room Ahlberg placed an an-

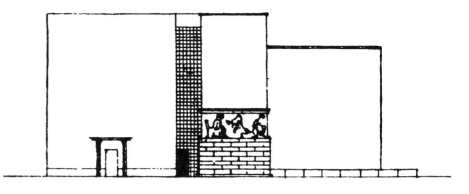

184. Municipal library competition entry, side elevation, Viipuri, 1927.

cient form—a high conical vault with an open skylight at the apex. This form, with its opening, admitted light in a mysterious glow very much like the Pantheon in Rome although, because of the low angle of the sun even at its maximum elevation in Gothenburg, direct rays of sunlight could never shine directly on the floor.[9] This, of all the sources for the Viipuri Library, is probably the only one that may be interpreted as an inspiration for the grid of conical skylights. Ahlberg's building was well published in Scandinavia and abroad and appeared in his own book on twentieth-century Swedish architecture well before the Viipuri competition was held. Thus even if Aalto had not seen the building at Gothenburg, he could not help but be familiar with its main aspects.[10]

The section (184) shows that the interiors of the library would also have exhibited a decidedly classical flavor, especially the columned entryway at the end of the main reading room. The spatial conception of the entry progress was a dramatic one, culminating in a grand finale. The arriving reader, after ascending inside the high, narrow passage of the entrance stairway, would pass through a low-ceilinged vestibule into a high, but somewhat murky lobby and cross an even lower-ceilinged space to emerge suddenly into a long well sunk at the bottom of a brilliantly lit, three-story space—a very powerful architectural device. In the center of the sunken space a narrow, open stairwell was placed as a barrier to turn entering readers left towards the broad stairs at the end of the well, which led up to the control desk and the great surrounding space of the main reading room above. Below the well, there was a basement level for special and oversized books to which one would descend by the narrow stairway in the center of the well.

Second Version

On February 29, 1928, Aalto was awarded the contract to prepare design development and construction drawings for the library,[11] only weeks after he had landed the commission for the Turun Sanomat. It might have been too much for a small independent office to have major projects simultaneously spreading across the entire width of Southern Finland, but the Viipuri Library was to undergo many changes before any on-site supervision would be needed. By the end of August 1928, however, Aalto did produce a second version of the design (185), which incorporated many of the same features in plan, but its two- and three-dimensional characteristics place it clearly in the realm of his newly developing modern style found in the Turun Sanomat, the courtyard of the Co-op, and the facade of the Tapani apartment block.

The changes evinced by the revised scheme (186) show that he kept the entry stair as it was but projected a wing forward to adjoin it, thus giving the building a simple L-shaped mass with a paved forecourt like the House of Culture across the way. Essentially, the second version utilizes the same major spaces as the competition project with the ad-

dition of a few refinements. The dark, tube-like main entrance was altered to become a metal and glass enclosure open to the entrance plaza facing the street.[12] The first floor entry lobby was similar, but now the stairway at the entrance, which connected to the administrative offices upstairs, was removed from view behind a wall on the right. Also to the right of the entry was the children's library with the control desk for that division located between its reference and circulation sections. On axis with the main entrance stair, the main path of circulation, as before, led through a doorway and into the depressed pit area. There again, a turn to the left led along the pit up the stair to the main control desk located, as in the original, at the end of a grand, brilliantly skylit space; but even at this stage Aalto appears to have elected not to take advantage of the building's site and refrained from opening windows into the park along the east wall of the upper level (187). Behind the main control desk, at the head of the stairs, a wide entryway, now stripped of the classical columns which divided it in the first design, opened to a balcony leading around the perimeter of a squarish room rising from the floor below.

Other changes are perceptible at this point: the shape of the control desk in the second version now has rounded corners to encourage the free-flow of circulation around it; and on top of the bookshelves lining the walls of the well area (188), Aalto has now drawn an arrangement of wide desks forming a long U-shaped reading table surrounding the well on the upper level in lieu of a balustrade.

On the upper level, through a columned opening on the side facing the street, a large reading room with metal frame windows overlooked the street and the House of Culture.[13] Beneath this, on the first floor, was to be a lecture hall which stretched along the main facade and had no windows, just as in the competition drawings. And of course the glass-walled stairway on the north end of the building had not been changed and showed on the

site plan as the same notch that appeared earlier.

The new exterior treatment (189) called for a stone base as before, but this was reduced to little more than a few courses. Above it was a smooth stucco wall punctuated by the large steel-sashed windows of the reading room and control hall and the smaller windows of the support facilities, capped by a thin projecting cornice. The site perspective (190) and model (191) reveal the project's new nature most dramatically, emphasizing its boldest form, the five-story-high glass stair lobby over the main entry stair. This steel-mullioned cage of glass alone places the building clearly in the mainstream of the Modern Movement and prevents anyone from mistakenly judging it merely as an example of denuded classicism. The drawing also depicts the proposed House of Culture across Aleksanterinkatu with a series of clean, volumetric balconies facing its plaza.

The new plans, however, were not approved easily. The flat roof design drew expressions of doubt from the jury who apparently considered the skylight design something of a problem. The site also caused problems, and the jury proceeded to seek the opinions of a number of independent architects including Oiva Kallio, Uno Ullberg, and Georg Fraser. Aalto's colleagues, however, for the most part approved his ideas. Finally, after reviewing the plans, the building committee decided on May 4, 1929,[14] to ask the City Council to approve the drawings and issue a permit, but a new set of difficulties arose. A lengthy fight now broke out over just where the library would best serve the community. The business community, which was probably responsible for the original site selection, argued that the library along with the proposed House of Culture should serve to attract people to the city's most active business street and thus remain on the planned site. Several civic and cultural leaders, however, notably Otto I. Meurman, Chief Architect in charge of town planning, and Uno Ullberg, City Architect, vociferously fought to have

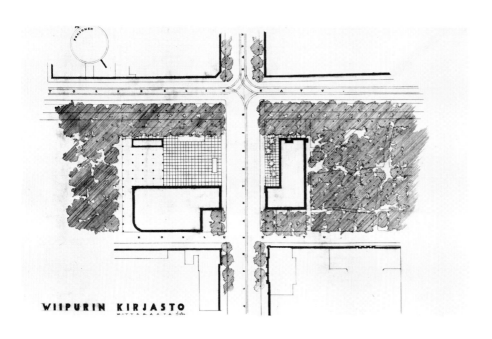

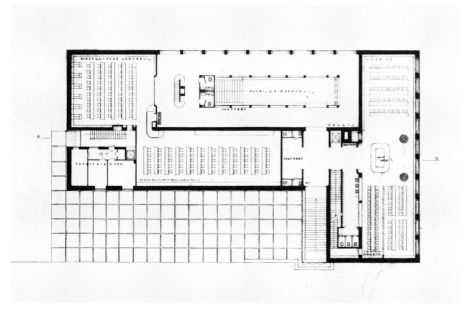

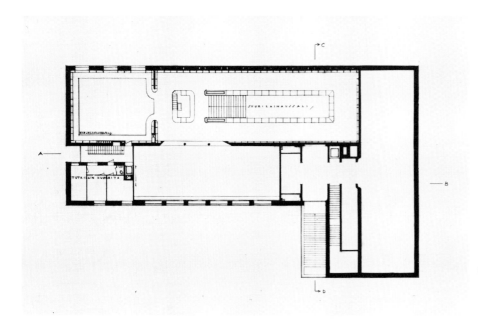

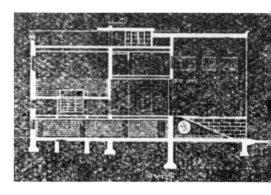

185. Top: Municipal library, second version, site plan, Viipuri, 1930.

186. Middle: Municipal library, second version, ground plan, Viipuri, 1930.

187. Left: Municipal library, second version, upper level plan, Viipuri, 1930.

188. Above: Municipal library, second version, section, Viipuri, 1930.

117

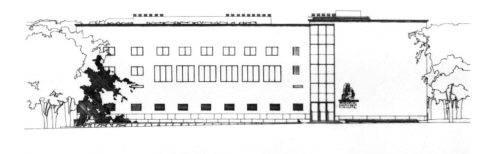

WIIPURIN KIRJASTO

189. Top: Municipal library, second version, main elevation, Viipuri, 1930.

190. Middle: Municipal library, second version, perspective, Viipuri, 1930.

191. Above: Municipal library, second version, model, Viipuri, 1930.

it moved on the grounds that the complex would spoil the linear effect of the green space of Torkkelinpuisto stretching through the town.[15] On November 12, 1929, the City Council decided to put off any decision until the 1931 budget was made up.[16] This controversy, understandably, set off a bitter internal struggle within the building committee and there ensued a period of legal maneuvering surrounding the election of an entirely new set of trustees.

The forces for change finally triumphed, and the site Meurman advocated was designated[17] three blocks away at the eastern end of Torkkelinpuisto where it adjoined another smaller park to the south which encompassed the site of the Cathedral of Viipuri and related to the open space of athletic playing fields to the south and east. If built upon, Meurman had asserted, this new location would link the two parks and merge them into one.[18] Aalto was pleased at the opportunity and redesigned the building to fit the new site. He moved his office to Helsinki in the summer of 1933, and on December 14, 1933, submitted his new (third) design. Two weeks later, on the 28th,[19] the City Council accepted the plans and construction began on April 12, 1934, with the city of Viipuri itself carrying out the excavation of the site.

At this point, the citizens of Viipuri became alarmed about the removal of trees and over 600 people signed a grievance protesting the project. They were pacified when they were promised that every tree removed would be replaced by one of the same species and size.

The construction of the building, completed in August of 1935, was the chief reason that Aalto switched his office from Turku to Helsinki,[20] for it would have been virtually impossible to supervise the construction from a distance. The supervision must have presented difficulties even from Helsinki, but unlike the transfer to Turku when he moved his practice to the actual site of his job, the lure of the capital and its awakening business interests, combined with the shaky nature of

118

the Viipuri commission, prevented Aalto from thinking about setting up practice in south Karelia. It is possible also that he considered it an unsuitable and far too provincial location for an architect of international stature, a role in which he was beginning to see himself.

Site Changed: Third Version

The new site (181, 192) permitted Aalto to construct a building which was truly open on all sides.[21] Except for a small service edge, the library did not abut directly on any street and was literally a building surrounded by park. The main approach to the building, which spans the boundary between the park and the cathedral grounds and forms an elision between the two, is from the north through the eastern end of Torkkelinpuisto. The entry vestibule, projecting slightly into the park, is faced with a contrasting dark material to give it emphasis. The grand staircase attached to the lobby is a dog-leg stair, glazed on the eastern side with the same square mullion pattern that the preceding design had incorporated and which appears even in the competition project on the side elevation walling in

192. Municipal library, final version, main entrance, Viipuri, 1935.

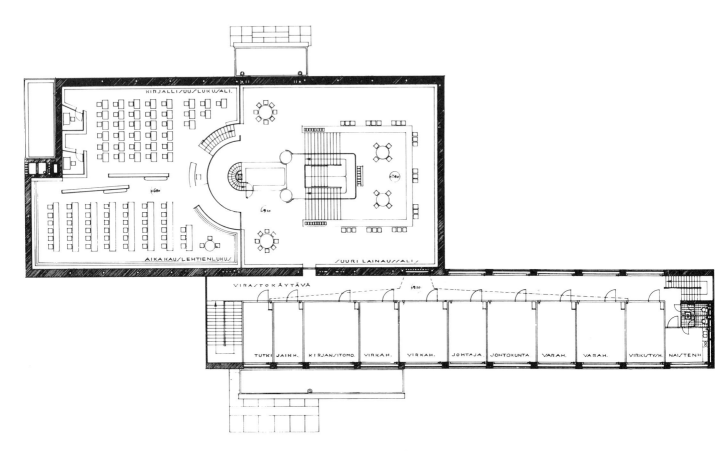

193. Municipal library, final version, plan, Viipuri, 1935.

the staircase niche. The lecture hall, along the front facade as before, was now stretched out to the right of the entry and glazed on that face from floor to ceiling. The children's library is entered from the south through the park alongside the cathedral site.

Aalto described the process by which he arrived at the final Viipuri design in the following, somewhat abstract terms:

While designing the Municipal Library in Viipuri (I had a lot of time at my disposal—five long years), I spent a great deal of time making children's drawings, representing an imaginary mountain, with different shapes on the slopes and a sort of celestial superstructure consisting of several suns, which shed an equal light on the sides of the mountain. . . .[22]

The account continues in the same picturesque vein:

. . . From these seemingly childish drawings sprang a combination of plans and sections which, although it would be difficult to describe how, were all interwoven. . . . This basic idea consisted in grouping the reading rooms and the lending rooms on different levels, like on the slope of a moun-

tain, around a central control desk uppermost in the building. Above everything was erected a sort of solar system—the round conical skylights.[23]

Despite this account, and Aalto's claim to have completely redesigned the building to fit the new site, the final form of the library bears a strong resemblance to the first and second versions. The massing is essentially that of two rectangular volumes joined in a lapped manner along one common surface (193). The longer, lower volume houses the entrance hall and grand stair, with lecture hall on the ground level and staff offices above on the second floor; the main volume contains the mechanical plant, children's division, and periodical room on its lower levels, and the great, multilevel complex of reference and circulation divisions above. This complex itself is comprised of two volumes which are vertically lapped, the lower volume being the high-ceilinged reference room whose space flows into that of the upper volume, the two-level circulation division.

From the main entry vestibule on the south, the lobby leads up a broad flight of steps to the wing housing the reference-circulation complex. At the top of the steps, one can either turn left to enter the lower reference room or continue on several paces, and turn right to reach the circulation division. After this 90° turn to the right, the progress is remarkably similar to that of the earlier schemes. One passes through a narrow opening of a short flight of stairs to a large open landing surrounded on all sides by the main upper level. The landing, devoted to special and foreign books, is the equivalent of the well in the earlier schemes. Now, however, the entrance to the landing, or well, is on axis with the overall space, instead of at right angles to it, and so the ascent to the upper level requires a 180° turn rather than the 90° turn of the early plans. This turn is effected by means of an elegant switchback, with a pair of stairs returning to either side of the first flight and depositing the reader in front of the circulation desk on the upper level (194). As in the second design, the balustrade which surrounds the well on the upper level is topped by a wide ledge forming a U-shaped reading table.

What may have been a problem in the earlier plans—control of access to the reading material shelved at the lower well level—is now handled in an elegant and ingenious manner. A U-shaped handrail serves to direct the traffic by dividing the landing and the upper pair of flights in two. The base of this U discourages the ascending reader from alighting at the landing and urges him to continue upward, to the right or left, channeled by the legs of the railing along the inner sides of the upper flights. After passing the control desk at the head of the stairs, he may if he wishes return along the other outer sides of the stairs to the lower landing where he now has access to the books.

In general terms, the effect of the passage from a somewhat dark, low-ceilinged space into a spacious, brightly lit volume is still the one Aalto had observed in Asplund's Stockholm Library. At Viipuri, however, it ultimately comes

194. Top: Municipal library, final version, circulation department entry stairway, Viipuri, 1935.

195. Above: Municipal library, final version, reference department, Viipuri, 1935.

closer to the older forms of the Roman atrium and the Renaissance courtyard, as the light enters not through windows but directly from above, through the grid of conical sectioned portholes which pierce the ceiling spanning the double complex.

The other half of this volume, the high-ceilinged reference division (195), corresponds to the balconied two-story reference room of the second scheme; spatially it lies in the same relationship to the open-welled circulation spaces in both old and new designs. Now, however, the upper level of the circulation area is totally open to the space beyond so that the two areas comprise a single, two-level volume.

The break in floor levels of this single volume occurs at the mid-point of the complex and a semicircular element is used to soften the effect of the dividing drop, to give interest to each separate level, and to denote the location of their central control points. The lower level, used by readers seeking reference material, is entered by turning left from the lobby and ascending via a short ramp which curves up and around the semicircular glassed-in librarian's office at the front of the reading room. This room is also connected directly to the upper level of the circulation area. A curved flight of stairs ascending to the adjoining area follows the semi-circle around on the opposite side of the office. The closed stacks are located beneath the auditorium and part of the circulation area. This level is reached via both the main stairway and another concealed spiral staircase with a booklift in the center, which stands like an axle almost the height of the building and connects the librarian's stations in the circulation, reference, and children's divisions.

Many have been under the impression that in this building Aalto created a totally windowless library, but in fact only the two sections of the reference circulation complex are treated without conventional fenestration. All the lower public spaces were lighted by large, fixed sash windows facing out into the park (196). Beneath the reference-circulation complex are housed the children's library and the periodical (or actually journal-reading) room, each with totally independent external access. The entrance to the journal room is from the only street frontage to the east, and the children's division is reached from the park beside the cathedral to the south. Thus, from the standpoint of public access, the final version of the Viipuri Library was a very different building from the earlier ones, as both Aalto and Meurman claimed. It was also a building that looked very different from each side or approach.[24]

Many features that are responsible for Viipuri's importance as a heroic example of modern architecture seem, from the evidence, to be present only in this final version of the design. It appears to have advanced to a far more modern position in terms of architectural theory than any of the buildings from the Turku period. In fact the final design was begun as the last of these buildings, the Paimio Sanatorium, was being completed.

Like Paimio it incorporated radiant heat panels for the heating of the interior, but unlike Paimio, the panels were concealed behind the plaster surfaces of the ceiling. Also because of the structural depth of the concrete needed to clearspan the masonry box of the Viipuri Library, the skylights, although basically the same as those used at the Turun Sanomat and Paimio, here have a special character. The light is reflected off the conical soffits of the skylight sides (197). This effect of reflection and diffusion of light over a wide area of readers below was explained by Aalto in a series of sketches. While this was a very elegant design decision, to a certain extent it appears to have grown out of unavoidable structural considerations.[25]

These skylights were supplemented by a system of "wall-washer" fixtures that in their reflection would duplicate the dispersion of light from the skylights and thus maintain the same quality of light day and night. Aalto said that he utilized this reflection off the wall to cast light on the books and not in the readers' eyes. He described it as making "a contract between the book and the reader."[26]

One of the more dramatic technical features incorporated in this building was the ventilation system. Since some of the building possessed no windows, and those in the other sections were for the most part large, fixed sashes of single panes of plate glass, Aalto's solution for supplying fresh air to the interior was obviously of great interest in a country that abounds with appreciation for the outdoors. The supply of fresh air was provided by a forced air duct system which pumped it from the basement through plenums located within the exterior walls and into the rooms via a series of diffuser grills. The stale air is forced through exhaust outlets upward through risers in the exterior walls and out the top. Aalto's early concern for this aspect of environmental comfort, which first showed itself in the railway employees' flats, reached an extreme stage in his ambitious efforts to ventilate this sealed building. He retained this type of concern in his repertoire of basic methodology from this point throughout his practice.

Nevertheless, none of the many innovations in this building has attracted anything like the interest aroused by the acoustical treatment in the ceiling of the lecture hall (198), which was the ultimate solution of the experimental designs Aalto had been producing over the last several years, namely those for the Tehtaanpuisto (173) and Vallila (152) churches. According to Aalto, the shape of the reflecting surface was dictated by the room's use; it was designed to allow not only for lectures but also for discussion among people seated around the room. It was therefore necessary for sound to travel from back to front as well as vice versa. A person speaking from the rear had to be audible not only to those around him but also to those up front and on the podium. This was accomplished by giving a wave-patterned cross section to the ceiling of clear pine strips. The form of the ceiling is basically that of a sine curve with every other trough raised to only half amplitude.[27] However, the acoustical diagrams traditionally shown with this building fail to take into account the distance the sound must travel before its first reflection, and it is probable that the effect works in practice because of the addition of a hardwood floor to aid in the distribution of sound to each part of the room. The section drawing is also misleading for it fails to consider the room's 30-m length. It would be difficult and disturbing not to be able to see the face of a speaker that one could hear with such ease. This is perhaps the reason that Aalto made provision for dividing the hall into smaller units when the need arose, but the result of this division is not taken into account acoustically.

The seven bays of the acoustical ceiling correspond rhythmically to the windows, the troughs falling on line with each mullion, but in other ways the ceiling almost denies the existence of the glass wall. It drops well below the head of the windows like a heavy swagged drape of wood hung against the glass. The projection of the ceiling stops about 10″ short of the glass line, and the soffit is closed by vertical strips of wood.

This building, like its immediate predecessor in Aalto's career, contains such an extensive number of significant features that it can be treated justly by devoting a full length work to it alone. However, it is in no way the polished work, presenting evidence of attention to every last detail, that Paimio is. The Viipuri interiors, as built, were splendid, and the derivations of the furnishings alone deserve to be included in any history of modern design theory. Nonetheless, the building is not at the level of the Paimio, which is characterized by a ceaseless attention to the quality of detail that makes every surface and fixture a new and surprising event.

At Viipuri Aalto's performance is less flashy, as if it was no longer necessary to prove his standing as an established master of the modern style either to himself or to his peers. He now possessed enough assurance to go beneath the skin of the building and fluently integrate the modern esthetic into his handling of volumetric, functional, spatial, and environmental relationships with a freedom and skill he had never before shown.

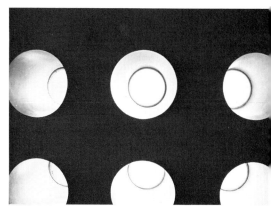

196. Above right: Municipal library, final version, entrance to children's library, Viipuri, 1935.

197. Right: Municipal library, final version, reading room skylights, Viipuri, 1935.

198. Below: Municipal library, final version, lecture-meeting hall ceiling, Viipuri, 1935.

10
Establishment in Helsinki and New Ambitions

Stadium Competitions

In the spring of 1933, immediately before he moved to Helsinki, Aalto took part in the competition for what was later to become the stadium for the Olympic Games planned for 1940[1] but subsequently postponed by the outbreak of war. For this project he used the profile that he had entered in the competition for the Independence Monument and its site plan. The stadium (199), entitled "456," was projected as a shallow-rimmed dish of concrete, partially set into the earth, with a smooth, deep, concrete fascia rising vertically from the upper lip edge of the oval perimeter. This was presumably to protect those seated in the rear rows and give visual substance to the sharp, shallowly raked edge of the bowl. The only addition he made to his previous design was to extend the rows of the stands further back, well over the entrance plaza, pull the corresponding section of fascia back as well, and add a roof (200). To protect and support this additional section, Aalto projected a series of nineteen monolithic concrete bents of an unequal T-shape. Their long, narrow cantilevered arms by which the roof was supported were counterbalanced by shorter concrete luglike arms protruding outward from the stadium wall, where each was tied to the earth by a slender steel column. Their mass gives the impression that the lug arms alone counteract the overturning effect of the slender

tapering bents which support the flat concrete roof and cast a deep shadow against the smooth fascia, forming a center of interest on the facade (201).

Appropriately, this is where Aalto chose to locate the main entry. Access to the interior of the stadium from the main entrance is by a ground level concourse that leads circumferentially around the oval and directly inward through any of the series of vomitoria. The 456 project reveals a stadium that is as starkly simple as the ruined Greek temples he had sketched on trips to the Aegean. The only modern element visible inside, other than the vomitoria, is the adventurous form of the slender roof structure (202). Apparently this was as far as his thinking had taken him by submission time, because opposite the triumphal entrance he sketched a scoreboard but left the seating panel beneath it unfinished. This shows in the section as well as the plan. This version is then little more than a preliminary design. Of the twenty-eight entries, Aalto's placed lowest within the group that would be asked to continue to the second phase of the competition that autumn.[2] Among those who took prizes were Erkki Huttunen, his partner H. V. Schreck, and also Martti Välikangas. Pauli Blomstedt, as well as Yrjö Lindegren and Toivo Jäntti, the winners of the second phase (and the final constructing architects), took the lowest mention along with Aalto.

Aalto's entry in the competition the following October, which dealt with development of the designs projected in the first, was called "Terra."[3] It was designed to take full consideration of the natural rolling site, preserving the hills and allowing construction only where the land was flat (203).

By the second part of the competition it was decided that the Olympic Games would be held in the stadium and it should be designed accordingly. At the southern end of the stadium, to one side of the triumphal entry, Aalto placed a tall concrete pylon to carry the Olympic flame.[4] The main approach to the stadium was shifted so that one only reached the lateral plaza at the side from the direction of the grand pathway leading to the triumphal entrance at the south end of the oval (204). Along this widening axis he placed a grand esplanade at the end of which—standing at a right angle to the lateral plaza—were the main turnstiles. It is essentially the same scheme of entrance as the 456 design but with refinements, especially in the relation of the building and pedestrian walks to the site (205). Near the main entrance he designed a series of natural, free-form motifs to be used as a series of outdoor dining terraces for the restaurant. He took the earth's contour lines from the map given with the competition program materials and simply converted each to a terrace of that shape and height. On the en-

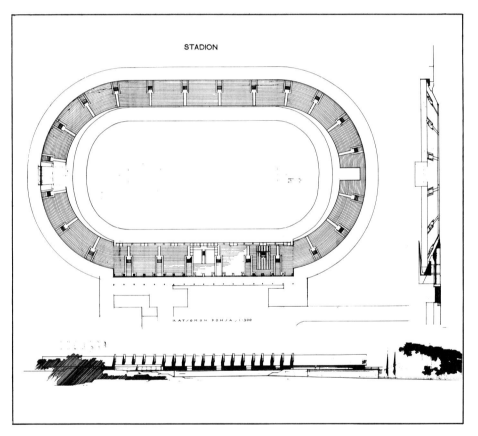

STADION

KATSOMON POHJA 1:200

199. Left: National stadium competition entry, part 1, plan, Helsinki, 1933.

200. Below: National stadium competition entry, part 1, perspective, Helsinki, 1933.

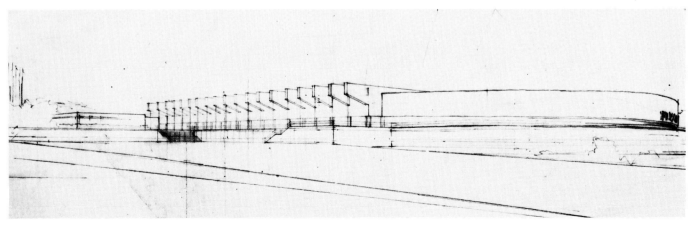

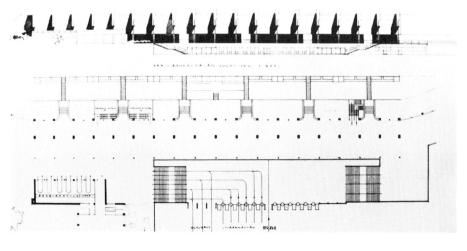

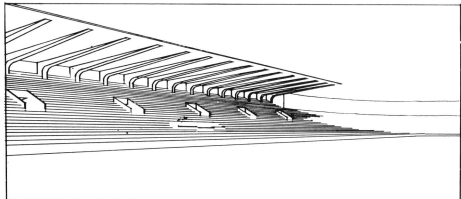

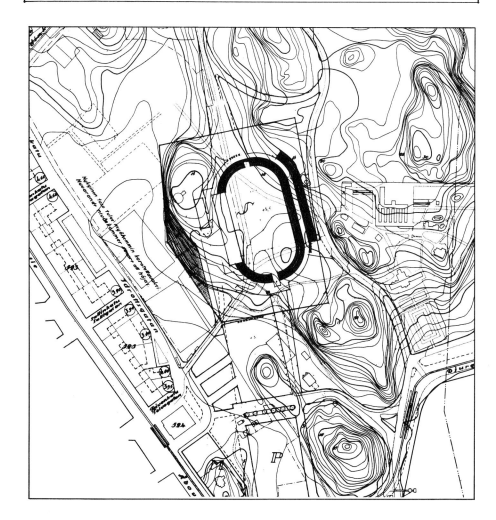

201. Top: National stadium competition entry, part 1, elevation and plan of entrance gate, Helsinki, 1933.

202. Middle: National stadium competition entry, part 1, perspective, Helsinki, 1933.

203. Bottom: National stadium competition entry, part 2, site plan, Helsinki, 1934.

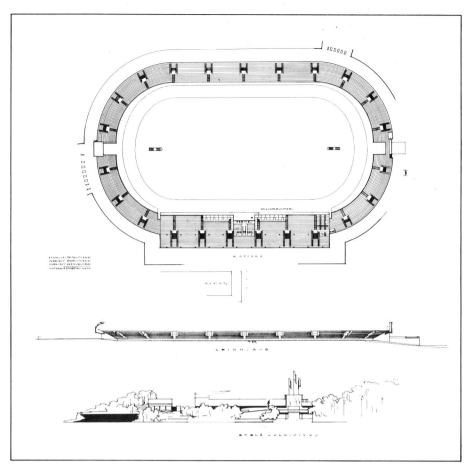

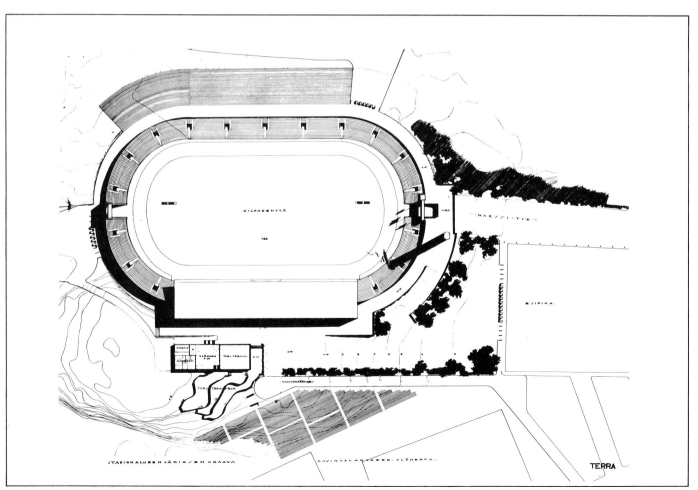

204. Left: National Stadium competition entry, part 2, plan, Helsinki, 1934.

205. Below: National Stadium competition entry, part 2, seating layout, Helsinki, 1934.

trance side of this area he placed a series of stepped berms where people could sit and sun themselves as they waited for the games to begin. He also did this on the other side of the stadium near the main automobile approach. Alongside the pedestrian way, which leads from the turnstiles to the main stadium entrance, is a driveway that ends in a turnaround at the entrance next to the restaurant coffee shop. This was to be used for heads of state and other VIPs visiting the games. The vacant space under the stands, particularly the grandstand, was utilized to create a wide concourse where Aalto located a large bar in the center bay with a high window wall that opened directly out to the field (206).

The system of cantilevering the grandstand has been changed in Aalto's second version so that the bent supports are no longer used. The seats and fascia stretch back even farther, to the point where the lugs had formerly reached, and are now supported by columns, while the canopy is a ribless tapering flat slab supported in midspan by columns in line with the perimeter of the main body of the stadium. As a consequence, the enlarged grandstand structure has a smooth facade, but the view from the stands

under the canopy is no longer unobstructed by supporting columns.

The obvious fact is that he found that there was no practical way to cantilever the distance shown on the original project. Of course this is precisely why competitions are organized in two stages—to make those bold ideas of the preliminary phases realistic and buildable before a decision to award the commission is made.

This competition remains one of the landmark examples of pre-war Finnish architectural activity: not only did the best designers compete, but they evolved schemes that represent almost every strain of modern architectural theory with respect to this building type.[5]

While Aalto was continuing to seek commissions that would sustain his practice in the capital, he began to design a private residence for himself in the suburb of Munkkiniemi. Before he moved his domestic and professional life to that location, he lived and worked out of the small apartment in the center of the city.[6] At the beginning of his residence in Helsinki, the main job in his office was the construction of the Viipuri Library, but there was nothing to be expected after that was completed, so he continued to seize every opportunity to compete that became available to him.

206. National Stadium competition entry, part 2, perspective and section, Helsinki, 1934.

Tampere Railway Station Competition

The preliminary competition for the railway station in Tampere was announced in October of 1933 and was due for submission on January 10, 1934.[7] Except for the prototype house competitions for *Aitta*, Enso Gutzeit, and Insulite, this far more elaborate contest attracted sixty-seven entries, the highest number in any competition in the history of Finnish architectural practice.

The competition called for the design of a major station located beside the main line connecting Jyväskylä and Central Finland with Turku and the southwest. The station itself was to sit at the end of one of Tampere's main streets. Of all the prize winners and mentions published in the review in the *Arkkitehti*, only K. N. Borg fails to display a fully developed Functionalist style.

Aalto's entry (207), submitted under the name of "Loko,"[8] cleverly combined vehicular access to the station from the main street with the underpass necessary to connect the two sides of the railyard embankment by means of a "roundabout drop-off." From that point a canopy

207. Railway Station competition entry, site plan, Tampere, 1934.

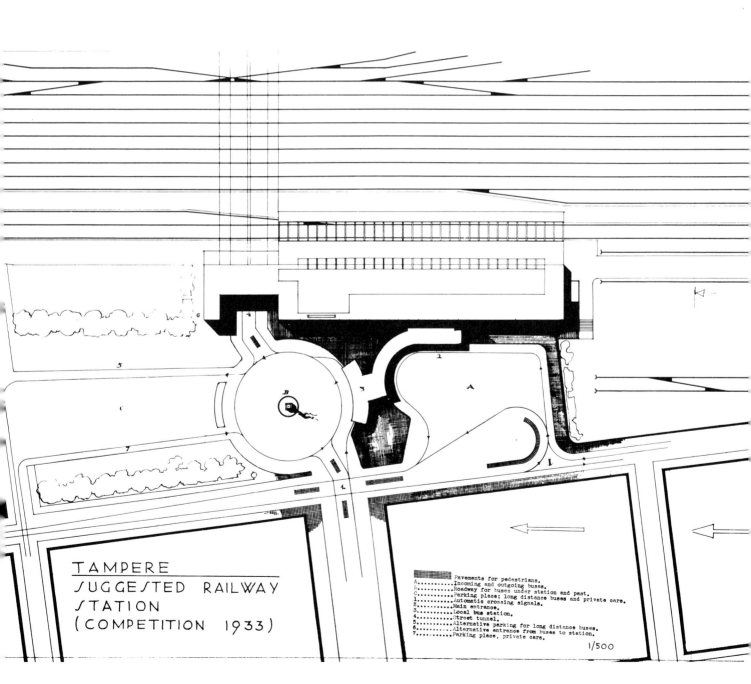

TAMPERE
SUGGESTED RAILWAY
STATION
(COMPETITION 1933)

Pavements for pedestrians.
A............Incoming and outgoing buses.
B............Roadway for buses under station and past.
C............Parking place; long distance buses and private cars.
1............Automatic crossing signals.
2............Main entrance.
3............Local bus station.
4............Street tunnel.
5............Alternative parking for long distance buses.
6............Alternative entrance from buses to station.
7............Parking place, private cars.

1/500

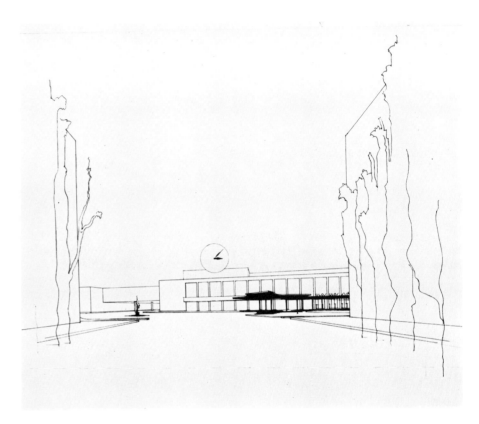

208. Top: Railway Station competition entry, facade, Tampere, 1934.

209. Middle: Railway Station competition entry, perspective, Tampere, 1934.

210. Bottom: Railway Station competition entry, interior perspective, Tampere, 1934.

211. Opposite page: Railway Station competition entry, platform shed perspective, Tampere, 1934.

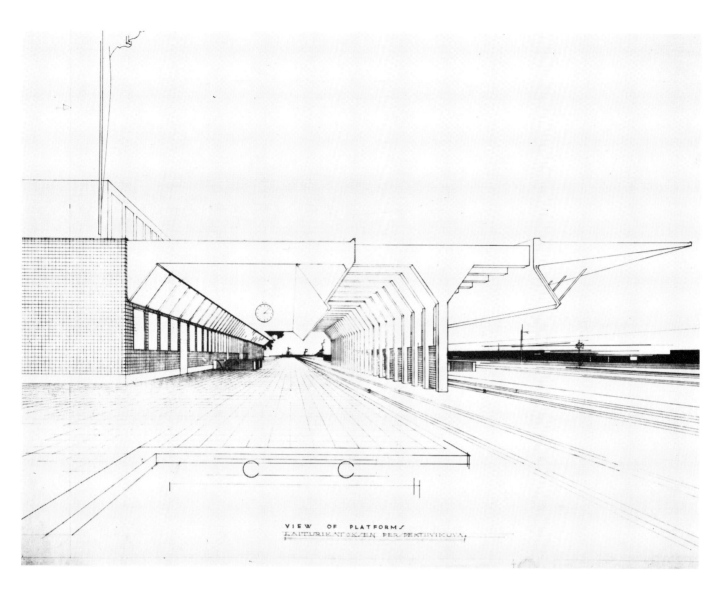

VIEW OF PLATFORMS
LAITURIKATOKSIEN PERSPEKTIIVIKUVA.

connects with a covered walk which curves around to the main entrance of the station. Passengers from connecting buses also alight in this area. This canopy can be even more directly related to Le Corbusier's Centrosoyuz project than can the Paimio entrance canopy finished the previous year.

The projected building (208), by the nature of the site requirements, was in most entries a long, shallow mass about two stories in height. One of the program requirements evidently was the incorporation of a clock into the design, for all entries show rather large clocks on the facades or towers of their stations. Aalto's design (209) is in concept and detail the simplest of all those published; it shows a building composed as a completely rectangular solid in the form of a glazed colonnade and surmounted by an enor-

mous circular clock, in itself two full stories in diameter. This minimalist play on the nature of the building as a line and the clock as a dot or circle is an example of nonobjective design used by many teachers and theorists of modern design during the late twenties and early thirties.[9] The basically facadal concept has a single, full-length concourse across which incoming and outgoing passengers pass to reach a single portal giving access to the track area above and in the rear. The interior perspective (210) shows a double-height concourse with a mezzanine set well back from the glass wall of the facade and carrying a full-length mural incorporating directional signs and advertising slogans for the shops below. Stretching across one end of the concourse on the mezzanine level is a restaurant. For the platform shed (211) Aalto speci-

fied that the structure be constructed of reinforced concrete T-shaped frames with one leg cantilevered to support a roof over the platform for the outer of the mainline tracks. The inner platform was similarly roofed with a flat ceiling, but the train tracks were open to the sky between the frames.

The elementary geometric image underlying the general concept of this station—the line and the dot—is emphasized in the perspective where the bucolic setting of the boulevard, lined with sharply vertical Lombardy poplars, frames the simplified composition of the station. Perhaps it was even too simple and stark in its use of scale and form to please the jury, which was led by Guunar Taucher, Väinö Vähäkallio, and Oiva Kallio.[10]

Helsinki Exhibition Hall Competition

The exhibition hall in Helsinki, which stood on the corner of the Turku road and Eläintarhantie adjacent to the stadium site, was destroyed by fire in 1933, and a competition was quickly organized to provide a design for a new one. Several of the entering schemes for exhibition halls were covered by long parabolic roof structures, including the first prize winner by Pernaja and Ypyä.[11] Once again the entire range of results or at least those that were published in the review were modern and Functionalist in spirit, and if anything, Aalto must have felt challenged. Many of the people taking the prizes in these years were either his age or younger.

His entry "MP (212)," probably standing for Messuhalli Palkinto (Exhibition Hall Prize), was indeed a prize winner this time, if only third. From the outside the building seems to be a rather boxy, long rectangular mass with a tall window wall stretching across each of the two long facades, but the interior perspectives and section drawings convey the volumetric sense of an entirely different building. Aalto's building would be supported by a row of thin, flat, rigid concrete frames, tapering outward from the bearing to form a knee with the beam above. The interior space is somewhat like the woodworking shop at Zonnestraal (167)[12] and the ceiling resembles that of the reading-circulation room at the Viipuri Library. The flat bents along the wall serve to deflect the light, and the ceiling curves over the bents along the edge of the long wall to form a sun reflector that directs the light downward. This is the same type of ceiling that was employed in the proposal for the Sports Institute at Vierumäki. It is also used on the outside edge of the low wings located just off the great exhibition space.[13]

The ceiling, like the raw structure at Viipuri, is a long span concrete beam that is braced at the sixth point by a cross member that could also be used to hang displays and equipment from. Within the resultant square panel Aalto proposed to put a grid of large, round dished lighting fixtures that would fill in and balance the natural light reflected from the side.[14] On the front, or main entry facade, he proposed the same idea of a circular concrete canopy to connect with the curb of the street. Here again Aalto was able to draw upon his repertoire of established and borrowed forms and combine them in an interesting arrangement, but the process was not yielding any first quality results and definitely not producing any commissions. He persevered.

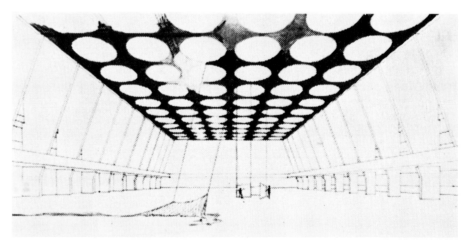

212. National Exhibition Hall competition entry, perspective, Helsinki, 1934.

Helsinki Central Post Office and Telegraph

Late in 1934 when Aalto turned in his entry for the Central Post Office and Telegraph in Helsinki, he must have felt it to be a futile gesture in some respects. The presence of Väinö Vähäkallio, Oiva Kallio, and J. S. Siren on the jury offered little chance of sympathy with what was by now a fairly recognizable style.[15]

The last competition he had won and continued through to construction had been the Paimio Sanatorium in early 1929. The last of the Paimio housing had been completed by this time, and except for winding up the Viipuri construction (the final stages of which were being supervised by Aarne Ervi), Aalto had no work at all and no prospects of any. Once again his entry did not even place, despite the fact that there were only fifteen entries. Nonetheless, his project was more progressive and basically more interesting than the entry that won first prize. At this point it is difficult to imagine why Aalto remembered himself as "always winning some prize," let alone "mostly winning first prize."[16]

The building in this case was not one of those medium-size public buildings that can be organized into one or two major spaces with a simple relationship to their respective support facilities. It (213) was to be a multistory, highly complex building, with multiple functions on every floor and some of them with disparate but nevertheless adjacent program requirements. The site was to be a location on Mannerheimintie, Helsinki's main street, just west of Saarinen's train station.

Aalto's project, humorously mottoed with a drawing of a pidgeon carrying a letter in its beak,[17] would have been a significant step ahead of the final version as built by Jorma Järvi and Erik Lindroos, which might well qualify as Helsinki's least attractive and interesting modern building. Though by no means a masterpiece, Aalto's scheme indicates a rational development and consideration for its surrounding environment. The basic idea is a division in architectural terms between those functions and services directly related to the public, which were located in one large and identifiable volume, and the rest of the postal administration offices, which were stacked in an open-well office block (214). The project gave him a chance to employ one of his favorite motifs in a particularly graphic way and in a purely graphic sense. The massing of the building works beautifully, identifying to all who view it which part is public and which is administrative. But since, in actuality, the entire operation is controlled by a single agency, this renders the unabashedly dual expression somewhat inappropriate. Looking more like a theater than a post office, the glazed fan shape rises like a clerestory over the similarly shaped public hall centered within the rectangular one-story base below. This room, in which postal services (215) would be available to the general public, contains a low counter running round the rear three sides. In the remaining area of the base are the ancillary functions necessary for the operation of a grand urban post office. This elegant wedge shape had been used by many architects to express the sight-line functions of theaters and cinemas, but Aalto's idea for the massing is closely contemporary with a theater complex project in Amsterdam by Duiker (216).[18] In the perspective drawn by Aalto to show the relationship between the station and the post office, the overall building seems so fragmented that it is obvious that few juries could rationalize it as a building.

213. Central Post Office and Telegraph competition entry, perspective, Helsinki, 1934.

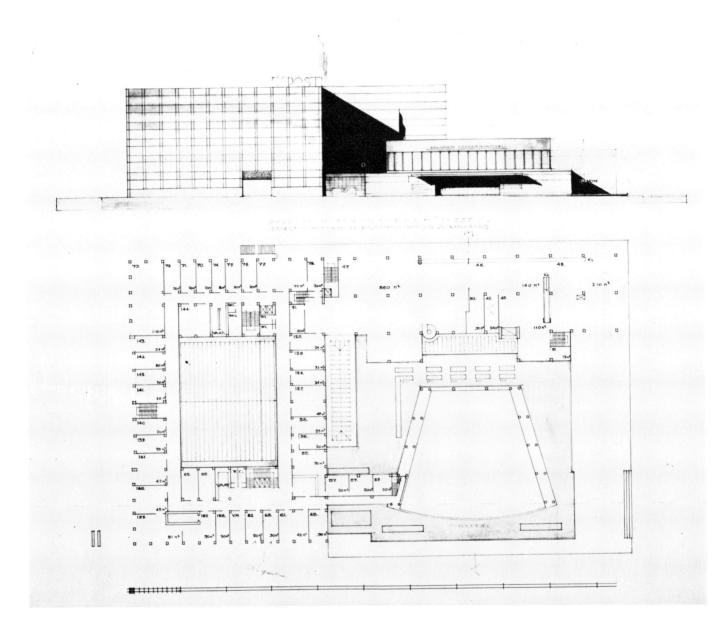

214. Top: Central Post Office and Telegraph competition entry, plan and elevation, Helsinki, 1934.

215. Above: Central Post Office and Telegraph competition entry, perspective of Main Hall, Helsinki, 1934.

216. Right: Project for theater in multipurpose commercial block, perspective, Amsterdam, 1934. Architect: Jan Duiker.

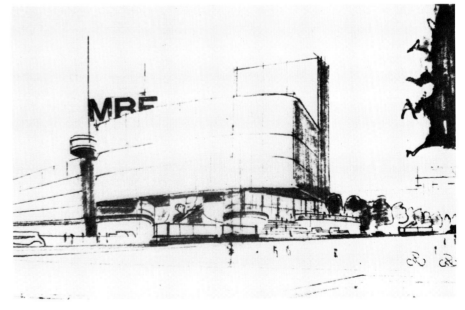

11
Recognition by Industry

Gullichsen Friendship

In 1935 Harry and Maire Gullichsen saw a chair designed by Aalto in a Helsinki shop window that aroused their curiosity, and some time later Harry contacted Aalto. It is quite likely that he made inquiries about him beforehand, but eventually Aalto was invited to submit ideas for the design of a new industrial plant at Kotka, the Sunila Cellulose-Sulphate Mill. Gullichsen was the manager of Ahlström, one of Finland's largest and oldest industrial holdings. The Ahlström empire had been assembled by Maire Gullichsen's grandfather and was enlarged by her father and her husband Harry to become one of the largest three companies in Finland. The Sunila plant was not owned solely by the Ahlströms for they were only one of five large corporate investors that founded it, but at that time Harry Gullichsen was the chairman of the board. He introduced Aalto to the board by saying, "Here is an architect who is well known outside Finland but hardly at all inside the country and who should be given a chance to prove what he can do," and added that he, Gullichsen, would personally take the responsibility.[1] Gullichsen was a modern man who not only wanted to live in a twentieth-century style but had given a modern air to the old and somewhat conservative Ahlström corporation. By 1936 Aalto had prepared a design that was ready for construction.

Industrial architecture in Finland occupies a unique position in the development of building forms and construction materials.[2] The main impact of the industrial sector in Finland is through the industry of paper and wood pulp production and the related support industries. Since the late nineteenth century, paper mills were constructed in Finland that followed the traditional forms of plants in other industrialized countries such as England and America. The main building material was brick since the remote sites required for such plants made the transportation of any other material difficult. Their forms were rectangular masses with segmental arched window heads but little or no articulation. The paper mill for Enso-Gutzeit at Valkeakoski by W. G. Palmqvist in 1928 is a late example of the soberly defined style that such buildings had arrived at. Industrialization took on a special meaning following independence when this, Finland's largest company manufacturing paper and wood products, took on the Finnish government as its principal shareholder. There was a constantly increasing demand for paper and pulp products during the first two decades of independence, and in the midthirties many facilities were expanded and new ones added to fill that area of profit opportunity. To ensure the expedient operation of processing wood into paper, every time a production mill was built, sawmill facilities, log plants, power plants, and housing had to be added also.

When Aalto was employed to work on the design of the Toppila plant at Oulu in 1930, it was only to effect cosmetic changes in the design already in the process of construction, and thus he did not possess a developed knowledge of plant design from the technical viewpoint. The system of cellulose sulphate production is a standard one, varying for the most part only with the size of the installation. However, since each building complex must occupy so much land area and be next to a source of water, the manipulation of the site plan to best advantage becomes a major task.

Sunila

In the design of Sunila (217) Aalto had to come to grips for the first time with a highly technical problem, and he basically adopted the established mode of designing such facilities.[3] In 1934-1935 Väinö Vähäkallio had designed and built a cellulose sulphate mill for Enso-Gutzeit at Kaukopää which is the same general prototype that Aalto used for Sunila. In its crisp, separated brick-clad masses, standing tall against the shoreline and linked by covered conveyers and hoppers whose exposed surfaces were finished in light-toned metal and concrete in contrast to the dark brick, it closely resembles Aalto's plant built two years later at Sunila, as well as others that came before it.

What, one might ask, makes Sunila different? The answer must be that it is primarily in the handling of the details that the best architectural efforts at Sunila can be recognized (218). It is in Aalto's use of horizontal and strip windows; the employment of the bowstring-type parabolic arches above the roof of the central building; the manner in which the building is integrated with the rocky site (he left trees standing even in the front of the mill); the emphasis on Vähäkallios' idea of painting all the conveyers, hoppers, and carriers a light tone to contrast with the red brick which is extended even to the dockside storage building (219). However, Sunila, when viewed within the tradition of Finnish industrial architecture, does not take the pride of place that many would assign to it.[4] Originally it had simple, clean facades, with the window openings arranged to give a regularized feeling, but the few simple forms of Sunila's first phase are all but lost today in an expanding collection of industrial hardware that protrudes everywhere from the

simple brick forms. The main facade of the central building, if it can be called that, has a clock mounted on the brick face and architecturally resembles Flodin's final version of the Tampere railway station. The entire plant is located on an island that had to be treated with respect. On the east side of Kotka harbor, which is mostly rock, the nature of the rugged terrain makes it virtually impossible to achieve an ugly or uninteresting relationship between it and the building. The site is a most beautiful place by one of the Baltic's natural deepwater harbors. It is, of course, a characteristic of many industrial buildings that they require sites on the shore. All the shore land on this section of the harbor has been reserved for Sunila's expansion should that be needed. The area of land on which the employees' village stands is, for the most part, hidden from the water by the mill and the industrial reserve surrounding the log-storage cove.

The village (220), started after the mill was nearly finished, has housing for all categories of plant staff.

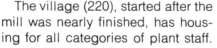

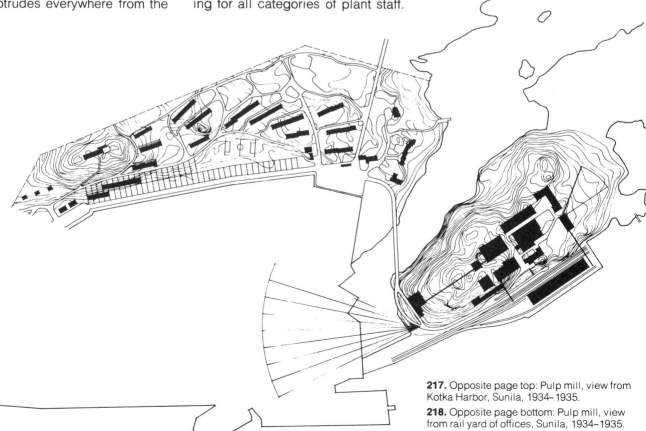

217. Opposite page top: Pulp mill, view from Kotka Harbor, Sunila, 1934–1935.

218. Opposite page bottom: Pulp mill, view from rail yard of offices, Sunila, 1934–1935.

219. Top: Pulp mill, dockside storage buildings, Sunila, 1934–1935.

220. Above: Pulp mill and village for employees, plan, Sunila, 1934–1935.

221. Above: Pulp mill and village for employees, central heating plant, Sunila, 1934–1935.

222. Right: Pulp mill and village for employees, engineers' housing, Sunila, 1934–1935.

223. Opposite page top: Pulp mill and village for employees, engineers' apartments, Sunila, 1936.

224. Opposite page right: Pulp mill and village for employees, main entrance to engineers' garden apartments, Sunila, 1935.

The main link between the plant and the village is by way of a bridge where the main gate of control is located. In a seemingly strategic aspect of the plan, the managerial, technical, and executive houses and garden apartments are located nearest the bridge approach. The only water frontage of the village is in this area. The remainder of the housing for the papermill workers is scattered up a gentle hillside parallel to the main approach road to the mill.

This village has been held up as a good example of industrial housing and planning for workers' convenience, but while there is merit in many of the housing forms, the village lacks any planning other than that the rows of apartments are located at a sufficient distance to ensure some privacy. There is no village center as such and there is no market of any significance, and if it were not for a store that located there subsequently, there would apparently be no provision for such services. The only other building beside the intercity bus stop is the central heating plant (221). The design of this called for a staggered facade like that of his own home in Munkkiniemi, completed simultaneously, but here it was to be complemented by a giant, overweight version of the Paimio stack.

Among the wide variety of housing types in the village two really stand out. The engineering staff residences are a series of attached row houses gently splayed at the joining walls to give the feeling that no two adjacent houses have exactly the same orientation. The splaying is accomplished by changing the alignment of a living room and stairway party wall so that it is no longer parallel to the opposite wall of the house on one side, while the house on the other side is set back and aligned in this new direction (222). The lower floor of this row type is finished in painted brick and the upper story in smooth white stucco. The garden walls continue the splay and the overall ground plan of the row is inevitably a fan shape (223).[5]

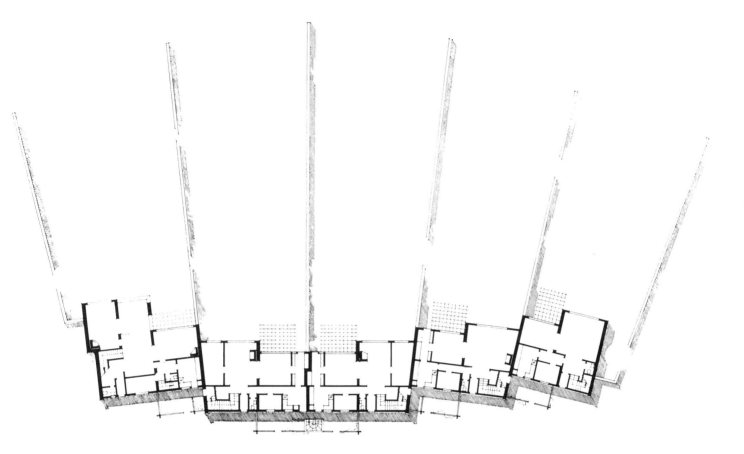

At the entrance to each of the engineers' apartments, away from the walled garden side, Aalto placed an enclosure of gridded poles (224) to act as a support for plant material that would eventually form a secluded entrance area open to the sky but not the adjoining entrances. It is the beginning of an appreciation of natural textures in Aalto's work that was to be found in most of his buildings for the next decade.[6]

The other unique type of multiple dwelling in the Sunila village is the so-called three-story terraced apartment (225) built in 1938.[7] This block consists of three levels of separate flats, each unit reached by a private entrance from the street. The lower flat is buried beneath the level of the hill while the upper two levels of flats are reached by a series of doorways located on the middle floor level at grade. The access to the middle flats is directly from the street level while the alternate doorways lead up a stairway one floor to the top flat.

The upper flats each have a private terrace and cross ventilation while the lower flats have a little planted area usable as a front yard and cross ventilation. The flats are extremely small in size and really unsuitable for family life, but the main drawback with this scheme is that since both sides must have vehicular access, the building is virtually surrounded by automobile traffic and a gravel street, preventing any possibility of privacy or appreciation of the immediate landscape.

Sunila finally offered Aalto the opportunity of acquiring serious patronage, and by applying himself diligently to the task, he won the respect not only of the Ahlström leaders but also those at Sunila who were representatives of other industrial fortunes. While constructing the mill and designing the village at Sunila, Aalto secured the commission for and built an almost direct copy of Sunila as a paper mill for Anjala at Inkeroinen including a complete employees' housing village. Throughout his career he was

225. Pulp mill and village for employees, stepped apartments, Sunila, 1938.

more or less constantly occupied with factories and housing for the Ahlström group, Enso-Gutzeit, Typpi, and others.[8] His friendship with Harry Gullichsen had indirectly assured him financial stability well into the sixties when Finland reached a saturation point in industrial buildings. He produced not only paper and cellulose sulphate plants, but glass factories, sawmills, regional and town plans, churches, clubs, houses, and many other types of buildings and projects for the industrial sector. It was Ahlström that provided the largest part of his commissions and in the postwar years, when he had little work of any other nature, he executed many such projects, although a lot of these were never built.

Artek and Furniture Designs

During the thirties Aalto and Gullichsen became fast friends, and the enthusiasm they both shared for the modern world spurred them on.[9] During these years Maire Gullichsen with Alvar and Aino Aalto formed Artek Company[10] to promote the manufacture and distribution of well-designed home furnishings and housewares. Maire Gullichsen was given the task of organizing and operating the functions of Artek while Aino Aalto took on the initial responsibility for choosing and supervising the production. To this day Artek is the exclusive distributor of Aalto furniture, and the Aalto and Gullichsen interests continue to control the organization.[11]

The move Aalto made to Helsinki had not only established him as an integral member of the city's architectural profession, but it also established his relationship to the business world and especially that of big business.

No study pretending to be a complete coverage of this period in Aalto's creative life can omit a discussion of his furniture designs, for it is perhaps more for his furniture than his architecture that he is known in the world, even today. In fact, Aalto's first international recognition came as a result of a show held at Fortnum and Mason's department store in London in 1933. The show, which was arranged jointly by the publishers of the *Architectural Record* and a group of Finnish commercial interests, was the first display of any of Aalto's work outside Finland.[12]

This strain of Aalto's career can be seen as an outgrowth of the idea, newly revived during the early twentieth century, that architects were qualified as designers of furniture, even when it was not directly related to buildings they were commissioned to execute. Catalogs of today's major modern furniture companies are still heavily dependent on chair designs produced by Marcel Breuer, Mies van der Rohe, Le Corbusier,[13] and others who practiced architecture as their main occupation. It is quite possible that it

was the example of some of these designers that led Aalto to venture into what is generally called industrial design and to extend his ideas into the realm of room furnishing. It is, however, more likely that he was influenced by the general tradition in architecture of providing designs not only for furnishings but the supplementary decoration of the environment as well, for as early as 1925 Alvar and Aino participated in the *Käsiteollisuus* magazine competition. Their involvement in this activity can be seen as a reflection of the time-honored tradition in Scandinavia, and particularly in Finland, of considering crafts and decorative arts part of the environment and therefore architecture.[14]

In his early furniture designs it seems most likely that Aalto was influenced by the furniture of Michael Thonet, constructed to utilize the structural and esthetic properties of steam-bent wood. The combination in these designs of functional purpose and pure use of a specific technology as a genesis for a unique esthetic effect must have impressed Aalto as it had so many others. Thonet furniture was perhaps the most frequently specified for houses and environments of modern architects before tubular steel frame furniture made its appearance in the fairs and showrooms of the midtwenties. Subsequently, Thonet even became the manufacturer for some of the tubular steel furniture designed by the Bauhaus masters.

Aalto's first venture into the realm of genuinely modern furniture design took place in 1927 while he was working on the Jyväskylä Civil Guard House. For the assembly hall in that building he designed a stacking chair made with straight legs and support, plywood seat and back. This chair, still in production (226),[15] is designed to stack in groups of up to six. It is made of a square birch stock, completely devoid of any ornamentation, and like the Thonet chairs, depends aesthetically on its structural materials. It is probable, however, that Aalto did not consider the possibility of bentwood as structural material in his

first designs because the technology seemed complicated and foreign to Finland.

Early in 1929, while Aalto was preparing in earnest for the 700 Year Exposition at Turku, his involvement in furniture production began in earnest. As one of the two principals involved in the fair design, he was sought out by Otto Korhonen, a local manufacturer of furniture and wood furnishings, to design the installation of his company's exhibit at the fair. The association that began then was to provide a long and rich history of design and technical experimentation that would yield many successful furniture designs. Korhonen asked Aalto to make suggestions for a flush drawer unit that his company was manufacturing, and Aalto produced the idea for a sculptural handle to be recessed along the top center of each flush drawer front. From that point on this item was produced as a design of Aalto's.

The most significant display in the Korhonen exhibit was a design by Aalto for a molded plywood chair supported on bent metal pipe. This was certainly due to his observation of similar examples of tubular steel furniture on his trips to Central Europe and Sweden. Apparently in the early stages of this chair's design some bentwood structural experiments were made but were deemed unsuccessful. Ultimately, a bent leg, made of rather thick members of wood replaced the pipe (227), but the design was not structurally resolved and was dropped except for children's furniture.[16]

The design of this early plywood shape would appear revolutionary in furniture technology and design of 1929 if it were not for the fact that similar shapes (228) had been manufactured by the A. M. Luther Company of Tallinn since 1900. These shapes, while not assembled as complete chairs, were used for inexpensive and easily maintainable benches in tramcars and for seating in railway stations and other public places in the U.S. and England. Luther's catalog carried a wide variety of shapes and curves molded from opposing plys of birch veneer. The

226. Wooden stacking chair, Jyväskylä, 1926–1929.

company had in fact won the Grand Prize for its woodwork in the Paris World's Fair of 1900.[17] Aalto visited the Luther factory, which Eliel Saarinen had enlarged, and certainly knew firsthand about the character and manufacture of these molded seating shapes.[18]

Aalto's initial failure to provide the Luther-type seat shapes with a successful wooden leg was ultimately overcome in the model called the "Paimio" chair (229) by making the laminated leg a closed form of veneered layers bound together with glue and cured in forms much like those Thonet had used earlier.[19] The Paimio chair was so named because it was evolved during the period of the sanatorium's design development and construction although it was not produced for it. The famous teacart is an adaptation of this closed circle structural shape.

In the early thirties Aalto entered a furniture design competition that was sponsored by a Viennese organization.[20] Most of the designs he submitted were to be constructed out of bentwood shapes. The design for a combination work and easy chair entitled "Arbeit Ruhe" (230) was a somewhat simplified version of a Thonet model, but it was shown with plywood seat and upholstered back. The design for a group of stacking tables was called "10 Stück 9 cm," in reference to the number of tables and the difference in height between the highest and the lowest, each of the ten being only a centimeter higher or lower than its adjacent member in the stack.

The most interesting piece submitted for this competition was an easy chair to be constructed in a cantilever fashion out of bentwood. The chair, entitled "Schnitt," depended on three spring supports joined in concentric fashion on each of two frames along the outer edges of the chair. The seat was to be an upholstered version of the molded plywood seat of the first chair he designed for Otto Korhonen.[21] The supports are awkward and demonstrate lack of familiarity with the structural nature of bentwood technology. In general the chair is a sort of amalgam of the cantilevered ideas of the pipe chairs of Breuer and Mies executed in a technique more befitting Thonet. Of course the compression of the bentwood forms by a heavy person would eventually break them, and it is not surprising that Aalto didn't win a prize for his efforts.

The main aesthetic and structural quality on which the two versions of the plywood chair depended was their curve—the small, constant radius that first Luther and then Aalto and Korhonen used to form the corners and ends of their various shapes. The latter team continued to experiment with methods of forming a bent structural support of laminated wood without utilizing a closed form. They solved the problem of structural supports finally, without either a closed form or steam bending, by means of backsawing the portion to be bent into leaves of wood which in their smaller cross sections could be formed around a radius. This invention (231), patented by Aalto,[22] made it possible to bend and glue, in a permanent right angle, wooden strips of sufficient thickness to be used as a structural support for a chair. The technique was finally put into production for a stool during the development of the final design for the Viipuri Library, about 1933. The potential universal usability and the (at that time) low cost of the nearly indestructable stool must have pleased Aalto and Korhonen greatly, and it was fairly predictable that these qualities of the design would make it a widely sold item in the realm of modern furniture.

Since 1876, designers had been experimenting with the possibility of an all-plywood chair,[23] but it would not be realized until the midthirties when Aalto and Korhonen produced the spring leaf support (232) and integrated it with the molded seat. It has been said that there is no precedent technology for this chair—which depends on a compression spring of birch veneers welded together—in the manufacture of furni-

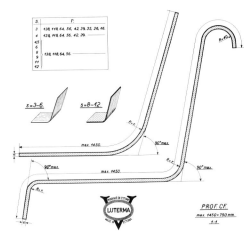

227. Top left: Plywood chair with laminated wood legs, Turku, 1929.

228. Top right: Molded plywood shapes as shown in Luther Catalog, Tallinn, 1911–1931.

229. Above: Paimio chair made of birch veneer layers, Turku, 1930–1933.

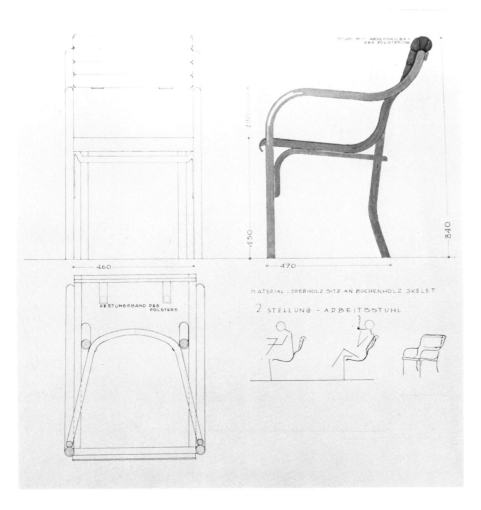

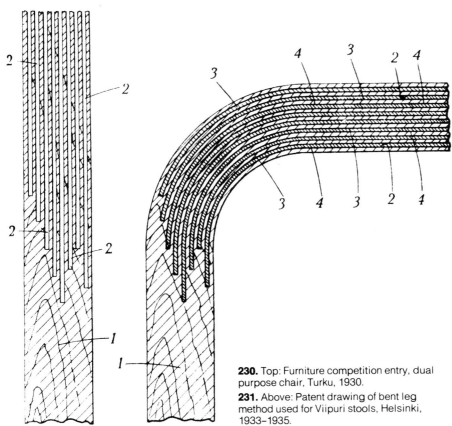

ture or wood products. Some inspiration, however, may be seen in the birch baskets and other wooden forms regularly for sale in the markets of Helsinki even today (233). This craft form is a long and well-developed tradition in Scandinavia and, unlike popular wicker techniques, depends on the use of thin but unsoaked strips of hardwood cut from freshly fallen trees to yield a molded, rounded corner. This type of basket is obviously partly a precedent for Aalto's technique. It even employs a similar width of strip.

Nonetheless, the adaptation of this technique to furniture design must stand as Aalto's major contribution in that area. The spring, made of seven layers of birch, is thickened at the points of greatest stress and reduced at the base end toward the rear of the seat. Like the Paimio chair, the molded seat was joined to the supporting legs only along the two extremities to give a more resilient nature to the body. The difficulty with the design of the molded seat for this and the earlier Paimio version is that while they are contoured to the profile of the human spine, no attempt was made to respond to the other human dimensions. Three-directional molding of plywood did come into use during the later thirties.[24] Aalto, however, made only limited experiments with those shapes which apparently did not appeal to him esthetically, and he produced relatively little along this line.

The spring leaf chair was produced in a variety of shapes and profiles; several upholstered versions and the most popular, a webbed sling model, are still in production. Utilizing the same spring leaf sandwich, Aalto produced a chaise lounge, an easy chair, and an overstuffed chair with wide arms that are almost traditional in feeling. One of the upholstered versions, with a high back and slight wing, was added by Otto Korhonen himself. This was also available with a pillow headrest of matching material.

Aalto's designs after the thirties depended more on the backsawn

230. Top: Furniture competition entry, dual purpose chair, Turku, 1930.

231. Above: Patent drawing of bent leg method used for Viipuri stools, Helsinki, 1933–1935.

leg bend and were conceived along straighter and more traditional lines. The bent form was ingeniously intersected with an identical shape at right angles to produce a fused leg, utilized both for a four-leg stool and a frame for the well-known glass-top coffee table. Still later he joined five of these bents to form a table or stool leg that had a splayed shape over its 90° profile, giving it the strength of a gusset. This leg component was joined to a plywood base to produce a stool or table.

Aalto's career as a furniture designer closely parallels his development as an architect.[25] During the late twenties and early thirties he searched for formal methods to break the bonds of traditional technology and esthetics and derive integral and beautiful furniture designs. During the late thirties he sought dynamic forms and bold technical methods to express more of the fluid, curvilinear feeling of the transfer of forces between the user of the chair and the floor on which the furniture rested. And during the later forties and onward he seemed to rely on a more or less classical definition of the chair, utilizing his bent-knee construction and some lamination that could be combined with plastics to give a more maintainable aspect to the furniture as a whole.

232. Top: Spring leaf-supported chair with molded plywood seat, Helsinki, 1935.
233. Right: Wooden baskets on sale at marketplace in Helsinki.

SEARCH FOR
A NEW STYLE

12

Vernacular and Romantic Precedents

Throughout the development of Western architecture romantic and classical modes have emerged and reemerged as the two extremes of the theoretical foundations of design. National and international styles as parallel expressions of these extremes have historically existed sometimes side by side and at other times exclusively on their own. The dialectic aspects of this coexistence might be said to have reached their pinnacle around the turn of the nineteenth century in Western Europe particularly in Germany where the international classicism of architects like Ludwig Hoffmann was in opposition to the folk romanticism of the Jugendstil. However, the motive forces behind these two distinct traditions could occasionally become amalgamated in a single style that while characterized by national overtones, was able to display a more universal identity and significance. In Finland National Romanticism had expressed a sense of Finnish ethnic and cultural identity; the neoclassical style of the twenties assumed a similar expressive significance in relation to the country's political existence as a newly emergent state with international aspirations.

Once the Functionalist exhibition opened in Stockholm it took only five years or so to complete the full transition to a Scandinavian version of the International Style which was essentially devoid of any national cultural characteristics. By the mid-

thirties most of the entrants and virtually all the winners in the national architectural competitions executed their designs in the new mode, and the lack of indigenous appropriateness or relevance seems to have aroused no objection. Finland's final emergence as a truly international theater for architecture had been realized. This conversion was complete except in the case of church architecture, where there was a lingering conservatism until the early forties.

It is possible that at least a small degree of Aalto's disenchantment with the International Style was related to his Finnish colleagues' comparatively greater success with the style that he had played a key role in introducing in Finland. It is possible, however, that his rebellion against it can be traced back even further to his numerous trips abroad during the late twenties and early thirties when his identification with the philosophy of CIAM and its members and their highly articulate dedication to the propogation of the "style" showed itself to be less than wholehearted.[1] But this disillusionment was only one of the factors that caused a marked change in the designs that Aalto produced in the second half of the thirties. His love of vernacular and romantic forms expressed during the early phase of his career had continued, even if only evidenced by a few traces, throughout his heroic period. The wooden buildings he executed in

Aläjarvi—the Youth Society building, the hospital, and his relatives' homes, as well as the Casa Laurén —while vaguely classical in conception and containing definite references to that style in their detailing, were essentially restatements of the traditional wood board and batten residential structures found in the northern part of the Baltic area.

Four Modes of Change
Within the realms of vernacular and romantic architecture there existed a wide range of techniques and forms that Aalto could draw on as precedents in order to express his departure from the mainstream of modernism.[2] In his own work of the previous 15 years the successful inclusion of at least a handful of romantic ideas shows that his interest in such precedents had never faded completely. These elements exist in his work on four levels: the planning and siting of buildings, the manipulation of volumes and shapes, the employment of textural effects, and the creation of special details to complete an effect founded on the previous three. Aalto gave evidence of working in a romantic or vernacular vein in each of these areas prior to the midpoint of the thirties.

In the planning and siting of buildings he was able to adopt the natural earth forms (contour lines) as part of his proposed design scheme "Terra" for part 2 of the Helsinki Stadium Competition. He also employed a somewhat formal version of a meander on the southern edge of the Paimio Sanatorium site to provide the patients, in his own words, "with a walk in the woods."[3]

The manipulation of volumes and masses in consciously nonrectangular or round-cornered forms was demonstrated in his proposal to build the Turku water tower as a curved volume. This shape, while basically formal in geometry, possessed an overall casual air and would have tended to blend with the smooth, rounded forms of the coastal plain of southwestern Finland far better than any of the rectangular proposals submitted. Perhaps the curvilinear shape of the podium of the Itämeri restaurant located within the Agricultural Co-op or the entrance canopy of the Paimio Sanatorium are clear indications of his special love for the nonrectangle as worthy of the central interest in a rectangular composition. His treatment of wedge- or fanshaped volumes such as the Enso-Gutzeit vacation house prototype Tuli also must be noted as a romantic precedent for his later style.

The most significant number of preexisting forms, found in his early and International Style buildings as well as his later works, occur in the realm of textural implementations. The thatched roof of the Craft Pavilion at the Tampere Fair in 1922 and the sod roof of the Villa Flora in 1925 are among the earliest examples of romantic textural treatment found in

Aalto's works. The range of textural effects is the most comprehensive of all the design elements to be seen in his developing style, and the most evolved of these was the textural surfacing of wooden buildings, recalling once again his earlier exposure to wooden buildings. The development of this motif can be traced through the board and batten facade painted in contrasting colors used at the Helsinki Fair in the construction of Carolus Lindberg's Tivoli area in 1920 and the natural version used on the sides of the chorus performing shell and platform at the Turku Fair in 1929.

Perhaps of all the planning and volumetric motifs that Aalto was to use in his personal revision of the International Style, the use of the free-form has been most noted. Whether it is true, as some have privately speculated, that Aalto took his lead from the work of such artists as his friend and associate Jean Arp, it is clear that he was engaged in the incorporation of free-form motifs in his designs as early as 1928. In October of that year, as he finished work on the Agricultural Co-operative in Turku, he designed for the Itämeri restaurant (to be located within that multipurpose building) a podium for a quartet.[4] The forms that he selected were those musical forms found in cubist and purist paintings and collages of the same period.[5] At least one plan (234) shows a configuration with a reverse curve something like a violin. The

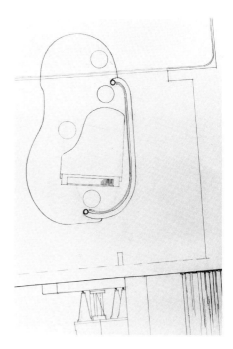

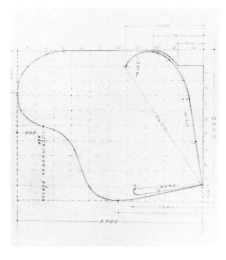

234. Music podium for Itämeri Restaurant in Agricultural Co-operative, podium plans, Turku, 1928.

most detailed design is more like the shape of a grand piano, which, of course, the platform (with its curving, parabolic reflector wall for the even dispersal of sound) was to contain. Nearly 3 m wide, by 3½ m long, the freely shaped form barely has any straight portions and only at one corner does the podium approach the orthogonal.

It is likely that Aalto appreciated the functional shapes of musical instruments as well as the power of their esthetics and that they thus held a dual appeal for him as did the Thonet chairs earlier.[6] He was not, of course, the first to realize this combined and rational beauty, but he was one of the earliest among architects. Because of his devotion to those principles he became identified as the master of the style that would employ free-form shapes in a rational manner.

The special details he introduced to call attention to some specific functional aspect of a building such as the slated columns in the children's department of the Viipuri Library were the last but not least of these ideas to appear in the development of his anti-International Style. Those columns and their subsequent evolution into fluted tile

piers and walls are more remembered by modern architects as evidence of Aalto's originality than any of the other techniques displayed.[7] The free-form twin fireplaces in the patients' lounge at the Paimio Sanatorium are another example of the unprecedented designs that Aalto created to supersede the standardized approach of the International Style.

There are at least two other aspects of the Viipuri Library which prefigure or herald the transition to a new mode in Aalto's work; both relate to his concern for the planting within and outside the building. The grand stairway adjacent to the main entrance (235) was provided with planting boxes, and vines sprang up from them along the glass wall separating the stairhall from the lobby proper.[8] The facade of the entrance projection of the children's library entrance (196) originally had a series of trellis poles attached to the southwestern corner; they were grouped in pairs with an additional single pole actually standing free just beyond the line of the corner. This would give an unusually bucolic feeling to a building that otherwise had a firm footing in the Functionalist style and would eventually

result in the visual obliteration of the corner by entwining vines.[9]

Transition by Experiment

The transition from the International Style to that highly individualized style with which Aalto became identified (and which has been referred to by some critics as a modern interpretation of expressionist forms) occurred between the competition for the Moscow Embassy and the outbreak of the war with the Soviet Union, between 1935 and 1939. The chief factor in this transition, the circumstance that enabled Aalto to make the rapid progress he did in coming out of the International Style, was the unusual opportunity of experimentation with new and untried forms and techniques afforded him by the competitions and commissions for the Finnish national pavilions at the Paris and New York World's Fairs and the Villa Mairea, the summer retreat for the Gullichsens.

This experimentation might be seen as a continuation of the experimental tradition within the International Style, but by this time that experimentation had subsided, at least among the leaders of the style. A more formularized approach was induced by the attempts of CIAM leaders and theorists to bring together a tighter set of constraints defining the minimum basis of International Modernism as a style; unfortunately, in most cases that was the maximum as well. For whatever reason, Aalto was or quickly became disinterested in this all-too-narrow basis for modern architecture and began to search for a better, more humanely tactile style both in forms and detail. One of his main themes, repeated in lecture after lecture around the world as a response to the machine-age philosophy of the International Style, was to assert that standardization, one of the chief by-products of the machine age, must be used to obtain the maximum amount of "flexibility" and variety, rather than be resigned to the dull and monotonous use of reduplicated forms.

235. Municipal Library, final version, grand stairway in main entrance lobby, Viipuri, 1935.

13
Romantic Modernism

The evolution of Aalto's rejection of the International Style can be traced from project to project and from project to project to building. A progressive accumulation of non-"International" or, more exactly, nonpurist forms and techniques is revealed in the designs of several key projects of the second half of the thirties in which Aalto clearly abandoned that style which as a young practitioner he so devotedly worked out and helped introduce in Finland. This progression, while basically a personal development, was nonetheless universal insofar as it alerted architects in other countries to the possibility of softening the outward effects of modernism and placing it, as a style, in a romantic and freely planned context. Aalto's own persistent statement that "the trouble with the rational style was that the rationalism didn't go deep enough"[1] hints at the root of his objections to the impersonal nature of the International Style and its harsh and somewhat southern orientation. The beginning of this marked change is chiefly revealed in the competition project for the Moscow Embassy from mid-1935 and in the design of his own house constructed between 1935 and 1936 but designed slightly earlier.

Finnish Embassy in Moscow Competition

In 1935, with Finno-Soviet relations continuing to have the appearance of a stable future, the decision was made to build a new facility for the Finnish Embassy in Moscow. The announcement of a competition to determine its architect was made in June 1935.[2] As the project had been given a rush priority status, the entries were to be judged on July 27. Among others the competition jury listed Yrjö Lindegren, winner and architect-designate of the Olympic Stadium, and Sigurd Frosterus, who had staunchly defended Aalto's innovative work in his writings. This competition jury must have been composed with some special balance in view because it was the first time in years that the once-controversial Frosterus had been asked to serve on a jury. It is possible, however, that he had reached the status of elder statesman—he was then 60 —and would have been presumed to have mellowed. (In fact he went on to live another 20 years.) But once again Aalto did not figure in the honors at the judging Ekelund won second, while O. Flodin, final winner of the Tampere Station, received third. First place was taken by Erik Lindroos, one of the architects who had just won the Postal Telegraph. However, as international tension was to accelerate over the next few years resulting in Russia's invasion of Karelia,[3] the project was postponed. It was eventually realized by Hilding Ekelund. Aalto's project, the title of which, "Ex Occidente" (236), conveys its non-Russian mood, has not been previously published. Nominally correct in spirit it can be seen as clearly avoiding any reference either to Constructivism, which by this time was in disfavor with the Soviet government, or to the more grandiose aspects of the International Style exhibited in such projects as Le Corbusier's entry in the Palace of the Soviets competition four years earlier. Aalto projected a quiet, full-blown version of the International Style, as might have been rendered by any mature designer practicing in that mode at the time,[4] but in this case softened even further by the addition of hanging, creeping foliage.

Aalto's complex (237)—housing an embassy and a consulate— would have provided a large forecourt for the arrival of officials and visitors with two separate dropoff points. From the street the building presents a simple string of elements stretching across the site. The main entrance is under a wing projecting from the second story level and supported over the forecourt on a dozen pilotis (his first use of this element). The ambassador's residence is at the left of the entrance, the embassy itself is in the center where the wing projects forward, the consulate is to the right of that, and resident staff quarters are in a wing projecting towards the back on the extreme right. The embassy banquet and conference rooms are in the wing projecting forward on the pilotis which is faced on the front with a smooth un-

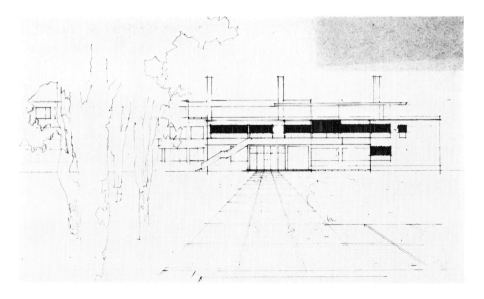

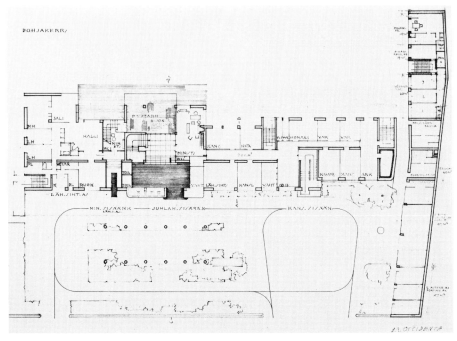

236. Top: Finnish Embassy competition entry, perspective view from garden, Moscow, 1935.

237. Middle: Finnish Embassy competition entry, ground floor plan, Moscow, 1935.

238. Above: Finnish Embassy competition entry, perspective from main approach, Moscow, 1935.

fenestrated rectangular end gable (238). Its glazed sides open onto the balconies which run their entire length and are screened with series of rough-hewn poles arranged in a vertical trellis to be planted with ornamental vines. This rough timber trellis with entwining vines is the first additive step in a long procession of such details and techniques that were to lead Aalto into a new realm of architectural design. It represented his first clear departure from the International Style, already well established in Finland. The trellis, with its rough outline against the sharp lines of the Functionalist building, points up the degree to which Aalto was leaning toward the romanticism of the vine-covered wall. In some other respects, the pilotis for example, there is still a close similarity with certain followers of the purist philosophy but in Aalto's general thinking these traits were to fade in their appeal.

Guided and buoyed up by his success as an industrial architect and as a beneficiary of the Gullichsens' good will, Aalto probably felt that he could put more of himself into his design theory than he had heretofore. Only tentatively had he previously applied his personal motifs, whether singly or in groups, to a simple International Style box. When the next opportunity appeared he departed sharply from his previous manner.

The transformation from the International Style to a modified expressionist mode overlaid with vernacular elements first became recognizable in Aalto's own house, designed in 1934 and constructed during the following 2 years.

In September 1935, Aalto, along with Väinö Vähäkallio, Erkki Huttunen, and Bertel Liljeqvist, was invited to participate in the competition for the factory and headquarters of the state alcohol monopoly ALKO.[5] The invited entrants were joined in public participation by eleven others. This building, sited on the western waterfront of Helsinki, was programmed to be a multistory complex of manufacturing, storage, and administration for a

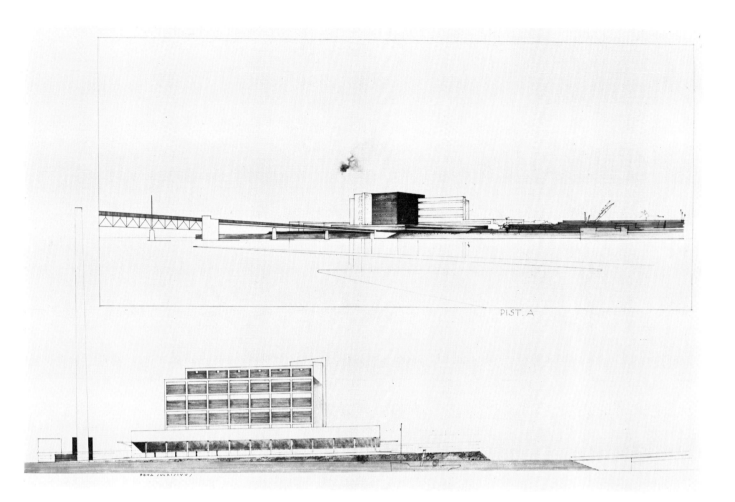

highly successful branch of the state-controlled industrial holdings. The project submitted by Aalto, entitled "In VINO veritas,"[6] was significant only in that it was his last completely Functionalist design. There is nothing in any of the drawings to indicate that a transition had begun in Aalto's work. This is perhaps because of the official and national nature of the building and Aalto's eagerness to secure one of the then-frequent commissions in the capital which were awarded as a result of competitions, a goal he had not yet achieved.

Aalto's building (239) called for a composition of three large volumes, two slabs with exposed concrete structures and brick infill set at 90° to each other, both of which were joined to the central element—a large cubic mass housing storage vaults and clad entirely in dark brick with only the smallest of windows. The entire complex rests on a base of wide, low buildings that covered nearly all the site plan. The program

called for the widest range of functions and considerations imaginable. In addition to both waterside and vehicular transportation facilities, there were to be rail sidings and the completely self-contained storage and delivery system for a coal-fired distillery.[7] When the results were announced, Aalto's project did not receive a prize but it was bought. Ironically perhaps, Väinö Vähäkallio won the competition with a crisp brick complex that incorporated into its massing along the ground floor a series of rounded corners and exposed contrasting structures not unlike some of Aalto's own contemporary forms.

239. Plant and office competition entry for State Alcohol Monopoly (ALKO), perspective and elevation, Helsinki, 1935.

Aalto's Own House

Aalto's house, designed to include his office, was built after he had established himself in Helsinki and exhibits a few clear examples of the new romantic ideas in his changing philosophy of design. The interlocking rectangular volumes of the building (240), comprised of a living area on the ground floor, a sleeping area above, and a double-height volume to house the office, were surfaced in two different materials, brick and wood. This contrast helps to define the individually articulated volumes and aids in the expression of the two-level and multi-use nature of the scheme. This expressive use of materials places the building in both Romantic and Functional styles at once.

Brick is used for the building's major structural walls. Although it is somewhat disguised by a coat of white paint, it constitutes one of the earliest uses of this material as an exterior finish on a residential building in Finland. The brick also rises to the upper story on the double-height volume projecting along the western facade that contains Aalto's office (241).[8]

The projecting upper volumes, which contain the sleeping portion of the house, were clad in clear-finished birch siding wrapped around three sides of the dwelling on the eastern half of the upper story. Though quite squarish and cubic in character, it must nonetheless be seen as the first of many such programmatically expressive forms that Aalto was to employ in his escape from the pure Functionalist style.

The flat, clear-finished wood surface of the projecting wing (242) is constructed of birch tongue-and-groove planking (custom-made) with a deep groove cut along the tongue edge.[9] When the wall is assembled, this groove shows up as a dark, thin shadow slightly less than $1/4''$ in width and located approximately $2''$ on center. The end joints of the planks are marked by this same kind of reveal, breaking the even rhythm of the striated effect. Thus while the overall effect continues to be vertical, this random breaking creates an effect of texture which, like the brick coursing, softens the sharp planes of the simple volumetric shapes and also adds another dimension of surface tension and contrast in addition to the shifting contrast of the volumetric forms themselves.

Another instance of Aalto's dissolution of volumetric forms through the use of contrasting textures is to be seen in the railing of the rear terrace on the upper story. Along the part of the terrace opening off the bedroom (where privacy is desirable), the railing maintains a solid, impenetrable form. The solidity is interrupted by a shift to an open horizontal railing which continues the rectangular form of the solid rail but allows a fuller view of the woods and fields to the south.[10]

In the plan (243) one can also observe several elements whose shapes diverge in subtle ways from the basic rectilinear forms of the building: the nonorthogonal counter in the studio, the splayed corner of the garage, and the chamfered end of the living room window shelf near the studio entrance. In each case this divergence from the straight and narrow Functionalist manner appears to be determined by rational considerations. The departure from conventional purist forms is justified on the basis of the necessity to respond to functional requirements. The esthetic effect created is one of subtle tension—a pulling off from the true and a dissolution of standard forms.

The most striking innovative romantic motif is created by the grouping of thin wooden shafts around one of the steel pipe columns at the southeast corner of the house adjoining the living room terrace. These clustered shafts, used here for the first time by Aalto, were not structural. Such shafts, however, did appear in many buildings of this romantic style during the late thirties although usually as a group of lashed poles forming a genuine structural support.

The house, in both living and office areas, incorporates some built-in tables of a shaped nature that

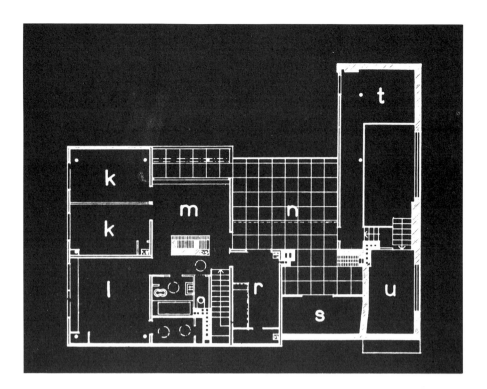

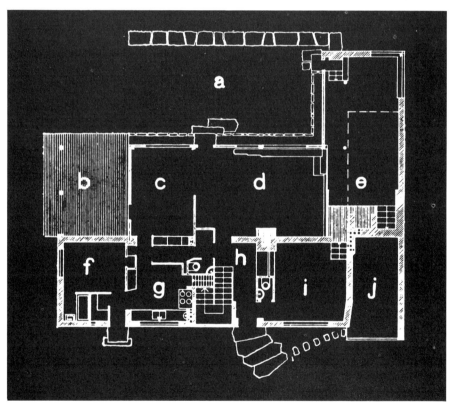

would be further developed in the following commissions. While this house was not really an experimental venture, Aalto nevertheless employed new forms and techniques in it, some of which would form a foundation for the wide repertoire of romantic motifs used throughout his later career.[11]

240. Opposite page top: Aalto's own house located in Munkkiniemi, rear view, Helsinki, 1936.

241. Opposite page middle: Aalto's own house located in Munkkiniemi, studio wing, Helsinki, 1936.

242. Opposite page bottom: Aalto's own house located in Munkkiniemi, detail of wood facing at rear terrace, Helsinki, 1936.

243. Top and above: Aalto's own house located in Munkkiniemi, plans, Helsinki, 1936.

14
A New Heroic Style

Finnish Pavilion Competition for Paris World's Fair 1937

In June 1936, while he was hard at work on at least two large pulp and paper mills, Aalto entered the competition for the Finnish Pavilion to be erected for the 1937 Paris World's Fair.[1] His hopes may have risen when he found that the jurors included Martti Välikangas, Yrjö Lindegren, and Erik Bryggman (the latter chiefly because he had built the last Pavilion at Antwerp in 1930), and indeed, when the awards were announced, Aalto took first and second prizes. This long overdue recognition must surely have buoyed his spirits and renewed his faith in himself.

Design credit was given jointly to those who worked on the projects in a manner rarely found in competitions. The first prize entry, called "Le Bois est en Marche" (244), was credited: Aino and Alvar Aalto, assistants Aarne Ervi and Viljo Revell. The entry winning second prize, entitled "Tsit Tsit Pum" (245), was credited: Architect Aalto's Studio, main assistants Aarne Ervi and Viljo Rewell. It seems virtually certain that these two men took a major part in the project designs since Aalto rarely shared credit with members of his office staff. Both men set up independent practices about this time and went on to substantial careers of their own. Each of Aalto's entries, designed for the triangular sloping site given by the competition, was organized in basically the

same way, merely presenting different articulations of the same volumetric solution. Both schemes feature a large volume located near the entrance on the upper part of the hillside linked to a garden at the exit and low point by intermediate exhibition levels and a high interior volume.

Le Bois est en Marche

The first prize-winning Le Bois est en Marche[2] (wood is on the move) employed as its central element a large rectangular volume with the by-now-expected double-height open-well skylit space (246). The concept called for a main entrance plateau of exhibition spaces and garden areas (including an open-air coffee shop) linked to a two-level main exhibition hall at the lower level of the site in the rear. The pavilion as built was quite faithful to the winning design, but the simplified nature of the drawings could not possibly describe the full array of features Aalto was able to incorporate into the final building.

The main exhibition hall (247), on the lowest part of the site, was rounded at the corners and clad in an embellished version of a fine, closely spaced board and batten system. Each batten was faced with a convex cover strip that projected beyond the batten; each board was concave to emphasize the battens and lend depth to the total effect (248).[3] The inside of the skylit volume with its circumferential balcony

resembled the stairhall of the Viipuri Library reference room. The skylights above displayed the same profile as those at Viipuri.[4]

The preliminary exhibition area (249), located on the upper level near the main entrance, contained a small, one-story skylit courtyard with a grid of thirty-two tall, slender wooden poles wired together at the top ends, recalling the profile of a young birch forest. This area (250) was entered from the garden by means of a progression of covered walks which conducted visitors along the side of the site from the point of entry. These walks were covered by flat roofs supported on clusters of poles lashed together to form column supports. This motif, appearing for the first time at the Paris Pavilion, proved an eloquent and emotional means of expressing both the romantic and rational uses of Finland's chief exports, wood products. This type of lashed pole support (251) is of primitive derivation recognized in the traditional vocabulary of raftmakers, campers, and scouts[5] who improvise constructions from such forest materials as young trees and vines. Aalto probably learned this method of wood construction from his father who was a surveyor in the densely forested areas of Finland[6] and an expert woodsman familiar with such basic techniques as lashings for making temporary camp furniture and surveying aids.

A third style of pole aesthetic em-

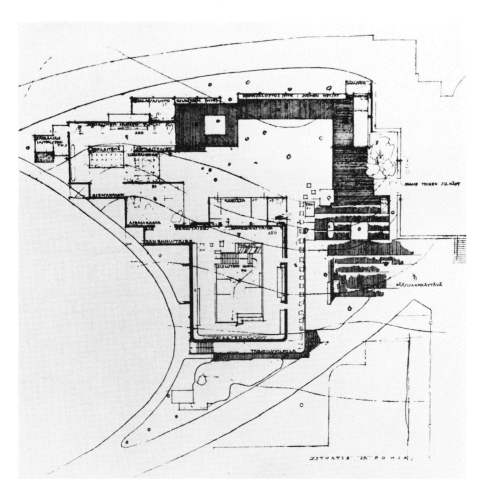

244. Left: Finnish Pavilion competition entry for the World's Fair, plan of Le Bois est en Marche (first prize), Paris, 1936.

245. Below: Finnish Pavilion competition entry for the World's Fair, plan of Tsit Tsit Pum (second prize), Paris, 1936.

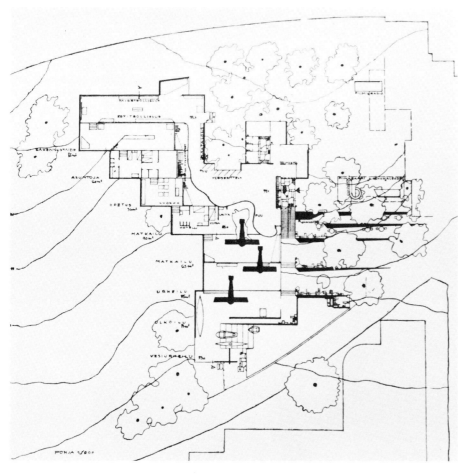

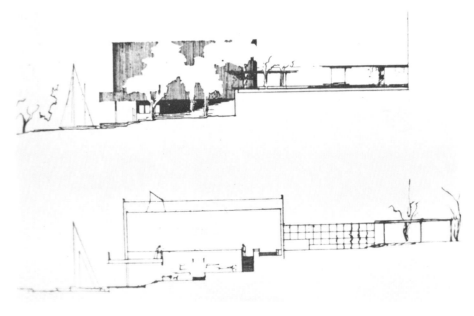

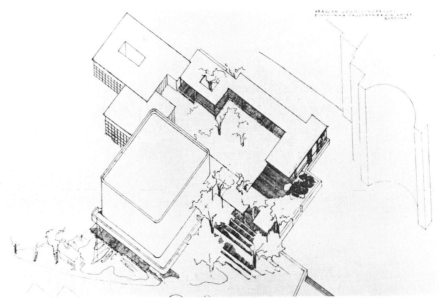

246. Top: Finnish Pavilion competition entry for the World's Fair, sections of Le Bois est en Marche, Paris, 1936.

247. Middle: Finnish Pavilion competition entry for the World's Fair, isometric of Le Bois est en Marche, Paris, 1936.

248. Bottom: Finnish Pavilion at the World's Fair, completed entrance to main hall, Paris, 1937.

249. Top: Finnish Pavilion at the World's Fair, completed preliminary exhibit space, Paris, 1937.

250. Middle: Finnish Pavilion at the World's Fair, completed entrance garden, Paris, 1937.

251. Bottom: Finnish Pavilion at the World's Fair, lashed column detail, Paris, 1937.

252. Above: Finnish Pavilion at the World's Fair, column with slats, Paris, 1937.

159

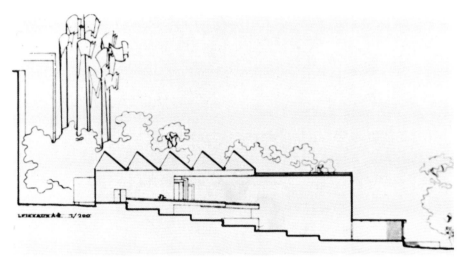

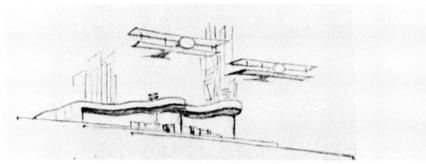

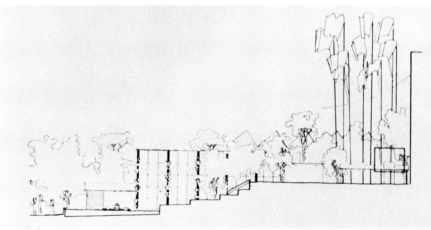

253. Finnish Pavilion competition entry at the World's Fair, section and perspectives of Tsit Tsit Pum, Paris, 1936.

ployed in the exhibition area consisted of using medium-size tree trunks as single supports, which were then given special emphasis by the attachment of three vertical fins along the middle three-quarters of each column. This device (252), like the slats on the columns of the Viipuri children's library, prevented people from brushing or inadvertently touching the shaft or trunk and, at the same time, gave visual and structural weight to the column along its weakest unbound length, a kind of modern entasis.[7]

Such features as the curvilinear free-form pool in the rear garden, the grid of low outdoor lighting fixtures, and the use of photographs laminated directly to the balcony baluster were typical of Aalto's efforts to utilize the widest range of techniques to create interest in Finland, not only by means of the exhibit but through the building as well.

Tsit Tsit Pum

Tsit Tsit Pum, Aalto's second prize-winning entry,[8] though published in the competition review, has till now escaped proper analysis. This scheme (253), designed for the same site and employing a stagger-type plan technique similar to Le Bois est en Marche, is conceptually different because the slope of the ground is broken up into equal risers and equal steps on which the exhibit could be housed. The entire complex would have been covered by a high, single-story roof, located at a constant level, thus giving the bottom level the highest ceiling height and the top level the lowest, or about half the height of the lower levels. As in the actual pavilion there was to be an outdoor garden at the top level descending parallel to the building in a series of terraces along with stairs adjoining the side of the main pavilion and also echoing its slope. The entering visitor would have worked his way down the various levels step by step and out into the garden, then returned through the tiered garden to the point of entry at the highest part of the site.

This proposal (254), if built, would have employed a set of romantic textural motifs similar to those for Le Bois est en Marche but in an entirely different manner. The most striking feature called for—a balcony with a free-form, undulating, curved baluster—was located near the front of the large interior volume connected to the uppermost exhibition level. This use of curvilinear form represents Aalto's first projected use of bold shape that was to be treated as the main design element in the Finnish Pavilion at the New York World's Fair nearly 2 years later. The central focus of the exhibition itself was to be three wooden-framed biplanes suspended from the ceiling to create the illusion that they had just taken off from the balcony. While this did not precisely constitute an architectural feature, it does indicate a continuation of the project's romantic nature through display technique.

The five topmost levels (245), those to one side and just beneath the balcony, were illuminated through five angled, roof-top monitors creating a skylit double-height spatial effect like that used at Viipuri;[9] here, however, the staggered stepped space is delineated as a curving-edged volume. This, the first informal use of the stepped, skylit volume that was eventually to become perhaps the single most prominent motif in Aalto's work, stands in sharp contrast to the formal manner in which he had thus far employed it either in Le Bois est en Marche or in the earlier buildings. Later this form was used in virtually every one of his buildings, and while never with precisely the same shape, it was almost always in an informal and nonorthogonal manner. The very use of this space in itself may constitute for Aalto a kind of fulfillment of his romantic notions.[10]

In the garden, on the side border of the site at its highest point, a small grouping of eight tall, randomly spaced, slender flags was specified, symbolizing (like the grid of the courtyard supports in Le Bois) the visual and emotional quality of the Finnish birch forest that provided the country's major exports of wood and pulp products.[11] On the side of the main building, facing the tiered garden, Aalto proposed a giant portico designed to shield a floor-to-ceiling window wall from the sun. Supported on four massive wooden posts with vines wrapped around them to create a soft, bucolic profile, the portico completes the romantic feeling and links the garden with the building and its interior in a direct manner. In fact the overall concept of the project could be viewed as a garden hillside with one portion of the site roofed over to form exhibition space. In spite of the reduced number of elements shown on these drawings, Tsit Tsit Pum incorporates a complete range of Aalto's romantic repertoire. The only notable omission is the ribbed, striated or batten-type surface found not only in Le Bois est en Marche but in many of his other buildings of the later thirties.

Aalto's completed Paris Pavilion (248) of 1937 was emotionally significant for those Finns who considered Finland's contact with the outside world important. It not only replaced Saarinen's 1900 Pavilion as a symbol of national pride, but in that same cosmopolitan center of world culture it was an outstanding design employing indigenous Finnish materials.[12] Aalto's pavilion was in at least two respects more important than the Saarinen predecessor: it was a basic and modern example of the truly new Finnish style of Functionalism, and it displayed an emotional tie to the oldest buildings in Finland's history by adapting the materials and forms of those buildings to a contemporary mode. For the first time this building shows a full-scale orchestration of Aalto's motifs and clearly reveals the extent of his immersion in this new departure from the prevailing modern style.

While it is possible that the influence of Aalto's industrial patrons, with their heavy financial involvement in the Finnish wood and pulp industries, made itself felt in the competition judging, it should also be noted that Bryggman, Lindegren, and Välikangas[13] were on the jury and must have viewed Aalto's departure from the standard approach to International Modernism with some sympathy. Each one of those designers had been responsible for architecture in his homeland that was certainly adventurous for its time although not revolutionary. Therefore they were in a position to judge the new style of Aalto in its proper context. It is coincidentally interesting to note how often during Aalto's career that whenever he won a prize, one of these three was on the jury.

After winning the Paris Pavilion competition Aalto served as a jury member on two competition panels —for the Temppeliakio Church in Helsinki and the planning competition for the Frenckell area in Tampere.[14] During this period he also produced other designs that continued to provide a format for the evolution of his new romantic modern style—his entries in the competitions for an art museum in Tallinn, Estonia, and the University Library at Helsinki, as well as the commission for the interior of the Savoy Restaurant in downtown Helsinki.

Tallinn Museum of Art Competition

In February 1937, when the international competition for the Museum of Art in Tallinn, the capital of Estonia, was due for submission, Aalto was among those who entered projects. Operating without the assistance of Ervi and Rewell, Aalto evidently had considerable trouble making a workable solution out of the ideas on which he hoped to base the project.[15]

Volumetrically, his solution (254) consisted of a pinwheel arrangement of linked volumes of varying shapes located around an open double-height courtyard. All but one of these volumes are housed beneath a single roof plane. The volume separately expressed is a wing containing the executive offices of the museum and an Estonian national folk art collection. This is comprised of a two-story space dis-

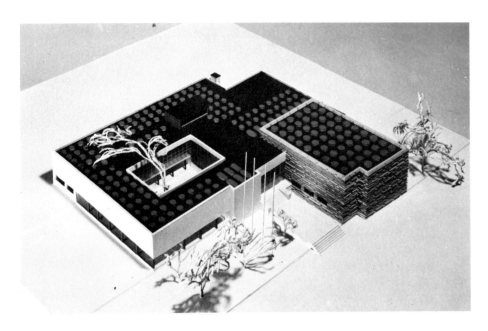

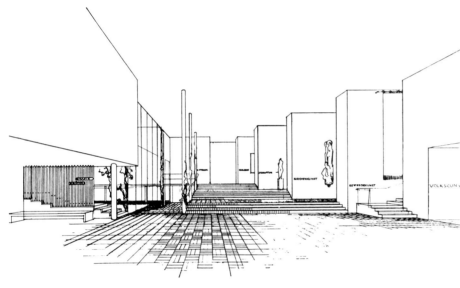

254. Top: National Art Museum competition entry, model, Tallinn, 1937.

255. Above: National Art Museum competition entry, perspective of main stair, Tallinn, 1937.

tinguished from the rest of the museum building by a slightly raised roof level and a rough masonry finish on its interior and exterior walls. This surface may perhaps be seen as a sort of deliberate quotation of National Romantic rusticism used here as an expression of the ethnographic material to be housed in the space.

While certain features, such as the conical skylights penetrating the entire roof surface, are borrowed from the Viipuri Library, the overall plan is organized in the same stepped, offset manner as both Paris Pavilion projects. It especially resembles the second-prize entry Tsit Tsit Pum but the clarity of that design as well as the completeness of its elaboration are missing here. The stepping of the vista from the entry (255) is dramatic but abbreviated, and unlike the Paris design, it shortcircuits rather than follows the main progression route through the exhibits. The entrance leads directly to a gentle three-stage stairway bordered on its left by a window wall which faces the central garden court. Each of the progressively narrower landings is linked to the next by only five shallow steps, and each landing opens to the right into a different gallery.

The main galleries are arranged in echelon with the folk art galleries and are connected in such a way as to permit the visitor to make a complete circuit of the museum in a smooth, flowing progression. At the same time, however, the wedge-shaped entrance stairway functions as a center from which the galleries radiate in a spiral or pinwheel fashion,[16] enabling the visitor to enter individual galleries without having to pass through any other galleries at all. At the top of the stairway, which is only a half story higher than the starting point, a circuit can be made around the periphery of the building through galleries circling the courtyard and ending back at the main entrance.

The scheme expressed in the drawings of the Tallinn Museum proposal is elegant but somewhat understated, and only the entrance stair hall, with its effect of exaggerated perspective created by its narrowing width, is visually organized. The strong perspective vista is a motif that can perhaps be discerned in Aalto's earlier designs, but certainly playing a less bold and less important role than in this project.

Moreover the echelon motif (256), while used here as a strong interior planning motif, is not really expressed volumetrically. Externally it is quite regularized and in this respect is something of a throwback to the earlier period when Aalto was more completely immersed in the International Style. The offset planning technique, however, is important in its appearance here, for it prefigures certain building plans of his later career in which the staggered arrangement was used to generate subtly variable relationships in form.[17]

Here (257), as in the Paris Pavilion designs, Aalto gives evidence of his belief in creating a psychological link between interior and exterior. The drawings show climbing vines entwining the tall columns just to one side of the stairway and adjacent to the courtyard, which provides a transition between inside and outside in spirit. Other bucolic touches visible in the scheme are a row of closely spaced wooden poles screening the return from the exhibition sequence into the main entrance hall and a basketweave pattern brick floor. These, however, seem somewhat superficial rather than integral and necessary aspects of the museum plan.

Helsinki University Library Competition

The Viipuri Library had finally been completed in August 1935 and was received with much acclaim from an increasingly widespread audience. A great deal of attention was focused on its innovative and uniquely Aaltoesque motifs, and Aalto was encouraged to repeat them in succeeding projects. The distinctive conical skylights perforating the ceiling of the Viipuri circulation/reference complex, for exam-

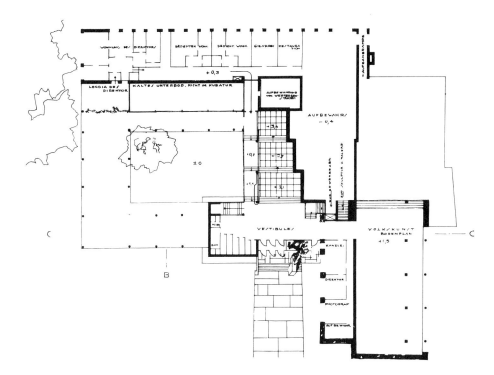

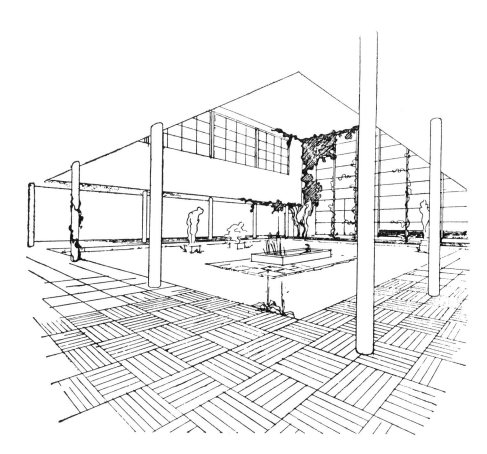

256. Top: National Art Museum competition entry, ground plan, Tallinn, 1937.

257. Above: National Art Museum competition entry, perspective of courtyard, Tallinn, 1937.

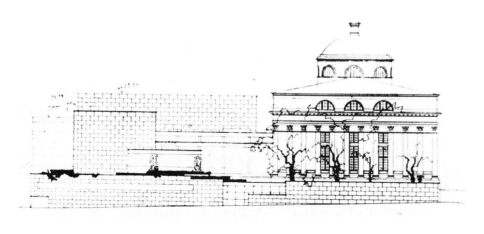

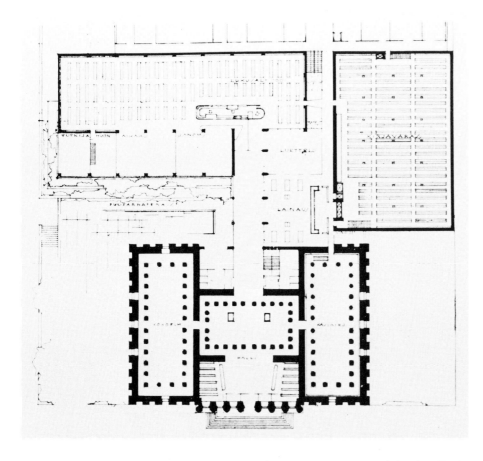

258. Top and above: Helsinki University Library expansion competition entry, alternate scheme plan, Helsinki, 1937.

and built by Carl Ludwig Engel between 1836 and 1845[18] and was supplemented in 1903 by the addition of a semicircular cast-iron stack structure by Gustaf Nyström, one of the leading architects of his day and a lecturer on history, theory, and design at the Technical Institute.[19] The program for the new building called for an annex to the rear of the old building, away from Engel's famous Cathedral Square in which not only the cathedral, but the university, library, and other civic buildings were located.

The competition continued into a second phase in June of the following year, and when the final judging had been completed, it was announced that Aarne Ervi, Aalto's protegé and former employee, had won first prize. Aalto took second place. All the five contestants invited to participate in the competition's second stage (out of the original twenty-four) chose to eliminate Nyström's cast-iron structure, which was in all likelihood in accordance with the program. Aalto submitted two schemes, or at least two variations of a similar arrangement, for the final competition, both under the motto "ERI," meaning "different,"[20] an obvious reference to the fact that his designs, unlike those of some other competitors, made no attempt to emulate the style of the revered neoclassical library which they would adjoin.

Proposal B (258) involved an asymmetrical, L-shaped echelon arrangement somewhat reminiscent of the Viipuri Library, with large volumes faced in ashlar with subsidiary glazed portions. The proposed annex was to adjoin the old building in such a way as to create a terraced garden court enclosed on three sides but open to the south to serve as the entrance to the annex. Internally the treatment was fairly standard with individual spaces allotted to separate functions, and with the exception of the snubbed-corner control desk in the main reading room, it is a surprisingly traditional and regimented design for Aalto at this time.

Aalto's first proposal, A (259), was

ple, soon reappeared in the Paris Pavilion, Le Bois est en Marche, and in the project for the Tallinn Museum. Similarly, the praise elicited by the undulating ceiling of the Viipuri lecture hall was surely responsible for Aalto's increasing experimentation with undulating curvilinear forms which he began to use more frequently and on a bolder and grander scale.

In October 1937, a competition was announced for an extension to the existing Helsinki University Library. The library was first designed the more interesting one. It consisted of two interlocking volumes which, though similar in massing to proposal B, were articulated somewhat differently on the exterior. The outside walls (260) were to be faced with a smooth stucco surface, presumably to match the cream-colored surface of Engel's library. The ground floor stage was rusticated and set off from the smooth facade above by a deep, overhanging cornice slab, echoing the relationship between the basement stage and the upper portion of the old building and giving an impression of classical proportions equivalent to those of the neoclassical buildings around Cathedral Square and throughout the university area.[21] The basement stage of the wing, which flanked the court on the left, housed administrative offices. The other floors of that wing (including the cellar) were primarily for book storage.

The most striking element in the entire complex, however, is the main reading room (261), located up one story on a level with the main floor of Engel's structure. For this room, Aalto produced a design of a pronounced romantic nature, sculpting the entire space with a boldly proportioned curvilinear form. He opted for the high, open, skylit interior volume as he would in many later buildings, but this is the only instance in which he combined it with a free-form, textured wood surface. The individual motifs have their source in the Viipuri Library, but the combination of the two here yields a particularly grandiose effect. By restricting the undulations to the north wall of the room, Aalto has given the design a strong directional quality of great visual power.

The apparent mass of the ceiling is supported on a row of eight rough-hewn piers that are trussed together in a V-column in order to visually gather the forces from the sloping line of the curving wall and the rectilinear structural system above. The library drawings show that the undulations of the ceiling are not strictly free-form, but for Aalto they probably served the

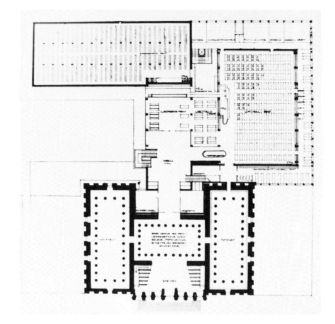

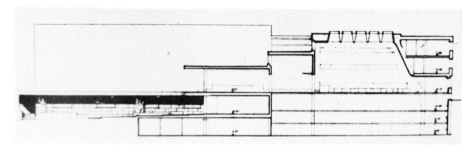

same function as free-form motifs would—to accent and humanize a larger, more regular building.[22] The plane of the batten surface continues beyond this pier line to the north wall of the building to give the reader a secure feeling as if he was under a kind of bright, warm blanket of natural material. The controlled free-form element was also displayed in the shape of the main desk next to the high, vertical wall. While serene and quiet, the room was in contact with the outside environment through both the north win-

259. Top: Helsinki University Library expansion competition entry, main scheme plan, Helsinki, 1937.

260. Middle: Helsinki University Library expansion competition entry, section, Helsinki, 1937.

261. Above: Helsinki University Library expansion competition entry, interior perspective, Helsinki, 1937.

262. Helsinki University Library expansion competition entry, perspective toward courtyard, Helsinki, 1937.

dow wall and clerestory window at the topmost edge of the south wall. The latter window, however, would have admitted a distressing quantity of direct sunlight even in Helsinki's extremely northern latitude, and the avoidance of sunlight was exactly what Aalto had gone to such effort to achieve in Viipuri. It was, in fact, the alleged rationale behind the design of the conical skylight. In view of the presence of the same skylight in the University Library design, the south window is inexplicable.

Yet another drawback in the design was the acoustic quality of the spectacularly designed reading room. Since the reflector shape was directly opposite a high vertical wall, it would probably have bounced sound around excessively. At any rate it would have required expert acoustical analysis to ensure the quiet needed in such a space.

Ironically, Aalto's failure to win the competition was probably caused by his attempt to blend his design with the classical nature of the Engel building by wrapping ashlar style decoration around the lower floor of his proposed new entry court to match the original building (262). Engel and his buildings have always occupied a revered position in the minds of Finnish architects, and while Ervi's Functionalist box was not directly sympathetic with the original building, Aalto's pronounced romanticism must surely have been deemed unacceptable as an addition to such a classical-style landmark.[23]

Savoy Restaurant

The interior design commission of 1937 for the Savoy Restaurant (263) with its custom furnishings and fixtures offered Aalto a chance to experiment with the possibilities of creating an environment in his newly developing mode through essentially nonarchitectonic means. This entailed the application of his romantic modernist motifs on a more superficial, but at the same time more intimate decorative level than he had done in any previous project of this period. It was also

Aalto's first commission for a public space in Helsinki.

The most dramatic element in the room—an existing space located atop a downtown Helsinki building—is the long row of closely spaced wooden boards mockingly arranged to simulate the knee brace system of a rural farm building. (Aalto himself referred to it, with tongue in cheek, as a manger.[24]) In reality, the "braces" supported nothing, but screened a row of vent sashes placed at the top of the wall and opening out into the elevator foyer. Around these boards, vines were entwined to complete the folksy effect of the interior of a rural structure. Sheltered beneath this bucolic canopy were a line of banquet tables, flanked by low, perforated screen walls; this motif of closely spaced round holes superficially recalls the pattern of Aalto's familiar skylight grid, but in fact had appeared on the theater doors of the earlier Agricultural Co-operative in Turku.

In the middle of the restaurant, serving as its focal point and centerpiece was located a free-form table, the room's other major design element, recalling the free-form music stand of the restaurant in the Agricultural Co-operative. The table's kidney-shaped top rested on a battened base that resembled the exterior undulating wall of the Lapua Pavilion. This table, the chairs, and the lighting fixtures were designed especially for this commission. The ceiling lighting was provided from recessed fixtures and diffused through specially designed wooden lattices and more intimate lights were suspended low over the banquet tables. The Aaltos also designed a chair for the terrace made of bent slats of birch, resembling traditional garden furniture, but formed to fit the contour of the human back and bottom. The designs provided for much of the glassware were characterized by a reversing free-form shape that was intended to recall the formless nature of the fluids they would hold. These vases and bowls, so often associated with the Savoy commission, were in fact

263. Savoy Restaurant, view of interior, Helsinki, 1937.

designed the previous year for a Scandinavian glassware competition (in which, in fact, they did not receive a prize).

The individual details of the Savoy, primarily executed by Aino Aalto, are in themselves not advanced over any of Aalto's contemporary work. The restaurant's importance lies in the fact that they were finally able to execute a commission in the capital—a sort of advertisement of the element of the Aalto style where the local general public could see it firsthand. The somewhat superficial aspect of the bucolic anti-Functionalism as it appears here may be interpreted as a result of an effort at popularization or commercialization, but one they must have taken pleasure in nonetheless.

15
Mastery of a New Rationalism

Stepped Apartments At Kauttua

The stepped housing group for the Ahlström workers in the Kauttua area was begun as a project during 1937 while the Paris Pavilion was fresh in Aalto's mind. The site plan (264) shows that he planned to have four blocks located on three sides of a steep slope, with each block accessible from the top of the hill as well as from the path along the base of the building complex.

The largest flats on the terrace side are intended for families, while the others are smaller and suitable for couples. The entire block (265) (the drawing for which is captioned "Terrassitalo") is reminiscent of architecture on the Bay of Naples and, in fact, bears a general resemblance to many hillside dwellings in Southern Europe.[1] The unique elements in the design of these buildings are the pole railings and trellises on the balconies and around the doorways (266, 267), resembling those proposed for the Moscow Embassy two years earlier. The incorporation of poles and free-forms in Aalto's designs is perhaps rooted in his appreciation of nature. Both eventually appeared at the Villa Mairea, his masterpiece of residential architecture.

Villa Mairea

Maire Ahlström Gullichsen had been raised on the Ahlström estate in Noormarkku near the west coast of Finland where her parents lived a conservative life in a house furnished in the French style that was traditional in international upper-class milieus.[2] After her marriage to Harry Gullichsen, they moved to Helsinki where they were to have an apartment which Gullichsen decided should be furnished in the modern style. Maire was charged with carrying out the project and told to spare no expense in doing so.[3] It was this project that led to her introduction to Helsinki's contemporary design scene (such as it was) and brought her into contact with such Functionalist designers as Alvar and Aino Aalto. In 1935, the Aaltos and Gullichsens (together with N. G. Hahl) founded Artek O. Y., the modern Finnish design firm which, among other activities, was to be responsible for the production of Aalto's furniture and the sponsorship of the highest quality of contemporary Finnish design.

By 1937 the Gullichsens decided to construct a summer house on the Noormarkku estate.[4] Their children were school age and such summer retreats were traditional in Finland. They asked Aalto to design their summer house and virtually gave him *carte blanche* to make it just as he thought it should be and let nothing else guide him. The couple's liberal attitude was described by Maire Gullichsen: "We told him that he should regard it as an experimental house; if it didn't work out, we wouldn't blame him for it."[5]

This house was to become more than just a commission for Aalto. The design of the "Villa Mairea," as it came to be known, allowed him to amalgamate in a single structure all the ideas that he had only been able to express episodically in his recent buildings. It had been 2 years since the completion of Aalto's own house, and in that time he must have had many new ideas and second thoughts over and above those that were excluded from the earlier construction because they were too expensive. Unlimited freedom of expression and an unrestricted design budget would constitute a rare opportunity for any architect, but as it happened to be Aalto's first house for a private client, he set his sights at the highest level of design that he could conceive.

The working method that Aalto used in most of his buildings can be observed quite clearly in the development of Mairea. It seems that his basic method was to record all the ideas that he was considering in the first drafted form of any project. This does not mean that he put anything extraneous in the design. Most of Aalto's first states during this period, in fact, appear to be Spartan (268),[6] if not actually skimpy, with proportions that are timid in comparison with the well-published, soft-pencil sketches that in some cases preceded them. Unlike the sketches, which in the minds of many later architects stand as testaments of sensitivity with respect to design methodology, the first

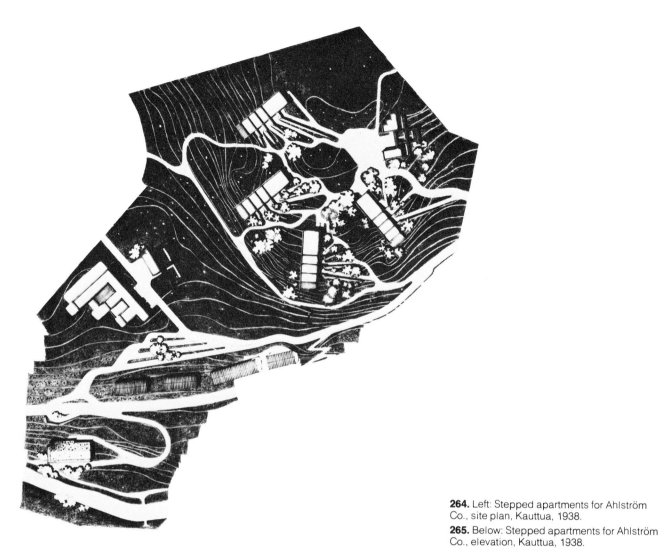

264. Left: Stepped apartments for Ahlström Co., site plan, Kauttua, 1938.

265. Below: Stepped apartments for Ahlström Co., elevation, Kauttua, 1938.

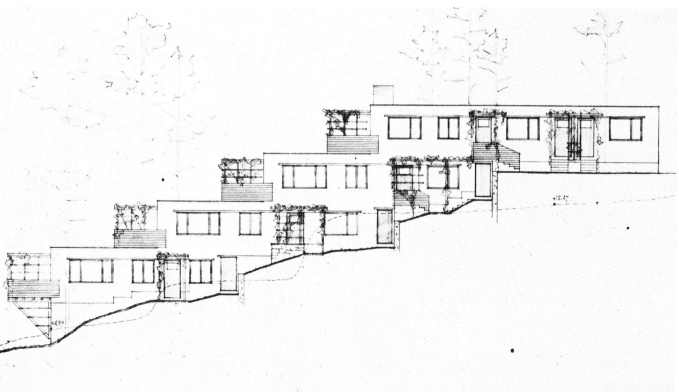

drafted form was the only basic idea
that was drawn to scale and could
be used as a working model by
Aalto himself. The development of
the final design was accomplished
by a progressive refinement in the
definition of forms and an increase
in prominence of certain distinctive
shapes. What had originally been a
respectable but unexciting Functionalist summer house grew into a
full-blown masterpiece of individ-
ualistic style, overflowing with innovative and original motifs.

The interim drawings (269) and
sketches leading to the final design
show this in a number of ways:
walks became thicker and bolder;
rounded forms appear where none
existed in earlier studies; when
such forms had been utilized previously, they were augmented and
given even stronger curvilinear profiles.

The progression illustrated in
Mairea appears to be a sort of stylistic "ontogeny recapitulating phylog-
eny." The evolution of spatial and
decorative motifs traced in Aalto's
major designs in the immediately
preceding years (i.e., the Moscow
Embassy competition, his own
house, and the Paris World's Fair
Pavilion project) was summarized in
the design development of the Villa
Mairea.[7] In the drawings for this
house we can see in a more connected stage-by-stage progression,
Aalto's arrival at a complex, virtually
unique collection of romantic architectonic expressions.

According to Aalto's original concept, the Villa Mairea was to be an
L-shaped house set within a walled
or fenced garden. The house
itself was sited on the line of the
east wall and just inside the south
wall or approach side. The resulting
courtyard in the interior angle of the
L was to be the main lawn for relaxation and recreation and the location
of the swimming pool, sauna, and
veranda. The house itself was arranged with the living and entertain-
ing rooms on a split level along the
southern leg of the L with a south-
facing balcony overlooking the approach drive and the older Ahlström
mansions in the distance. Along the
south wall of this wing Aalto placed

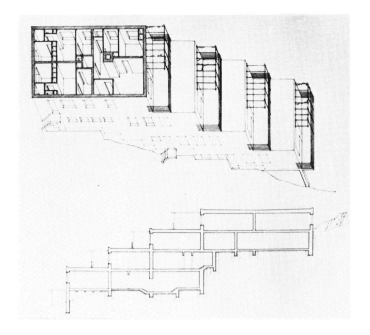

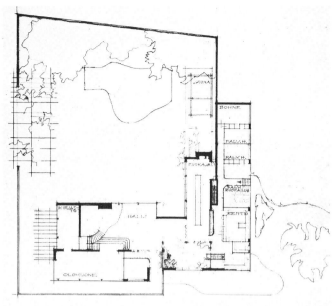

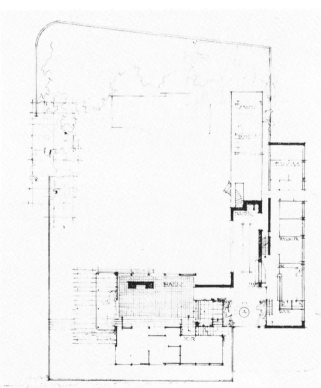

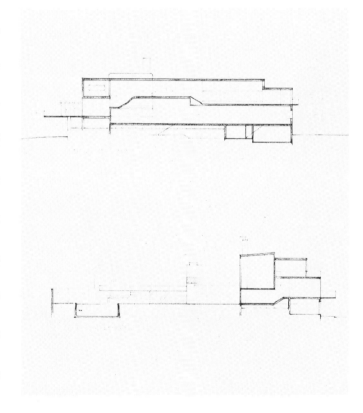

266. Opposite page: Stepped apartments for Ahlström Co., entrance terraces, Kauttua, 1938.

267. Top left: Stepped apartments for Ahlström Co., isometric and section, Kauttua, 1938.

268. Top right: Summer villa for Marie and Harry Gullichsen, Villa Mairea, first state, plan, Noormarkku, 1937.

269. Above left: Villa Mairea, second state, plan, Noormarkku, 1937.

270. Above right: Villa Mairea, first state, sections, Noormarkku, 1937.

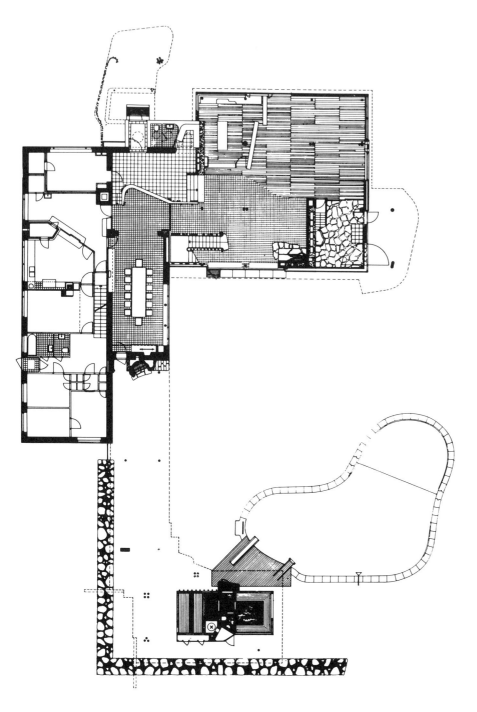

271. Above: Villa Mairea, final state, plan, Noormarkku, 1937.

272. Opposite page above: Villa Mairea, second state, elevation, Noormarkku, 1937.

273. Opposite page below: Villa Mairea, completed house, studio floor with flower room beneath, Noormarkku, 1938.

an art gallery. The rear of the wing was designed as the sitting room with a massive free-standing fireplace partially hiding the garden from view. The floor was shown here as tile on the presumption that this area would handle most of the traffic to the upstairs. At the extreme western end of the wing was a flower-arranging room with a trellis stretching beyond.[8]

The wing along the eastern line of the garden wall was comprised of the entry space with the dining room to the north, the kitchen outside the dining room, and the servants' quarters beyond, further to the north. At the extreme southern end of this wing a small office was provided for Maire's use as director of Artek. North of the dining space was a covered veranda with the sauna at the end and adjoining that a swimming pool. The free-form shape of the southern edge of the swimming pool was identical to that of the podium used in the restaurant in the Agricultural Co-op in Turku in 1930.[9]

The sections (270) reveal a unique arrangement in the sitting room ceiling, which is raised even higher than the floor line of the studio on the second level above and exposes the form of the studio as a special element. At a still higher level—again split by half a floor height—is the master bedroom. As a design it is an interesting arrangement of domestic architectural spaces, even if some of the adjacent uses are slightly in conflict.

The final version (271), as far as the overall plan is concerned, is just a pavilion for relaxation in the woods with no garden wall to protect or obstruct the view in any direction. (The Ahlström estate was, after all, a private ground.) The wing that stretches northward is the same in development as it was in the original concept; if anything is changed it is that the dining room has been shortened to provide a more intimate space. The majority of changes that occur are on the wing along the southern edge of the house. The art gallery has been removed and replaced with a multipurpose space which has movable partitions capable of forming any type of arrangement that might be desired, for the display of paintings or for the various social functions which were envisioned for Villa Mairea.[10] Because dancing was a popular pastime with the Gullichsens, the floor was a heavy Norwegian beech parquet that abuts the tile floor of the sitting room in a free-form line. The fireplace has been transferred to the corner of the sitting room, thus opening up the view to the garden and pool beyond.[11] The stairway has been moved to the glass wall of the garden facade, giving it an open effect screened by a random row of poles on each side. At the western end of this portion of the house is the flower-arranging room, but now it is incorporated within the rectangular line of the wing.

This house was to be not only the base of operations for Maire Gullichsen's activities as director of Artek and as organizer of special exhibitions for that company, but also a place where she could fulfill the training she had received as an artist.[12] One of the main features was thus the studio on the second level (272) that was expressed separately from the remainder of the house. It was shaped as a trapezoidal solid with rounded corners and clad on the outside with the vertical fins employed on the main building at the Paris Pavilion. In the final scheme (273) this form is retained but slightly reduced in height. It rests partly on top of the flower-arranging room, cantilevering out to the west to form a canopy for that space below. This studio element—the dominant form at the Villa Mairea—can be seen as such from all views except the service wing along the east.[13] The master bedroom has been shifted to the second floor, and there are no longer any split levels in the arrangement.

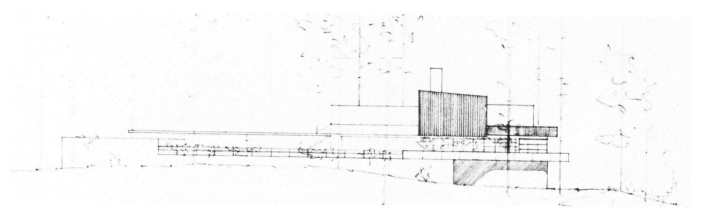

274. Top: Villa Mairea, completed house, entrance view, Noormarkku, 1938.

275. Above: Villa Mairea, completed house, pool and sauna (sauna finished later), Noormarkku, 1938.

The addition of a variety of free-form elements changes the spirit to one more playful than that of the original version. The flat entrance canopy (274)—supported on informally attached banded poles which form columns and tripods—is a free-form shape that stretches forward from the house to the driveway in a warped version of a parallelogram. The swimming pool (275) is brought forward toward the house and is shaped somewhat like a kidney in plan. Free in its form, it adjoins the sauna and covered walkway leading to the house. At the rear edge of the large fireplace in the sitting room a free-form niche extends this spirit of curvilinear form in a nonfunctional, ornamentally playful fashion.

The outdoor chimney (276), while never used again, shows Aalto's ability to juxtapose two traditional forms. A rock-vaulted fireplace and a rough masonry stairway with flat pieces of stone for the treads are combined on the chimney at the north end of the house to create a rustic conversation piece at the end of the dining room wing. The clever and simple use of caning to wrap large steel pipe columns in pairs (277) transforms what might be a brutal structural necessity into a soft, natural, touchable object in the middle of the sitting room.

In the execution of the Villa Mairea, Aalto exploited Harry Gullichsen's invitation to experiment to full advantage.[14] Derivations from motifs he had already used and developments of new forms and techniques produced a complete repertoire of architectural ideas which could be drawn upon in combination or permitted to yield a seemingly endless variety of architectural characters. But the building itself (278)—a landmark in his career—provided Aalto as well as others proof that he was capable of producing architecture of an extraordinary high level if the commissions were forthcoming and if time and money could be available to serve the highest standard of design.

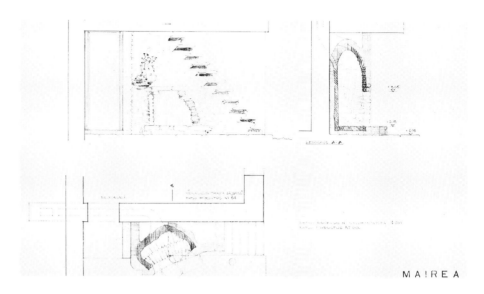

MAIREA

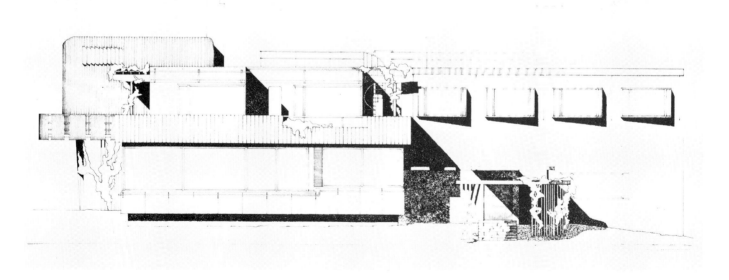

276. Top: Villa Mairea, final state, outdoor fireplace, Noormarkku, 1938.

277. Middle: Villa Mairea, completed house, living room details, Noormarkku, 1938.

278. Above: Villa Mairea, final version, southern elevation, Noormarkku, 1938.

16
Transition Complete

New York World's Fair: Competition for Finnish Pavilion

The culmination in the development of Aalto's romantic or anti-Functionalist style was his participation in the competition for the Finnish Pavilion at the New York World's Fair for 1939–1940.[1] Thus Aalto was afforded his third major opportunity in three years to design without serious budgetary limitations—first the Paris Pavilion, then the Villa Mairea, and now the Finnish Pavilion in New York. He rose to the challenge in what may well have been his most extreme departure from the Functionalist creed. Winning commissions for the pavilions in two consecutive World's Fairs was not only an unprecedented feat for a Finnish architect but for an architect in nearly any other country as well. That alone must have given Aalto a pronounced sense of confidence, in great contrast to his first few years as a practicing architect in Helsinki when he won nothing.

The competition unfolded at what must have been a lightning pace. The announcement was made in March 1938 and the due date was May 9, just two months later.[2] The reason for this haste was clear. The pavilion had to be designed and constructed within a mere eleven months before the opening. Since Aalto had just finished the Paris Pavilion, he must have had an advantage over the other ten competitors. Lending support to this sup-

position is the fact that his designs for New York were to some extent based directly on certain features incorporated in his Paris projects. It would be even understandable if the competing architects felt this advantage at that time. Moreover, the two architectural members of this panel, Välikangas and Lindegren,[3] had also been on the Paris Pavilion jury. Perhaps in a modestly sized architectural community such as that in Finland a frequent repetition of the same jury members might be inevitable, but whatever the case Aalto surely didn't suffer from the presence of either Välikangas or Lindegren. The competition was entered by relatively few architects for an open or public contest, which may also have been a factor in the outcome. At any rate even Aalto must have been surprised when his office won all three prizes. The credit for each entry varied slightly but all were produced in Aalto's office. First prize was won by a project (279) entitled "Maa, Kansa, Työ, Tulos"[4] (Country, People, Work, Products) credited to Alvar Aalto and assisted by architects Stenius, Urpola, and Bernoulli.[5] Second prize was taken by a project (280) mottoed "Kas Kuusen Latvassa Oravalla,"[6] which is an abridged line from a Finnish children's song, and was credited simply to Alvar Aalto. Third prize (281) was called "U.S.A. 39"[7] and was credited to Aino Marsio-Aalto. Each project was essentially the same volumetrically, probably

because the program called for an interior space design that would exhibit Finland's culture and commerce in two- and three-dimensional displays. The volume in which the exhibit would be housed was a long, windowless rectilinear solid with a ceiling height of 52' (16 m), equivalent to four stories. The main feature was to be a restaurant where visitors could eat a light, typically Finnish snack and view motion pictures and documentaries about Finland.

The pavilion, and ultimately Aalto's authorship of it, was particularly important to the Finns. Not only did it provide them with another chance to test their mettle in an international forum, but the American context gave the project an additional interest, especially to Aalto who was enthusiastic about America at this time. Some of his Americaphilia could be attributed to the fair's theme, the "World of Tomorrow,"[8] which not only encouraged modernity, but unlike previous international expositions, virtually required it.

When Eliel Saarinen won second prize in the Chicago Tribune competition in 1922, most Finnish architects were pleased and took pride in the feeling that Finnish designers were the equal of those anywhere.[9] Later, however, when Saarinen announced his permanent relocation in the United States, the first major European architect to effect such a transfer,[10] many of those designers must have been shocked at his

abandonment of his native land. Aalto may not have realized fully that he had replaced Saarinen as a leader in the philosophical sense, but it must have crossed his mind that by winning the New York Fair Pavilion competition, he would also be in a position to think seriously about a move to America.

Three Schemes, Three Winners

Of the three Aalto entries the third prize winner, U.S.A. 39 (282), presented the fewest new ideas and an only slight free form in its solution. Like the other two entries it provided a high central space flanked by balconies and included a cinema, dining space, and coffee shop. The cinema (283) was located under a wedge-shaped balcony and was shielded from glare and ambient light by a plenum extended above. The only other opportunity to create architectural interest was the use of poles and exit stairs which served the exhibition balconies located opposite the cinema. The drawing (281) shows an interesting (but for this time in Aalto's career somewhat timid) curvilinear free-form effect.

279. Top: Finnish Pavilion competition entry for the World's Fair, first prize winner, perspective, New York, 1938.

280. Middle: Finnish Pavilion competition entry for the World's Fair, second prize winner, perspective, New York, 1938.

281. Left: Finnish Pavilion competition entry for the World's Fair, third prize winner, perspective, New York, 1938.

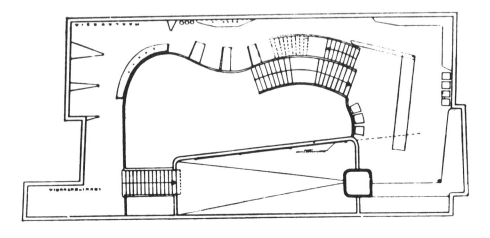

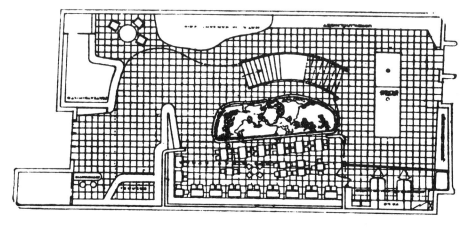

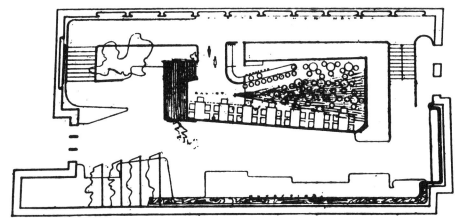

282. Top: Finnish Pavilion competition entry for the World's Fair, third prize winner, upper level plan, New York, 1938.

283. Middle: Finnish Pavilion competition entry for the World's Fair, third prize winner, ground level plan, New York, 1938.

284. Above: Finnish Pavilion competition entry for the World's Fair, second prize winner, upper level plan, New York, 1938.

This was created mainly by the balcony rail above and supplemented by a planting area in the center of the main space on the entrance level. There were to be a few trees, plants, and vines scattered around the various levels to give the romantic look that was by this time so much a part of Aalto's thinking.

The second prize-winning solution (284) was a clearer attempt to incorporate romantic elements within the same volume. The motto, taken from a children's song, means "the squirrel has a nest in the top of a spruce tree." This seeming frivolity was nearly a literal description, for within the overall pavilion scheme of a skylit, two-level courtyard like those of Viipuri and its successors, Aalto suspended the lightproof cinema (285) in a sort of nest, high up in the air, level with the balcony. It was to be free standing along two sides and set off by a grouping of poles placed just at the main entrance to the Pavilion, thus creating the effect of a volume floating among the treetops. It is evident that Aalto found it an interesting challenge to design a lightproof screening room, for in each of the entries he handled the problem in a distinctly different manner. In this version, the cinema was designed as a long, wedge shape which would be constructed of two interlocking horizontal baffles (286) that screened the direct rays of light, yet permitted one to look outward to the exhibits and also allowed a free air flow. Aalto's desire to achieve an inventive design with such dramatic tension—a brilliant, skylit, double-height courtyard with a secure and dark nest hung in the middle—imposed a severe technological challenge. By incorporating this technical solution into his design he achieved a highly dramatic and romantic impression of a single space in which light and dark were juxtaposed. Except for its bucolic aspect, however, this building is somewhat unromantic for this period of Aalto's work in terms of planning and in its forms. Nonetheless, within this rather squarish geometry Aalto managed to achieve a significant degree of freedom and subtlety

through the use of display cases
and platforms in varying sizes and
shapes. Whether or not it was uneth-
ical to present more than one entry
in a national public competition in
Finland, it was certainly not good
politics to present three. But not
only did Aalto present three entries,
he provided two alternatives for the
entry that finally won first prize: a
two-level scheme and a three-level
scheme. Altogether that amounted
to four possible chances out of a total of fourteen on which Aalto could
count to express his ideas for the
design of the fair pavilion and to secure the commission.[11]

The two alternatives were essentially the same but their geometrical
configurations differed (279, 287).
Both schemes employed stacked,
curvilinear, undulating plywood
screen walls along one side, balanced asymmetrically against low
balconies on the opposite wall.
They differed mainly in the character of the undulating wall, and in
each case the projection area was
behind a different part of it. One version of the wall (288) was delineated in giant sweeping rolls while
the other (289) was given a more
controlled, staccato pattern of undulations. The final exhibition, while
basically of the latter type, incorporated some of the spirit of both.[12]
Whether or not there is any correlation between the collaborative
credit given for the project and the
richness of its design, the winning
project is certainly far richer in
ideas than any of the other prize entries. The overwhelming feature—a
50' (15 m) high display wall constructed in a small room in four staggered undulating layers—was a
powerful and unprecedented visual
display then and remains today just
as unrivaled an image of architectural form.[13]

The first mentioned of these two
schemes (288), the three-level version, was designed with a large curl
at the end near the entrance that
was coordinated with a circular
ramp leading to the exhibition area
on the topmost level behind the
three-tiered plywood curtain wall.
The other end of the wall curved out
over the main volume to allow for the

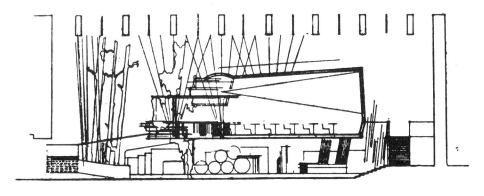

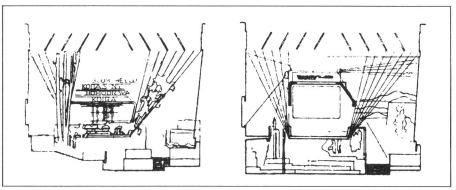

285. Top: Finnish Pavilion competition entry
for the World's Fair, second prize winner,
section, New York, 1938.

286. Middle: Finnish Pavilion competition entry for the World's Fair, second prize winner,
section, New York, 1938.

287. Above: Finnish Pavilion competition entry for the World's Fair, alternate first prize
winner, perspective, New York, 1938.

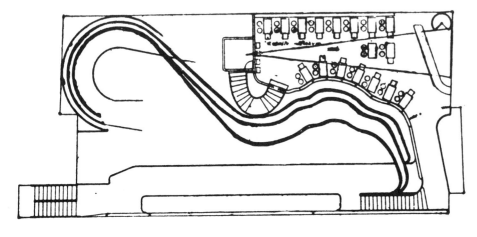

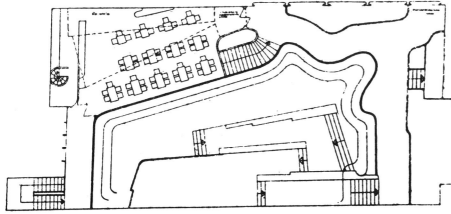

288. Top: Finnish Pavilion competition entry for the World's Fair, first prize winner, upper level plan, New York, 1938.

289. Above: Finnish Pavilion competition entry for the World's Fair, first prize winner, alternate upper level plan, New York, 1938.

290. Opposite page above: Finnish Pavilion for the World's Fair, interior view, New York, 1939.

291. Opposite page below: Finnish Pavilion for the World's Fair, final plan, New York, 1939.

placement of a closed, free-form cinema tucked behind it on the second level. In a final concave turn it swept across the rear wall to the opposite balcony. The second, or two-level, version (289) incorporated the undulation into the total geometrical solution in a slightly greater degree than its alternative. Angling away from the main entrance along the left wall to conceal the wedge-shaped cinema on the second level, the plywood curves are arranged in a pair of open folds that stretch across to the opposite balcony. This version of the plywood screen-wall is closer to the final one built in New York (290, 291) than the giant sweeping curves of the former. Both sketches of the wall are the same in essence and are really patterned after the special effect of the northern lights called "curtain aurora." Such natural phenomenon as the constellations and aurora were used by Aalto as sources for various architectural designs and artworks throughout his career.[14] There is, however, at least one additional source worth mentioning here for the undulating curved surfaces he

so often used from Viipuri onward and that played such a large role in supplanting the Functionalist's forms as well as in the derivation of Aalto's own individually romantic modernism. Since Aalto means wave in Finnish—as of the sea or the scientists' oscilloscope—one is tempted to speculate that his growing involvement with these forms entailed a sort of spiritual identity with his own name.

Exhibition Pavilion

The main difference between the winning projects and the finally constructed one was that the cinema was moved to the wall opposite the curtain display as it had been in Aino Aalto's scheme U.S.A. 39 (283), but it was raised up to the balcony level looking out on the main volume of the building (292). This alteration of Aalto's basic concept of contrasting the open space of the exhibition area and the enclosed space of the cinema/restaurant may have been determined by the final site allocated to the Finnish Pavilion.[15] The pavilion was located at the end of a standard row of attached national pavilions which meant that one side could have windows opening to the outside, and the opportunity to have a restaurant with a view was one the Finns must have been reluctant to forego.[16] The necessary lightproofing was finally provided by placing the projection screen on the rear wall in a light baffle depressed deeply into the wall surface and ringed with small concentric light traps.

The entrance pattern proceeded down the center of the pavilion (293) between the great display surface of the plywood curtain and the exhibition space beneath the restaurant balcony. At the rear visitors were directed up the spiral stairway and back along the balcony where the café cinema was located (291), then around to the opposite side behind the curving wall to the final exhibition areas, and back to the rear again where the information desk and exits were. It was a spiral system that allowed the flow of visitors to enter, walk through the exhibit,

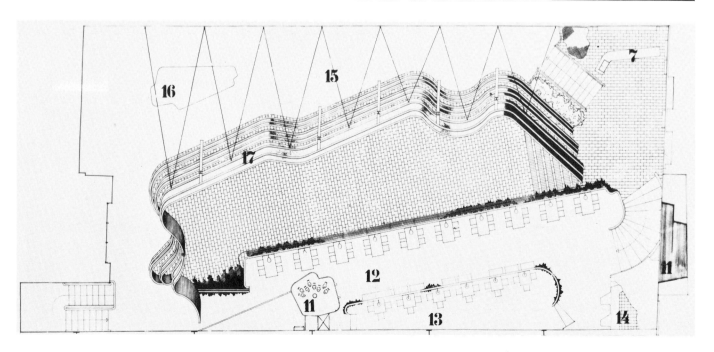

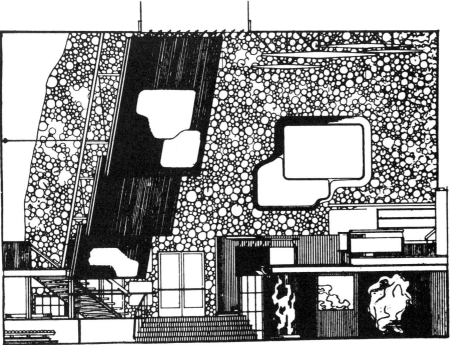

292. Top: Finnish Pavilion for the World's Fair, interior view looking toward balcony, New York, 1939.

293. Above: Finnish Pavilion for the World's Fair, final design, end wall showing projection screen, New York, 1939.

294. Opposite page above: Finnish Pavilion for the World's Fair, cinema balcony, New York, 1939.

295. Opposite page below: Finnish Pavilion for the World's Fair, view of restaurant windows from outside, New York, 1939.

and exit without once retracing a step. As one mounted the spiral stairway to the cinema, it was possible to look directly upward and see the screen because the recessed baffle enclosure was opened downward and to the left to allow visitors to become involved with the kinetic experience even as they were climbing. The café-cinema balcony was a long fan- or wedge-shaped space (294) that contained two rows of dining tables along its entire length with seating for fifty-eight people. The ceiling-mounted light and film projection booth were located at the opposite end from the projection screen. (This free-form box, covered with the striations of fine wood battens that were employed in earlier projects, resembled the painting studio at Villa Mairea which was constructed about the same time.) Meals were served at a counter to one side and below the projection screen.

At the main entrance visitors emerged from beneath an upper level balcony directly into the high space. The ceiling-high, four-tiered, undulating wall dominated the entire volume as it curved and folded to the rear and across the end of the space. The exhibit was arranged on four levels, the upper three being display surfaces. The lower one was located directly beneath the soffit of the first balcony and on a slightly raised platform which had the same profile as the display wall. The exhibit was organized from top to bottom in accordance with Aalto's winning motto, "Country, People, Work, Products" (290). Large photographs mounted directly on the surface of the curving plywood wall illustrated the first three. Products were reserved for eye-level view on the main floor and were displayed like items in a department store window or in Aalto's own words "like a country store."[17] The upper parts of the wall not covered by photographs, which were laminated directly on the surface, were textured by the small, randomly spaced wooden battens found in many of Aalto's projects and buildings during these years.

The objects displayed—arranged entirely by the Aaltos and their assistants—included many wood products traditionally associated with Finnish industry, especially those of bent and laminated construction such as propeller blades, skis, axe handles, etc. Most prominent, however, was the bent plywood furniture which included nearly all Aalto's furniture prototypes then in production. He had been given full control of the exhibit on the strength of his involvement in the display of Finnish products in Paris 2 years earlier. This time, unencumbered by any collaborators, the Aaltos brought into play the full extent of their design training, their cultural heritage, and their love of designed and natural forms to achieve a totally balanced ensemble of varied objects. They were probably also inspired by the importance given at that time to display windows in fashionable department stores around the world. The wall itself continued the display of Finnish plywood and formed wood technology. It was constructed from panels made in Finland by a manufacturing process not unlike that used to make Aalto's furniture, and like his laminated furniture, the panels of the wall were formed by bending the material around only one set of parallel axis.[18] In design and construction methods, the New York Pavilion is closer to his furniture than any other of his contemporary works in architecture.

One of the manageable techniques for producing this wall might have been to use a preformed, scaled shape. The thin, wide shavings rolled from the blade of a hand plane are one such shape that comes to mind. By stacking three shavings one on top of the other, edge to edge, the form of the curtain wall of the pavilion could have been produced in scale form. Aalto had experimented with shapes in wood that had these ribbonlike properties during the development and manufacturing of his laminated furniture with Otto Korhonen of Turku in the late twenties and early thirties. He later called them "abstract experi-

ments in wood." In fact the sweeping curve of the plywood wall in the alternate version (288) of the first prize winner closely resembles some of those sculptures made by Aalto out of what seem to be scrap pieces from the manufacture of the Paimio chair. When these were shown in an exhibition in London in 1933 and a London Times critic implied that they were just leftover pieces from the manufacturing process displayed as art, Aalto was defensive.[19]

The Finnish Pavilion attracted the interest of architects and critics alike, and for many architects it remains the one significant design that has yet to be eclipsed in its boldness and romantic modernism. Although the impression it made at the time is without question a tribute to Aalto's ability as a designer, he was fortunate in one respect. The pavilion was located in what might have been an obscure site. It was at the end of a row of nine national pavilions facing an open mall called the Court of Peace which was near the eastern edge of the fairgrounds and far away from the main access gates.[20] There were, however, two aspects of the site that made it favorable for the recognition Aalto naturally hoped for in this truly international setting: first, it was located next to the large United States Pavilion which closed off the eastern end of the main axis of the mall and would be the most visited pavilion during the fair; and second, its end location made it possible to have windows which in turn opened up the possibility of architecturally expressing the pavilion's identity on the end elevation. This elevation (295) facing the U.S. Pavilion was treated in the by-now-expected romantic vein through the use of natural materials in contrast to the fair's standard stark white stucco architectural treatment. The strip of windows that allowed the diners to look out toward the space directly to the east was shielded by a rustic sun control device in the form of randomly spaced wooden birch saplings entwined with vines growing from the planting bed beneath. This arrangement stood slightly away

from the stucco facade because the window strip was framed by a shallow projecting arrangement. Since the poles extended both above and below this bay, they created a shadow pattern on the stucco wall and provided variation in texture and light.

While most of the textural motifs may not have been much advanced beyond those of the Paris Pavilion and the Villa Mairea,[21] certain details did appear that had not been used in Aalto's repertoire before: the undulating birch handrail of the spiral stairway baluster; the continuous perforated light baffle handrail (292) angled over the cinema-café balcony and its small bentwood supports; and the use of irregular free-form cutouts of birch veneer arranged in a montage to form a portion of the soffit under the curved display wall. Another new motif utilized on the wall above the cinema-café windows was a giant aerial photo of an archipelago of southern Finland whose natural and free-form pattern echoed the curves of the wood components used by Aalto in the overall design of the pavilion and in its details. Perhaps the most interesting new textural detail was the utilization of end-grain slices from birch saplings to create a mosaic that acted as a sound-absorbing wall.

The technical features employed by Aalto in the New York Pavilion might, at first glance, seem routine for his buildings of this period, but once again there are techniques not previously used in his work. The lighting was carefully controlled to dramatize the displays by bathing the undulating wall evenly from recessed lamps located in a ceiling trough. The light was directed toward the displays and shielded from the cinema by use of a louvered diffuser-reflector system. The lighting in the cinema was carefully designed to prevent interference with the projection lanterns by means of a small, low-wattage, fixed table lamp designed by Aalto to control the light on the dark, nonreflective table tops (294). Natural birch egg-crate diffusers were employed in the soffits of the cinema-

café balcony to enable the use of standard American fluorescent and incandescent fixtures for effective display lighting.

Perhaps the most unusual technical feature was Aalto's system of ventilation. Since New York's summer heat was a factor for which he had not yet had to design and since the pavilion had to make careful use of controlled light, air circulation presented problems.[22] Air was supplied to the large interior volume through horizontal slits located in the surface of the base of the uppermost tier of the undulating wall and also through ducts located underneath the café-cinema floor. The diffusers of the latter were integral with lighting fixtures that were embedded in the base of the balcony baluster to highlight its finned surface. This fusion of ventilation and lighting in the same fixture cluster was one of the earliest design resolutions of such an integration.[23] The air, once it was dumped into the openly planned volume, was literally churned around by another Aalto invention or perhaps re-invention—a playful version of the old-fashioned ceiling fan comprised of belt-driven, wooden airplane propellers and mounted above the café-cinema.

If the Moscow Embassy project represents the first appearance of the romantic and textural details and the Paris Pavilion represents a full repertoire of such elements, then the New York Pavilion must stand as the ultimate statement in achieving an emotional, anti-Functionalist style.

Conclusion

Aalto's departure from the International Style and the use of his modern version of Finnish romantic design to focus attention on his pavilion and homeland was a somewhat less bold statement in the context of the New York World's Fair than it would have been in Europe. It must be remembered that there was little true International Style at the World of Tomorrow Fair.[24] The predominating brand of modern architecture that appeared at the fair recognized the oncoming European style only in a somewhat mannered fashion, emphasizing primarily the streamlined and rounded forms of industrial designers. The most advanced designs vaguely resembled the expressive modernism found in Erich Mendelsohn's commercial architecture of the late twenties.

The New York World's Fair Finnish Pavilion exemplified the final stage in the calculated and nearly mathematical progression of Aalto's own development of a romantic alternative to the International Style, the style which he had sought out from afar and focused on during his formative years as a designer. Unlike Functionalism which spread widely in Finland following the Stockholm Fair in 1930, Aalto's romantic modernism—though derived from Finnish and Baltic design traditions and rationales and thoroughly appropriate for Finland—was such a personal style that it could not be readily followed by others and was perhaps too subtle and intricate to be formularized (to the extent that would be necessary for others to adopt it—some of course did try).[25]

Despite the fact that the evolution of this unique style took only four years from its timid but style-breaking appearance (in the trellis of the Moscow Embassy project and the poles on Aalto's own residence) to its full blossoming in the Villa Mairea, it was carefully built up to form a comprehensive mode of design which could vie with the best and most established Functionalist traditions in Aalto's own work such as the Paimio Sanatorium and Viipuri Library. Except for the retention of a few selected details, he never returned to that style he fought so hard to bring to the forefront in Finland.[26] The transition, when completed, left Aalto not only identified as a respected architect of international reknown but one who viewed the world from a special vantage point—a position that philosophically could encompass the best of the modern derivatives of classicism and romanticism simultaneously and yield designs that were as advanced technologically as those of any of his peers.

INTERNATIONAL
RECOGNITION

17
Hopes for a New Career

During the late 1930s when Britain and the United States became havens for those fleeing the spreading Nazi influence as well as a sort of promised land for those seeking a wider theater of practice for their talents, both countries received a substantial influx of architectural talent from continental Europe.[1] The United States had been the scene of great building activity in the twenties and even during the depression years, and nearly all the European designers had to take notice of the important American developments in the skyscraper and the single-family house for the middle class.

USA

During the thirties many Finnish architects expressed their fascination with American culture through the mottoes of their competition projects which were sometimes couched in American slang. Aalto himself had been interested in America and its buildings even before he entered and won the competition for the Finnish Pavilion of the 1939 New York World's Fair. In fact he had sought information about the U.S. from Hakon Ahlberg as early as 1930.[2] When he began to receive visitors from the U.S. and Britain—as a result of the publication of the Turun Sanomat and Paimio Sanatorium in architectural journals in those countries during the mid-to-late thirties—his interest in the West and its architecture was undoubtedly significantly intensified. The

first such person to visit Aalto and his buildings was the British journalist P. Morton Shand who had been instrumental in arranging for a show of Aalto's furniture at Fortnum and Mason's store in London in 1933.[3] And during the summer of 1936, Aalto and Viljo Rewell invited James M. Richards, already a prominent journalist and author, to Finland to visit Aalto's recent buildings.

During the summer of 1937 a chance meeting took place that was to affect Aalto's career for much of the next decade. Two noted California designers, William Wilson Wurster, an architect in Berkeley, and Thomas Church, a landscape theorist and author, along with Church's wife, accidentally stumbled on Aalto's house in Munkkiniemi during a tour of Scandinavia. The friendship that began when they were met at the door by the Aaltos was to enrich all their lives. When Wurster and the Churches departed after their tour of Helsinki, which was personally conducted by Aalto, an early renewal of their friendship seemed remote. Aalto, however, definitely intended to establish contact with architects in the U.S., and by the following spring he had made contact on many levels with the architectural community there. When his office corresponded with Wurster about some furniture that the latter had ordered from Artek, the letter included an inquiry for Richard Neutra's address.

However, Aalto's major line of communication with the U.S. in the spring of 1938 concerned the first major international retrospective of his works which opened at the Museum of Modern Art in New York in March.[4] He was expected to appear at the opening but was not able to do so because of the timing of the announcement for the New York World's Fair Pavilion competition. Although the competition was not officially announced until later that spring, it can be assumed that advance knowledge of it made Aalto realize that he would not be able to spare the time to travel to America for the March opening. The World's Fair competition, of course, had to be handled simultaneously with the University Library competition also due in May.

During this time Aalto participated on the jury for a planning competition for the Kemi area and designed and executed the forestry products pavilion (296) at the Lapua Agricultural Fair. The pavilion itself was a truly free-form, undulating wall which curved in convex and concave folds. The wall was constructed of straight, tall, slender poles joined tangentially at a constant height to give the appearance of a curtain in the forest magically suspended from the sky. It was, of course, designed simultaneously with the undulating walls of the New York Pavilion competition and the same analogy to the curtain aurora would be applicable here.[5] The roof

296. Below: Forestry Pavilion at Agricultural Exhibition, elevation, Lapua, 1938.

297. Bottom: Forestry Pavilion for Agricultural Exhibition, interior view, Lapua, 1938.

is flattened so that the freestanding curtain of wood poles driven in the ground would be the only observable form. The overall rustic effect also recalls the particular character of the young birch forest which springs up so rapidly in that region of Finland. Inside, he used the same type of rustic poles (297) that he had employed at the Finnish Pavilion in Paris the previous year as well as the same device he had previously used of grooving rough tree trunks to receive three smooth splines along most of their lengths, thus keeping hands off the natural bark shaft and visually strengthening the column effect.

About this time Artek began to exhibit in its catalog a free-standing, collapsible screen made of clear birch battens joined at their tangents by a fabric hinge. This screen could be used as a temporary divider like the traditional folding screen but in a material, color, and general free-form geometric pattern visually compatible with the Aalto furniture. Unlike the already-built forms at Lapua and New York, however, the screen does not remain plumb and vertical but tends to slump slightly. This of course produces another interesting effect even freer in form but basically contrary to the one that Aalto used on all the other applications. In all cases, however, whether the battens are arranged horizontally or vertically, they run parallel to the undulating folds of the wood surface.

The use of this motif here, as pure shape, almost sculpture, represents a final level of abstraction in the development of the free-form in Aalto's work. Once again the projects and commissions for fair and exposition designs afforded him the opportunity to experiment and introduce new techniques into his repertoire.

In October 1938 Alvar and Aino Aalto made their first trip to the U.S. The purpose of the trip was to settle certain details concerning the design and construction of their prize-winning Finnish Pavilion for the New York World's Fair to be opened the following spring. They were met at the boat by Harmon H. Goldstone, a young architect who had visited Aalto two years earlier and was among the first writers to introduce Aalto to the U.S.[6] Goldstone worked in the office of Wallace K. Harrison at the time, and had formed a private company with Harrison and Lawrence Rockefeller to import Aalto's furniture. Goldstone, who had numerous contacts in New York society, introduced Aalto around town and made sure that he met the cultural leaders of the day.

Aalto is remembered by those who met him on that first trip to the U.S. as having been enthusiastic about his New York visit and the opportunity to circulate in that architectural society. This was more significant than might be thought, for Aalto could speak little English. Nevertheless, he charmed an audience that came to hear him and see slides of his work by using gestures and simple phrases to describe his feelings about his work. He made a similar impression when he visited Cranbrook Academy that autumn at the invitation of his former countryman Eliel Saarinen who was not only the director of the arts and crafts school but also the architect of its campus. Aalto also visited other architectural schools where he delivered talks and acted as guest critic. At New York University's Bryant Park architectural school he delivered a talk entitled "The Attack of a Problem."[7]

In addition to their activities in and around New York, the Aaltos received an invitation during the late autumn of 1938 from Wurster and the organizers of the Golden Gate Exposition (to be held early in the spring of 1939) to exhibit their furniture and fabrics in the decorative arts section. Aino was responsible for the design and execution of the sample dining room which they sent. Harmon Goldstone assisted her in trans-Atlantic logistical problems as he had also aided the Aaltos with the New York Pavilion.

When the Aaltos returned to Finland late in the autumn of 1938, they resumed work on the nearly completed Villa Mairea, the stepped apartments for workers at Kauttua, and the Sunila pulp and paper mills. They also executed a design for the Blomberg Film Studio at the edge of Helsinki.[8] The latter scheme incorporated the spatial and formal motifs that Aalto had recently developed, but as at least one critic has pointed out, he utilized these forms in a geometrically freer interplay reminiscent of his later cultural and civic complexes for various cities in Northern Europe. During the winter of 1938–1939 Aalto made an attempt to base himself in the U.S. He apparently tried to study English because when he arrived in New York in March 1939 to supervise the final installation of the Finnish Pavilion and exhibition, he was able to communicate much better, although by no means fluently. Even before the fair opened he was busy charting a lecture tour of the U.S. and had sought out Wurster to arrange a series of lectures for him at Berkeley. Although the Berkeley lectures never materialized, he did deliver such a series at Yale University in April and May immediately after the opening of the New York Fair.[9]

In one way Aalto's engagement in this lecture tour represents little more than his response to invitations which are typically offered to somewhat celebrated and pace-setting architects during their travels. The content of the series, however, reveals the nature of his commitment to architecture and his intent to involve himself in more than just a lightweight travel slide presentation. The first lecture, held at New Haven on April 14, dealt with the "Problem of Humanizing Architecture" and was designed to cover Aalto's personal experiences as an architect. It was similar to the lecture given at the Museum of Modern Art in New York the previous autumn,[10] but more carefully prepared and more sophisticated in its presentation. The second lecture, delivered in two parts on April 18, dealt with psychology and the problems of humanization in town planning, including the problems of protecting the identity of the individual in large concentrations of dwellings. On April 25 he lectured on the small dwelling and its relation to town planning and mass production. On May 2 he discussed the collective function of public buildings and the protection of the individual against the mass experience. Finally on May 9 he lectured on designing a dwelling for a family who collected art and illustrated his talk with slides of the still-unfinished Villa Mairea. In fact the entire series was carefully tailored to promote Aalto's work and was illustrated with his finished buildings. The high theoretical level of these discussions underscores Aalto's interest in dealing with the profound social and philosophical aspects of architecture and planning and his ability to deal with them in a skillful and intellectual way. He had not ventured so deeply into the area of theory since his early professional days.

By mid-May Aalto was in the Los Angeles area systematically visiting the work of his old CIAM colleague, Richard Neutra.[11] Aalto's interest in Neutra's practice is significant since it is not usual for an architect to pay such attention to the work of a competitor of equal status or at least to one whose architectural philosophy was so strikingly different. Of course it is true that Neutra, as a member of CIAM, had bona fides as a serious modernist of international standing that few West Coast architects possessed. Aalto, however, may also have considered that Neutra was not only one of the earliest Europeans to make the transition from one side of the Atlantic to the other but in 1939, the most successful. Neutra, of course, was not a well-established architect before emigrating, but it nevertheless must have intrigued Aalto to see the flowering of his colleague in a newly adopted homeland.

Aalto arrived in San Francisco on May 25 to see his new friend William Wurster and that very evening he was asked to lecture at the San Francisco Museum of Art.[12] During their ten-day stay in the Bay Area, the Aaltos were treated not only as internationally important visitors but also with the informality reserved for close friends. The warm reception given them by Wurster and the Churches enabled Aalto to relax and quickly adapt to the casual West Coast lifestyle (298).[13]

In San Francisco Aalto organized a meeting with Wurster, Gardner Dailey, Thomas Church, and others to discuss an adventurous proposal he had conceived for an Institute for Architectural Research. His proposal called for informal research programs and laboratories combining the resources of universities and industry to evaluate the social implications of technical developments in the building field, the aspiring objective being the public good. This was certainly an avantgarde and pioneering position for him to take in the community of American architects at that time and it seemed doomed to failure given the conservative bias of that group.

In reading the notes taken at the San Francisco meeting—a sort of brainstorming session held on June 1, 1939—one basic theme seems to have been expressed by Aalto: that a great deal of technical research and development going on in the United States was not being evaluated or appropriately assimilated by the architectural profession. Here again, as in his lectures, Aalto emphasized the social implications of architecture. He proposed to investigate "human reactions" to various developments focusing on social as well as scientific and physiological research.[14]

By and large, however, the Ameri-

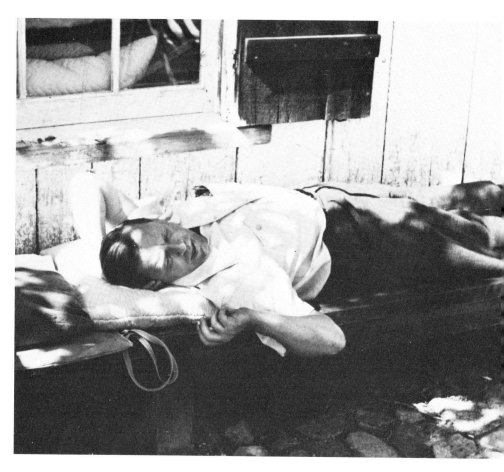

cans seemed caught up in specific practical problems. Their responses to Aalto's proposal appeared somewhat limited as if they had failed to grasp the broad scope of his approach. Issues raised by the other participants concerned the lack of understanding in the United States of the architect's role, the threat to the architectural profession of the "free, speculative sketch," provided by contractors, and public resistance to modern architecture in general. They seemed resistant to consideration of other-than-technical problems, and it was suggested, for example, that a group which confined itself to technical matters would "make more progress" than one also concerned with esthetics. The possibility of an excessive devotion to aesthetics seemed to worry them, and one of the group, Ernest Born, attacked what he described as the monastic mentality of the Cranbrook Academy. That school, then under the direction of Eliel Saarinen, was cited as an example of a group that had originally been concerned with such research val-

298. Photograph of Aalto sleeping on a bench at Gregory Farm in California, 1939.

ues but had not lived up to them. They asked numerous concrete questions regarding the precise organization of the group and seemed unable to cope with the broad implications of Aalto's proposal.

Among other things his proposal seems to have been designed to create a position for himself in order to secure some sort of professional foothold in America. It was probably a response to the enormous potential represented by the activity of the new world's construction industry compared with that of tiny Finland as well as to the uncertainty of the European political conditions, particularly Finland's tenuous position between the Nazi and Soviet structures.

Nonetheless Aalto's desire to establish such an international network of architects and theorists, as well as his concern with the physiological and psychological aspects of the environment, was somewhat ahead of its time, especially in the United States. It recalls, in fact, the socio/psychological approach to esthetics of Aalto's early friend and mentor, Yrjö Hirn.

As Aalto departed the Bay Area for the return trip to New York, his adopted base, he might have been discouraged that little of a concrete nature, besides two suggestions to contact various foundations, had been put forward by his associates. Upon his return to New York, however, probably feeling that he had failed to communicate his ideas to the Americans effectively, Aalto mailed to Wurster what he termed an article of some 1200 words.[15]

On reading this text one perceives the urgency of his feelings and his sense of an impending deluge of technological advances from the American industrial behemoth that not only would outstrip humanity's ability to cope with them in a humane way but would ultimately overwhelm society. He stressed the fact that current building materials research laboratories were insufficient and concentrated too much on the technical rather than the human factors of architectural materials—that the social sphere of this research was being neglected. Schools of architecture, he urged, should combine other related disciplines in the curriculum to approximate what we call "environmental design" today. It was an impassioned plea for a kind of self-enriching network that was essentially an elaboration of the working method Aalto himself used on many of his major projects during these years. Having delved bravely into many of the problems himself, he realized that he had just begun to scratch the surface and was calling for assistance from his colleagues.

Aalto who had developed an affinity with America, was exhibiting his best and noblest thoughts in response to his experiences there. Whether or not he realistically thought of emigrating to the U.S. at this time, he surely considered it a possibility.

When he returned to Finland later that summer he must have thought a great deal about America and the contacts and friendships he had been able to cultivate in a relatively short time. He made his first visit there only the previous year and, at forty, was at the peak of his abilities and had more than enough energy to meet the challenge of building a career in a new and exciting setting. His close and continued association with the U.S. was projected by Aalto in a letter to Wurster in which he proposed the establishment of a new magazine to be called "Pro Memoria Re." Its headquarters, he asserted, ultimately should be in America. The journal, which was to be edited by Aalto and Gregor Paulsson, an architecture professor in Uppsala, Sweden, was intended to be a cultural/political periodical.

The expressed aim of the magazine was apparently to bring to the attention of a general public "the symptoms of 'sociobiological responsibility' in the fields of culture, social life, industrial life and politics"![16] It was to deal in an apolitical way with building "new standards of values . . . to replace the present nihilism" which the proponents of the magazine held to be causing the period's chaotic conditions. As a weekly pamphlet, initially published by the two founders from Sweden and Finland, it was hoped that it would be written by "persons from the elite of the so-called democratic countries" having a personal knowledge of the questions on the program. At the beginning of December Wurster responded that he would favor such an association but by that time the Soviet Union had invaded Finland and the Winter War had begun; little or nothing more was ever mentioned about the project. It is probable that Aalto's concern with the conditions he found on his return to Scandinavia and the mounting probability of war with Finland's giant eastern neighbor impelled him once again to reach out for contact with and support from abroad. Events must have raised some doubt in Aalto's mind about whether or not he would ever be able to make his planned return to the U.S.

18
War Years

Winter War

Faced with the prospect of aggression and lasting war, Aalto must have felt that his plans to cement the ties he had formed with America during his relaxed and reassuring summer abroad were indefinitely put off and that efforts to create a base of operations there might never be realized. A housing exhibition in which Aalto had invited Wurster to participate was never held because of the Winter War. It must have been a doubly frustrating time for Aalto, because the Karelian Isthmus was taken from Finland during this period, thus sealing off Viipuri, the major city of that region. This city's isolation meant that Aalto's most recent and much acclaimed civic building, the Viipuri Municipal Library, was no longer visitable and that one of the major centers of building in Southern Finland would no longer be a source of commissions.[1] Since he had become a respected figure in the community of Viipuri, while still not having received a major commission in the capital, this was a particularly unfortunate state of affairs for Aalto. Much more serious, however, was Finland's seemingly helpless situation against a vast power like the Soviet Union. As in all war-torn countries architectural activity for all practical purposes had ceased. Most of the work that Aalto was involved in at this time was for his main patrons, the Gullichsens. In addition to the completion of the Villa Mairea and the stepped apartments at Sunila and Kauttua, he produced housing designs for the Ahlström headquarters in the industrial town of Karhula 75 miles east of Helsinki, as well as a master plan for the Kymi district in which Karhula is situated. He also continued work on the workers' village at the Anjala paper mill which was begun the previous year at Inkeroinen only a few miles to the north of the Ahlström headquarters.

As a dependent Grand Duchy or territorial possession, the Finns' homeland had been subjected to attack from the East and the West for centuries, but now they experienced the most extreme threat of their 20-year period of sovereignty.[2] Nothing in their history could have prepared them for the new form of war that had just emerged, the brutal air attacks on their defenseless cities. The peace-loving but tough-minded Finns cried out for help. Aalto himself wrote a long memorandum addressed to his influential friends abroad. His plea opened with the assertion, which would become a dismal commonplace over the next few years, that this war—aimed directly against the civilian population—was different than all those which preceded it. He saw the inhumane destruction of defenseless country villages and their people as the most brutal expression of war yet devised. Because of this, he argued, traditional measures of "humane" assistance were inadequate. His plea for help centered around the defense that could be afforded by what he called fighting planes. He said: "Fighting planes are the only and real 100% humane protection of the civilian population."[3] His scheme for aid to Finland was centered on three points of action: first, the effort of everyone to "work for a quick change of public opinion" that would recognize a new conception of humane assistance; second, assembling voluntary formations of fighting planes (to be used only for defensive purposes); and third, to protest throughout the civilized world against the concept of total war. He maintained that the battle was not Finland's alone; but at this point those countries that were still neutral hoped to sit the war out.

It was the aspect of the air attack that he dwelled on as if he could hardly believe it himself and expected any reader of his memorandum to have difficulty in fully grasping the effect of this desperate moment for Finland. He further pleaded for an organization of "intellectuals, technical men, artists and literary people" that could work to change and ratify support of his scheme. In closing he urged all who read the memorandum to do as the Norwegians had done, to circulate a protest in the press and among their friends regarding Finland's welfare.

The "memorandum," awkwardly translated into English, was the desperate outcry of a man in the middle of perhaps the greatest peril of his life, calling in his own impassioned way on those of his friends who he thought would be in a position to provide effective help. People like Maxwell Frye in England and William Wurster in the U.S. were correspondents of Aalto's during this period and received this memorandum. (During the war Wurster wrote "Beautiful Letters" to Aino and Alvar Aalto supporting them and the resistence to aggression.)

That winter and the preceding autumn marked one of the few periods in Aalto's early career in which he didn't enter any competitions, because none were held during the war. This period came to an unsatisfactory conclusion with the peace treaty signed in Moscow on March 13, 1940.[4] Within two weeks Aalto was back in New York to handle some alterations on the Finnish Pavilion for the second season of the New York World's Fair.[5] He also tried to drum up support for his plans for the construction of new towns in Finland where displaced Karelians would be able to settle in an orderly fashion. He had been chosen by the Finnish government to "take charge of the enormous reconstruction problem involving the development of homes for 500,000 people including construction of twelve entirely new cities and the repair or reconstruction of more than 40 hospitals destroyed in the war . . ."[6] It is probable that he hoped to find help in the U.S. from a foundation or from some other source that would be able to offer technical assistance. This is undoubtedly why he came into contact with the Alfred F. Bemis Foundation, a fund established at the Massachusetts Institute of Technology to support research and development in new construction techniques for housing, particularly prefabricated and modular techniques for low-cost housing. This foundation was instrumental in his appointment as a visiting professor at MIT, which took place at this time.[7]

This period of travel must have been an uneasy one for Aalto, for within two weeks of his arrival in the U.S., German troops invaded Norway. Immediately following that, Wurster wrote to Aalto at the Hotel Wyndham in New York where he had always made his base, expressing his relief that Aalto was again safe in the U.S. But Aalto probably didn't see it quite that way. At that point Finland was still able to maintain her neutrality and (in that same summer) had granted transit permission to both the German and Russian armies.

MIT Professorship

Aalto evidently remained in the U.S. that spring. On July 24, 1940, an MIT press release stated that Aalto was in Cambridge and would be joining the faculty of architecture late in the autumn term after he made a return trip to his homeland.[8] This appointment was arranged by John Burchard, then Director of the Bemis Foundation. Burchard had urged Walter Roy MacCormack, Dean of Architecture (and a traditionalist), to hire Aalto.[9] This of course was when MIT's neighbor institution Harvard had hired Walter Gropius and other prominent U.S. schools had also secured Bauhaus personnel to either administer new design programs or teach the new international modernism as staff members.[10] It is important to keep the link by which Aalto was introduced to MIT in mind. He had by his own account come to America "mainly in connection with reconstruction plans in Finland," i.e., the housing problem growing out of the Winter War, which accounts for the Bemis Foundation's interest in sponsoring him. The press release announcing Aalto's appointment emphasized the research nature of his background—"The importance of research carried on at the Institute will be enhanced by knowledge and methods developed through research on reconstruction in Finland under Mr. Aalto's direction"[11]—and noted specifically that his presence was made possible through the cooperation of the Bemis Foundation.

The reason that Aalto could not begin the autumn term on time was

that he had just become aware, probably in a letter from Aino, that there was to be a competition for some 580 apartment units for the HAKA group that were to be located in the northeastern quarter of Helsinki. He planned to return in October just after the competition entries were due. The open competition for the HAKA housing was entered by 31 firms, including, along with Aalto, many of the architects who had joined him in creating Finland's reputation as a significant generator of modern architecture. The competition was won by a relatively new team on the Helsinki scene, that of Hugo Harmia and Woldemar Baeckman, with Ekelund and Välikangas on the team winning second prize. Hilding Ekelund by himself took third, and Ervi and Aalto both had mentions or their entries were bought.

Aalto's scheme was an interesting one, composed of four high-rise towers with a single-loaded corridor on each floor. The massing of the individual buildings was designed as a segment of a curve, or "fan arrangement," with the apartments located on the convex side of the curving plan form. The project was called "Etelä," meaning south, the general direction that the splaying apartment buildings were to face. Aalto's design, which prefigured his much acclaimed similar design for an apartment facing the harbor in Bremen, Germany,[12] was probably too Westernized in its use of 12-story blocks of flats and that is probably the reason why it did not receive any prize. This project marks Aalto's first full-blown use of the fan, or splayed shapes as a planning tool. He had employed it on the housing scheme for Stenius in a 1934 proposal, but there only the straight line forms of the buildings were located in a radial pattern responding to the contours of the shore-front site in Munkkiniemi. For the HAKA competition he not only splayed the buildings slightly in relation to each other, but the forms of the buildings themselves are fan shaped in plan. Presumably many of the apartment units were to be that shape as well, as they finally ended up in the block at Bremen.

Aalto returned to the U.S. in late September before he was scheduled to begin his first three months as professor of architecture at MIT, but the records of the school indicate that he suddenly departed for Finland on October 17.[13] This was probably due to the renewed threat of war between Finland and the Soviet Union following Germany's successes in the early part of World War II and the breakdown of the negotiated relationship between Germany and the Soviet Union. The situation was further complicated by the resignation of president Kallio on December 19, 1940,[14] making it urgent that Aalto, given the delicate balance of Finnish politics, return to his home and family at once. The complications of the war would prevent Aalto from returning to MIT until after its conclusion, and although many sources claim that he was teaching there in 1941, there is no evidence to support that.

In spite of his abbreviated stay at MIT that fall, Aalto did remain long enough to produce, along with a group of his students, a plan (299) for an idealized new town to be built in connection with Finland's industrial reconstruction. The principal evidence of this study is a single drawing, frequently published as a demonstration of Aalto's interest in housing and planning. The drawing consists of an inset plan with vignettes located around the circumference and connected by lines to the various parts of the town that they depicted. The plan itself shows a town located on an isthmus with a free-form shore line drawn in a deep, undulating line of linked circular segments. On the isthmus are four hills or areas of high ground drawn in a curiously stylized manner with the formality of concentric circular forms. The elements of the plan are distributed loosely along the contours or between the hills on the flat area of the topography. The multiple dwelling units are located on the sides of the hills while the civic center and single family houses are located on the flats. The

299. Plan for development of a model town in Finland, detail, Helsinki, 1940.

various vignettes are for the most part taken directly from Aalto's recent buildings in Finland.[15] The single family houses were the same as those for the engineers at Inkeroinen, and the stepped apartments on the hillsides were similar versions of those at Kauttua and Sunila. Aalto described this design as being constructed on biological lines.[16] This may be a reference to the fact that the apartment groupings are independent units located around the heart of the scheme, i.e., the town center. The factory is located on the periphery out of the organic system of the town design.

The overall impression made by the drawing is of a quick and simple proposal seemingly produced for an amateur public rather than for the eye of a professional or student. The drawing is usually dated 1941 but since Aalto was back in Finland before November 1, 1940, the date must be listed as 1940.[17]

World War Engulfs Finland

Following the winter of unrest and uncertainty, it must have become clear that war was imminent. This was confirmed when, following Germany's invasion of Russia in June 1941, Russia commenced aircraft bombing of urban centers in Southern Finland. Finland's military had

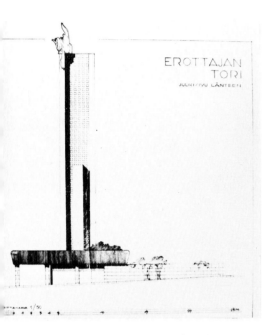

EROTTAJAN
TORI
JULKISIVU LÄNTEEN

300. Plaza competition entry for train turn-around and air-raid shelter entrance for Erottaja area, Helsinki, 1941.

been preparing to resist the Russian attack (with the help and counsel of the Germans), and the first priority was to retake the Karelian Isthmus lost during the Winter War. They did so during the summer of 1941.

Preparations were made by everyone—civilians, government, and industry—for a long war.[18] Finland, which had been in a period of depressed economy and uncertainty following the Winter War, had to reorient itself and its people to the planning of new facilities for the protection of its citizens and, after the recapture of Viipuri and the remainder of Karelia, the reconstruction of regained and war-ravaged lands. For Aalto, this consisted of involvement in his country's building programs on three levels of professional activity:[19] the design and construction of three distinctively different defensive and protective structures such as air raid shelters and hospitals; the expansion and relocation of industrial complexes, mainly those of the Gullichsens; and the planning of towns and areas to provide the need for housing and administration of the population in a time of crisis.

Air Raid Shelter Competition

Aalto's first opportunity to participate in the war effort came in May 1941 when the competition for the construction of an air raid shelter and tram plaza for Erottaja, one of the key intersections in the center of Helsinki, was announced. The designs were not due until October, three months after the war began. Of the sixteen entrants Aalto was selected as the first prize winner.[20] The jury consisted of Birger Brunila, one of the *Arkkitehti*'s most expressive journalists, Uno Ullberg, Erik Bryggman, and Hilding Ekelund, among others. In according Aalto's design the honor of first place they were almost certainly granting official recognition or sanction to their most famous colleague at a time that called for solidarity. They, along with others in the architectural/cultural community, must have been as relieved and happy as Wurster had been the

year before to know that Aalto was safe and nearby. He was, after all, Finland's only internationally prominent architect at this point. His work had been exhibited during the previous three years in New York, Copenhagen, Oslo, Zurich, and Milan.

Aalto's design for the shelter (300), which was never realized, consisted of an underground, or rather understreet, complex including a series of ventilated rooms and facilities, and a street-level entrance pavilion. The pavilion was mounted by a tall slender triangular prism of concrete with an ornamental shrub at the top. This was not merely to add beauty, but presumably to serve as an unlighted beacon to indicate the location of the shelter in the smoke and densely polluted air of a bombing attack. The Y-shaped intersection where Mannerheimintie, Esplanaadi, and Boulevardi converge, at which the shelter was to be located, was designed to permit trams to turn around or branch off the main line separately from vehicular traffic and pedestrian access to the shelter. The traffic engineering aspect of this scheme is a comprehensive treatment of those systems in conjunction with each other. The subterranean shelter space was actually built by others but was ultimately redesigned by Aalto in 1951 as a series of underground public lavatories and shops.[21]

Planning Projects for Government and Private Industry

During the war there were periods of relative calm for sections of the country and within these periods Aalto was able to apply his talents to various strategic projects for the government and for industry. In 1941 he began a master plan study (301) for Harry Gullichsen of the Kokemäki River valley, which extended from the town of the same name to the sea. This area, which surrounds the city of Pori, was once under the sea and is still considered one of Finland's prime agricultural regions. Moreoover, it is the home region of the Ahlström headquarters located in the town of Noormarkku. In conceiving a plan for the preservation and growth of this area, Aalto was able to involve himself in the most practical aspects of planning theory, specifically those of an active agrarian and distribution center and its socioeconomic life. The area to this day is base for many Ahlström factories and companies, as well as one of Finland's main sea resort areas.

This project was beneficial in preparing Aalto for participation in a limited competition for the planning of another river valley, the Oulujoki, and its relation to the port city, Oulu. Aalto and the only other participant, Bertel Strömmer, also submitted designs for a separate but related facility, the Merikoski power plant. These two projects were due in December 1942, and the results were announced the following month. Aalto was awarded the overall planning commission while Strömmer received the one for the power plant. It might seem as if Aalto had been denied what, for an architect, would be the most exciting part of the project. In this case, however, the design for the power plant only involved cosmetic architectural treatment on a technical scheme that had been predetermined, while the planning project was one of the most interesting in all of Finland. The Oulujoki River contains a long and dramatic series of cascades, one of which, in the vicinity of Oulu itself, became a site for that country's most massive concentration of hydroelectric facilities at about this time. Although the area Aalto was to deal with only included the rapids and plant controlled by the city of Oulu, his scheme did have far-reaching importance for those plants that would later be built up river. The entire scheme, begun with the founding of the Oulujoki Company in 1941, was completed in 1958.[22]

Aalto's scheme (302) involved the planning on and between a cluster of islands in the river in the center of Oulu. He zoned some of them residential, others recreational, and still others institutional, principally educational. The University of Oulu was projected for the one it now occupies. These projects which enabled Aalto to experiment with the nature of town and regional planning actually marked the beginning of his career and reputation in this field, for he had neither formal training nor practical experience in such matters before he executed the industrial estates and factories of Sunila and the Ahlström Company headed by Harry Gullichsen.

Aalto's design for the power plant (303) is reminiscent of his style during the early to midthirties and is particularly akin to the competition projects for the Tampere Railway Station and the pulp mill at Sunila. This proposal for the Merikoski plant was also essentially the same design which his protegé Aarne Ervi used in the midfifties for one of the Oulujoki's upstream plants.[23]

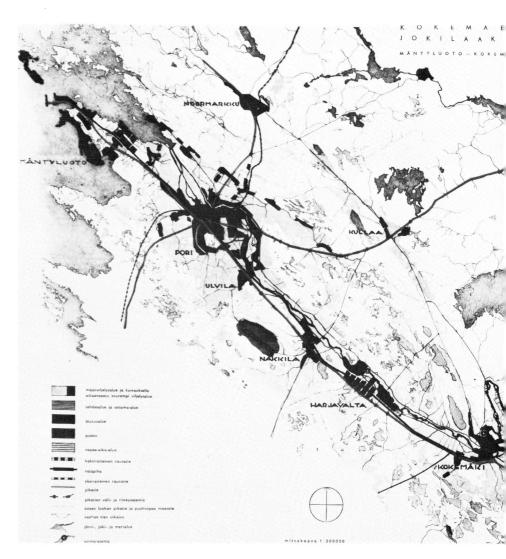

301. Master plan of Kokemäki River valley for Ahlström Co., Helsinki, 1941.

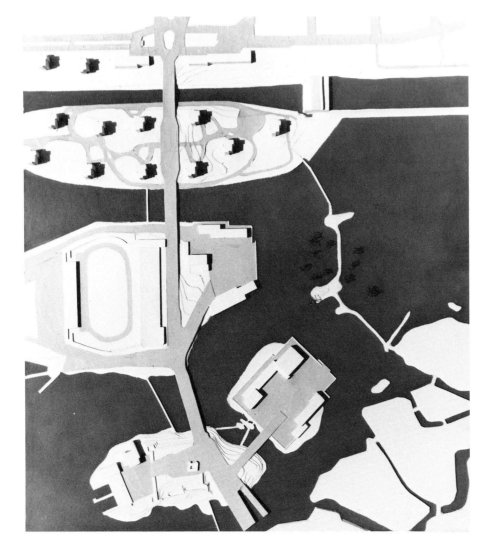

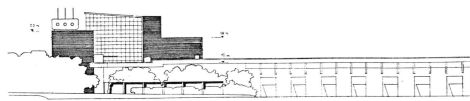

Also during this period Aalto began studies for a new town for Enso Gutzeit, the government-controlled company at Säynätsalo on an island in the lake country south of Jyväskylä. The site, only a few miles off the highway connecting that city with Southern Finland, is a hilly, lightly forested island at the northern end of one of the largest lakes in that part of the country. The plan he executed is not unlike the final plan project with which he won the competition for the town hall and center in 1949 and which was constructed in the following period.

The site design (304), finished in 1944, consisted of a town hall and apartment units located around a large triangular open space; the main building which was the town hall, was to house administrative offices, a library, meeting rooms, and shops for the village. The overall spatial concept is like the final scheme except that the town hall is actually located on the apex of the triangular space on high ground rather than at its base, on the level portion of the site.

In the plan we have Aalto's favorite plan form—staggered rectangular blocks.[24] These rows of blocks, while parallel in relationship to each other, form the two sides of the long triangular space adjoining the corresponding pathways. An echelon, not unlike that of the Viipuri Library massing, was used on the town hall design, but like the administration building at the Technical University at Otaniemi designed some years later, there are connecting links between the staggered masses which form courtyards. The design of the site is that now-familiar form in his work identified as the fan shape. This type of land shape formed by staggered blocks was shown in material presented to the CIAM conference in Brussels in 1930 for the garden houses.

The scheme for the town hall as it was built was later changed to include a fully enclosed courtyard, but both have much in common. They are variations of another one of those Aalto motifs, except these are based on the idea of a Roman

302. Top: Town plan competition entry, model of town center, showing rapids and islands, Oulu, 1943.

303. Above: Power plant competition entry for Merikoski, elevation, Oulu, 1943.

304. Opposite page above: Village plan for Enso Gutzeit Co., plant, Säynätsalo, 1942–1944.

305. Opposite page below: Group of Finnish architects touring in Germany, 1943; Aalto left center.

atrium, which influenced him from his earliest days as a young designer.[25]

This period in Aalto's life was a difficult one because the state of war that existed between Russia and Finland was extended to Russia's allies, and on December 9, 1941, two days after the Japanese attacked Pearl Harbor, Great Britain declared war on Finland. No actual fighting ever occurred between the troops of those two countries. The U.S. never issued a declaration of war on Finland, but it must have saddened Aalto to be even marginally on the opposite side from the friends and colleagues abroad to whom he had appealed for help for his homeland during the Winter War.[26]

As allies of the Nazi regime, Finnish architects were placed in an awkward position during the war. However, despite Aalto's claim to the contrary, he had at least some cultural contact with architects of the Third Reich when in 1943 he, Suttinen, and Ervi and Rewell made a trip to Berlin at the invitation of Ernst Neufeurt. They were taken around to see the architecture of Nazi Germany and introduced to sculptors, artists, and architects working there at the time (305).

During 1943, Aalto continued to produce designs for Ahlström and other industry-related sites,[27] but little of significance was presented for him to undertake until 1944 when he executed, together with Albin Stark, a design for a projected town center in Avesta, Sweden,[28] similar to the one proposed for Säynätsalo two years before. The general idea for Aalto's proposal was that of an open courtyard that was enclosed only around three-fourths of its perimeter, the missing quarter being at one of the corners. The geometric organization is the most significant aspect of the drawing (306). The complex is composed of two major masses, presumably to house the places of assembly and the library, linked in the form of a slightly rotated quadrangle joined by gently angled, nonorthogonal, one-story wings. The tension between this

subtle rotation and joining of the buildings' elements and the rigid geometry of the rectangular town square open space gives a feeling reminiscent of such Italian Mannerist compositions as Giulio Romano's Palazzo del Té in Mantua,[29] where the parts and detailing are out of alignment, purposely set off from the regular geometry of the basic scheme. In the project for Avesta, Aalto capitalized on the nature of the surroundings, creating interest by playing on the geometric

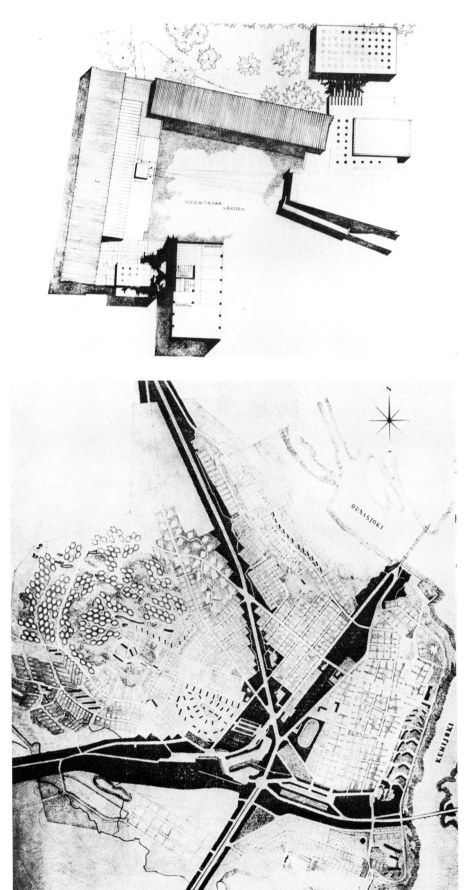

perceptions of the building's audience.

This project, along with the Säynätsalo plan, is the first appearance of the town center scheme that Aalto evolved through various projects from the end of the war to his death. The large expressed masses of the elements of the Avesta project's plan, splayed or angled according to their internal functioning, are directly reflected in all those executed later. The subtle geometric alignment was used in many of them as well. The design departures embodied in these planning and urban design techniques grow directly out of the developments that Aalto had made in narrower architectural terms over the previous decade in bringing himself out of the International Style.

In 1944, the last year of the war, Aalto was actively engaged in designing for industry as well as for the Finnish state.[30] He was involved in work on eleven different projects of varying size and type, more than in most pre-war years. He was, in a real sense, an important figure in architecture in his own homeland, perhaps for the first time.

This prestige was reflected in the role he was to assume in leading a team of architects responsible for the town and regional planning of the areas devastated by the war. When the Germans withdrew from Lapland in the autumn of 1944, that region was in a critical state and Aalto and his colleagues began, even before the war ended, to plan for its rebuilding. The central focus of their efforts was the design and rebuilding of Rovaniemi, the capital city of that somewhat desolate region, located near the Arctic Circle. The scheme has been published many times and is dated 1945, the year of the study's first stage of presentation.[31]

The study (307) has been the subject of much praise and is always cited as evidence of Aalto's keenly developed ability in the area of town planning. The radiating open spaces, often likened to a star or the antlers of a reindeer, are for the most part sited along the traditional

306. Top: Town center competition entry, model, Avesta, Sweden, 1944. Architects: Alvar Aalto and Albin Stark.

307. Above: Town plan for rebuilding and development, plan, Rovaniemi, 1944–1945. Architects: Alvar Aalto with planning team.

paths of access to Rovaniemi before the war. The addition of the open spaces along those routes allowed for Rovaniemi's future expansion and gives the plan its basic character. Many facilities have, in fact, recently been added to the town which only in the last few years has neared its ultimate projection as a regional center for culture and distribution.

One of the most significant departures for planning in Finland shown on this drawing (308) is the inclusion of North American style single family houses, each complete with a garage and driveway, located on adjoining elongated hexagonal-shaped plots. The house and garage are drawn at right angles to each other but parallel to one of the six sides of the plot, and each plot is joined to its neighbor on one or more edges, forming a hexagonal module. This type of suburban development had been observed by Aalto on his pre-war trips to the U.S., and judging from its inclusion here, it must have impressed him. Not only the style but the geometry as well was the result of his visit. He had seen the Hanna house by Frank Lloyd Wright at Palo Alto when Wurster and others were guiding him through the Bay Area of northern California.[32] The hexagonal plots, joined in almost every case in a different manner, give a wide variety of overall land coverage to the residential development. This kind of systemic diversification was always one of Aalto's major themes—the type of weapon he used to fight the oppressive regularity of normal industrialized housing.

In addition to the planning projects begun during 1944, Aalto undertook industrial expansion for both the Ahlström and Strömberg factories. For Ahlström he designed a machine shop for its headquarters at Karhula that was completed in 1945, and for the Strömberg appliance company he began a meter factory and housing estate, both of which were completed in 1947.

The interesting aspect of these two building projects is that the meter factory is executed in a rather

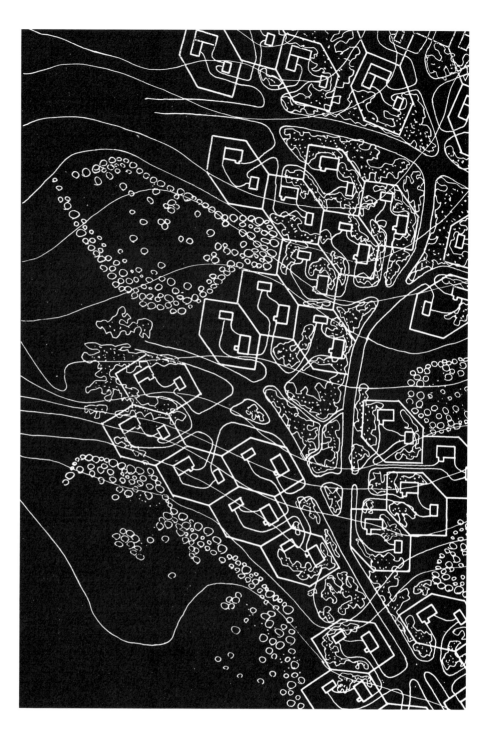

low-key International Style while the housing is composed of two-story units with wooden siding and pole aesthetic very much like that of the housing at the Anjala plant in Inkeroinen.[33] The juxtaposition of these two diverse elements to express two different types of utilization further underscores Aalto's persistently reaffirmed theory that people require humanized architecture. He chose to realize that quality through the romantic modernist development of the wooden vernacular ar-

308. Single family house neighborhood development, plan, Rovaniemi, 1944–1945.

chitecture of Finland's traditional past.

The war had taken its toll of Finland and of Aalto especially.[34] It had halted his efforts to develop international communication among architects and others who, he had hoped, would be inclined to speak out against the International Style, as it had come to be known by that time, and the predictable regularity that withheld variety and interest from the modern interpretation of architecture.

The year 1944 was a year of mixed emotions for the Finns. It brought them much grief since the final year of the war spelled defeat, but finally the relief of settlement and peace. At about the time of the Normandy invasion the Soviets shrewdly chose to retake Karelia and did so with surprising ease. But soon the resolution of the war was imminent, and it became clear that the Russians did not intend to occupy any more of Finland than that which they felt necessary for strategic defense. After the peace treaty was signed in Moscow on September 19, Aalto was once more able to turn his thoughts to establishing himself in America.

Of all the immediate post-war commissions, the one that perhaps best shows Aalto's consistency is the addition to the Ahlström sawmill at Varkaus in late 1944. The company had outgrown the operating capacity of the existing plant, a shed building with bow-string roof trusses, and to this shed Aalto added a high penthouse structure to house the incoming log conveyors and the outgoing removal conveyor (309). The penthouse was formed as a grouping of free-form volumes with striated surfaces, similar in manner to forms that appeared (although on a more purely decorative scale) on such pre-war projects as the Villa Mairea and both fair pavilions. The structure, whose striated wooden surfaces resemble (as others have observed) the board and batten of traditional vernacular sheds,[35] is held in place by a metal angle structure and rests on the existing load points of the original building. It has been said that the grouping of the forms that make up the penthouse expresses and was inspired by the functioning of the sawmill process.[36] While this is probably true to an extent, the composition, with its particular proportions and shapes had a certain pure abstract and organic geometry in itself characteristic of Aalto's work at this period.

The Varkaus sawmill, with its freeforms and interlocking volumes and projections, is clearly akin to the Villa Mairea, also, in fact, an Ahlström building, and while one cannot assume that Aalto was consciously trying to create a "company style," the two buildings must at that time have stood out very clearly from other contemporary architecture and given the distinct sense of belonging to the same family.

The aesthetic of the building cannot truly be described as industrial because similar forms had been used by Aalto in the nonindustrial Villa Mairea and both fair pavilions. However, in this return to the freeforms of the pre-war years, Aalto did extend their application on an ambitious scale, seizing the opportunity offered by a building that contained a more-than-average amount of industrial complexity and enabling him to achieve a final expression of extraordinary style and even some complexity.

It had been industrial buildings that had made his career financially stable in the midthirties when he concentrated all his efforts on Sunila in order to establish his reputation in industrial circles. Now Aalto was able to take advantage of the Varkaus commission and the opportunity it offered him to project once again a striking image of his new style within the industrial community. He had depended on industrial commissions, especially those for Ahlström for 10 years, and at the end of the war it was evident that that would be the case for another decade.

It was not, however, until the spring of 1945 that he began to chart his return to the U.S. and his part-time post of Research Professor in Architecture at MIT.[37] By June he had written William Wurster, who in the meantime had become Dean of the MIT School of Architecture, to help secure a permanent visa for him and his family.[38] He then evidently planned a significant change in his life. The war had changed the face of Europe and undoubtedly Aalto had changed too, but at the end of the war he seemed even more prepared to take up where he left off in 1940.

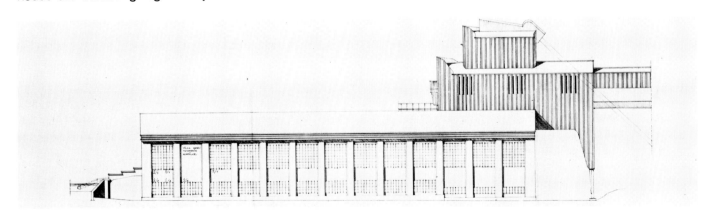

309. Sawmill extension for Ahlström Co., Varkaus, 1944–1945.

19
Return to MIT

Teaching Post

During the pre-war period Aalto, like many visitors to the U.S., had been impressed not only by the relative wealth of the private educational and research institutions but also by the level of involvement on the part of leading members of society in the making of a new type of social order under the Roosevelt administration's New Deal. He was probably remembering the flexibility of the pre-war American economy when he wrote to Dean Wurster requesting information about his forthcoming stay in the autumn of 1945, for he boldly suggested that MIT, along with the U.S. Office of War Information, might sponsor a "journey" for him to survey war damage in European countries.[1] It would, he asserted, be a relevant subject for a series of lectures he proposed to present on his arrival in Cambridge. His letter was enthusiastic, and he nearly overran the pages with ideas he proposed to introduce as part of his teaching responsibilities. Travel between Finland and the major part of Europe in 1945 was slow and uncertain; one was required either to pass through Stockholm by air or to take a circuitous route over sea and land through southern Russia. The extravagant air passage his proposed European junket would necessitate was not fundable under MIT's strict budget.[2] Moreover the nature of Aalto's participation in the school, as outlined by Wurster, was more that of a visiting studio critic

than a lecturer on theory or research topics, although the option to experiment with his future role in the school was left open.

He arrived to start teaching when the fall term began on November 5, 1945, and little out of the usual was recorded during the term. However, on his Christmas break he traveled to Spring Green, Wisconsin, to visit Frank Lloyd Wright. He was clearly impressed by what he found at Taliesin and was so enthusiastic that on his return to MIT, he wrote Wright and asked if he would take his son, then studying engineering in Helsinki, into the fellowship training program[3] the following autumn. This, however, never came to pass.[4] In fact Aalto never succeeded in bringing any of his family to America while he was teaching at Cambridge. The rising transportation costs made it unfeasible.

Starting with the next academic year and continuing through the late forties, Aalto spent increasingly less time teaching at MIT.[5] The reason was that by the autumn of 1946 he had been chosen as architect for the new seniors' dormitory, and it was thought to be in the best interest of all for Aalto to confine himself during his limited time in Cambridge to work on that project.[6]

Seniors Dormitory (Baker House)

Basically, Aalto divided his time at MIT into semi-annual visits while the construction and planning were un-

derway, and each of these visits was less than six weeks in length. Even without the abbreviated schedule it would have been necessary, for legal reasons, for him to associate with an American firm. The firm selected was Perry, Dean and Shaw of Boston[7] and they, along with a representative from Aalto's own office,[8] produced the design drawings and contract documents under Aalto's periodic supervision.

The Baker House, as it was named on completion, is an undulating, six-story wall of dormitory rooms located on a single-loaded corridor system with an entrance floor and connected pavilion devoted to common functions of student residential life. Like most of his buildings, it was the subject of endless soft pencil sketches by Aalto himself. It is in these studies that one can perceive the basic idea evolving for the development of the building. The earliest sketches show that the famous undulating wall was not embodied in the original concept but rather evolved in the process of refining the siting of the building. This, as well as the emergence of a full range of Aalto's textural and volumetric manipulations, can be detected in examining the drawings Aalto produced in the various stages of design.

The building is situated on the north bank of the Charles River facing Memorial Drive in Cambridge, Massachusetts, and from the beginning was envisioned as having a di-

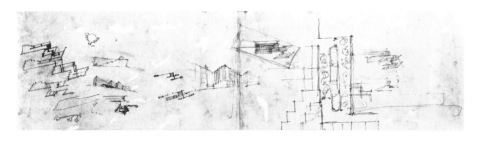

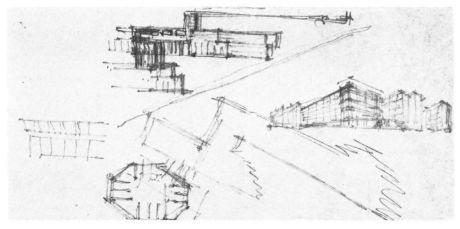

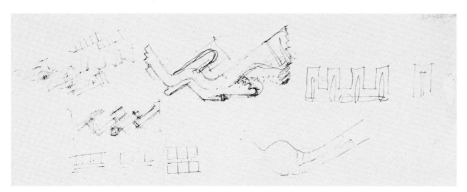

310. Top: MIT seniors dormitory, first state, sketch, Cambridge, Mass., 1946.

311. Middle: MIT seniors dormitory, second state, sketch, Cambridge, Mass., 1946.

312. Center: MIT seniors dormitory, third state, sketch, Cambridge, Mass., 1946.

313. Above: MIT seniors dormitory, fourth state, sketch, Cambridge, Mass., 1947.

314. Opposite page above: MIT seniors dormitory, fourth state, sketch perspective, Cambridge, Mass., 1947.

315. Opposite page below: MIT seniors dormitory, final state, sketch perspective, Cambridge, Mass., 1947.

rect relationship with the river. The first state (310) shows a wealth of ideas based on the central theme of a pavilionized grouping of dormitory rooms, connected by long single-loaded corridors. It was to be oriented so that the windows of the rooms on those links faced in a southerly direction toward the river. A thumbnail perspective of this treatment in the center of the drawing shows that at the outset he conceived of the project in terms of a laterally layered arrangement, or wings arranged in echelon like many of his previous buildings. The right end of the sketch shows that the north side of the building, adjacent to the rectangular automobile-turnaround at the entrance, was also to have a stepped treatment that was orthogonal with the line of the riverbank. The building, because of its proximity to the main buildings at MIT, was to be entered from the north on the side opposite the river front. The two-point perspective sketch gives the distinct impression of being at an angle to the viewer and therefore to the lines of the lot itself.[9] It is likely that it was through this type of constructed view that Aalto first entertained the interesting idea of turning the entire building at an angle to the plot in contrast to the other buildings on the drive which were basically parallel to the river.

Turning the structure at an angle enabled Aalto to give most if not all dormitory rooms on the single-loaded corridor some view of the river and all a southern exposure, thus relieving the gray severity of northern winters. Aalto said that the curvilinear version was conceived to counteract what he considered to be "the powerful and inhuman monotony. . . [of] the ground plan of a normal American city with its checkerboard netting."[10] This statement may not have reflected his thinking at the earliest stage of the dormitory's development, but the possibility and inherent virtues of the nonorthogonal siting must have struck Aalto immediately upon composing the perspective sketch.

By the second stage (311) the complex was firmly turned at an angle from the drive, with the clustered or pavilioned rooms arranged in a loosely orthogonal overall plan, presumably to wed the geometries of both the river bend and the angled residence wings. The perspective shows the same staggered or sawtoothed profile, but the ends of the wings are staggered also, giving a rounded impression to the whole view from the river.

Much of this effect is also evident in the third state (312), but here the stagger, or wings, have been separated by a short link and the cluster has assumed an even more prominent position. The clusters are located at the river ends of two of the residence wings and have the rooms arranged radially in rounded tower pavilions. These towers, shown in a sketch near the lower edge of the drawing, reveal the first germ of Aalto's ultimate curvilinear line. But even though it was expressed as a planning motif, the rounded form is not integral with the overall profile of the building. After three different stages Aalto had still not reached the final form of the design. This is characteristic of his working method during this period. His habit was to patiently digest the

nature of the problem while he was producing designs for the solution and to progress through constant reevaluation and an ever-tightening series of ideas to the highly original designs that characterized most of his work. The drawing containing the fourth and final plan state (313) shows just how much he retained from all the previous states.

Basically the plan consists of a two-part building—the flowing, double-curved wing of residential cells oriented toward the river and sun and the adjoining circulation system of halls and stairs along the north face. From the central convex curve, the main independently articulated element, the student common room, projects into the triangular garden inscribed by the rotated building and Memorial Drive. To the west, at the extreme end of the residence wing, a staggered end cluster is still shown with a large central hall space outside the rooms. Other sketches on the same sheet also reveal that Aalto was still interested in an echelon arrangement of freestanding rectangular volumes,[11] one of them accented with a cylindrical tower facing the athletic fields to the

north. The same sketch seems to indicate that the east end was also staggered, but there is no sign of any central space.

The perspective sketch (314) that closely follows this development shows the south side of the building with a form exactly as it was finally constructed. The details of the facade, however, were not finalized and developments continued.[12] Here the straight portions of the dormitory wing were horizontally delineated. This may indicate the presence of sun shades, but the representation of large areas of vinelike materials (315), probably ivy, suggests that their true function was textural—such as a trellis to support the vines. The facade also seems to be rendered with a series of vertical lines which may have been intended as supports for the trellis but which gave the facade an articulated effect. On the final form, as shown in an architectural model (316), the trellis has been moved to the central section spanning all three of the curved portions of the facade. The basic wall material is shown as brick.

This Aalto took from buildings of

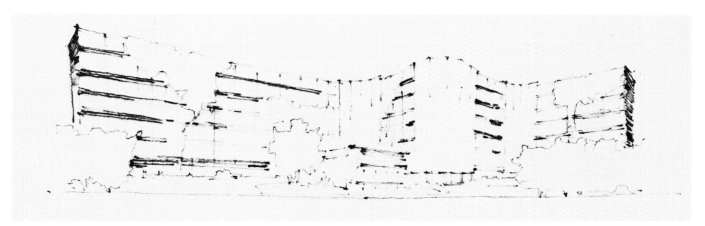

205

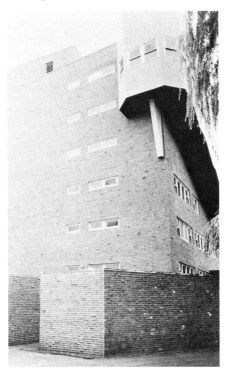

316. Top: MIT seniors dormitory, final state, model, Cambridge, Mass., 1947.

317. Above: MIT seniors dormitory, corner of north face in completed building, Cambridge, Mass., 1949.

318. Above right: MIT seniors dormitory, stairway glazing in completed building, Cambridge, Mass., 1949.

319. Opposite page: MIT seniors dormitory, final state, elevation, Cambridge, Mass., 1949.

many of America's older universities in which brick was traditionally employed as a finish material and on which ivy usually grew, sheathing the facade in a natural material like that drawn by Aalto for the seniors' dormitory. This was Aalto's first use of natural-color brick as a sheathing fabric on a nonindustrial building. Aalto's awakening to the potential of this old material probably grew out of his travels in the U.S. and England where brick had been used for centuries not only structurally but also on exposed exterior surfaces. On most American university buildings, however, the vines engage di-

rectly to the wall. What Aalto apparently had in mind in specifying a trellis was a modern more architectonic interpretation of this traditional motif although in the final version he found such a device to be impractical. Instead he opted for a texturized brick surface to supply the romantic quality that he clearly desired for the university building.

This particular textured brick surface is one that has been used by many designers and builders to give interest to the brick walls of single family houses and apartment groups.[13] It is composed of a dark red Flemish bond with random clinkers and fused double bricks, some preshattered, projecting from the wall to provide texture and shadow and to break up the surface. It should be mentioned here that Aalto admired Frank Lloyd Wright's use of brick and had heard him lecture on its beauty and economy as a building material.[14]

Of all the unique motifs featured in this building, perhaps the most influential single aspect, and therefore the most important, is the long straight-run stair (317) stretching across the northern facade. As the main access stairs in many of his buildings Aalto had been employing a multilevel, straight-run stair as a primary architectural element beginning with the Turun Sanomat plant and offices nearly two decades earlier. In Baker House, however, he used that type of stair as a main exterior design element for the

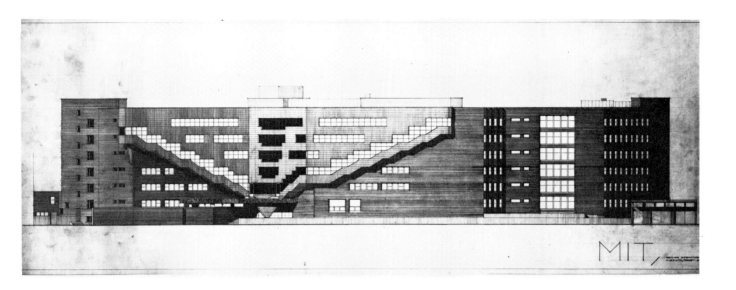

first time. Here each floor is virtually the same in plan, but a variety of hallway shapes is created, primarily because the landing, entrance, and lounge are in a different location on each floor.

The entrance facade on the north side is a curious arrangement having many shifting planes, corners of varying size, and irregular fenestration, but it is the massing of the projecting stair volume with its lower edges directly expressing the line of the straight-run stair that dominates the entire composition of the facade. The projecting volume, which houses not only the stair but also a lounge for each floor, was originally meant to be clad with copper sheets. Eventually, however, the price was scaled down and the finish material was specified as large ceramic tiles, something like those he employed in many later buildings. In the final building, much to Aalto's dissatisfaction, the surface, which was constructed by others, materialized as a pink stuccoed wall.

The fenestration (318) of the stairway itself is perhaps the most unorthodox aspect of the dormitory design. A continuous row of wooden, triple-sash, double-hung windows, located at the baluster line of the stair, is offset at each landing and linked by one double sash at the midpoint of each run of treads and risers. It has been shown in a recently published drawing of the north elevation (319) that the entire

area was designed as a continuous metal sash window unit, analogous to strip windows. Strip windows were used above in the individual floor lounges which also were housed in the mass.

The most curious detail of this fenestration was the triangular fixed sash called for under the double-hung sash on the slope of the baluster. This produced a general rhythm of three-to-three-to-one units stepping unevenly along with the runs and landings of the stair. The great proportion of this strange glass wall system is reminiscent of removable glazing systems found on summer houses in the Baltic region.

The building that finally emerged from these design drawings was a compromise but Aalto occasionally referred to it with fondness.[15] One of the points that he would particularly single out was the variety in size and shape of the students' rooms.[16] This type of variety, in fact, is one of the qualities that in later years he would include in his definition of flexibility in building.

The building was in the full process of construction in October 1948, with some decisions as to material, texture, and fenestration yet to be decided, when Aalto had to desert his teaching duties and the dormitory's development and return to Helsinki where Aino had been stricken with cancer. He remained constantly near her in Helsinki until her death in January 1949.

Aalto only returned once more to

teach at MIT and that was for a few weeks in October 1950[17] as a sort of visiting critic. In February of the following year he permanently resigned his position as Research Professor at the Institute.[18] Altogether the total time Aalto spent at MIT amounted to less than one academic year. The fact that most studies of Aalto inevitably include this position of professorial rank as an achievement is a somewhat misleading claim. It is fair to say that many people remember his presence there fondly and are gratified that they had a chance to be exposed to him as a teacher and a colleague, as well as a colorful and vital human being.[19] It is too much, however, to attach any significance to a nine-month career even for such a great and unique architectural thinker as Aalto. The prestige of an international teaching post probably helped him bury his regrets that he was not given a professorship in his own country when he applied for it, but the enthusiasm that he showed in 1940 when first hired and again in 1945 when he entertained the idea of establishing an office in the U.S. soon faded. Like many active designers his practice came first, and it is evident that the time-consuming trips to teach a few months, or sometimes only a few weeks at a time, must have created many obstacles to his burgeoning practice in Finland and provided little stimulation as he progressed into his maturity at midcareer.

20
Aalto at Midcareer

When Aalto died in May 1976 he had been practicing as an architect for fifty-four years and when Aino died in January 1949 he had reached the exact midpoint of his career.[1] During the first half he developed from a young provincial, impressed with and operating under the influence of a classical dogma, to become one of the chief exponents of the International Style, or Functionalism, as it was called in Scandinavia. His dissatisfaction and, to some extent, failure with that style encouraged him to seek other means of expressing the spirit of his homeland and his own personal sense of relationship with the environment and the world. By 1949 he had transformed his architecture into a personal and romantic modern style that set him apart from the other Functionalists and modernists.

When Aino passed away, he was on the verge of yet another departure in theoretical development that, like his earlier one, would soon be put into practice.

Aino Aalto

It is difficult to evaluate Aino Marsio Aalto's (320) contribution to the partnership so often listed in the credit lines of competition reviews and publications of their work. Scandinavia in general and Finland in particular have been associated with an early emergence of equal roles for women in the working world. Even more developed is the role of Scandinavian women as fully qualified members of the architectural world. From the time of their marriage, Aino and Alvar are generally listed as equal authors, but there are some significant exceptions which point to a certain division of roles. The Villa Flora was credited only to Aino, while several projects and competitions fail to mention her at all. This, however, may be due in part to the editors of the publishing journals. The most troubling attribution is that which centers around the work produced for Artek. Aino is credited not only with administering the firm, but also with designing a number of the objects produced. It is particularly in this area, when it was a matter of crafts and furnishings, as, for example, in the interior design for the Savoy Restaurant, that she was frequently credited alone.[2] In general Aalto's name was left off these, while Aino's was omitted from some of the architectural commissions.

She is remembered by many of their international friends as a quiet woman who was the stable background against which Aalto's more flamboyant personality was free to flourish.[3] Being four years his senior, she may have had a slightly different perspective on their life, but she seemed above all to be supportive of Aalto and his lifestyle. If she was a guiding light, she must have left a large, vacant area in Aalto's life when she passed away.[4]

Evaluation

In spite of Alvar Aalto's extraordinary development as an architect in the thirties and forties, he was not generally recognized as a truly unique modern architect in the first half of his career. Siegfried Giedion only listed Aalto as a modern master in 1954, more than two decades after he had first become familiar with his works and about fifteen years after he visited them. His career had begun in a time when the world was experiencing sweeping changes and in a country that had more than a nominal desire to express its independence. His development as an architect had, like his homeland, experienced widely conflicting trends in influence, but in a country of independent isolationists he became an internationally minded protagonist of the International Style, later reverting somewhat to the opposite position.[5]

Aalto above all was resourceful, and in two areas he was to use his training and character to his own advantage. Not only was he able to digest and assimilate what he was taught and all that he observed, but his fundamentally dynamic personality fueled the constant promotional efforts he made in the furtherance of his career. In establishing contacts and friends he traveled widely with few resources at hand to do so. In the early years, this was mainly to observe buildings, view environments, and meet people all

of which would reinforce the thoughts he held that were alien to the traditions of his homeland. In later years it was to spread his reputation and seek commissions.

Both as a theoretician and a writer[6] he tended to be withdrawn and even secretive. He did give lectures but for the most part they consisted in slides and illustrations of his own work that didn't require exact, on-the-spot intellectualizations. In his research and reconnaissance he was not only lucky but brilliantly astute in finding the right sources; architecture is basically an imitative art and he knew just what to borrow.

Aalto's career encompassed the widest imaginable range of architectural activity and there is satisfactory evidence that he could muster the resources and propose, with an extraordinary sense, just what should be expressed for a particular building and how it would create the most interest for those who lived and worked in it. He also had enormous self-confidence that he could create buildings that would be unique. What is more he had a wide range of activities besides architecture. He designed furniture, organized exhibitions, and took part in Artek's promotion of modern arts and crafts for the home.

Specifically, in the first half of his professional career—the twenty-seven years between his graduation and Aino's death—he exhibited a rare consideration for all the environmental aspects of architectural design. His observance of technical principles in the areas of ventilation, heating, lighting, acoustics, solar orientation; his understanding of natural site qualities, of the necessity for privacy, and his consideration for people's feelings, were probably not rivaled by any architect in the twentieth century, with the exception of Frank Lloyd Wright.[7]

His particular way of dealing with the technical side of these considerations often led to unorthodox collections of forms; the result was an architectural expression very different from that of his contemporaries. His career had developed in a time when construction methods were traditional. Stucco was the established Baltic surface technique, and when the white surfaces of the International Style began to appear in his work, they were executed as in other countries of Western Europe, through the medium of smooth white stucco. Brick was seldom used in Finnish architecture except in industrial buildings. Aalto, probably through his observation of vernacular and monumental brick architecture in England and America in the late thirties saw that the material could be used in various combinations to create rich effects and textural interest like that of his Baker House dormitory and later buildings until it was replaced by what has been referred to as his "second white period."[8] The buildings in his middle period were executed in brick, but they are not just remakes of those found in another culture. In executing the Pension Bank and Otaniemi buildings and the House of Culture for Finland's Communist party, he was able to bring to them not only the programmatic translations of the forms already in his repertoire, but he also went forward and developed his own individual, local techniques and his own manipulation of brick texture and details.

The buildings of this period tend to be based on rather simple ideas of arrangement that, in the main, are worked and reworked until the final design is revealed by adding (as in the development of the Villa Mairea) progressively more elaborate features and details that become the outward essence of the building when constructed. The considerations of environment, while in his mind from the beginning, only first appear in the middle phases of design development.

Aalto's buildings must be characterized in two basic ways: firstly, the rational spirit with which he respected the requirements of the program and the needs of the human beings who would use the building, and secondly the forms and physical aspects with which he chose to express that spirit. Having been one of the major architects who helped spread the influence of rationalism in Scandinavia, he tired of the movement's puritanical nature quite early, saying:

It is not the rationalization itself which was wrong in the first and now past period of Modern architecture. The wrongness lies in the fact that the rationalization has not gone deep enough. Instead of fighting rational mentality, the newest phase of Modern architec-ture tries to project rational methods from the technical field out to human and psychological fields.[9]

He didn't feel that this was in conflict with the early history of Functionalism but was only an edification of it. By the forties Functionalism as a theoretical base had disappeared from his work. In his working method of the forties the big, soft pencil that he held loosely to touch the paper in a deliberate shaking motion, blurred the crisp, rational forms that had been so attractive to him in Turku, Paimio, and Viipuri. Later he was perhaps able to look more closely at this and said:

The social, human and technical demands which are found alongside psychological factors and which concern each individual and each group, their rhythm and the effect they have on each other, are so numerous that they form a maze which cannot be worked by rational methods.[10]

He had striven in the late twenties for the firm establishment and acceptance in Finland of the basically foreign style of rational construction. His style in the thirties, however, was an amalgam of those rationalizing tendencies which he later criticized, together with an emotional sense of how the building would be experienced by the user. His style, moreover, was influential. Pauli Blomstedt's entry in the Kotka town hall competition, praised for its Constructivist extremes, was taken from Aalto's winning project in the Paimio competition the previous year.[11] Aalto's buildings of this period were similar in detail, perhaps because his feelings toward the users could not be established in a theoretical sense as easily as those of the program per se. His design style changed slowly, like his outlook, tending toward the mellow, soft, and outwardly informal buildings of his middle years. Aalto's work in its basic form combined the sober organization of rational planning and construction with motifs taken from his collected repertoire of domestic traditions and imported techniques.

Aalto's career was long and prolific. Before 1949, in addition to some sixty projects that never reached the contract stage, he produced over 100 buildings ranging in size from a weekend house to giant industrial complexes. With the exception of Le Corbusier and Wright, few architects in the twentieth century have produced as many projects and buildings as Aalto. Yet he is still being characterized by those buildings from the thirties that earned him respect as a truly modern architect. Paimio, the Viipuri Library, Turun Sanomat, and perhaps Sunila in that order are the buildings for which he is remembered. It is true that some of his later buildings have been praised highly, and within architectural circles, it seems that nearly every Aalto buff has his own obscure favorites; but these four buildings alone have caused his name to be passed down to succeeding generations of architectural enthusiasts and students as a key developer of thought and form in buildings in this century.

21
First Helsinki Buildings

During the period of construction of the seniors' dormitory at MIT and his teaching involvement there, Aalto was busy at home with the design and construction of housing and factories for his industrial clients. In 1946 he had participated in an open competition for the town hall at Nynäshamn, Sweden.[1] His entry, called "Song of the Pines," won no prize. At the same time he produced a design in collaboration with Albin Stark for a seven-story apartment building in Nynäshamn. In 1947 he produced design projects for the Johnson Company headquarters in Avesta, Sweden, and designed a laundry and sauna for the Strömberg factory at Vaasa. He began the comprehensive master plan in the area surrounding Imatra to accommodate the Enso-Gutzeit facilities and a population of 100,000. He also commenced designs for Enso-Gutzeit's factory at Säynätsalo.[2] In addition to these industrial commissions, he produced a design for the United States Information Services Library in Helsinki.

The year 1948 was a pivotal one for Aalto. Not only did he receive the commission for the Engineer's House in Helsinki, but he participated in two major competitions that would both yield him commissions and elevate him to a level of national prestige that he had not previously known. Sadly these designs, begun with Aino, would be finished long after her death.

Pension Bank Competition

The competition for the National Public Pension Institute headquarters, to be located in Helsinki, drew no less than forty-two entries. The roster of entrants numbered the names of nearly every architect of quality in Finland. The jury included Erkki Huttunen, Väinö Tuukkanen, Aulis Blomstedt, and Yrjö Lindegren.[3] Aalto won first prize with his motto "Forum Redivivum,"[4] over the competition of a host of younger colleagues. Among the other prize winners and mentions, nearly all of whom had worked for Aalto at one time or another, were Viljo Rewell, Heikki Siren, Ragnar Ypyä, and Aarne Ervi.

At the time of this competition the site (321) for the Pension Bank headquarters was on the west side of Mannerheimintie, opposite Töölö Bay to the east, on the hillside now occupied by the Inter-Continental and Hesperia hotels and the Air Terminal. Like the final site further to the north, along the same line of travel, although larger to permit a larger program, it was a trapezoidal-shaped plot bordered by streets on all sides. In his now familiar fashion, Aalto provided an alternate to his proposed scheme, labeling the second motto simply "Forum Redivivum/B." Both schemes solved the basic program in the same manner. B, however, incorporated into its site a small parcel (on the block south along Mannerheim-

intie) to be linked to the main plot by bridging over the street at the second-story line. By doing this Aalto was able to orient the complex away from Mannerheimintie, splaying it so that its axis is no longer quite parallel to that of the main street. Essentially, however, both schemes recognize that the straight orientation of Mannerheimintie is the main consideration.

The primary entry (322), labeled simply "Forum Redivivum," is a pinwheel arrangement of three large volumes linked and connected by lower wings. The three major elements, compositionally, are the Pension Bank proper, a twelve-story office building, and a concert hall for approximately 500 people. These sit in an asymmetrical balance around three sides of a two-level entrance plaza along the main street. Projecting from the rear of the concert hall, toward Töölönkatu, the rear street, a block of flats for Pension Bank workers is indicated.[5] At the northeast corner of the site is shown a garden atop the parking garage. The low wings connecting the main elements contained shops, restaurants, and other dependencies and auto parking beneath the broad, tile-surfaced decks of the upper plaza.

Both the overall composition (323) of the grouping of this project, so responsive to its sloping site, and its varied massing show a strategic recognition of the view

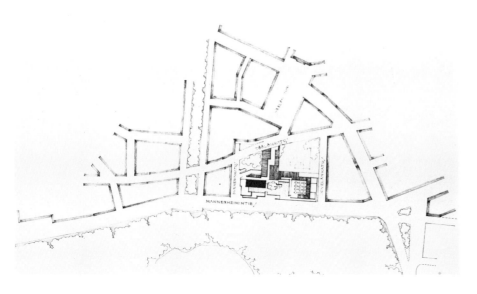

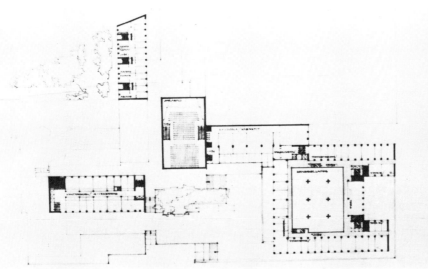

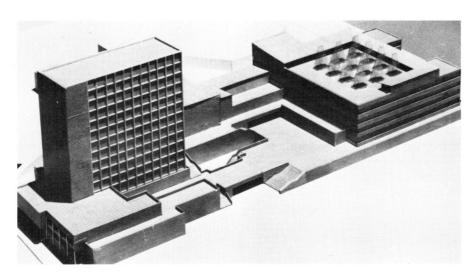

321. Top: National pension bank competition entry, scheme A, site plan in Töölö area, Helsinki, 1948.

322. Middle: National pension bank competition entry, scheme A, plan, Helsinki, 1948.

323. Above: National pension bank competition entry, scheme A, model, Helsinki, 1948.

from Mannerheimintie as one approaches from the center of Helsinki. However, it is the architecture of the large, five-story Pension Bank block (324) itself that is the most dramatically new expression of Aalto's ideas. All the buildings are shown clad in dark red brick, his first use of that material on any building of civic importance in Finland. With some few exceptions, it was a unique material for that type of use in Finland.[6]

The general spatial concept of the Pension Bank building (325) called for a large interior volume four stories high to be ringed with offices on balconies above and around all sides. The space was designed to be lighted by twelve large, mutifaceted skylight lenses in the ceiling, the entire arrangement supported on six massive cruciform piers with a reverse taper. The sheathing of the building is a continuous strip-windowed brick facade. Although the interior volume was much reduced in grandeur, the general scheme of this building is quite like the building as constructed in 1956. The triple-glazed skylight lenses projecting both high above the roof and deeply below the ceiling are a conscious attempt to create an indoor environment for the cold climate of the region that would be equivalent to that in southern latitudes of more open skies.[7] He employed this detail in many of his later buildings where he wanted a large interior volume for public nonassembly use. Each of the skylights in the Pension Bank is contained on a one-story-high coffer to prevent the direct rays of the sun from penetrating to the interior space.

Aalto's alternate B scheme (326) included the same basic buildings in generally the same manner but proposed to incorporate an adjacent block to the south into the site thus extending the complex to the main boulevard of Töölö district which adjoined Mannerheimintie at a right angle and from there ran straight up the hill to the west. Extending the site to Hesperiankatu enabled Aalto to produce a different geometrical solution. The land parcel resulting from the enlargement was essentially triangular rather than trapezoidal, and the longer, nonorthogonal alignment of Töölönkatu and Mannerheimintie gave him more opportunity to employ his favorite splayed technique. He kept the massing of the Pension Bank building and plaza elements parallel with Mannerheimintie but turned the high-rise block and other buildings at a gentle angle more or less bisecting the triangle inscribed by the two major edges of the site. The two-level plaza arrangement facing the east and Töölö Bay Park is the same, but along the upper street the buildings of that side of the complex are oriented to Töölönkatu. This change in geometry involved the housing block, the concert hall, and a long row of commercial shops forming a bridge over Dunkerinkatu, one of the local streets running down the hill.

In the L-shaped building (327) in which the row of shops and concert hall are housed, he placed a formal vehicular access drop-off and turn-around. On the extreme northern border he placed the block of flats to form a formal upper plaza with the northern face of the concert hall at the highest level of Töölönkatu.This plaza, linked in an offset manner to the one on Mannerheimintie, together with the corresponding staggered relationships between the flanking buildings, is reminiscent of those urban plazas that he had seen on his travels to Italy. The complex, as in some of its Italian counterparts,[8] is linked by means of the upper plaza to the open marketplace which in this case is the Töölö district at its western end. This B scheme is the version for which Aalto won first prize (328). It is the more resolved of the two plans in its relationship to all parts of the topography, the community, and the handling of the buildings' programmatic functions.

The traffic access on both schemes is basically the same. An underground (329, 330) or covered vehicular entrance located off Dunkerinkatu runs through the property to Kivelänkatu, the northern bound-

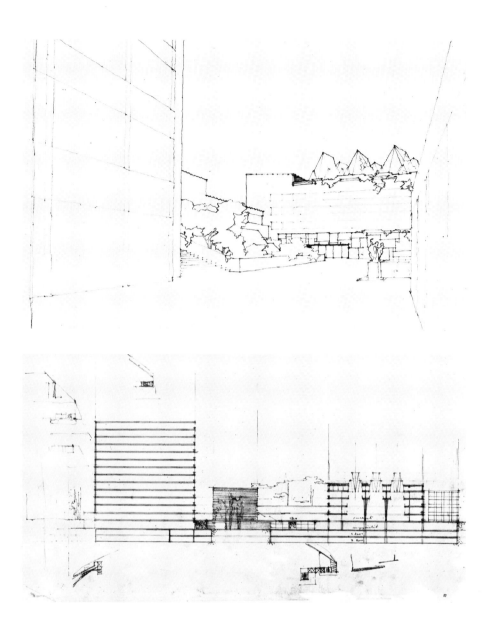

ary, and connects to a large parking garage located just beneath the highest plaza level along the western edge of the site. Both projects show a strongly developed sense of modern urban design considerations, but the B scheme is the most comprehensive in its solutions. A final and perhaps accidental result of the reorientation away from the axis of Mannerheimintie is that it would have enabled a person approaching from the center to attain a clearer and more monumentally imposing view of the high-rise Pension Bank block. For the final version (331), executed on a triangular site further to the north, it is clear that Aalto was able to draw on his experience in designing to even further utilize the geometrical nature of a site of this shape. Sadly, however,

324. Top: National pension bank competition entry, scheme A, perspective, Helsinki, 1948.
325. Above: National pension bank competition entry, scheme A, section, Helsinki, 1948.

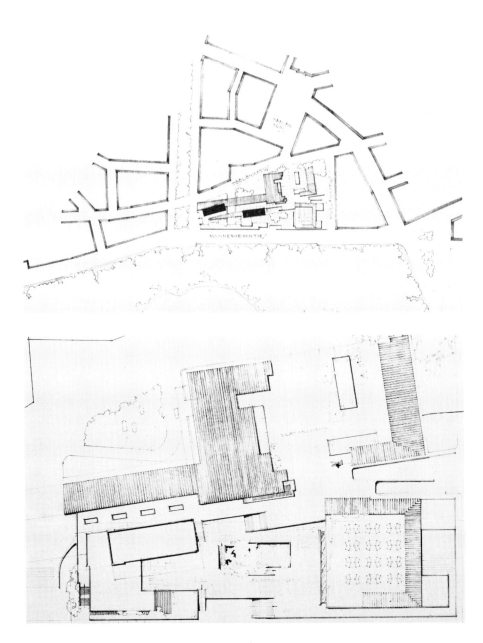

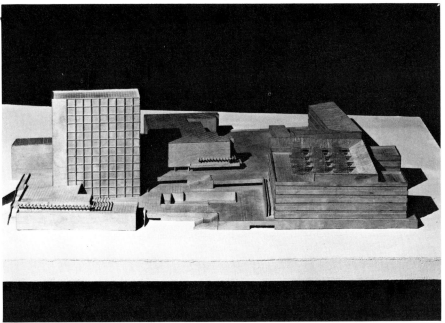

326. Top: National pension bank competition entry, scheme B, site plan in Töölö area, Helsinki, 1948.

327. Middle: National pension bank competition entry, scheme B, plan, Helsinki, 1948.

328. Bottom: National pension bank competition entry, scheme B, model, Helsinki, 1948.

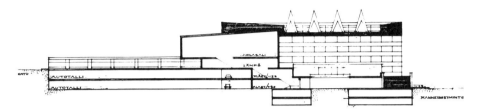

ЫКК△UБ B

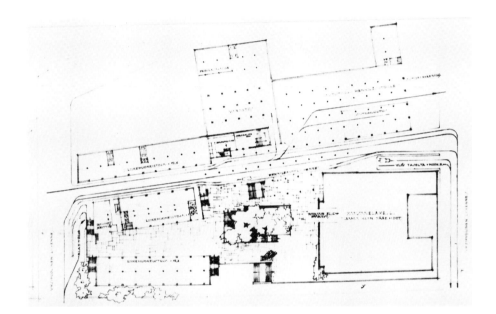

329. Top: National pension bank competition entry, scheme A, site section, Helsinki, 1948.

330. Middle: National pension bank competition entry, scheme B, basement plan, Helsinki, 1948.

331. Bottom: National pension bank headquarters, main view of entrance, Helsinki, 1956.

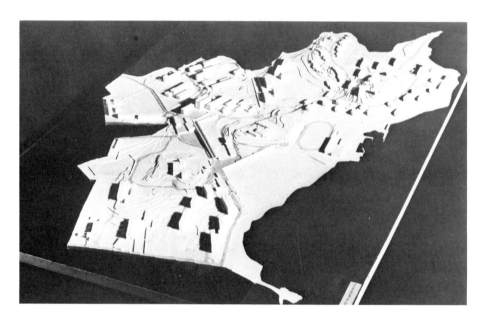

332. Site plan and administration complex competition entry for Helsinki Technical University at Otaniemi, model, Helsinki, 1949.

the new site presented neither the same neighborhood nor the same topographic features.

The buildings in both schemes demonstrate significantly less evidence of the romantic and vernacular influences of his distinct prewar style. They seem to indicate a certain redirection towards the general crispness of the International Style, but Aalto's use of brick, the delineation of plant materials on the roof, and the kind of paving stones used on the plazas still show that he was not returning to the severity of the style he had struggled to throw off.

Helsinki Technical University Campus Plan Competition

The building, or project, that is closest in spirit and style to the Pension Bank competition project is Aalto's prize-winning entry in the competition for the overall campus plan for the Technical University and its main classroom complex, to be set in the Helsinki suburb of Otaniemi, near Tapiola. This competition, which again attracted a wide range of participants, was announced on November 10, after Aalto had departed for MIT in the autumn of 1948. It was probably the first project to occupy his thoughts when he returned to be with Aino during the final days of her life. When the competition results were announced in April 1949 she was listed, along with Aalto, as first prize winner for

the movingly entitled "Ave mater alma morituri te salutant."[9] Both were graduates of the university, as were the younger husband and wife team of Heikki and Kaija Siren, who tied for second place with a team headed by Aarne Ervi.

The competition called for the design of a land-planning project that would provide for the new campus, ancillary activity centers, and housing for the school, as well as for adjoining facilities for the National Research Institute. In addition, it required a specific architectural design for the main academic center of the university.

The planning project (332) that Aalto produced combined the central recreation facilities complex, housing for both faculty and students, a research complex, and even a small commercial complex. The design was the first total design for comprehensive town facilities that Aalto was to execute for a public client. The entire community is planned on a peninsula directly across the inlet from Aalto's home district in Munkkiniemi.[10] Although the main access to the estate is by automobile, the single road that links the peninsula in the two directions of Munkkiniemi and Tapiola is located along the highest ground where the trees are larger and more developed. This produces a feeling of privacy and tends to insulate the facilities from outside disturbances. Slightly below this roadway and the secondary roads leading from it outward to the edges of the peninsula, Aalto located most of the housing, and on the next lower level he located the academic and research facilities. The pedestrian links were designed to take the existing landscape into account. One of the principal avenues of physical transportation in the Baltic region is the footpath, and even today in Southern Finland, long and ancient paths are maintained by the constant wear of traffic.[11] To provide access on this level, Aalto used a series of curving paths interlocking at tangent points.

He utilized medium-rise, slab-type buildings, as well as tower units and attached garden-type row housing. The orientation of the individual buildings, especially residential units, is determined with respect for the contours of the site, the view, and the angle of the sun. Most apartment buildings are located with their windows facing either east or west, but within the groupings he generally faced each building in a slightly different direction. In some cases, to take advantage of the beauty of the Baltic archipelago seascape, he would turn a dwelling around the perimeter toward the water.

Aalto did ultimately build many of the facilities called for in this plan, but some were built by the Sirens and some by others.[12] Of all those built by Aalto, the most important and best known is the main academic complex of the university. The project which was produced for the competition is somewhat different from the design finally constructed by Aalto, but the organizational idea and the siting are essentially the same.

The design for the complex in the original project (333) is located on a slight rise in land on the site of an old private estate. Like many of the town center designs produced in this period, this one is based on a system of two independent geometries, each staggered to give an echelon effect. The angle of difference between the two systems in this design, however, is not a subtle one but rather a bold splay of 120° inscribing a broad garden on the side away from the street. From this garden one could walk out to the residential, the recreational, or even the commercial facilities of the campus without encountering automobile traffic. On the vehicular approach side was a traffic circle from which the academic and research complexes were linked to the main roadway.

The northern portion of the complex (334), being the largest group of connected buildings, houses the administration and several academic departments, including that of architecture. These departments were to be housed in a series of parallel wings, echeloning in such a

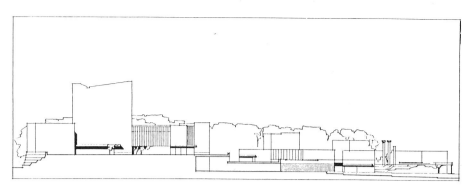

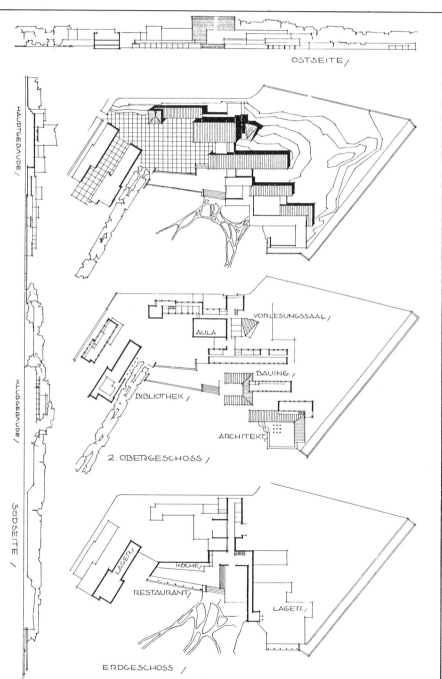

333. Top: Site plan and administration complex competition entry for Helsinki Technical University at Otaniemi, elevation, Helsinki, 1949.

334. Above: Site plan and administration complex competition entry for Helsinki Technical University at Otaniemi, site plan of classroom and administration group, Helsinki, 1949.

217

manner that the angle created between the line of the edges and that of the axis of the wings was roughly 45°. This meant that, to have a consistent exterior line, the wings had to be progressively shorter, each one situated at a somewhat greater distance from the connecting wing of the main lecture hall than the next. Opposite this grouping, at the obtuse angle, is the library. This angle was established by Aalto's retention of an old tree-lined path, formerly in the yard of the old estate.[13]

The entire complex had as its center of balance a three-chamber lecture hall nearest the access road to the northwest. This is the one weak element in the original scheme, and since it was to function as the center of the composition and, of course, as the central lecture hall of the entire campus, it was programmatically the most important space. Aalto later redesigned this element, replacing it with the massive splayed wedge that has become the chief architectural symbol of the school.

From the high ground on which the loosely aligned, open-ended quadrangle was placed, the topography stepped down in two stages to the level ground of the open space. It has been incorrectly pointed out that this type of stepping arrangement for a multiwinged building is related to the design produced for the town hall competition at Säynätsalo in the same period. In fact it more closely resembles the earlier competition sketches for Säynätsalo and some of the studies previously discussed for the development of the MIT dormitory.[14] The School of Architecture facilities, located at the extreme end of the staggered wing, are shown as a sort of undeveloped version of the massing that he used for the Viipuri Library building. The basic idea of the stagger is retained in the final version as it was built in 1964 and arranged essentially the same way, but the staggered units were later linked by a bisecting hallway running through the departmental units. It produces a series of back-to-back, open-ended courtyards which

began to reappear in his work during this period, most notably in the new design for the town hall at Säynätsalo in the same year of 1949.[15]

A New Life

Ironically, after Aino's death, with the commissions for the general plan and main building at Otaniemi as well as the Pension Bank and the general flow of housing and industrial work created by Finland's expanding market economy in the postwar era, Aalto had much to look forward to professionally. His practice was suddenly occupied with nationally important projects, and for the first time in his life he must have felt truly sure of his recognition inside Finland as an architect of international prominence. This feeling of heightened national stature was probably one of the factors that led him, after a brief visit in the autumn of 1950, to resign his position at MIT in February 1951. This decision ended his tie with teaching in a formal sense and any notion in his own mind or anyone else's, that he would ever practice outside Finland.

He did not, however, sit back and rest on his laurels. Later in 1949 he submitted entries for two competitions, winning the Säynätsalo town hall contest but losing the one for the seafront passenger terminal on the Helsinki harbor.[16]

The building known as the Sea Harbor project, built by the winners, Hytönen and Luukkonen, is on a site near the high rocky park at the harbor entrance known as Beacon Hill.[17] The program called for facilities to accommodate liners and connecting ship service from Finland's Baltic neighbors. It required large waiting and disembarkation lobbies, ticket offices, restaurants, and cargo and automobile handling areas, as well as public parking. A two-story scheme was indicated because of the need to separate passengers from other transport.

Aalto's solution (335), called "Entrez en Paradis," shows us once again a departure from the highly developed romanticism of his previous years. His style seems to be tending, at this point, towards a cer-

tain structural rationalism, with each unit set apart both volumetrically and in treatment of material. He did include a gently stepping garden on one side of the sharp concrete and brick structure as a response to the nature of the harbor and the desirability of outdoor waiting during the mild Baltic summers (336). There is nothing particularly striking about this design; rather, it seems to rest on an understated simplicity of form and use, and could probably be adapted to almost any function connected with the harbor or the city. The MIT dormitory was perhaps the final work in the style of romantic modernism that he developed, but it would never again occupy the position in his thought that it had in the late thirties and forties.

The other competition of 1949, the Säynätsalo town hall, would probably have been given to Aalto without any contest if it had been for a private client, but as Enso-Gutzeit, the sponsoring entity, was a government-controlled industry, it was necessary to hold an open competition. Much has been written about the nature of the building that was derived for this small industrial community near Jyväskylä (337), and it does seem to occupy a pivotal position in Aalto's career.

Firstly, it was to some extent the building in his postromantic phase which best combined some of the romantic features that he retained, such as the brick, the exposed wooden structure on the interior, and some trellis work. Secondly, it seems to signal a return of interest to such Mediterranean features as the atrium courtyard scheme. At least one scholar has likened it to a Roman patrician's house. Thirdly, it carries on the tradition of echelon planning found earlier in his work. Finally, and perhaps of most significance, it brought Aalto into contact with Elsa Mäkiniemi, an architect in his office called Elissa.[18] After a long association with him as job captain on this project, she married him and became his partner in 1952. The building (338) may be the clearest bridge between the two halves of Aalto's career.

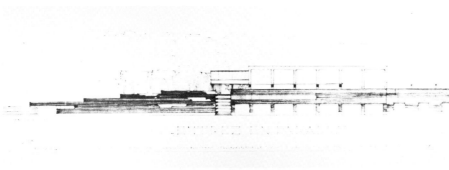

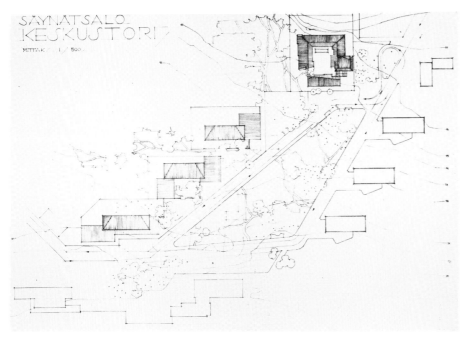

335. Top: Sea Harbor facilities competition entry, perspective, Helsinki, 1949.

336. Middle: Sea Harbor facilities competition entry, elevation, Helsinki, 1949.

337. Above: Town Hall competition entry for Enso Gutzeit Co. plant and village, site plan, Säynätsalo, 1949.

338. Above right: Atrium courtyard in Town Hall, Säynätsalo, 1950-1952.

22

Epilogue: Carrying on an Aalto Tradition

During the last 27 years of Aalto's career he built and designed many buildings and objects that, while always fresh and exciting, were clearly patterned on the developments of the first half of his career. It may sound obvious and even natural that a designer would stand on his earlier achievements, but in Aalto's case the motifs and techniques were retained as a repertoire to experiment with and to yield new and different styles completely apart from those of his previous career. It must be left for a separate study to sort out the second half of his career, but the blend of characteristics of his later work can only be seen as a restudy of those discoveries made before. In Aalto's later career, three major aspects of his designs—the volumetric and planning, the technical, and the textural—were combined and permuted into an ever more polished and integral style. One can, even on superficial examination of the Aalto material, detect differing phases and corresponding styles, but the period of Aino's death is the earliest time in his career when there was no repetition of phases. After this period he reached back into his past and utilized the developments he alone thought important.

Planning and Volumetric Motifs
In the execution of various planning proposals and site plans for projects, Aalto's steadfast inclination

was to preserve some natural aspect of the site. This often took place as a reinforcement of a contour line, as in the earthen steps of Seinäjoki and Säynätsalo, but is also evident in his major Central Plan for Helsinki where he adopted the edge of Töölö Bay as the access roadway and locus line for a string of cultural institutions. He also included in the same design a giant arrangement of fan-shaped plazas leading from the town center to the concert hall. In site planning, the form preferred is the wedge or fan arrangement taken from his established vocabulary. The character of these motifs vary according to use. In the 1952 cemetery proposal for Lyngby, Denmark (339), Aalto utilized long, narrow, wedge-shaped planting forms, stepping down a sharp incline radially inward to a ravine. The pathways bordering these forms are themselves straight, although rarely parallel, and different in length. In his own summer house at Muuratsalo built in 1953, he linked a series of outbuildings to the main part of the house by arranging them in one direction, along a gently curving spiral or fanned line. More frequently he arranged groups of buildings in a nonorthogonal manner, slightly fanning or opening the space from one building or mass to another, and so on. This device, recalling the Avesta plan, is incorporated in the planning of nearly every later building and project.

The volumetric motifs are of wider range, but the one most frequently employed in this area of design was also the fan or wedge shape.[1] The previously mentioned Bremen apartment building has apartments of wedge-shaped units linked into an overall fan-shaped tower. The town hall at Seinäjoki (340) possesses a double wedge-shaped gable above the council chamber that, from most angles, resembles a perfectly bisected gambrel roof form borrowed from American vernacular architecture. It is clad in a dramatic warm blue tile. While the Finlandia Concert Hall in Helsinki, with its giant wedge-shaped, fragmented rear wall, resembles Melnikov's much earlier Tramworker's Club in Moscow, it is developed from Aalto's own vocabulary, from the Villa Mairea onward. Each volume in the series of linked volumes projecting from the outside wall in the Wolfsburg Cultural Center is different and yet all reveal a family relationship running through their subtly varying shapes and sizes. Each volume is wedge shaped in plan and is linked to the others in a fan-shaped line (341). Ironically, Aalto used the wedge shape as the primary massing scheme for the Maison Carré in Paris to set it apart from its sloping hillside site and again in both section and plan for the main lecture hall of the Technical University at Otaniemi, where it produced a kind of geometric counterpoint not found in earlier works. This building was

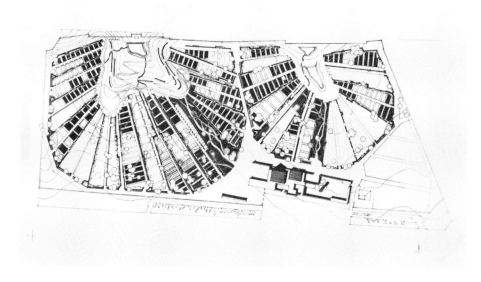

339. Left: Cemetery master plan, Lyngby, 1951.

340. Below: Town center development, view of town hall with church, Seinäjoki, 1953–1967.

conceived plastically, as a piece of sculpture, then worked as a building. The volumetric derivations from his early work are by no means limited to the outside of buildings. Again at Wolfsburg (342), as in the final building for the Pension Institute at Helsinki, he used the earliest of those volumetric motifs, the double-height skylight space with its lowest level expressed as a sunken area of the upper. In both cases it was employed as a library. But, perhaps the most expressive use of the fan shape was to be in the House of Culture in Helsinki,[2] with its wide auditorium and concert hall wrapping around a convex angle of view of more than 90°. The rear wall is also broken up into segments which reflect a change in the seating panel depths inside the auditorium.

Technical Innovations

The technical implementations that he began in the thirties and even earlier continued to be a part of his designs, and he continued to be intensely involved in the technical aspects of his own designs, particularly acoustics. In some cases he acted as his own consultant.[3] The microvent gravity air ventilation systems that he used for the Villa Mairea and other buildings were employed in the Vuoksenniska Church at Imatra and the ceiling or wall of nearly every assembly area he built in the second half of his career.[4] He designed special lighting fixtures to light the paintings at the Maison Carré. The triple glazed skylights of the Pension Bank (343) and the Academic Bookshop in Helsinki give the volume below a special feeling of close contact with the light and yet withstand the crushing weight of heavy snow loads. The major technical development to appear in his work after 1950 was the introduction of the long span of assembly hall structures located along the direction of the lines of the site, as in the main hall at Otaniemi (344) and the parish church at Wolfsburg.[5]

As a basis for his design of the Central Plan for Helsinki he incorporated a comprehensive transportation scheme which utilized his

341. Top: Cultural center, view to main entrance, Wolfsburg, 1958–1963.

342. Above: Cultural center, interior view of library, Wolfsburg, 1958–1963.

343. Opposite page above: National pension bank headquarters, view of skylit consultation chamber, Helsinki, 1956.

344. Opposite page below: Helsinki Technical University, auditorium interior of main building, Helsinki, 1964.

knowledge of traffic engineering and vehicular access. This knowledge was applied to the problem of ringing the Töölö Bay with traffic. This, however, was catastrophic for the relatively low and manageable traffic density of Helsinki, since it would have eliminated the park surrounding the bay, a precious natural feature. His skylights, though based directly on his early experiments, continued throughout his career to be an endless device for solving the problems of providing natural light to exhibition spaces such as in the two museums at Jyväskylä and the libraries in each town center design. Although they are all different (342), each provides light without direct sunlight by utilizing the baffle arrangement that he used in the Vierumäki Sports Institute project.

Textural Motifs

As his style matured he substituted some new textural motifs for earlier modes. He continued to use the undulating wooden ceilings of Viipuri in the Wolfsburg Cultural Center (345) and in the Maison Carré.[6] However the use of wood as an exterior material, like the fine battens of the Paris Pavilion and the Villa Mairea, was generally replaced by vertical convex, colored, and glazed ceramic tiles of a similar profile (346). They replaced the banded wood strips on columns as well.[7]

His interest in experimenting with brick surfaces was the most notable textural retention during the 1950s and early 1960s. Until he switched to what George Baird called the "white style" of stucco walls, nearly every building was made of brick. The House of Culture (347) with its stacked bond units, tailored especially for the varying curves of the rear wall of the auditorium, was a high point in the use of brick for monumental buildings. It is probable that Aalto singlehandedly pioneered the use of this material in Finland, which is now applied widely for all building uses. His own summer house, whose experimental nature is the subject of much talk and discussion, appears to be a collection of brick office samples

rather than any particular design by Aalto, thus revealing his evident fascination with the material.

Many textural motifs—the use of trellises and striated surfaces for example—faded from use and were gradually replaced by more sophisticated building materials such as bronze and marble. A slightly folksy, bucolic effect was eventually superseded by finely proportioned facades such as the Enso-Gutzeit building (348). In that structure, supposedly derived from the generative lines of Engel's harbor-front buildings, the marble-clad parts are shaped to respond geometrically rather than texturally.[8] Here, as in many other buildings of his later career, Aalto gradually evolved away from the experiments of the late thirties and in some respects eased back into the mainstream of International Modernism as it had developed. But those breakthroughs and innovations that had long ago taken him away from the International Style provided the centrex for his work until he died and caused his designs to stand out from any other master of the Modern Movement.

345. Above: Cultural center, interior of main auditorium, Wolfsburg, 1963.

346. Left: Cultural center, interior view of main lobby, Wolfsburg, 1963.

347. Left: House of Culture, exterior wall of auditorium, Helsinki, 1955–1958.

348. Below: National headquarters of Enso Gutzeit Co., view of exterior from market-place, Helsinki, 1962.

Notes

INTRODUCTION

1. The generation analogy and the term "second generation" were first used by Henry Russell Hitchcock in *Architecture: Nineteenth and Twentieth Centuries* (London: Penguin, 1958), pp. 363–391. Aalto was first added to this group by Siegfried Giedion. Siegfried Giedion, *Space, Time and Architecture* (Cambridge, Mass.: Harvard University Press, 1949), pp. 453–492 (8th printing).

2. Now that Alvar Aalto has passed into the annals of history, perhaps the previously protected material will be more accessible to a wider group of scholars.

3. Two notable exceptions are Fredrick Gutheim's *Alvar Aalto*, (New York: Braziller, 1960), and Eduard and Claudia Neuenschwander's *Alvar Aalto and Finnish Architecture* (Zurich: Verlag für Architektur, Erlenach, 1954).

4. The name reverently used to refer to Alvar Aalto by the staff members in his office.

5. Wolfgang Pehnt, *Expressionist Architecture*, (London: Thames & Hudson, 1973), pp. 194–202. Denis Sharp, *Modern Architecture and Expressionism* (London: Longmans, 1966), pp. 131–142. See also Julius Posener, *From Schinkel to the Bauhaus: Five Lectures on the Growth of Modern German Architecture*, (London: Lund Humphries for the Architectural Association, 1972).

6. See V. E. Khazanova, *Soviet Architecture of the First Years of the October Revolution 1919-1925* (Moscow: Nauka, 1970).

7. See Stanford Anderson, *Peter Behrens and the New Architecture of Germany*, unpublished doctoral dissertation, Columbia University, New York, 1968; and Jacques Paul, *Modern Architecture and the German Classical Tradition*, unpublished doctoral dissertation, University of London, 1972.

8. See Raija-Liisa Heinonen, thesis in progress, *Functionalism in Finland*, Helsinki University.

1. AALTO'S EARLY YEARS

1. Interview with Alvar Aalto conducted by P. D. Pearson in Aalto's studio, Helsinki, Finland, August 15, 1974. It seems that he frequently repeated this particular story to interviewers.

2. Interview with A. Tuukanen, architect, Helsinki, conducted by R.-L. Heinonen, Curator of Archives, The Museum of Finnish Architecture, Helsinki, July 1975.

3. The year is reckoned by the claim that when he was nine years old, "he was living in a town of 3,200 people"; this is from his introduction to Albert Christ-Janer's book, *Eliel Saarinen*, (Chicago: University of Chicago Press, 1948). The census for 1900 shows

Jyväskylä alone with 3,031 people to be the only settlement of that size in central Finland.

4. Alvar Aalto, introduction to Albert Christ-Janer's *Eliel Saarinen*, op. cit., p. ix.

5. The National Romantic Style, popular in Finland, began to wane after the turn of the century, and by the time Aalto graduated from his professional course the influence had expired totally. Surely some of his later work which exhibits a decidedly romantic and Finnish overtone is related to this movement if only inadvertently.

6. Interview with Alvar Aalto cited above in note 1.

7. For a complete discussion of the early period of independence, see Eino Jutikkala and Kauko Pirinen's *History of Finland*, 2d ed. (New York: Praeger, 1974), pp. 227–259; and L. A. Puntila's *Political History of Finland 1806-1966*, (Helsinki: Otava, 1974), pp. 102–122.

8. L. A. Puntila, op. cit., pp. 102–122.

9. Interview with Hilding Ekelund, (architect, b. 1893), Helsinki, August 1974, conducted by P. D. Pearson and R.-L. Heinonen at The Museum of Finnish Architecture.

10. *Encyclopaedia Britannica*, 1966, vol. 9, p. 283. According to Puntila, op. cit., the moderate Social Democrats were given new spirit and reacted to their previous dominance in Parliament.

11. S. Pranzell, *Memoirs*, Stockholm, 1965.

12. Interview with Hilding Ekelund cited above in note 9.

13. Ibid.

14. Nils Erik Wickberg, *Finnish Architecture* (Helsinki: Otava, 1959), p. 81.

15. Ibid.

16. Marika Hausen, *The Helsinki Railway Station in Eliel Saarinen's First Versions*, Art History Study Series (Helsinki: Helsinki University, 1977), p. 76.

17. J. M. Richards, *A Guide to Finnish Architecture*, (London: Hugh Evelyn, 1966), p. 75. This is also contained in Van de Velde's memoirs, *Geschichte meines Lebens*, Munich, 1962.

18. Nils Erik Wickberg, op. cit., p. 85.

19. See Leonard K. Eaton, *American Architecture Comes of Age* (Cambridge, Mass.: MIT Press, 1972), pp. 186–192, 205–206.

20. Richards and Wickberg, op. cit., seem to feel that the "facility" was one associated with the National Romantic designers originally.

21. In the library of the School of Architecture at the new Technical University (formerly Polytechnic Institute) exists a copy of Alois von Wurm-Arnkreuz's *Sieben Bücher über Stil und Mode in der Architektur* (Mit 74 Abbildungen aus den Jahren 1863-1913 als 50-Jährige Zeitspiegelung in einem Lebenslauf). (Wien und Leipzig: Verlag von Moritz Perles, 1913), with margin notes by the donor Gustaf Nyström. These sketches and characters in pencil depict a bold and inventive style of neoclassical architectural details.

22. Yrjö Hirn, professor and lecturer on aesthetics and the psychological basis of art appreciation at Helsinki University, was a forceful figure in the establishment of a basis for Finland's culture as an independent yet integral force in the development of modern interpretation of art. He was contemporary with the major theorists dealing with this subject. Kirmo Mikkola, who probably spent more critical interview time with Aalto than any other scholar, has confirmed Aalto's friendship with Hirn in his article "Aalto as Thinker," *Arkkitehti*, 7/8 (1976), p. 20.

23. Yrjo Hirn, *Origins of Art* (London: Macmillan, 1900), p. 5.

24. From the turn of the century the exercise of preparing measured drawings of Finland's

medieval churches was part of every student's training. Professionals involved in National Romantic causes made journeys to visit and record these source monuments; see a spectacular watercolor rendering of a wooden church at Saloinen by Armas Lindgren dated July 24, 1906, now in the collection of the National Museum in Helsinki.

25. The original drawings of this project have only recently been donated to the Museum of Finnish Architecture. Close examination of the main elevation reveals one amusing if not important half-erased cartoon of a hatted gentleman relieving himself against the wall of the church. This seems to be more in keeping with Aalto's sense of humor as it was later to become known in the circles of CIAM.

26. Catalogue Department of the Finnish National Fair Commission, *Fifty Years of Finnish Fairs* (exhibition catalog) (Helsinki, 1971), p. 17.

27. Lauri Kuoppamäki, "Suomen Messujen Hallinnon Sunnitelma," *Kotimainen Työ*, no. 12 (1921), p. 504.

28. Interview with Hilding Ekelund cited above in note 9.

29. Interview with Alvar Aalto cited above in note 1.

30. Ibid.

31. Since land surveyors would be in the forest for many days, it must be presumed that they were qualified woodsmen as well. Temporary camp furniture and some basic instruments would be rigged of rough poles lashed together. The interior of the Gothenburg Congress Hall reveals that the bolted arches were made of strips of dimension lumber and finished naturally. They resemble a present-day laminated wood arch.

32. Interview with Alvar Aalto cited above in note 1.

33. One might also be inclined to extrapolate backwards from the Gothenburg Hall to the proposed Helsinki project in regard to that system of construction. It seems quite possible that the lightweight construction methods employed at Gothenburg may reflect those which were projected for the earlier Helsinki fairs for the erection of similar large and low-cost temporary structures.

34. In Scandinavia the influence of classical styles in the 1920s seemed to be Roman or Italianate, particularly Renaissance, rather than Greek. See early works of Gunnar Asplund in *Gunnar Asplund 1885-1940*, edited by Homdahl, Lind, and Ödeen with an essay by Hakon Ahlberg (Stockholm: Tidskriften Byggmastaren, 1950). Works of others in Hakon Ahlberg's *Modern Swedish Architecture* (London: Benn, 1925).

35. Tessanow's classicism was simple and even humble in character. Also Gunnar Asplund's Woodlands chapel in Stockholm's South Cemetery built 1818–1820 exhibited this classical quality.

36. Hermann Muthesius had introduced this mode to Germany to meet rising needs in housing with designs of simplicity and rationalism. See his *Das Englische Haus*, Berlin, 1904–1905; see also Nikolaus Pevsner's *Pioneers of Modern Design*, (London: Pelican, 1960), pp. 32–38.

37. Göran Schildt, *Alvar Aalto, Luonnoksia* (Helsinki: Otava, 1972). The travel sketches from his first trip are dated 1924.

38. Interview with Hilding Ekelund as cited above in note 9.

39. Particularly the modular divisions of Wagner's Karlplatz Station built 1899–1901.

40. The Functionalist manifesto called "Acceptera" (to accept) was published privately in Stockholm in 1931 and was signed by its editors Gunnar Asplund, Wolter Gahn, Sven Markelius, Gregor Paulson, Eskil Sundahl, and Uno Ahren. This is the foundation document of the Functionalist style as it was called in Scandinavia. Aalto reviewed the Manifesto in the *Arkkitehti* in October 1931 and spoke positively about the goals of that movement.

41. A recurrent theme in Aalto's work.

42. There is no other need for the diagonal braces except to brace the system as employed on lighter-weight roofs.

43. Many Baltic band and choral shells prefigure this structure, but it appears to be in keeping with the most contemporary acoustical theories of its time.

2. PROFESSIONAL PRACTICE

1. In a new spirit and perhaps even a democratic mood the newly independent state began a policy of open competitions for the selection of architects for its major civic buildings. To some extent this policy has carried over to the present.

2. He seemed to have a high regard for this site and its surrounding monuments of architecture. In the Enso-Gutzeit building he claimed that the genesis of the skin was a remake of the proportions of Engel's buildings which faced the marketplace and harbor.

3. "Jamsan Kirkkokilpailu," *Arkkitehti*, no. 1 (1926), p. 10. Site plan showing roman lettering in review of competition results, pp. 1–13, signed by Waldemar Wilenius. The shell form tile block shown on the site plan of the Gothenburg Fair may not have been drawn by Aalto, but he would have come in contact with it in Bjerke's office in 1921.

4. Alvar Aalto, "Maalarit ja Muurarit" *(Jouaimies* 1921) reprinted in Goran Schildt's *Alvar Aalto Luonnoksia* (Helsinki: Otava, 1972), pp. 11–15.

5. See J. M. Richards, *Guide to Finnish Architecture* (London: Evelyn, 1966), p. 64.

6. This partial pinwheel type of arrangement was one of the major methods of architectural composition of the "Beaux Arts" schools. See Harbeson, *A Study of Architectural Design* (New York: Pencil Points Press, 1927).

7. This building points out the understanding of two early phases of Hermann Muthesius' Deutscher Werkbund; the earliest influence of simple forms decorated with indigenous details as found in the work of Philip Webb and C. F. A. Voysey, and the next phase that introduced the architecture of ancient Greece and Roman as a source for inspiration.

8. Unfortunately the library was mostly destroyed during a Russian air raid on Helsinki during World War II, making impossible any detailed scholarly analysis of books and journals to which Aalto might have had access. There exist no accession lists of the Technical University prior to that time.

9. Alvar Aalto, "Between Humanism and Materialism," speech and lecture held at the Central Union of Architects, Vienna, Austria, Summer, 1955; first published in *Der Bau*, no. 7/8, pp. 174–176. Reprinted in *Alvar Aalto Synopsis: Papers of the Institute for History and Theory of Architecture* (Zurich: Swiss Federal Institute of Technology, 1970), pp. 19 –21. This has been verified by Raija-Liisa Heinonen in an interview with Teuvo Takala, Aalto's model maker and draftsman at that time; 1977 Finnish Museum of Architecture Archive, Helsinki.

10. Goran Schildt, *Alvar Aalto, Luonnoksia*, (Helsinki: Otava, 1972); see travel sketches Aalto made abroad. It was Schildt who first published this proof of Aalto's link to the Mediterranean.

11. Aalto would have been familiar with a purer version of Palladio's famous window, but consciously avoided that form in favor of his own.

12. There were many methods of proportioning facades, etc., at that time. See "Warnung vor Akademismus und Klassizismus" by Werner Hegemann and Leo Adler, *Wasmuth's Monatshefte* (1927), p. 3. This article on design methods used in Copenhagen is illustrated by a student project entitled "Entwurf zu einem Badehotel" executed by Arne Jacobsen under the direction of Professor Ivar Bensten. Nikolaus Pevsner supports this contention, adding simply that it is an "old German style composition." The latter is taken from an interview with Dr. Pevsner conducted by P. D. Pearson, London, July, 1975. However, the overall composition of the facade bears a strong, almost cartoonlike resemblance to Peruzzi's Palazzo Massimo alle colonne, Rome, presenting in exaggerated form the already extreme Mannerist proportions of the latter's two rows of strangely framed small windows in the upper stories and the feeling of excessive load on its Doric-columned portico. See also Pieter Singelnberg's *H. D. Berlage*, (Utrecht: Dekker Cunbert, 1972), pp. 101–110.

13. See Robert Brucemann and Donald Prowler's "19th Century Mechanical System Designs," *Journal of Architectural Education* 30, no. 3 (February 1977), pp. 11–15. A long overdue appraisal of the early attempts to ventilate buildings with gravity air.

14. Nils Erik Wickberg, *Finnish Architecture* (Helsinki: Otava, 1959), pp. 42, 114. In Finland this was mostly in wood.

15. The surprising aspect centers around the fact that Aalto's buildings were ornamentally correct, not that they were classical in nature. Jyväskylä in 1926 largely consisted of low Baltic classicized wooden buildings.

16. Aalto was by no means the first architect to rediscover this as an essential consideration in the design and erection of architecture.

17. "Furniture for Common Homes," *Kasiteollisuus*, no. 2 (1925), p. 35, designs for a group by Aino and Alvar Aalto.

18. Interview with Clive Wainwright, Department of Woodwork and Furniture, Victoria and Albert Museum, conducted by P. D. Pearson, London, August 22, 1975. The revival spoken about here is one of design spirit.

19. William Morris Company, *Furniture Catalogue*, London, 1921.

20. Taking the shortest route on his trip or honeymoon to southern Europe, he would have passed through Vienna via Poland.

21. The barracks building published in all the standard works on Aalto was first listed in Fredrick Gutheim's *Alvar Aalto* (New York: Braziller, 1960). The actual date of this building is 1927 and in its details represent a later thinking on Aalto's part; nevertheless it was part of the scheme as originally planned.

22. Not all the building's details were realized. The mock pediment seems to have been left off and there are alternate versions on file in the Aalto Atelier which indicate stairways at the ends.

23. Since they are related to the Greek influence it may be considered a less surprising form. But just prior to this in 1921 was the first published appearance of *The Palace of Minos at Cnossos*, London, 1921.

24. The inventive nature of the overall stairhall design with aligned courses and ornamentation is spiritually Victorian, but the details in themselves are not.

25. Her later reputation as a designer of decorative objects and furnishings relates to the fine-grained nature of the drawings of the interiors. She being four years older and ahead of Aalto at the Poly would have had a greater exposure to this vocabulary as taught by Gustaf Nyström.

26. Italianate influence could have been im-

ported from secondary sources, but there is little evidence to deny the direct appreciation of Italy as such.

27. It is rather the Italian Renaissance and its revival of older modes that influence the classical revivalists of the early 20th century. See Peter Behrens' Hagen Crematorium, a take-off on San Miniato in Florence. This has been exposed by Stanford Anderson in "Behrens' Changing Concept," *Architectural Design*, February 1969, pp. 72–78. This article is an excerpt of Anderson's excellent but yet unpublished thesis on Behrens.

28. Alvar Aalto, "Kirkkotaiteestamme," *Kasiteolisuus*, no. 3 (1925), p. 51.

29. It is likely that they spring from the popularity of Russian neoclassical influence. The monumental architecture of Russian cities, particularly St. Petersburg, acted as a model for much of the wooden buildings in the countryside and small provincial towns where a version of the high style was desired.

30. Nils Erik Wickberg, op. cit., p. 83.

31. Nearly every Finnish town had (and many still do have) a wide range of wooden buildings of this nature. Jyväskylä was no exception.

32. The older and less technically derived structural framing systems of such buildings showed Aalto that structure could be achieved in a nonorthodox manner.

33. There are many examples where the space at the towrail of a stair is expressed. Aalto himself often employed a coving on the inside of the baluster in his buildings. He never again used the expression of a void inscribed beneath the smooth line of the baluster to give the saw tooth arrangement found here.

34. This may be due to the nature of the drawings; although they are signed, they may have been intended for a stage preliminary to construction.

35. Asplund used this unusal combination in his Skandia Cinema in Stockholm built in 1922–1923, see *Gunnar Asplund 1885–1940*, edited by Hemdahl, Lind, and Ödeen, essay by H. Ahlberg (Stockholm: Tidskriften Byggmastaren, 1950), p. 49.

36. Aalto's later style is more complex and founded on a wider range of architectural theories, but it does include the two divergent modes of his early work.

37. Piazza del Popolo in Rome and Piazza San Carlo in Turin both have twin churches. At least the former of these was known to Aalto as he had previously used its name for his motto in the Houses of Parliament Site Plan Competition.

38. It is mysterious that he made no attempt to create a Baroque-style planning link between the main street and the approach artery near his recently finished building.

39. European city plans after Pope Sixtus V and André Le Nôtre obviously owe both men a debt. Aalto's plan does also.

40. L. I. Linqvist should not to be confused with Selim Lindqvist, architect who pioneered the use of reinforced concrete in Finland.

41. This church, which stands in a grouping of trees located in the center of an otherwise open square, was the focal point of the town's main civic space.

42. At this date Aalto had not been given the commission for the Civil Guard House. He only placed second in the competition just a few months earlier. Yet it seems unusual that he did not use his design for that part of the city plan.

43. League of Nations Competition program announcement, *Arkkitehti*, no. 9 (1926), pp. 166–167.

44. Not the creed of the "golden age," but

adapted forms taken through toned-down revival styles of Europe.

45. Asplund's Stockholm Municipal Library built in 1923 served as a source for the Viipuri Library as well. See Hakon Ahlberg, *Modern Swedish Architecture*, op. cit., p. 126.

46. The facade design is composed only for the first stage of construction while the suggested extension shown on the ground plan indicates that the portal would not be in the precise center or at any geometrically regular location.

47. This scheme of the open multileveled courtyard with a stair along one edge was observed by Aalto in Gunnar Asplund's design for the City Hall annex in Gothenburg. Aalto used this motif many times in his career; the stair in the Viipuri Library (now Viborg, Russia) is a version and so is the escalator in the Academic Bookshop in Helsinki.

48. This spiral motif has been in use in bronze work since the second half of the second millenium. See N. K. Sanders, *Prehistoric Art in Europe* (Baltimore: Penguin, 1968), pp. 182–187.

49. Gunnar Asplund had produced a number of designs utilizing the broken pediment like that of Alberti's. See designs for Carl Johan School in Gothenburg in *Gunnar Asplund 1885–1940* edited by Homdahl, Lind, and Ödeen, essay by H. Ahlberg, op. cit., pp. 108–110.

50. The interior dating from two years later is plainer and less strictly classical. However, the general tradition of country churches was observed here.

51. The interiors of many country churches in Finland exhibit a Spartan character with a minimum of ornament and classical detailing. This is true of the earliest medieval churches and the styles that followed down to present times; therefore it cannot be fully equated with a modernizing tendency on Aalto's part.

52. Poul Henningsen, a major force in Scandinavia, chiefly because of his technical and architectural writings in the Danish journal *Kritisk Revy*, caused Aalto, among others, to consider a more scientific basis in the design of buildings and fixtures.

53. Only SAFA members were allowed to participate in open competitions. There were and still are qualified architects in Finland who are not members of that organization.

54. See Leonardo Mosso, *Alvar Aalto* (exhibition catalog) (Helsinki: Ateneum, 1967), p. 18.

55. Interview with Alvar Aalto conducted by P. D. Pearson in Aalto's studio, Helsinki, Finland, August 15, 1974.

56. These areas, all residential neighborhoods, are near the central zones of their respective cities today, but in the late twenties were slightly more remote.

57. See Hilding Ekelund, "Italia la Bella," *Arkkitehti*, February 1923, pp. 27–31.

58. The Jämsä Church and the Taulumäki Church are in the same area of central Finland.

59. Tampere was then the "God-city" of Manchester, England.

60. Aalto was probably not totally familiar with the round towers of German Romanesque cathedrals, such as those of Mainz, Worms, and Laach, but he might have had knowledge of the Ancient Porta Nigra and Romanesque cathedral at Trier. However, it is more likely that he knew of the 10th-century cylindrical campanile of San Apollonaire in Classe near Ravenna. While Scandinavian architects in the 1920s were influenced by Italian Renaissance architecture, freestanding cylindrical companiles were not found in that vocabulary.

61. Leonardo Mosso, op. cit., p. 29.

62. Many have written of the stripped-down classicism as a transitional style preceding the Modern Movement. See especially Nikolaus Pevsner, *Pioneers of Modern Design* (London: Pelican, 1960), pp. 179–217.

63. The same type of cloud formation is found in the perspective of Saarinen's first prize-winning solution for the Helsinki Railway Station Competition in 1904.

3. TURKU: CLASSICAL FOUNDATION

1. Being a normally ambitious person, Aalto quite naturally sought out new opportunities in Turku. He duplicated this to some extent when he moved to Helsinki in 1933, securing many commissions from business leaders he encountered there, as well as national leaders in the capital. To some extent he attempted this type of self-promotion when he spent the better part of 1938 in the U.S.A. Hopes for an American practice as described by Aalto in an interview conducted by Heikki Hyytiainen, architect. November 1973, at Aalto's studio Helsinki were never accompanied by the effort needed to make them a reality.

2. The term "heroic" in relation to modern architecture refers to the period between 1917–1937 when architects were attempting to produce buildings of a high degree of excellence—those that were as completely realized as any in the history of architecture. The term was coined by Peter Smithson in a special issue of *Architectural Design* which surveyed the "heroic" period. See *Architectural Design* 35 (December 1965). The period died, he claims, around 1929, just after Paimio had been constructed.

3. The community of architects was by necessity small. When the Aaltos moved there, only 10 other architects practiced in Turku, one of those being the City Architect Ilmari Ahonen.

4. Turku had suffered two major losses; first, the transfer of the capital during the early part of the 19th century to Helsinki, which included such cultural institutions as the university; second, a fire that leveled most of the city in 1864. As an alternate port for commerce Turku retained its dominance due to its more convenient access to northern ports. With the coming of independence Helsinki flourished markedly in the first decade, but as the center for a significant segment of commerce and culture Turku recovered easily. This recovery and a realization by the publishers of *Arkkitehti* of Turku's importance as a major area producing architectural and building activity led to special issues in 1928 and 1929 devoted to the Turku scene.

5. See Nils Erik Wickberg, *Finnish Architecture* (Helsinki: Otava, 1959), pp. 66–69.

6. Hilding Ekelund, introduction to Erik Bryggman, exhibition catalog, The Museum of Finnish Architecture, Summer 1969, p. 7.

7. Ibid.

8. In a climate that required double glazing in the winter season, this through-the-wall method of ventilation would not appear to be anything out of the ordinary but might explain Aalto's apparent concern for this environmental consideration, thought by the outside world to be uniquely characteristic of his work.

9. See Otto Antonia Graf, *Die Vergessene Wagnerschule*, Schriften des Museums des 20. Jahrhunderts, Vienna (Vienna: Verlag Jugend und Volk). Profusely illustrated book showing many facades with geometric polychromatic decorations. Plates 6 and 49 show designs for apartment blocks with shops decorated in a similar vein.

10. This is a version of Mendelsohn's Tageblatt addition executed in 1921–1922. See Wolf von Eckardt, *Erich Mendelsohn* (London: Mayflower, 1960), pp. 11–12. It is probable that the original source for all the "intempled" openings is Olbrich's Palace of the Secession in Vienna.

11. Many designers in the vanguard of the International Style observed industrial and utilitarian examples of architecture that led them into the mainstream of modern architecture, but in Finland Aalto would have been able to observe the buildings of Selim A. Lindqvist which, though many were executed in the style fashionable before independence, did exhibit a quality of design that was related to the nature of the construction and function.

12. This unusual color scheme (similar to the one shown on the jacket of this book) was employed in the Skandia Cinema in Stockholm by Aalto's friend Gunnar Asplund in 1922–1923. Hakon Ahlberg characterized Asplund's use of such a color combination as frolicsome play. The exuberant and playful Aalto obviously found his friend's attitude refreshing and inspiring. See *Gunnar Asplund 1885–1940*, edited by Homdahl, Lind, and Ödeen (Stockholm: Tidskriften Byggmastaren, 1950); Ahlberg's essay, p. 46; illustrations, p. 49.

13. The now famous lighting fixture was in comparatively wide use around this time. Bryggman had used it for his Hotel Hospits Bertel, and Mies van der Rohe specified it for the Tugendhat House in Brno, Czechoslovakia.

14. Interview with Hilding Ekelund, Helsinki, August 1974, conducted by P. D. Pearson and R. L. Heinonen at the Museum of Finnish Architecture.

4. HOUSING DESIGNS

1. This system developed by Juho Tapani, a Turku manufacturer, had been used for the first time in an apartment building of 1913 by architect Alexander Nyström. Later it was employed in the construction of several buildings, bridges, and summer houses. See *Rakennustaito*, nos. 6–7 (1920), pp. 57–58.

2. The use of a multipurpose room hardly qualifies this suite for comparison with the free planning of the architects of the International Style at that time, but by the same token it was seen by many as a departure from those principles then emerging as the foundation for Scandinavian Functionalism. See Asko Salokorpi, *Modern Architecture in Finland* (London: Weidenfeld and Nicolson, 1970), p. 33.

3. The park, known as Puololonmäki, contains the Art Museum and is the main open space of central Turku, but the rear yard linking the apartment building to the park is cluttered with lower wooden buildings.

4. See Le Corbusier and Pierre Jeanneret, *Oeuvre Complète, 1910–1929*, pp. 128–129. This aspect of Aalto's building does not qualify it as an example of modern architecture under Corbu's rules.

5. It was nearly a standard part of an architect's professional activity to experiment with the implementation of building systems, particularly those that employed manufactured components. Le Corbusier had used a sandwich panel of his own design in the Maison Monol in 1920 just before he abandoned a career in brick manufacturing.

6. The presence of this balcony seems timid compared with work by engineers like Maillart and Fressinet, but not having seen these works firsthand Aalto was nevertheless able to find an adequate source. This does not represent the level of boldness exhibited by Le Corbusier in the garden stairway of his Maison Plainex in 1927.

7. Alvar Aalto, "The Influence of Construction and Material on Modern Architecture," lecture held at the Nordic Building Conference, Oslo, Norway, 1938. Printed in *Arkkitehti*, no. 9 (1938), pp. 129–131.

8. Small vacation houses in Finland are an integral part of a wide sector of the population's summertime life.

9. The mark, used in the period from Independence to 1963, when it was revalued, was exchanged at about 193 to the pound sterling, or 41 to the dollar. See *The Bankers Almanac 1926 to 1930* (Thomas Skinner, director), Croydon (U.K.), 1926.

10. This summer villa is still standing in Alajärvi and is now owned by a member of the Aalto family; it is reported to be in a dilapidated state. See *Arkkitehti*, no. 5 (1929), pp. 74–75. Also in the same year other completed projects were published in five other articles, but this is the only one credited to her alone.

11. Alvar Aalto, *Aitta,* October 1926, p. 63. The atrium house, or at least a house with a central area that was directly accessible to most of the other rooms on the ground floor, was a traditional type in Ostro-Bothnia and in Scandinavian log houses as well. The early ones had a roof that could be opened to the sky when cooking was done on an open fire.

12. Ibid., p. 65.

5. INTERNATIONAL MODERNISM

1. *Turun Sanomat,* Oct. 14, 1928; the article states that the new Sanomat headquarters has been under construction for almost two months.

2. Johan Sigfrid Sirén, known principally for his Houses of Parliament, the commission for which was attained by a competition and only just under construction at the time of this jury.

3. Asko Salokorpi, *Modern Architecture in Finland* (London: Weidenfeld and Nicolson, 1970), p. 22.

4. *Arkkitehti,* no. 11 (1928), p. 171; results listed. This is one of the key splits in the branching-off of the modernists in Finland.

5. *Arkkitehti,* no. 2 (1929), p. 31. News review of SAFA meeting in December where Aalto showed photographs from his travels in France and Holland.

6. These two designs, sharing much in common at this point, are somewhat of a mystery in regard to their dates. Aalto's designs dated June 6, 1928, show this type of vitrine, store-front arrangement. Since the Suomi Competition was only announced in July of that year, it would seem that Aalto might well be the earliest of the two to produce the design, but it is clear that the cross-fertilization of design ideas was taking place between the two.

7. In the program of these two projects, the display of the printed word was to play a unique and integral role. Each had a screen on which propaganda was to be projected. Slogans must have been projected on the screen located on the top of Tatlin's tower project, but no description of it seems to have been recorded. The Pravda project drawings show a large display screen located at the third and fourth levels, tilted over the sidewalk below to display the full page makeup of two pages. Misconceptions regarding rear screen projections led architects enthusiastically into design projects that were new and interesting but often unworkable.

8. From that point on he used concealed, interior drains and began to take into greater account the ventilation of the interiors of his buildings, especially combining that aspect with the heating.

9. While in Western Europe that summer he toured the newly constructed concrete architecture of Jan Duiker in Holland and Andre Lurçat in Paris; see note 5 above.

10. The progression of designed shapes for these columns has been confused due to overzealous early dating of the building. The basic plan in its earliest form was a simple post and beam structure, as shown on the drawings in the Aalto Atelier dated June 22, 1928. By September 1929 the bell-shaped capitals in the paper storage vaults beneath the press room appeared on the drawing, but the configuration above remained the same. An engineer's drawing produced at Christmas time gives the first canted shape to the piers, like Markelius's Gothenburg Auditorium; see Stefano Ray, *Sven Markelius* (Rome: Officina Edizioni Roma, 1969), pp. 51–57.

11. Sven Markelius's Gothenburg Auditorium has earlier and similar shaped concrete bents carrying the main roof load. These expressed shapes are the direct influence on Aalto's Turun Sanomat, but Aalto combined the crisp geometry of Markelius's structure with a more fluid expression used in a bell-shaped supporting system by Maillart in a Zurich brewery to yield his own rationalized version of a concrete flooring system. See Max Bill, *Robert Maillart Bridges and Construction* (London: Pall Mall Press, 1969), pp. 157–164.

12. The shape with the canted profile was the final shape indicated on the drawings dated December 31, 1928. The uniquely shaped, dropped panel in the ceiling was added during the construction phase in January 1929 to give extra shear resistance.

13. As it is today, a credential of some finished work in an acceptable style was required for the most part to maintain an air of self-confidence when one entered international professional circles. In the 1920s and 1930s when transportation and the mails did not provide for instant communication, such promotion was a necessity, and Aalto used his first purely modern building as his calling card in Europe.

6. HEROIC AGE: MASTERY OF THE STYLE

1. The Turun Sanomat building has always been regarded by outside critics as the building that fully launched Aalto in his career as an internationally prominent modern architect, but this was not the case within Finland. The newspaper plant was in full view in Turku, and while located in an out-of-the-way place in relation to the main body of culture in Helsinki, it could be dismissed by many as being at odds with tradition as well as being executed by a pushy, unlikable colleague. Paimio certainly gave Aalto new belief in his ideas, and in winning the commission for such a large building of public use he could no longer go unrecognized at home.

2. Aalto had made a trip to Paris to attend an International Congress on Reinforced Concrete Construction, held between May 21 and 24, 1928. See *Boewkundig Weekblad Architectura,* no. 24 June 15, 1928), p. 188. He stopped in Rotterdam to visit the Trade and Craft Fair held that summer, and visited Duiker with whom he had become acquainted at the concrete conference. The additional publication of Duiker's Zonnestraal Sanatorium in July 1928 clearly gives Aalto knowledge of this source. See *Boewkundig Weekblad Architectura,* no. 29 (June 21, 1928), pp. 225–232.

3. This was the primary method of dealing with convalescing tubercular patients in the 1920s and 1930s. Special centers such as Davos, Switzerland, were proliferated with hospitals constructed with this type of treatment in mind. See Thomas S. Carrington, *Tuberculosis Hospital and Sanatorium Construction* (New York: New York Association for Study and Prevention of Tuberculosis, 1911).

4. Perhaps Aalto's relationship with Duiker will never be exactly detailed, due to Duiker's untimely death in 1935 and Aalto's reluctance to discuss this aspect of his career.

5. It was used also in a design project for a large resort hotel by André Lurçat dated 1927. However, the overall character of a sanatorium including its window shape is even more a precedent for Paimio. The single-loaded corridor of Lurçat's patients' wing, promenades, and stacked sunning terraces is the same as that Aalto employed at Paimio. Lurçat's project, dated 1928–1929, while geometrically rectangular, is organized in the same manner. See A. Lurçat, *Projets et Realisations* (Paris: Vincent, Freal et Cie, 1929), pp. 50–54 and 85–88.

6. The courtyard stair tower of the Civil Guard's Club House, though by no means unique for the neoclassical style of Finland, indicates Aalto's earlier concern with and preference for the functionally expressive qualities of certain forms, in this case circular and semicircular.

7. For a detailed treatment of Duiker's works, see the Dutch periodical *Forum* 22, no. 5 (November 1971), and no. 6 (January 1972).

8. The reinforced concrete ribs of the dome of Sirén's Houses of Parliament constructed in the latter part of 1928 attracted much attention in Finland. See *Arkkitehti*, no. 12 (1928), pp. 189–190.

9. See visitors' booklet *Varsinais-Soumen Tuberkuloosiparantola* (Turku: Kirjanpaino Lolytypos, 1924), pp. 55, 56. Construction photographs show brick construction.

10. This is meant in the sense given to it by Reyner Banham and not in any of the transmogrifications to which the term has been subjected since its coining.

11. Open-cage elevators were built into systems of apartment blocks in Paris and other European cities since the turn of the century, but their use as an external design feature would appear to be an original idea of the Russian Constructivists. See Vesnin brothers Pravda Project Vittorio de Feo, *USSR Architecture 1917–1936* (Milan: Editori Riuniti, 1963), p. 100; see also Anatole Kopp, *Ville et Revolution* (Paris: Editions Anthropos, 1967).

12. The idea of a free-form curvilinear shape nosed against a rectilinear system of design to create what the Bauhaus painters referred to as a center of interest was utilized by many before Aalto employed it in 1930. Its first appearance in his work was in the restaurant in the Co-op building where he placed a free-form counter as the centerpiece. Le Corbusier had used such curves in the garden walk of the Maison Cook of 1926, in the living room open well of the Villa Stein of 1927, and other such examples too numerous to list. The concave form of the Paimio canopy and its correspondence in plan with the circular automobile turnaround below is similar to the same element in Corbu's Centrosoyus project for Moscow of 1928. Except for a single rounded end and a difference in size, they are the same. It was used by Aalto as mentioned previously in late 1928 in the Itameri restaurant.

13. These dual fireplaces were backed by a steam radiator to give off heat even when there was not an actual fire.

14. This lobby has been altered and is now fitted out with a free-form glass booth for a reception desk.

15. Interview with Alvar Aalto by H. E. Hyytiainen in November 1973 at Aalto's studio in Helsinki.

16. Alvar Aalto, "Between Humanism and Materialism," lecture held at the Central Union of Architects in Vienna, Austria, Summer 1955. Printed in *Der Bau*, nos. 7–8 (1955), pp. 174–176.

17. Ibid.

18. *Arkkitehti*, no. 12 (1928), p. 191.

19. *Arkkitehti*, no. 2, (1929), p. 21.

20. Ibid.

21. At this point in his life Aalto had won three major competitions in his country, each yielding a commission. During the early days of Functionalism for Aalto and perhaps many other Finnish architects, this was one of the main methods of securing commissions for their practices.

7. INTERNATIONAL STYLE BECOMES FUNCTIONALISM

1. He also collaborated with Max Ernst on the design for a restaurant located in a theater in Zurich.

2. The design of the pylons and the lightweight construction methods were used in the Helsinki Fair of 1920 and the general form and decoration was again used in a giant version for the double pylons of the Gothenburg Fair in 1924.

3. Pylons, it seems, were an essential part of fair design in the Baltic during the early 20th century, but not as information points and not grouped informally as Aalto had specified.

4. Many Russian propaganda pavilions were planned to have high lightweight pylons to attract attention and inform the Soviet citizens. These towers often contained graphics and were designed to express their lightweight structural members including cables. N. Pachov, a student under Vhutemas' direction, in 1927 executed a project for a propaganda pavilion with pylons. See Anatole Kopp, *Architecture et Urbanisome Sovetiques des Annees Vingt Villes et Revolution* (Paris: Editions Anthropes, 1967), p. 417.

5. See Le Corbusier et Pierre Jeanneret, *Oeuvre Complète 1910–1929*, 8th ed. (Zurich: Les Editions d'Architecture, 1965), p. 174. Also E. Lissitski's Press Pavilion at the 1928 Cologne Exposition had graphics applied to the outside.

6. V. E. Khazanova, *Soviet Architecture of the First Years of the October Revolution 1917–1925* (Moscow: Nauka, 1970), p. 175.

7. See P. A. Aleksandrovana and S. O. Chan-Magomedov, *Ivan Leonidov* (Milan: Franco Angeli Editors, 1975), p. 36.

8. *Arkkitehti*, January 1930, p. 2.

9. *Arkkitehti,* March 1930, pp. 46–47. A wide variety of shapes for this water tank as shown in the review.

10. This is one of the earliest references to Aalto's well-known character as a heavy drinker. Many countries had prohibition laws during this period and it must have amused Aalto to title his water tank Wolsted Act.

11. Rational thinking in hydrostatic terms is not limited, however, to a single most efficient profile.

12. Stefano Ray, *Sven Markelius* (Rome: Officina Edizioni Roma, 1969), pp. 14–16.

13. This technique of architectural presentation utilizing only line and black or shadow tone was popular with architects and students in European and American schools in the late 1920s and early 1930s who wanted to express themselves in a manner that could not be associated with the tonal wash drawings popular with those working in the Beaux Arts' style.

14. It seems that the woodworking shed executed with timber trusses and plywood gusset baffles at Duiker's Zonnestraal Sanatorium may well have provided inspiration. It is important to remember that fair buildings and crafts exhibition halls for summer festivals usually had no substantial light, and designers of these buildings had to solve the problem of lighting a space with the available daylight. Aalto applied many of the things he learned from the building of these temporary spaces to problems that arose throughout his practice.

15. This quite advanced design was perhaps too much so, for the jury selected the slightly more conservative design of Erik Bryggman which was ultimately built. See Anna-Lisa Stigell, *Erik Bryggman* (Ekenäs: Ekenäs Tryckeri Aktiebolag, 1965), pp. 32–35.

16. The general area of Helsinki has both hills and valleys, but this site was specified to be on a part of a plateau. Perhaps it was selected purposefully to present an extra problem, but it was the portion of the site nearest the major streets of access.

17. Aalto might have gleaned special knowledge from his travels in and around European capitals, but other designers in this contest should have exhibited a similar experience.

18. Asko Salokorpi, *Modern Architecture in Finland* (London: Weidenfeld and Nicolson, 1970), p. 17.

8. INTERNATIONAL FRIENDSHIPS AND TRAVELS

1. Though Stockholm was closer he must have had a strong desire to move to Helsinki at this time.

2. Interview with Hilding Ekelund, Helsinki, August 1974, conducted by P. D. Pearson and R. L. Heinonen at The Museum of Finnish Architecture.

3. Hilding Ekelund's Rememberances of Aalto, *Arkkitehti*, 7/8 (1976), p. 28.

4. See *Die Wohnung für das Existenzminimum* (Frankfurt: Englert & Schlosser, 1930), p. 40. A conference review edited by Siegfried Giedion for the 1929 CIAM Meeting held in Frankfurt. List of participants on pp. 39–40.

5. Interview with Alfred Roth, conducted by P. D. Pearson, Zurich, February 1974.

6. CIAM Report for Brussels.

7. Similar theories had also been advanced by Heinrich Tessanow. See Gerda Wangerin, *Heinrich Tessanow* (Essen: Gerhard Weiss, 1976), pp. 83–87.

8. *Arkkitehti*, no. 2 (1930), forepage 5. News section covering applications.

9. There were undoubtedly bad feelings against the young Aalto at that point.

10. Interview with Marcel Breuer, via telephone from New York City, January 19, 1974, conducted by P. D. Pearson.

11. Interview with Mrs. Walter Gropius conducted by P. D. Pearson, London, February 13, 1974. Erno Goldfinger has confirmed this.

12. Interview with Erno Goldfinger, architect, conducted by P. D. Pearson, London, December 1973, at architect's home in Hampstead, U.K.

13. Only the ceiling of the apse is parabolic in shape; the side walls are straight but splayed open towards the nave. The introduction of rationalized acoustical design into church architecture at this time was unpopular and foreign to Finland. Church design was the last area of architecture to be affected by functionalism. The jury's unhappiness with the inappropriate modernity yielded a second competition with a traditionally styled entry by Sonck as winner and architect of the realized church.

14. These cusps produce what acousticians refer to as "dead spots" where no sound can be reflected.

15. Finnish Arts and Crafts Society, *Pienasunto* (exhibition catalog) (Helsinki, 1930), pp. 27–32.

16. Ibid.

17. See note 4, above. The idea of designing a dwelling for "the living income earner" that would satisfy the material and "mental" needs of its occupant at a "bearable" rent was one of CIAM's more utopian preoccupations, revolving around the still controversial issue of the "Existenzminimum." Giedion observed some of the practical difficulties inherent in architects' attempts to provide relevant solutions, noting that "the necessary scientific foundations are still lacking." He adds: "On the occasion of the Frankfurt Congress experts in other sciences had been called in, but in order to replace instinctive

groping by real scientific security, further cooperation with hygienists and sociologists will be necessary." S. Giedion, *Space, Time and Architecture* (Cambridge, Mass.: Harvard University Press, 1949), p. 9.

18. The Aalto apartment in the Agricultural Co-op was published in the *Arkkitehti* 19, no. 6 (1929), p. 90, and attributed to Aino Aalto.

19. This design also appeared in the *Nordic Building Conference Catalogue* published in Helsinki in 1932.

20. Aalto must have seen many sources for this type of layout in modern architecture during his travels around Europe. Mies' Tugendhat House could even be reckoned as such, but too much should not be made of this.

21. Enso-Gutzeit is a governmentally controlled industry specializing in timber and wood products.

9. VIIPURI LIBRARY

1. "Viipurin Kaupungin Kirjasto," *Arkkitehti*, no. 3 (March 1928), p. 38.

2. This park still exists today and is the major green space in the central area of the town renamed Viborg, USSR.

3. However, it can easily be compared as well to Hakon Ahlberg's Arts and Crafts Pavilion at the Gothenburg Fair in 1923. Aalto had most assuredly observed that building in its construction stages while in the employ of Bjerke. See Hakon Ahlberg, *Modern Swedish Architecture* (London: Benn, 1925), pp. 143–148.

4. A nearly identical sunken space arranged with stairs was the central feature on the 1929 proposal for the Vesnin brohers' Lenin Library in Moscow. Aalto's is surely earlier but the scheme by the Vesnin brothers is clearly advanced in terms of its modernity. See Anatole Kopp, *Ville et Revolution* (Paris: Editions Anthropos, 1967), p. 526.

5. See Giuseppe Marchini, *Giuliano da San Gallo*, Monografie Studi III (Florence: University of Florence, Instituto di Storia del Arte, 1943).

6. Villa Väinöla had been originally planned with a two-story central hall.

7. This type of low-relief posed figures were popular with neo-classical architects in many parts of Europe. The Musée de l'Art Moderne in Paris, built for the 1937 World's Fair, may have been one of the last to employ it.

8. Although he was an architect his chief contributions to the development of the field have been through his lectures and writings.

9. See Hakon Ahlberg, *Modern Swedish Architecture* (Lodnon: Benn, 1925), p. 145.

10. See note 3 above.

11. *Viipurin Kaupungin Kirjasto* (Viipuri Municipal Library) (Viipuri: Viipuri Library Board of Directors, 1935), p. 20.

12. Actually he had discreetly used this motif before in the competition project where he placed a four-story window wall on the north stairway which was recessed in a niche, but in the execution of the second version he obviously felt bold enough to bring it out front.

13. Aalto utilized a recent proposal which called for the municipal assembly hall to be located on the side of Aleksantrinkatu opposite the library site. To reinforce his scheme he specified that the House of Culture, as the hall was referred to, would have included in its program a balcony restaurant to house the facility of an old and well-known private dining establishment.

14. *Viipurin Kaupungin Kirjasto*, op. cit., p. 21.

15. Interview with Otto I. Meurman, conducted by P. D. Pearson and R. Heinonen at The Museum of Finnish Architecture, Helsinki, July 1975.

16. *Viipurin Kaupungin Kirjasto*, op. cit., p. 22.

17. Interview with Otto I. Meurman, cited above in note 15.

18. Ibid.

19. *Viipurin Kaupungin Kirjasto,* op. cit., p. 24.

20. The completion of the Paimio Sanatorium was the last of the Turku commissions, and at that point in the midthirties Helsinki was full of design opportunities and was linked directly by airplane to the major centers in Finland as well as Stockholm, Gothenburg, and Copenhagen. Alfred says theat Aalto traveled by plane as far as Belgrade when he attended the Athens conference in 1933. By this time he was already situated in Helsinki.

21. One face bordered on a street, the others on parkland.

22. Alvar Aalto, "Abstract Art and Architecture," *Werk,* February 1969, p. 43.

23. Ibid., p. 44.

24. Interview with Alvar Aalto, conducted by P. D. Pearson in Aalto's studio, Helsinki, Finland, June 26, 1975, and interview with Otto I. Meurman cited above in note 15.

25. The principles of lighting that Aalto used in the design and placement of fixtures for the Turun Sanomat, Paimio, and all later buildings were probably inspired by the lamps of Poul Henningsen published in his *Kritisk Revy.* However, as early as April 1927, an article by H. Kjaldman appeared in the *Arkkitehti* covering the full range of lighting problems and solutions available to modern architects.

26. Interview with Alvar Aalto, August 15, 1974, conducted by P. D. Pearson in Aalto's studio, Helsinki, Finland.

27. This is only an explanation of how the shape itself is derived in conceptual terms; the actual design is in practice a complex process based upon the exact reflections needed for an even distribution. Again most of these principles had been made familiar to Aalto in articles by Henningsen and others in the journal *Kritisk Revy.*

10. ESTABLISHMENT IN HELSINKI AND NEW AMBITIONS

1. In 1933 it was not known that the stadium would be for an Olympic contest; it only developed that this would be the case during the course of the competitions. The Olympic games were not held in 1940 but in 1952.

2. Of the total twenty-eight entries only 15 were invited to proceed to the next stage of the competition. Aalto received a "second bought" category which is comparable to a mention in the competitions of Western countries. At that point in the competition each of the mentions and those receiving higher awards received some money to participate in Part II.

3. A reference to Aalto's recognition of the earth and the working of it as a special consideration in such a large project.

4. Not required in Part I of the competition.

5. All the drawings for these two competitions are located in the archives of the Museum of Finnish Architecture.

6. Aalto had an apartment in which he worked and lived. In 1936 William Henderson, RIBA of London, then a young architectural graduate, visited the Aalto office and has reported that they were very busy working on competitions and, not having enough drawing boards, had removed all the doors from their hinges and set them up for drafting.

7. *Arkkitehti* 30 (August 1933), forepage 7.

8. *Arkkitehti,* January 1934, forepage 1; February 1934, pp. 26–29.

9. This basic design exercise was used at the Bauhaus and also appears in the work of many painters of the early 20th century. See the work of Kasimir Malevitch, Wassily Kandinsky, and Kurt Schwitters from the middle of the second decade on.

10. This group of romantic enthusiasts may indeed have chafed at the geometrical nature of Aalto's solution, but the first prize winner as selected by them was equally rectilinear in profile.

11. It would seem from the quality of the long-span structures in this competition that a full knowledge of the known possibilites of reinforced concrete had reached Helsinki as soon as any European capital. Many of the solutions submitted employed reinforced concrete because structural steel shapes capable of long spans were not realistically avaialbe in Finland.

12. Aalto's use of this motif is for both lighting and structural purposes, just as Duiker had employed it at Zonnestraal.

13. This type of perimeter skylight or light trap was the exact profile on which he based most of the windows in his libraries from the sixties.

14. This combination of concrete coffers and large dished lighting fixture resembles the construction photographs of the Viipuri Library in the book about its planning and construction. See *Viipurin Kaupunkgin Kirjasto,* (Viipuri: Viipuri Library Board of Directors, 1935), p. 31.

15. In architectural competitions certain charactersitcs of some designers can be detected even with the most anonymous procedures. The jurors, which included Sirén, probably sought a modern design but one that would quietly respect Sirén's neoclassical styled Houses of Parliament standing on the opposite side of Mannerheimintie from the Postal Telegraph site.

16. Interview with Alvar Aalto conducted by P. D. Pearson in Aalto's studio in Helsinki, June 26, 1975.

17. One of his less creative labels.

18. Dated 1934, Duiker's Theater and Commercial Block for Amsterdam was contemporary with Aalto's Post Office project. See *Forum* (Amsterdam) 22, no. 6 (January 1972), p. 90.

11. RECOGNITION BY INDUSTRY

1. Interview with Maire Gullichsen Nyström, conducted by P. D. Pearson at Villa Mairea, July 15, 1974, Noormarkku, Finland.

2. See Kyosti Ålander, ed., *Industrial Architecture in Finland* (Helsinki: Association of Finnish Architects, 1952); essay by Viljo Rewell, p. 5.

3. His Oulu plant in 1930 was only a surface treatment and his knowledge of paper and pulp mills would have begun at that time. He would, however, have been able to see other such plants in southern Finland.

4. In the total picture of modern industrial architecture in Finland Aalto's accomplishments are not as significant as the rest of his works when compared with their counterparts. The dockside storage building with its curved laminated wooden roof beams is an exact copy of Sven Markelius's basic structure for the Introduction and Information Pavilion at the Stockholm Exhibition in 1930.

5. These houses for the engineering staff are in groups of five arranged with five adjacent gardens to form a fan. The logo that Aalto designed for the Sunila organization representing the five shareholders consisted of five elongated wedges arranged in a fan.

6. This early use of the pole aesthetic was concurrent with the proposed but unexecuted use of a similar expression for his own house in Munkkiniemi.

7. Altogether Aalto produced six different types of multiple dwellings at Sunila.

8. After the Gullichsens opened the doors to the executive level of industry, Aalto secured many commissions for industrial plants and villages. This contact and its resultant buildings were to form the key to his economic success.

9. Interview with Maire Gullichsen Nyström cited above in note 1.

10. Ibid.

11. The Gullichsen/Ahlström interests now own less than half of Artek.

12. "Standard Wooden Furniture," *Architectural Review* 74 (1933), p. 221.

13. It is a strange testimony to contemporary designers that the now classic chairs continue to be sought after and imitated more than later furniture designs.

14. The arts and crafts tradition has always been closely allied with and sometimes integral with architecture in Finland. See Marc Treib's "Gallen-Kallela: A Portrait of the Artist as an Architect," *Architectural Association Quarterly* 7, no. 3, (July/September 1975) pp. 3–13. The Society of Arts and Crafts in Finland has always sought the involvement of architects. Aalto among many others participated in their exhibitions and proceedings. See any annual publication *Ornamo* (Helsinki: Suomen Koristetaiteilivain Liito Ornamo).

15. It is sold primarily with a webbed seat and back rather than the plywood of the earlier model.

16. Interview with Pekka Korhonen, technical director of the Korhonen factory, conducted by P.D. Pearson and R.L. Heinonen at Korhonen factories near Turku, July 15, 1975. He reported that the chair legs deformed under continued use.

17. The original patents for the use of casein glues and a hot plate press were granted to Christian Luther (claimed to be a relation of Martin Luther) in 1892 and 1896 respectively. From 1884 Luther experimented with, and from about 1892 onward manufactured, a strong light chair seat made of molded plywood slats. Many of his products were exported to the United Kingdom, Belgium, Germany, and Holland. In London these products were sold primarily for tea chests and rubber chests by Venesta Ltd. Luterma, as the factory was ultimately named, was destroyed during the war, but has been rebuilt and is still producing plywood. See Andrew Dick Wood, *Plywoods of the World, Their Development, Manufacture and Application* (London: Johnston and Bacon, 1963), pp. 72, 90, 225–226. Eliel Saarinen had also experimented with bent wood furniture and knew of Luther's products for he designed and executed an extension to the factory in Talinn in the 1920s.

18. He had traveled to Tallinn when a newly graduated student for *Arkkitehti* magazine; from an interview with Alvar Aalto conducted by Heikki Hyytainen, November 1973, at Aalto's studio in Helsinki.

19. Some forms and braces used today in the Korhonen factory resemble those used by Michael Thonet. See Karl Mang, *Bugholz-Möbel-Das Werk Michael Thonet* (exhibition catalog Palais Liechtenstein) (Vienna: Hans Thonet, 1965), p. 7.

20. Interview with Aalto, June 26, 1975, conducted by P. D. Pearson at Aalto's studio in Helsinki.

21. This was a basic shape manufactured for 30 years by A. M. Luther Co.

22. Aalto secured patent rights for this back curved bending technique. See British Patent No. 423.686, applied November 8, 1933, accepted February 6, 1935.

23. Giuseppi Morandi was granted a British Patent No. 156.015 on January 6, 1921 for a design of an all wood chair laid up in thin plys of veneer. The entire chair was made in this technique including the legs which in form resemble the profile of the bent-leg stool Aalto designed in 1929.

24. Charles Eames was one of the pioneers in the design and use of three dimensionally formed shapes in plywood. See *Work of Charles and Ray Eames,* University of California at Los Angeles exhibition catalog, 1977. This catalog shows a plywood nose form for a 1939 military aircraft. See also Charles Eames' and Eero Saarinen's prize-winning molded plywood chairs in *Organic Design* (New York: Museum of Modern Art, 1941), pp. 10–17.

25. He continued to develop ideas taken from others in an experimental mood and eventually evolved from them a series of special forms and techniques unique to his work.

12. VERNACULAR AND ROMANTIC PRECEDENTS

1. The fact that he appeared at CIAM conferences more infrequently as the years went on is an indication that his enthusiasm for that organization's professed style had waned. His lack of highly articulate verbal skills in an international context probably made him feel somewhat ill at ease.

2. Finland's repertoire of vernacular modes is perhaps as wide and varied as in any European country, and national romantic enthusiasm for some of them had been popular in Aalto's youth.

3. Interview with Alvar Aalto, June 26, 1975, by P. D. Pearson in Aalto's studio in Helsinki.

4. Sketched faintly on the podium is the outline of a grand piano and three stools where other members of the quartet would be stationed. By the mid-1920's, these forms began to appear in the work of Jean Arp. See Herbert Read, *The Art of Jean Arp* (New York: Abrams, 1968), plates 34 (Winged Configuration, 1925), 67 (*Clock,* 1924); and Carola Giedion-Welcker, *Jean Arp* (New York: Abrams, 1957), plates 7 (*Egg Board,* 1922), 9 (*Torso,* 1925), and 14 (*Objects Arranged as a Writing,* 1928).

5. Aalto was a great devotee of modern art and developed many personal friendships among painters and sculptors of that period. A number of painters experimented with the shapes of musical instruments in thin ink. See the works of Picasso, Braque, and Gris in Werner Hartmann, *Painting in the Twentieth Century,* vol. 2, (London: Lund Humphries, 1965), pp. 77–80 and 85–95; and Robert Rosenblum, *Cubism and Twentieth-Century Art,* rev. ed. (New York: Abrams, 1966), plates ix (Georges Braque, *Still Life with Violin and Pitcher,* 1909–1910), 38 (Pablo Picasso, *Bottle, Glass, Violin,* 1912–1913), and 43 [Georges Braque, *Oval Still Life (Le Violin),* 1914] in Part One, *The Foundations of Cubism: II, Picasso and Braque, 1909–1911* and *III: Picasso and Braque, 1912–1924.*

6. The use-related form of objects always seemed to fascinate Aalto, which may be a simple explanation for his facile use of architectonic forms in a manner that could be easily perceived by observers of his works.

7. These vertical slats which were applied to the round concrete columns in the children's library were to keep fingerprints off the plaster in the middle section of the column. As a form they resembled or perhaps abstractly represented the fluting of classical columns. Aalto made use of this motif in his breakdown of the International Style.

8. These were evidently installed just at the building's completion in 1935, by which time Aalto was beginning to show signs of change. It is likely that Aino Aalto had a share of the responsibility in the final outfitting of the Library and is chiefly responsible for this bucolic addition. This is confirmed in an interview by Aarne Ervi who assisted Aino in that work. Interview conducted with Ervi at his home in Helsinki, June 1975.

9. Along with the curving full forms, the planned and controlled use of vines seems to have been the earliest indication of a new aesthetic in Aalto's work.

10. One of Aalto's most repeated theories was that standardization must serve the architect to yield a flexibility that would present a wide variety of design alternatives. *Alvar Aalto Synopsis: Papers of the Institute for History and Theory of Architecture* (Zurich: Swiss Federal Institute of Technology, 1970), p. 13.

13. ROMANTIC MODERNISM

1. *Alvar Aalto Synopsis: Papers of the Institute for History and Theory of Architecture* (Zurich: Swiss Federal Institute of Technology, 1970), p. 15.

2. *Arkkitehti,* no. 6 (1935), forepage 21; list of amount of prize awards and jury: Jussi Paatela; Johan Roiha, engineer; and A. Hackzell, minister.

3. This moment in 1935 was something of a high point in relations between Finland and the Soviets during the pre-war era. See L. A. Puntila, *Political History of Finland 1806–1966,* 2d ed. (New York: Praeger, 1974).

4. The program called for a dignified ·style building. Perhaps the delicate nature of relations between Finland and Russia and the Soviet government's denouncement of modern architecture, especially that of their own Constructivist group, made it imperative to require architecture of a less modern expression under the Stalinist regime. However Aalto's, Ekelund's second prize-winning project, and all the other projects reviewed in *Arkkitehti* exhibited a decidedly modern character. *Arkkitehti,* no. 7 (July 1935), pp. 109–112.

5. ALKO, a state owned company, controls all alcoholic beverages sold in Finland, imported as well as locally produced.

6. Reference again to Aalto's reputation as a drinker. In fairness, many of the mottoes of other competitors have equally poignant meanings. See *Arkkitehti,* no. 4 (1936), pp. 58–64.

7. Large quantities of coal, the primary fuel for this facility as constructed, are delivered at dockside and stored in an open yard.

8. The wall of the western facade contains windows to permit sunlight in that extremely northern latitude to penetrate into the studio. On the evidence of interior photographs the largest window in the upper middle portion of the facade (and therefore the double-height space behind it) was temporarily closed off during the war years to maintain blackout conditions.

9. This type of pattern with a slightly wider pitch was later much imitated by plywood siding in many Western countries. It was employed as a standard texture in the vocabulary of popular houses executed in the modern style from the 1950s on. The siding on Aalto's house was originally "bright" and meant to be maintained periodically as one would the bright work on a yacht. This was the aspect of required maintenance built into the Villa Mairea that has enabled it to be continually revived throughout its existence.

10. Because the grounds were originally less foliated and because of the open plot to the south, the view was unobstructed for quite a distance.

11. It was not a luxury house by later standards but presented Aalto's first opportunity to experiment with aspects of housing and residential design for a mass clientele. See Brian B. Taylor, "Methods of Construction and Rational Empiricism," *L'Architecture d'Aujourd'hui* 191 (June 1977), p. 113. Aalto's quote regarding this aspect of design has been published in other sources as well.

14. A NEW HEROIC STYLE

1. The announcement was made in April of 1936 and the entries were due for submission in June. See Museum Archives Competition file, Museum of Finnish Architecture, Helsinki.

2. Competition review, *Arkkitehti,* nos. 6–7 (1936).

3. The corner batten covers were sanded and finished in a clear varnish to emphasize the outermost surface and give the effect of a corrugated surface made of wood. Perhaps this had originally been made as a test model out of corrugated paper and simply retained. It is the first use of Aalto's well-known finned surfaces.

4. As at Viipuri the Pavilion at Paris had structures and conical skylights in one plane. The basic material at Paris was wood while at Viipuri it had been concrete.

5. The technique for assembling these poles is found in many manuals for camping and woodmanship including the Scout handbooks of most countries. See Clifford W. Ashley, *The Ashley Book of Knots,* (Garden City, N.Y.: Doubleday, 1944), pp. 342–343.

6. Interview with Alvar Aalto conducted by P. D. Pearson in Aalto's studio, Helsinki, Finland, August 15, 1974.

7. Although the strips were secured to the trunk or shaft they were probably of more value visually than structurally.

8. "Tsit Tsit Pum" is a sound similar to that made by a marching drummer. Here again as in his first motto the reference to marching is intended to indicate that wood was on the move or making a breakthrough in its use as a source of consumer products.

9. In both buildings the level of the roof is constant, but the floor levels vary to give low and high ceiling volumes.

10. In the sense that the pure volumetric form is broken down into a multilevel form that follows the contour of the earth, the building or volume is related to the romantic base of the earth.

11. Aalto, who used rough but mature birch trunks as supports in the same area of the building, recalled in abstract form the most dazzling effect of the Finnish landscape with its densely spaced straight shafts of young birch saplings reaching up to the sky for light.

12. In some cases Saarinen's buildings had also been based on the older wooden buildings, but whereas he used the forms of Karelian log buildings, Aalto used forms and details found in the houses of Ostro-Bothnian villages. Albert Christ-Janer, *Eliel Saarinen* (Chicago: University of Chicago Press, 1948).

13. The jury consisted of a former partner, a teacher, and a supportive associate. Each knew and respected Aalto and his work, but not one could have expected the type of building designs he produced for this competition. Yet it is likely that they knew his designs when they were presented for jury.

14. It was the custom to select the jury members from the winners of previous national SAFA-sanctioned competitions.

15. He did not place in the competition awards; Museum Archives Competition file, Museum of Finnish Architecture, Helsinki.

16. The vista of parallel free-standing walls at right angles to the axis of travel had been used in the examination suite at Paimio Sanatorium.

17. Many designers had used the idea of an irregular pinwheel as an organizational tool. Many of Frank Lloyd Wright's Prairie Houses were based upon it. Asko Salokorpi has found that echelon planning had been a popular notion with Martti Valikingas while a student at Helsinki Polytechnic Institute some years before Aalto graduated.

18. See J. M. Richards, *A Guide to Finnish Architecture* (London: Hugh Evelyn, 1966), pp. 53–54.

19. Nyström's addition was a semicircular stack area located at the rear of the building.

20. One of the few straightforward and less humorous mottoes ever utilized by Aalto. It was fashionable to be as inventive and as clever in the selection of one's mottoes as it was in a design and solution.

21. This area, laid out by Engel, is one of the oldest in Helsinki and architects have always treated it as a special resource. After all, at that time most of the buildings were just approaching their 100th anniversary, giving them an extra sentimental importance.

22. "Free form" usually refers to a shape that appears to be constructed without an orthodox system of geometry: lack of constant radius and exactly repetitive line length and positions. Architecturally any nonregular curved corner geometrical volume might loosely be described as free form. In this case the term could be applied because Aalto intended the interior to contrast sharply with the sharp-edged rectangular forms of the rest of his design. This is the only instance in which he combined the use of the round skylight and an undulating ceiling, but in the lecture hall of the Technical University at Otaniemi, a curving acoustical shape was combined with a series of light trap-type skylights.

23. Aarne Ervi's first-place scheme was not more traditional, but as a modern design it was perhaps considered more appropriate than Aalto's scheme.

24. Interview with Maxwell Fry conducted by P. D. Pearson at Fry's office in London, December 15, 1973.

15. MASTERY OF A NEW RATIONALISM

1. See George E. Kidder Smith, *Italy Builds* (New York: Reinhold, 1955), pp. 30–31.

2. Interview with Maire Gullichsen Nyström, conducted by P. D. Pearson at Villa Mairea, July 15, 1974, Noormarkku, Finland.

3. Ibid.

4. Ibid.

5. Ibid.

6. First state here refers to mechanically drawn plans and sections, etc., not freehand sketches.

7. Nearly all the romantic forms from the previous projects appear in a refined form in the Villa Mairea. It is one of only two luxury houses that Aalto executed, the other being the Maison Carré outside Paris designed and built between 1956–1958.

8. The flower arranging room, referred to by the owner as the Japanese flower arranging room, is a combination of curved elements like the enormous china sink and such wooden elements as the trellis. It is located directly beneath the studio. The larger size of the studio projects to the west and is supported by an engaged pole arrangement, creating a small, rough portico.

9. This pool as constructed was one of the earliest versions of the free-form or kidney-shaped swimming pools built in the U.S.A. in the early forties and elsewhere later on. See the large free-form pool in G. E. Kidder Smith, op. cit., pp. 190–191.

10. Aalto had erroneously hoped that the Gullichsens would develop an interest in collecting art works in a major way but that was overruled by them. In the final version he provided for the display and exhibition of a smaller number of works by incorporating a system of linked movable partitions in he south area of the living-sitting room.

11. As a summer house conceived as a pavilion in the woods, the view of the forest was increased by shifting the fireplace. The massive window units were designed and constructed to be individually removable to create the effect of a rustic pavilion, but only once was a unit removed. To provide ventilation in this fixed glass house Aalto provided a ceiling plenum where fresh air could be brought in by gravity air flow through small holes located in the revealed joints of the clear birch ceiling planks.

12. As a young woman, Maire Gullichsen had trained in Paris to be a painter. Interview with Maire Gullichsen Nyström, cited above in note 2.

13. Ibid. This was to be Maire Gullichsen's corner of work and pleasure on both levels. According to her, she produced only one painting in that studio.

14. This is the type of experimentation that Aalto had in mind when he referred to the private house as a laboratory. See Brian B. Taylor, "Methods of Construction and Rational Empiricism," *L'Architecture d'Aujourd'hui* 191 (June 1977), p. 113.

16. TRANSITION COMPLETE

1. Aalto's breakdown of Functionalism was completed at this point. This building represents his first attempt without any significant influence from the International Style.

2. A short period of time, but as architect of the previous Pavilion at Paris, Aalto must have had prior unofficial knowledge of the competition.

3. Selected because they were on the Paris Pavilion jury.

4. See *Arkkitehti*, May 1939, p. 116.

5. Ibid.

6. Ibid.

7. Ibid. This entry is supposed to have been submitted by Aino Aalto secretly without Aalto's knowledge; but given the nature of their small and open office, that seems unlikely.

8. As an enthusiast for America during this period of his life he probably envisioned it as something of a world of tomorrow. See Hakon Ahlberg's remembrance of Aalto in *Arkkitehti* Vol. 73, no. 7/8, p. 26.

9. In spite of the fact that for this competition Saarinen altered his style to one that was vaguely Chicago in character and certainly American in flavor, his design was and still is to some extent a subject of pride in the minds of Helsinki architects.

10. Adolf Loos had traveled to the U.S.A. for only an extended visit in the 1890s, and Richard Neutra relocated there in 1923, but was not an independently practicing architect before his move. Saarinen seems to be a decade or more earlier than the main wave of well-known architects fleeing the strife created in Europe by the Nazis. See Siegfried Giedion's essay *Richard Neutra*, (Zurich: Editions Girsberger, 1950), p. 8.

11. Probably not illegal in the strict sense but given the quiet, gentlemanly nature of the architectural profession in Helsinki it could be considered bad taste or at least brash. This seems to be an unprecedented number of entries by a single office in the history of open architectural competitions in Finland since that policy began just after its independence.

12. The undulating wall and basic layout of the final scheme was a combination of the best aspects of the two alternatives, both being similar in spatial divisions to begin with.

13. As architects sometimes take to the spirit of revival, designs from the early works of modern masters are honored and brought once again to the surface and reemployed. This space which has the expressed admiration of nearly every architect who knows the photographs has yet to be so honored.

14. *Alvar Aalto Synopsis: Papers of the Institute for History and Theory of Architecture* (Zurich: Swiss Federal Instiute of Technology, 1970), p. 17. (Aalto article reprinted from *The Technology Review*, November 1940, pp. 14–16.)

15. The original program stated nothing about the possibility of windows in either side wall. See Archives, Museum of Finnish Architecture, Helsinki.

16. It gave them a view and an opportunity to place some architectural expression on the outside of the building, but it presented further problems with the cinema restaurant, located on the balcony adjacent to the windows.

17. See Karl Fleig, *Alvar Aalto 1922–1963* (Zurich: Editions Girsberger, 1963), p. 124.

18. Several critics have made a point of this. See Pekka Suhonen "Alvar Aalto and Finland the 1920s and 1930s," *Space Design*. no. 149 (January/February 1977), pp. 69–72, translation p. 5. Utilizing straight strips of wood to form his awned surfaces, Aalto limited himself to undulations in only one direction as he had in his furntiure.

19. See Alvar Aalto, "Thoughts from Finland," a speech given at the Architectural Association; reprinted in *Special Commemorative Publication*, (London: Architectural Association, 1965), p. 168.

20. There was an entrance gate in that area leading in from the Long Island Railroad to the east. *Souvenir Guide to the New York World's Fair 1939-40* (New York: New World's Fair Commission, 1939), pp. 41–43.

21. The Villa Mairea was actually finished after the fair pavilion had begun, but it is the original source for many of the details used at New York.

22. He was not able to solve the air circulation in his usually prescribed manner. In addition this space was to be relatively dark with dramatic display lighting which was characteristically different from his brightly illuminated and gravity-ventilated spaces like those at Viipuri and Paris.

23. A rustic if not crude dual systems fixture; but such ideas have only appeared in wide architectural use from the midsixties on.

24. Sven Markelius was one of the few European designers from the CIAM group besides Aalto to execute a building at the 1939–1940 New York Fair. Although a number of the Bauhaus staff had by that time emigrated to the U.S. few were asked to participate.

25. Aarne Ervi and Viljo Rewell, both former employees of Aalto's, attempted to incorporate romantic motifs in some of their works, but when they did not find any significant success, their enthusiasm eventually dissipated. *Viljo Rewell*, edited by Kyösti Ålander (Helsinki: Otava, 1966). For work of Ervi see N. E. Wickberg, *Finnish Architecture* (Helsinki: Otava, 1959), pp. 200, 208, 209, 226, 227.

26. The traces of the International Style that Aalto retained were quickly absorbed by the romantic nature of his later works and their identity lost.

17. HOPES FOR A NEW CAREER

1. See William H. Jordy, *American Buildings and Their Architects: The Impact of European Modernism in the Mid-Twentieth Century* (Garden City, N.Y.: Doubleday, 1972).

2. Hakon Ahlberg's remembrance of Alvar Aalto, *Arkkitehti*, vol. 73 (July/August 1976), p. 26. The date is reckoned by the fact that the trade fair that Ahlberg refers to in his article was the Pienasunto exhibit; see Finnish Arts and Crafts Society, *Pienasunto*, Helsinki, 1930, pp. 27–32.

3. "Standard Wooden Furniture," *Architectural Review*, vol. 74 (December 1933), p. 220.

4. Press release announcing opening of exhibition dated March 15, 1938, at the Museum of Modern Art. Museum of Modern Art, Archives Architectural Department, New York, Arthur Drexler, Curator.

5. The relationship of these buildings to the natural phenomenon was noted in the *Souvenir Guide to the New York World's Fair 1939–40* (New York: New World Fair Commission, 1939), p. 181.

6. Interview with Harmon H. Goldstone conducted by P. D. Pearson, New York City, January 15, 1974.

7. *Bulletin, School of Architecture and Applied Arts* (New York: Bryant Park Center, New York University, 1940), p. 5.

8. See Leonardo Mosso, Alvar Aalto (Helsinki: Ateneum, 1967), p. 57.

9. Letter to William Wilson Wurster from Alvar Aalto dated March 29, 1939. William Wilson Wurster Archive, College of Environmental Design Documents Collection, University of California, Berkeley, Professor Richard C. Peters, archivist.

10. Ibid.

11. Letter to William Wilson Wurster from N. G. Hahl dated January 12, 1938. Wurster Archive as cited above in note 9.

12. Telegram to William Wilson Wurster from Alvar Aalto dated May 24, 1939; also letter to same from Grace L. McCann Morley, director, San Francisco Museum of Art, dated May 12, 1939. Wurster Archive as cited above in note 9.

13. Wurster saw to it that everything was taken care of in relation to the Aaltos' visit. He enlisted Mrs. Church and Mrs. Gardner Dailey to coordinate their touring movements. He had arranged for an exhibition of Aalto's furnishings at the Golden Gate exposition then in progress and arranged for dinner engagements and even a trip to the countryside at the Gregory Farm where Wurster had designed some of the buildings.

14. As Adolf Loos had become aware of America's spirit in the 1890s, Aalto perhaps sensed industrial growth in the Americas that could significantly effect a change in architectural theory through cooperative research. Minutes of meeting dated June 1, 1939. Wurster Archives as cited above in note 9.

15. Letter of July 12, 1939, and article from Alvar Aalto; Wurster Archive as cited above in note 9.

16. Letter to William Wilson Wurster from Alvar Aalto dated October 25, 1939; Wurster Archive as cited above in note 9.

18. WAR YEARS

1. Viipuri, a distribution center, was one of the three major centers in southern Finland and as such was the site of potential commissions. The construction of the Viipuri Library had prompted him earlier to move to Helsinki to be in a central location in the "south."

2. It appeared extreme because Finland had never been threatened or attacked as an independent nation.

3. Memorandum sent to William Wurster from Alvar Aalto was undated, but it would have been at the beginning of the Winter War. William Wilson Wurster Archive, College of Environmental Design Documents Collection, University of California, Berkeley, Professor Richard C. Peters, archivist.

4. L. A. Puntila, *The Political History of Finland 1809–1966* (Helsinki: Otava, 1974), p. 169.

5. Letter to William Wurster from Alvar Aalto dated March 28, 1940; Wurster Archive as cited above in note 3.

6. Press release, Massachusetts Institute of Technology, announcing Aalto's appointment as Research Professor dated July 24, 1940. Institute Archives, Massachusetts Institute of Technology, Cambridge, Mass., Helen Stolkin, archivist.

7. The Bemis Foundation had been recommended to Aalto by Wurster the previous year. John Burchard, the first director of the

Bemis Foundation, contacted Aalto when he learned that he was to come to Cambridge to visit Walter Gropius in April 1940 and arranged for him to lecture at MIT while he was there. See letters to Aalto from Burchard dated April 8 and 18, 1940 as well as letters from Aalto to Burchard dated April 17, 20, and 22, 1940; Institute Archives as cited above in note 6.

8. Press release; see note 6 above.

9. It was John Burchard who first introduced the idea of adding Aalto to the MIT faculty. This has been confirmed by Mrs. John Burchard.

10. It must be presumed that the sympathy shown to Finland during the Winter War prompted the group interested in reconstruction, which included Aalto, to seek financial support in the U.S. References to Aalto's involvement in this reconstruction organization called "For Finland" are found in many sources. Aalto had mentioned its existence to Wurster in the previously noted letter dated March 28, 1940; see note 5 above. The organization, however, was not effective to any significant degree in securing aid.

11. Press release; see note 6 above.

12. The Bremen apartment block utilizing the same wedge-shaped units was designed and built between 1958 and 1962.

13. Letter to John Burchard from Alvar Aalto dated October 17, 1940 written from New York just before he sailed for Europe; Institute Archives, see note 6 above.

14. Puntila, op. cit.

15. Aalto's well-known architectural forms were used presumably to allow students more time to concentrate on the planning aspects of the exercise.

16. This biological or organic reference to towns and cities obviously did not originate with Aalto. In lectures and articles he depended on that reference to communicate his concern for a town as an organized environment. See Kirmo Mikkola, "Alvar Aalto's Influence on Town Planning," *Tilli*, no. 1 (1973), pp. 29–31.

17. Aalto did not return to MIT in 1941. This can be verified by an examination of his Personnel Study on file at the School of Architecture Office, Massachusetts Institute of Technology, Cambridge, Mass.

18. See K. Pirinen and E. Jutikkala, *A History of Finland* (New York: Praeger, 1974).

19. During the war, Finland's industry being only partially nationalized depended heavily on private owners of large industry and encouraged these leaders to participate in the planning of the war effort.

20. The underground shelter already existed and was not part of the design program.

21. See Eduard and Claudia Neuenschwander, *Alvar Aalto and Finnish Architecture* (Erlenbach-Zurich: Verlag fur Architektur), pp. 109–111.

22. Viljo Rewell and Aarne Ervi, *Industrial Architecture in Finland* (Helsinki: Suomen Arkkitehilütto, 1952), p. 28.

23. Ibid., p. 32.

24. This type of echelon arrangement in site planning to form a nonrectalinear open space was widely used by architects and students through western Europe, England, and America from the late 1930s on.

25. Not only was he influenced by Asplund's and Ahlberg's versions of an atrium, but his home district of Ostro-Bothnia contained many settlements and hamlets where the houses were arranged around small squarish courts giving a similar effect.

26. Feelings had obviously cooled toward Finland, but Aalto was able to maintain his friendships through normally infrequent letters.

27. The years of the war were the low point of building of any nature.

28. Kirmo Mikkola has listed this as a competition project; see his "Alvar Aalto's Influence on Town Planning," *Tiili*, Winter (January 1973), pp. 29–31.

29. The comparison here is with Giuliano Romano's contrived mannerism to achieve a noticeable discord. While Aalto was not seeking the same emotional response, he meant to utilize an observer's orthodox perception as a foil.

30. Suddenly his practice was alive with projects mostly industrial in nature. See Leonardo Mosso, *Alvar Aalto* (Helsinki: Ateneum, 1967), pp. 71–73.

31. The plan is Aalto's first complete, overall town plan and the cornerstone on which his reputation is based.

32. Aalto had been shown Frank Lloyd Wright's Hanna House when he visited Wurster in 1939. Vernon de Mars passed this information on to P. D. Pearson in a phone interview on May 15, 1977.

33. This disparate nature of two different expressions for two distinctly different building types was not unique to Aalto. Peter Behrens had developed a similar response in his practice by the first decade of the 20th century. Aalto made a special contribution to this theory, however, often utilizing the same materials for both types but achieving a complete aesthetic differentiation between the two types.

34. Finland was drained economically and had given up valuable country including Karelia for the first time.

35. The Neuenschwanders have compared this surface with the natural romantic shingle textures revived around the turn of the century. See these textures on older wooden churches in Nils Erik Wickberg, *Finnish Architecture* (Helsinki: Otava, 1959), pp. 38–45. See Eduard and Claudia Neuenschwander, op. cit., pp. 18–21.

36. The saw mill which existed at this location was a nonmechanized mill and Aalto emphasized the new process to change the form of the mill's architecture. The places within the mill where special operations are housed are represented by an expressed form on the outside of the mill.

37. Letter to William Wilson Wurster from Alvar Aalto dated July 14, 1945. William Wilson Wurster Archive, School of Architecture and Environmental Design, University of California, Berkeley, Professor Richard C. Peters, archivist.

38. Ibid.

19. RETURN TO MIT

1. Letter to William Wurster from Alvar Aalto dated July 14, 1945. William Wilson Wurster Archive, School of Architecture and Environmental Design, University of California, Berkeley, Professor Richard C. Peters, archivist.

2. Letter to Alvar Aalto from William Wilson Wurster, Dean of the School of Architecture, MIT, dated August 17, 1945; see Personnel Study, School of Architecture, Massachusetts Institute of Technology, Cambridge, Mass.

3. Letter to Frank Lloyd Wright from Alvar Aalto dated December 12, 1945; Personnel Study cited in note 2 above. In spite of his earlier visits Aalto's appreciation of Wright had taken some time to develop. By 1945 Aalto had become something of a student of American architecture and was, along with others, instrumental in bringing an exhibition of American architecture to the Ateneum in Helsinki. Aalto wrote the main article of the exhibition catalog, see *Amerika Bygger* (Helsinki: Ateneum, 1945), pp. 3–15.

4. Aalto's son remained in school at the Technical University of Helsinki and graduated as a construction engineer.

5. An examination of Aalto's personnel records and the relative correspondence shows that Aalto wanted to spend less and less time at MIT. Usually it was arranged by Dean Wurster that Vernon de Mars, a professional associate of his from San Francisco, would split the terms with Aalto. However, due to Aalto's constant rearranging of his residence period, that did not always prove to be the course followed. This has also been confirmed by de Mars in a letter to P. D. Pearson dated June 22, 1977; see Personnel Study cited above in note 2.

6. The Architectural School at MIT under Wurster's leadership supported Aalto's work on the dormitory project and required little from him in the performance of his teaching duties. See letter to Lawrence B. Andersen from William Wurster dated November 24, 1947; Personnel Study cited above in note 2.

7. The drawings were actually prepared at the offices of Perry Dean and Shaw. See Stanley Abercrombie, "Happy Anniversary Baker House," *Architecture Plus* 1 (July 1973), p. 60.

8. Olaf Hammerström traveled to Cambridge from Aalto's office and remained on the project throughout construction. Abercrombie, op. cit., p. 60.

9. Once upon a time all architectural students were required to be familiar wih methods of constructing perspective drawings, and the utilization of three-dimensional aspects of massings of buildings was demanded from them. Aalto could have easily been inspired by the resultant form of a selected sketch view, but this would only be normal practice for any designer.

10. A similar type of angled arrangement was also popular with American architects in the post-war era. It centered on the aspect of orientation to the sun with the primary face of the building being arranged 22 1/2° south of west to provide maximum control as well as light. It was well thought to have been a relief to the gridiron of urban street pattern usually laid out with the four primary parts of the compass.

11. This was another technique by which Aalto throughout his career was able to avoid the monotony of a long, single planar facade.

12. The well-known curving facade at MIT grew out of the combination of rounded or cylindrical form pavilions and adjacent straight wings, instead of being conceptualized as a smooth undulating wall, quite like the tilting expression constructed in plywood at New York 10 years before. The two similar forms have no common derivative.

13. In the 1930s and 1940s many single-family and semidetached houses were built in the U.S.A. with randomly rusticated brick walls to achieve a break-up of the regularized brickpattern. They were mostly incorporated in pseudo-Tudor or pseudo-English cottage styled dwellings.

14. *Alvar Aalto Synopsis: Papers of the Institute for History and Theory of Architecture* (Zurich: Swiss Federal Institute of Technology, 1970), p. 20.

15. This was Aalto's first major permanent building outside Finland, an aspect of practice that quite naturally presents difficulties.

16. *Alvar Aalto Synopsis*, op. cit., p. 20.

17. Personnel Study, School of Architecture, MIT, cited above in note 2.

18. Ibid.

19. Dean Harlan McClure of Clemson University, School of Architecture, and Vernon de Mars, architect, in Berkeley, California, among many others, have related to me various aspects of Aalto's brief stays at MIT from a student and colleague viewpoint.

20. AALTO AT MIDCAREER

1. Obituary of Aino Marsio Aalto, January 25, 1894–January 13, 1949, *Helsingin Sanomat*, January 15, 1949.

2. Karl Fleig, *Alvar Aalto 1922–1962* (Zurich: Verlag für Architektur, Artemis, 1963).

3. Interview with Erno Goldfinger, architect, conducted by P. D. Pearson, U.K., December 10, 1973 at architect's home in Hampstead U.K. Mrs. Walter Gropius has confirmed this as well.

4. Being Aalto's partner she was an integral part of his life. Many friends of the Aaltos have characterized the period immediately following Aino's death as an extremely difficult time in his life.

5. It seems to have been his constant will to achieve recognition at home by producing works and a life-style that were untenable to his countrymen. When aspects of theory that he believed in came into popular use he altered his belief once again.

6. He failed to include any of his own writings in either of the volumes he produced with the editorship of Karl Fleig. See Göran Schildt, *Alvar Aalto* (Jyväskylä: K. J. Gummerus, 1964).

7. Wright produced over 600 projects and buildings, perhaps the highest number by a single practitioner in the history of the art.

8. George Baird's "Lecture on Aalto" delivered at the Institute for Architecture and Urbanism, New York, April 18, 1975.

9. *Alvar Aalto Synopsis: Papers of the Institute for History and Theory of Architecture* (Zurich: Swiss Federal Institute of Technology, 1970), p. 15.

10. Ibid., p. 17.

21. FIRST HELSINKI BUILIDNGS

1. Leonardo Mosso, *Alvar Aalto* (Helsinki: Ateneum, 1967), p. 75.

2. He had produced design projects for buildings for that industrial town as early as 1944. See site plan dated 1944 of Säynätsalo, Museum of Finnish Architecture Archives, Helsinki.

3. Except for Tuukkanen all the men had been confirmed Functionalists.

4. During this period of his life he chose his mottoes from well-known Latin phrases; perhaps this reflects an increasing enthusiasm for classical aspects of architecture. George Baird has characterized the period following this as one in which Aalto attempted to build ruins, meaning of a classical nature. See George Baird, *Alvar Aalto* (New York: Simon & Schuster, 1971).

5. In the final development of this commission, the housing for Pension Bank employees was built at a separate location. In fact the location was the same block of the same street as Aalto's own house constructed in Munkkiniemi. The housing was built before the office building had begun.

6. However, there are some exceptions such as an office building by Eliel Saarinen in central Helsinki located on Keskuskatu next to Aalto's Rautatalo (or "Iron House") and, even earlier, the Knights House in Helsinki has a brick face to set off its Venetian Gothic styling. See N. E. Wickberg, *Finnish Architecture* (Helsinki: Otava, 1959), pp. 78, 87.

7. The top layer of this lens was sharply inclined upward like a mountain peak to quickly shed the snow accumulation, the lower two layers acting as a double-glazed window to seal out the cold. His experiments with the flat single-paned lens of Viipuri led him away from that simple form.

8. The Piazza di Spagna in Rome, as well as the Piazza del Popolo nearby, are obvious sources for the two-level aspect of this scheme.

9. In the light of Aino's death (prior to the submission date) this is an unusually macabre motto. Aalto was obviously moved, for Aino's funeral is remembered by many who experienced it as equally eccentric. Quite against Finnish custom of discretely disposing of a loved one's remains, Aalto had Aino's casket placed in an upstairs room of their home where friends could pay their last respects in person.

10. The land has now been developed by others.

11. Footpaths of ancient times exist in nearly every country, but in Finland it has been only in the last two decades that dense building developments and limited access highways have begun seriously to interrupt these pedestrian ways.

12. The well-known students' union on campus is by Reima Pietilä.

13. Aalto knew this site well as he had lived across the inlet in Munkkiniemi for many years.

14. Also the early echelon studies of the seniors' dormitory; as told to me by Dean Harlan McClure of Clemson University, School of Architecture, and Vernon de Mars, architect, in Berkeley, California, among many others, who have related to me various aspects of Aalto's brief visits to MIT from both a student and colleague viewpoint.

15. From the standpoint of massing, the source in Aalto's work for the echelon arrangements is the Viipuri Library. All other schemes are modifications.

16. An important link at that time as well as now, because a major portion of the passenger traffic to Stockholm passes through this facility.

17. The location that Aalto had chosen for his proposal of a stadium for the Independence Monument competition in 1929.

18. She has characterized this association with the statement that they got married with Säynätsalo.

22. EPILOGUE: CARRYING ON AN AALTO TRADITION

1. Referred to in several instances as splayed.

2. Built for the Communist Party of Finland. It has to some extent the basic function that the Worker Clubs had in Moscow in the first decade after the Russian Revolution. Perhaps this is why it bears a resemblance to Melnikor's tramworkers club.

3. He actually dismissed the acoustical consultant on the House of Culture and engineered it himself.

4. It is fair to say that relatively mild summers in Finland make this scheme more of a realistic system than it might be in Central Europe or the U.S.A.

5. Here he achieved an unusual effect by placing the primary structural bents so that they run in the direction of the lines of sight.

6. These wooden slatted ceilings were retained in very much the same nature as he had first employed them at Viipuri.

7. In the lobby of the Wolfsburg Cultural Center he used the tiles to recall his slatted columns executed in wood in Paris and Viipuri. The ultimate profile of this looks like a modernized, refined version of a fluted Doric column but instead springs from the vernacular.

8. This has been disclosed by Aalto and Fleig in *Alvar Aalto 1963–1970* (Zurich: Verlag für Architektur, Artemis, 1970).

Selected Bibliography

In general citations in Notes are not repeated here.

Aalto, Alvar. *Postwar Reconstruction; Rehousing Research in Finland.* Published privately in New York, 1940.

Aalto, Alvar. *Synopsis.* Stuttgart: Birkhauser Verlag, 1970.

"Aalto." *Space Design,* no. 149 (1977), entire issue.

"Aalto's Experimental Workshop Is Also a Vacation House in the Lake Country." *Architectural Forum* 100 (1954):152–154.

Ahlberg, Hakon. *Swedish Architecture of the Twentieth Century.* New York: Charles Scribner's Sons, 1925.

"Aino et Alvar Aalto, works." *L'Architecture d'Aujourd'hui* 20 (1950):1–37.

Akademie der Kunste. Exhibition Catalog: *Alvar Aalto.* Berlin, 1963.

"Alvar Aalto." *Architectural Record* 125 (1970):125–140.

"Alvar Aalto." *L'Architecture d'Aujourd'hui* 134 (1967):1–13.

"Alvar Aalto." *Arkitektur* 69 (1969): entire issue.

"Alvar Aalto." *Arkkitehti,* no. 1/2 (1958), entire issue.

"Alvar Aalto." *Arkkitehti* 65 (1968):23–58, 61.

"Alvar Aalto." *Arkkitehti* 73 (1976), entire issue.

"Alvar Aalto." *Progressive Architecture,* April 1977, pp. 53–77.

"Alvar Aalto—Finn Without Borders." *Architectural Forum* 112 (1960):116–123.

"Alvar Aalto in the Finnish Forest, the Virtuoso of Wood Puts Up a Civic Center of Brick. . . ." *Architectural Forum,* April 1954, pp. 148–151.

"Alvar Aalto; Sequenza fotographica di Richard Einzig sulla Concert Hall di Helsinki." *Casabella,* June 1972, pp. 27–33.

Alvar Aalto Synopsis: Malerei, Architektur, Sculpture. Eidgenossische Technische Hochschule. Zurich: Institute für Geschichte und Theorie der Architektur, Schriftenreihe.

"Alvar Aalto verk, 1922–1958." *Arkkitehti,* no. 1/2 (1958), p. 140.

"Arets Model." *Form* 45 (1947):22–23.

"Aresta stadscentrum." *Byggmästaren,* no. 23 (1944), pp. 434–436.

Arteo-Pascoe Inc. Exhibition Catalog: *Furniture of Alvar and Aino Aalto.* New York, 1937.

Baird, George. *Alvar Aalto.* New York: Simon & Schuster, 1971.

Baruel, J. "Alvar Aalto." *Arkitekten. Manedshaefte* (Copenhagen) 52 (1950):122–136.

Borräs, Maria Lluïsa. *Architectura finlandessa en Otaniemi.* Barcelona: Ediciones La Poligrafa, 1967.

Bunning, W. R. "Paimio Sanitorium, an Analysis." *Architecture* (Sydney) 29 (1940):20–25.

Burchard, John E. "Finland and Architect Aalto." *The Architectural Record* 125 (1959):126.

"Büro—und geschäftshaus 'Rautatalo' in Helsinki." *Werk* 44 (1957):103–108.

"Caise d'allocation vieillesse à Helsinki." *L'Architecture d'Aujourd'hui* 25 (1955):100.

"Caise d'allocation viellesse, Helsinki." *L'Architecture d'Aujourd'hui* 30 (1959):62–69, 82.

"Centrale kas voor ouderdomsvoorzieningen a Helsinki." *Forum* (Amsterdam) 13 (1958):54–58.

"Centre administratif et culturel de Seinajoki." *L'Architecture d'Aujourd'hui* 31 (December 1960–January 1961):14–15.

"Centre culturel à Wolfsburg, Allemagne." *L'Architecture d'Aujourd'hui* 34 (1964):58–63.

"Centre de Seinäjoki, Finland." *L'Architecture d'Aujourd'hui* 39 (December 1967–January 1968):4–13.

"La chiesa Italiana di Alvar Aalto." *Domus,* no. 447 (1967), pp. 1–7.

"Church at Imatra Finland." *Architectural Design* 29 (1960):111.

De Feo, Vittorio. *URSS Architettura 1917–1936.* Rome: Editori Riuniti, 1963.

"Designing Today's Furniture." *Interiors* 100 (1941):16–21, 40, 42, 46.

"A Dormitory That Explores New Ideas of Student Life." *Architectural Record* 102 (1947):97–99.

"Dos decoraciones interiores." *Nuestra arquitectura,* no. 6 (1941), pp. 214–215.

"Ecole Polytechnique d'Otaniemi." *L'Architecture d'Aujourd'hui* 25 (May-June 1954):68–71.

"Edificio per uffici e negozi 'Rautatalo' a Helsinki." *Casabella,* no. 208 (1955), pp. 6–15.

"The Enso Gutzeit Building, New Center for Helsinki and the Culture Centre of Wolfsburg." *Perspecta* 8:5–14.

"Fine della 'machine à habiter.' " *Metron,* no. 7 (1946), pp. 2–5.

"Finland." *Architectural Forum* 72 (1940):399–412.

"Finland i New York, arkitekter Aino och Alvar Aalto." *Byggmästaren,* no. 34 (Nov. 6, 1939), pp. 420–426.

"Finland, International Section." *Architectural Forum* 63 (1936):171–186.

"Finland pa världsutställningen i Paris." *Arkkitehti,* no. 9 (1937), pp. 137-144.

"Finlands avdelning pa världsutställningen New York." *Arkitekten,* no. 8 (1939), pp. 118–127.

"Finlands avdelning pa världsutställningen New York." *Arkkitehti,* no. 6 (1939), pp. 118–127.

"Finlands utstallning i New York." *Byggekunst* 21 (1939): 154.

Fleig, Karl. *Alvar Aalto.* New York: Praeger Publishers, 1974.

Fleig, Karl. *Alvar Aalto, Band I 1922–1962.* Zurich: Verlag für Architektur, Artemis, 1963.

Fleig, Karl. *Alvar Aalto, Complete Works.* Zurich: Editions d'Architecture Artemis, 1970.

Floquet, Pierre-Louis. "Les maitres de l'architecture nouvelle à Finland pays des villes lacs." *Batir,* October 1938, pp. 421–25.

Fogh, Fredrick. "Aalto in Italia." *Arkitektur* 16 (1972):24–32.

"Folkebibliotek i Viborg, Finland." *Arkkitehti* 41 (1939):24–28.

Giedion, Sigfried. "Alvar Aalto." *Architectural Review* 107 (1960):77–84.

Giedion, S. "Alvar Aalto." *L'Architecture d'Aujourd'hui* 20 (1960):5.

Giedion, S. "Uber Alvar Aaltos werk." *Werk* 35 (1948):269–276.

Goldstone, Harmon Hendricks. "Alvar Aalto." *Magazine of Art* 32 (1939):208-21.

Gutheim, Fredrick Albert. *Alvar Aalto.* New York: Braziller, 1960.

Gutheim, F. A. "Alvar Aalto Today." *Architectural Record* 135 (1963):135–150.

Hahl, Nils Gustav. "Alvar Aalto utställningar i Utlandet." *Arkkitehti,* no. 9 (1938), pp. 132–133.

Hahl, N. *Om konst och konstindustri.* Helsingfors: Arteks forlag, 1942.

"Hall des sports de Vienna." *L'Architecture d'Aujourd'hui* 25 (1954):72–75.

"Haus der Kulture in Helsinki." *Bauenwohnen* 12 (1958):310–311.

"Helsingfors kulturhus." *Arkkitehti,* no. 12 (1959), pp. 208–217.

"Helsingin Kaupungin uusi Keskusta." *Arkkitehti,* no. 3 (1961), pp. 33–44.

Hirn, Yrjö. *The Origins of Art.* London: Macmillan, 1900.

Hirn, Y. *The Sacred Shrine.* London: Macmillan, 1912.

"House of Culture at Helsinki." *Architect and Building News* 219 (1961):227–30.

"A House in Finland." *Architect and Building News* 165 (1941):96–97.

"A House Near Helsingfors." *Architectural Review* 85 (1938):175–78.

"Housing, Switzerland." *Werk* 55 (1968):637–664.

"Hovedkontor för Enso-Gutzeit Oy, Helsingfors." *Arkitektur* 7 (1965): 24–30.

"The Humanizing of Architecture." *Architectural Forum* 73 (1940):505–506.

"Institute of Technology, Otaniemi, Finland." *Architectural Design* 38 (1968):57–64.

Jutikkala, Eino, and Pirinen, Kauko. *A History of Finland.* New York: Praeger, 1974.

Khazanova, V. E. *Soviet Architecture during the Constructivist Period.* Moscow, 1970.

"Kirke og menighedscenter i Riola ved Bologna." *Arkitekten* 69 (1967):205–208.

Kopp, Anatole. *Ville et Revolution.* Paris: Editions Anthropos, 1967.

Koppel, Nils. "Villa 'Mairea,' " *Arkitekten* 42 (1940): 93–99.

Labò, Giorgio. *Alvar Aalto.* Milan: Il Balcone, 1948.

Le Corbusier. *Modulor 2.* London: Faber & Faber, 1958.

"Mairea, Marie och Harry Gullichsens privathus Norrmark." *Arkkitehti,* no. 9 (1939), pp. 134–137.

"Materialens och byggnadssättens inverkan pa modern byggnadskonst." *Arkkitehti,* no. 9 (1938), pp. 129–131.

"M.I.T. Dormitory; an Undisguised Expersion of Function." *Architectural Forum* 87 (1947):13.

Moderna Museet, *Alvar Aalto.* Stockholm, 1969.

Moser, Walter. "Die Arbeit in Atelier Alvar Aalto." *Werk* 56 (1959): 392–396.

Mosso, Leonard. *Alvar Aalto, teokset 1918–1967.* Helsinki: Otava Publishing Co., 1967.

Mosso, L. Exhibition Catalog: *L'Opera di Alvar Aalto.* Milan: Edizioni di Comunità, 1965.

Mosso, L. *La luce nell'architettura di Alvar Aalto.* Milan, 1960.

Mosso, L. "La luce nell'architettura di Alvar Aalto." *Zodiac,* no. 7, pp. 66–115.

Mosso, L., "Nel centro storico di Helsinki la sede . . . Gutzeit di Alvar Aalto." *Casabella,* no. 272, pp. 4–5.

Museum of Modern Art. Exhibition Catalog: *Architecture and Furniture: Aalto.* New York: The Museum of Modern Art, 1938.

Nässtrom, Gustaf. *Swedish Functionalism.* Stockholm: Bokforlaget Natur och Kutur, 1930.

Neuenschwander, Edward. *Finnish Buildings.* Erlenbach-Zurich: Verlag für Architektur, 1954.

"L'Oueuf de Poisson et le Saumon." *Werk* 36, no. 2 (1949):43–44.

Pagano, Giuseppe. "Due ville di Aalto." *Casabella* 12 (1940):26–29.

"Il pediglione finlandese alla biennale." *Domus,* no. 322 (1956), pp. 3–5.

Pehnt, Wolfgang. "Aalto in Deutschland." *Zodiac,* no. 7 (1962), pp. 176–181.

"Privathus Aalto." *Arkkitehti,* no. 8 (1937), pp. 113–115.

"Progetto per il museo a Aalborg, Denmark." *Casabella Continuita,* no. 236 (1960), p. 50.

"Projekt für den Wiederaufbau von Rovaniemi in Finnish Lappland." *Werk* 33 (1946):102–106.

Puntila, L. A. *The Political History of Finland 1809–1966.* Helsinki: Otava Publishing Co., 1974.

"Research for Reconstruction, Rehousing Research in Finland." *Royal Institute of British Architects Journal* 48 (1941):78–83.

Rewell, Viljo; Aarne, Ervi; and Ypyä, Ragnar. *Industrial Architecture in Finland.* Helsinki: Suomen Arkkitehtiliitto, 1952.

"Rovaniemi, Alvar Aalto Architect." *L'Homme et l'Architecture,* no. 7–8 (1946), pp. 51–58.

"Rovaniemi, a Finnish Reconstruction Project." *Architects Yearbook,* 1947, pp. 51–58.

"Rovaniemi, piano redatto da Alvar Aalto." *Metron,* no. 7 (1946), pp. 15–21.

Sachs, Lisabeth. "Studentheim des Massachusetts Institute of Technology, Cambridge, USA." *Werk* 37 (1950):97–102.

Salokorpi, Asko. *Modern Architecture in Finland.* London: Weidenfeld & Nicolson, 1970.

"Un sanitorium pour tuberculeux en Finland." *L'Architecture Française* 7 (1946): 2

Schildt, Görän. *Alvar Aalto.* Jyväskylä: K. J. Gummerus, 1964.

Schildt, G. *Alvar Aalto: Luonnoksia.* Helsinki: Otava Publishing Co., 1972.

Schildt, G. *The Sculptures of Alvar Aalto.* Helsinki: Otava Publishing Co., 1967.

"Senior Dormitory Massachusetts Institute of Technology." *Arkkitehti,* no. 4 (1950), pp. 53–64.

Sergeant, John. *Frank Lloyd Wright's Usonian Houses.* New York: Whitney Library of Design, 1976.

Shand, P. Morton. "Viipuri Library, Finland." *Architectural Review* 79 (1936):107–14.

"Shop for Finnish Designs Limited, Haymarket St." *Architect and Building News* 215 (1959):725–726.

Shvidkovsky, O. A. *Building in the USSR.* London: Studio Vista, 1971.

Smith, John B. *The Golden Age of Finnish Art.* Helsinki: Otava Publishing Co., 1975.

"Sonderheft Finland." *Das Werk,* April 1940, pp. 65–112.

Spring, Bernard P. "Aalto Revisited." *Architectural Forum* 124 (1966):70–79.

Die studentstadt Otaniemi." *Werk,* no. 46 (1959), pp. 389–391.

"Sunila, Architect, Alvar Aalto." *Focus* 1 (Spring 1939):13–26.

"Sunila sulfatcellulosafabrik." *Arkkitehti,* no. 10 (1939), pp. 145–60.

"Tavlingen om konstmuseum i Reval." *Arkkitehti,* no. 5 (1937), pp. 65–70.

"Tuberculosis Sanitorium at Paimio." *Architectural Record* 76 (1934):12–19.

"Tuberculosis Sanitorium at Paimio." *Modern Hospital* 72 (1949):79–81.

"Turun Sanomat, Newspaper Plant, Helsingfors, Finland." *Architectural Record* 68 (1930):510.

"Utvidgningen av universitetsbiblioteket Helsingfors." *Arkkitehti,* no. 6 (1938), pp. 86–96.

"Varldsutställningarna; New York World's Fair, The Golden Gate Exposition." *Arkkitehti,* no. 8 (1939), pp. 113–115.

"Vuoksenniska Church." *Arkkitehti,* no. 12 (December 1959), pp. 194–207.

Wickberg, Nils Erik. *Finnish Architecture.* Helsinki: Otava Publishing Co., 1959.

Zurich, Kunstgewerbemuseum. Exhibition Catalog: *Alvar and Aino Aalto.* Zurich, 1940.

"Zwischen humanismus und materiallismus." *Baukunst und Werkform* 9 (1956):300.

Photography Credits

Unless otherwise noted below, source for all illustrations is The Museum of Finnish Architecture, Helsinki, Finland.

Paul David Pearson: 13, 14, 15, 16, 28, 31, 32, 33, 41, 43, 64, 74, 78, 80, 82, 98, 101, 106, 117, 129, 130, 147, 162, 181, 183, 194, 197, 233, 316, 317.

Aalto Atelier, Helsinki: 61, 62, 63, 71, 72, 73, 87, 88, 89, 90, 91, 92, 93, 94, 95, 97, 127, 176, 185, 186, 187, 188, 189, 190, 191, 213, 214, 215, 230, 234, 296, 302, 306.

Raija-Liisa Heinonen, Helsinki: 8, 10, 11, 12, 44, 45, 46, 47, 48, 49, 50, 51, 59, 60, 65, 66, 67, 68, 69, 70.

Arkkitehti, Helsinki: 17, 18, 19, 52, 53, 54, 55, 56, 57, 75, 76, 77, 79, 86, 96, 99, 103, 104, 108, 118, 119, 123, 124, 151, 152, 160, 161, 180, 182, 184, 244, 245, 246, 247, 253, 258, 259, 260, 261, 267, 279, 280, 281, 282, 283, 284, 286, 287, 288, 289, 303.

Forum, Amsterdam: 137, 138, 139, 140, 141, 142, 167, 216.

Nauka, Moscow: 128, 156, 157.

Jyväskylä Municipal Archives, Jyväskylä: 35, 36, 37, 38, 39, 40.

Museum of Modern Art, New York: 22, 196, 223, 224, 235, 240, 241, 242, 250, 295, 320.

Erno Goldfinger, London: 177.

Jack Pritchard Archives, Newcastle University, England: 231.

William W. Wurster Archive, College of Environmental Design Documents Collection, University of California at Berkeley: 298.

Artek, Helsinki: 226, 227, 228, 229, 231.

Ezra Stoller: 290.

Index

Numbers in italics indicate illustrations.